NICHOLAS KALDOR

NICHOLAS KALDOR

Anthony P. Thirlwall

Professor of Applied Economics
University of Kent at Canterbury

WITH A FOREWORD BY
SIR DOUGLAS WASS

NEW YORK UNIVERSITY PRESS
WASHINGTON SQUARE

First published in the U.S.A. in 1987 by
NEW YORK UNIVERSITY PRESS
Washington Square, NY 10003

Library of Congress Cataloging-in-Publication Data
Thirlwall, A.P.
  Nicholas Kaldor.
  Bibliography: p.
  Includes index.
  1. Kaldor, Nicholas, 1908–1986.   2. Economists—
Great Britain—Biography.   I. Title.
HB103.K36T45 1987   330'092'4 [B]   87-22065
ISBN 0-8147-8177-2

Typeset in Andover 11/12pt by Gilbert Composing Services

Printed in Great Britain

To Clarisse for Nicky
and
To Philippa with love

'One crowded hour of glorious life
Is worth an age without a name'.

(Thomas Osbert Mordaunt, *The Bee*,
Edinburgh, 12 October 1791)

CONTENTS

FOREWORD

I count it a great privilege to be asked to write a foreword to this book. Nicky Kaldor was not just a close personal friend for whom I had a deep, if sometimes tested, affection. He was one of the two or three real geniuses that I have had the good fortune to meet. When, in September last year while I was on a visit to the United States, I read of his death, I was affected like the poet's friend, who on hearing similar news could only say over and over again 'Coleridge is dead'.

This book is both a timely and a worthy salute to Kaldor's life. It is at once a biography which traces the interwoven threads of his professional, political and personal development, and a technical description and appraisal of his theoretical work in the field of economics. It amply demonstrates the breadth of his intellectual curiosity and the originality with which he addressed himself to the problems he thought worthy of investigation. It shows him above all as a man who saw economics as a branch of study of man and his behaviour – but a branch of study that, because of its subject, can never be wholly free from value judgements.

I first met Kaldor when he was working as a special adviser to the Wilson Government of 1964–70. He had begun that period by concentrating on tax reform and had devoted his energies to the introduction of the Capital Gains Tax and the Corporation Tax, both of which he had advocated in 1955 in his Memorandum of Dissent from the majority report of the Radcliffe Commission on the Taxation of Profits and Income. As time passed, his restless energy took him into the mainstream of macro-economic policy, and this brought him into contact with a wide variety of Treasury officials. Exchange rate policy, the international payments mechanism, regional policy and investment incentives were all issues to which he addressed himself; and in all of these he had original and exciting ideas. He was immensely popular in the Treasury, even among those whose orthodoxies he challenged. This was not just because he was approachable and friendly. He was patient too, and listened to the arguments of people of all ages and all ranks who had experience of the practical problems which his ideas, if implemented, would encounter. He loved to hold court with his audience, treating a Whitehall meeting like a Cambridge seminar, often pacing about the conference room while his official colleagues listened in rapt attention as his thoughts unfolded. But he was no dogmatic theoretician, dictating his prescriptions to passive disciples. He welcomed argument, criticism and controversy. Above all, he heeded the objections of those concerned with the practical and administrative implications of what he wanted to do. He was the only economic adviser to Government that I have worked with who studied the administrative system and sought to fashion his ideas to what that system could bear. This sometimes led him to propose a change in the system itself, and in this field too his originality was a stimulus, not a threat to public service management.

What I found most refreshing – and this feeling recurred many times in the twenty years that I knew Kaldor – was the spirit of empiricism which informed his intellectual approach to economic problems. He was first and foremost an observer of the economic scene, collecting material at both the aggregate and the particular level; and he built his theories on the evidence he saw around him. The theories sometimes appeared far fetched, but he was always willing to see them scrutinised and tested according to their results when they were implemented. The Selective Employment Tax was one of his inventions, based on his theory of the causality of economic growth. But he was the first to insist, when it had been in place for a couple of years, that its effects should be studied by an impartial investigation to determine whether it was having the impact on employment and productivity that he had predicted. And when, with the change in Government, the Tax was abolished, he consoled himself to me one day by saying that this created a laboratory experiment for examining whether the effects of the Tax were reversible.

All this, though welcome, I found puzzling. I had expected someone trained in the neoclassical school of Central Europe to be very theoretical and abstract; what confronted me was the epitome of Baconian empiricism, someone more English than the English. And so, in conversation with him and in reading his work, I sought to unravel the explanation of this paradox. I found that he had certainly started his professional life as a neoclassical economist. In his early days, indeed, at the London School of

Economics, he was fascinated by Lionel Robbins' lucid exposition of
classical thinking, and he had no difficulty in embracing the
general equilibrium theory of Walras and the Austrians. But in the
early 1930s things began to change. The evidence of the Great
Depression, the writing of Allyn Young and then of Gunnar
Myrdal and Keynes, took him swiftly into the camp which
challenged the prevailing orthodoxy. Market imperfections and
failures needed to be explained and neoclassical explanations were
palpably implausible. Economies of scale and the inefficiencies
which excessive competition could generate also had to be
accounted for. Surpluses of labour and goods did not simply
disappear at a theoretical market clearing price. Aggregate
demand could be deficient, even in a world where market
restrictions were minimal. It was hardly surprising that Kaldor's
determination to explain why the textbook theories did not hold
water should take him into the Keynesian camp, the camp to
whose cause he remained faithful all his life.

Kaldor's empiricism and his passionate moral sense were the
two factors, I think, that impelled him to seek to contribute to
public policy-making. His first excursion into this field was when
he worked in Geneva in the late 1940s at the Economic
Commission for Europe. But his function there was analytical
rather than prescriptive, and it was not until he was appointed to
the Royal Commission on Taxation in the early 1950s that he first
tasted the heady nectar of making influential recommendations on
the way public affairs should be handled. His route to the role of
adviser on Government economic policy was not unlike that of
Keynes himself, whose entry too was via a Royal Commission –
that on Indian Currency and Finance. And like Keynes, Kaldor's
interest in public policy extended far beyond the shores of the
United Kingdom. Many foreign governments sought Kaldor's
advice, perhaps principally in the field of taxation policy, for it was
as an expert in tax reform that he was known abroad, particularly
after the publication of his work on an Expenditure Tax.

Kaldor's commitment to Keynesian economics, suitably adapted
to take account of the problems which full employment generates,
inevitably took him into conflict with monetarism when this creed
took root in the Anglo-Saxon world in the late 1960s. His attack on
it was partly theoretical, but he reserved his most serious
strictures for its weak empirical base, strictures which are now
accepted by all but a handful of acolytes. What worried him most
was that a simple but poorly based theory should have held such
sway over policy-makers, and his written work on the short-
comings of monetarism is shot through with indignation and at

times despair at man's intellectual fallibility.

It will fall to others, better qualified than I, to assess Kaldor's place in history. To link his name to that of Keynes is perhaps to make by implication too extravagant a claim. He produced no single explanatory theory of a kind and quality comparable to the *General Theory*. His canvasses, though impressive, had not that quality of bigness and historical significance that cause the observer to stop breathlessly before them. His written work consisted of a series of essays and papers not, with the exception of *An Expenditure Tax*, a book of sustained argument. But many of his miniatures were gems of exposition, argument and originality, and they were produced over a period of 50 years, from the early 1930s to the 1980s. His eight volumes of collected essays are a monument to the range of his interest and the originality of his mind.

It will always be a mystery to me, as it will to so many others, why his achievements were not crowned with a Nobel Prize. Perhaps he offended the economic establishment too much. Perhaps his progressive politics were not to the liking of the Committee of Award. We shall probably never know. But what we do know is that right up to his death the economics profession throughout the world paid homage to him by giving him the most prestigious platforms on which to lecture and teach. That accolade, I think, was more eloquent and more important to Nicky than a dozen formal awards. It is just that the Prize would have given such pleasure to his friends.

Douglas Wass
June 1987

PREFACE

To write this book on Nicholas Kaldor, I have read all his published works (see the bibliography) and some of his private papers and correspondence, although by no means all; I spent forty hours interviewing and recording him, in addition to spending many hours in casual conversation, and I consulted many of his academic and personal friends. He died while the book was being written, on 30 September 1986.

I was not brought up on Kaldor's economics. As an undergraduate at the University of Leeds I do not recall being exposed to any of his ideas or papers, not even his growth and distribution models. Perhaps they were too new, or I took the wrong courses. It was not until I started to develop my own lecture courses at the University of Kent in 1966 that I began to read some of his works and absorb his ideas. Fresh from the press in that year was his controversial Cambridge Inaugural Lecture on the *Causes of the Slow Rate of Economic Growth of the United Kingdom*. I believed him to be wrong in his diagnosis that the constraint on Britain's growth was a shortage of labour, but not in his stress on manufacturing industry as the engine of growth and on the causal impact of output growth on productivity growth working through scale economies, induced capital accumulation and embodied technical progress.

In 1970 an equally important paper appeared on 'The Case for Regional Policies', where he laid out for the first time his theory of growth, and regional growth rate differences, as a cumulative disequilibrium process. This too struck an intellectual chord and later Robert Dixon and I were to formalise the model under the title 'A Model of Regional Growth Rate Differences on Kaldorian Lines' (*Oxford Economic Papers*, July 1975). Kaldor approved the model, and it was at this time that we started to correspond, irregularly at first since he was a very forgetful letter writer with

xv

people he did not know well. When he did write, however, it was at great length, arguing every point in detail. Our correspondence blossomed further when quite independently we both became interested at the same time in the Harrod (foreign) trade multiplier. In 1979 I published a paper on 'The Balance of Payments Constraint as an Explanation of International Growth Rate Differences' (*Banca Nazionale del Lavoro Quarterly Review*, March 1979), the end-result of which turned out to be the dynamic analogue of the static Harrod trade multiplier, although I did not realise it at the time. It was only when Kaldor wrote a letter to *The Times* on the subject that my colleague Charles Kennedy referred me to Harrod's *International Economics* (1933) and I realised that I had reinvented the wheel.

It was at this time that I found my interests and thinking so close to Kaldor's that I determined to read the whole of his work. In the summer of 1979 I took a sabbatical term in Cambridge for that purpose. The more I read, the more I liked: the combination of the theoretical and empirical, and not the pursuit of theory for its own sake; the powerful intuition and insight, and the concentration on interesting topics of public concern. I found myself thinking more and more on Kaldorian lines and came to believe that a Kaldorian economics, or view of the world, could and should be written. My interest culminated in the formalisation of his two-sector agriculture–industry model of the development process which I tried to argue provides a general theory of growth and development applicable to both individual countries and the world at large (viz., *Oxford Economic Papers*, July 1986).

In writing this book, I am indebted to a number of individuals and organisations, not the least to Nicholas (Nicky) Kaldor himself, who gave me so much of his time to talk about his theories and of events and controversies of long ago. My intellectual debt to him cannot be measured. These conversations started in the summer of 1979, while I was a Visiting Fellow of King's College, Cambridge, and were renewed in earnest in 1985–86 when the Economic and Social Research Council very generously awarded me a Personal Research Fellowship for one year to finish the work, and Robinson College Cambridge elected me as a Bye-Fellow so that I could stay in Nicky's back garden!

Besides Kaldor himself, several other people helped me fit the pieces of his life and work together, including Mr Maurice Allen, Mr Christopher Allsopp, the late Lord Balogh, Professor Tibor Barna, Sir Alec Cairncross, Mr James Callaghan, Professor David Champernowne, Dr Colin Clark, Mr Sidney Dell, Professor Jack Gilbert, Professor Wynne Godley, Dr I. S. Gulati, Dr Geoffrey

Harcourt, Mr Denis Healey, Mr Douglas Jay, Sir Alexander
Johnston, Mr Arthur Johnstone, Lord Kahn, Professor Nicholas
Kurti, Professor Robert Neild, Mrs Giselle Podbielsky, Professor
Robert Skidelsky, Mrs Frances Stewart, Mr Roger Tarling,
Professor Brinley Thomas, Mr Ralph Vickers, Sir Douglas Wass
and Professor Thomas Wilson.

Some of the above and other colleagues read parts of the
manuscript and volunteered several comments. I would like to
mention particularly my colleagues at the University of Kent:
Professor Michael Allingham, Mr Chris Brown, Professor John
Craven, Mr Richard Disney, Mr Roger Hill and Professor Stephen
Holt. Julia Stevens at the University of Kent Library undertook
various bibliographical researches for me, and transcribed from
microfilm all of Kaldor's letters and references in *The Times*. I owe a
special debt of gratitude to Sir Douglas Wass, Professor Charles
Kennedy, Dr Robert Dixon and Mrs Frances Stewart who took on
the task of reading the whole manuscript. Without their advice
and encouragement, the book might never have seen the light of
day. Lastly, I express my gratitude to Mrs Tracey Robinson and
my secretary, Mrs Celine Noronha, for typing successive drafts of
the book.

One final word. The book is not a full personal biography on the
lines of Harrod's or Skidelsky's life of Keynes; nor is it an
intellectual biography in the sense of providing a new interpretation or critique of Kaldor. Rather, it is a straightforward attempt
to elucidate the work of a man who was one of the most
interesting, inspiring and influential economists of the twentieth
century, and who exerted a major influence on the economics
profession for over fifty years. I deliberately mix discussion of
quite complex theoretical issues with biographical detail, both to
lighten the economics and to put it into context. It is sometimes
said that in order to understand history, one has to understand the
historian. The same may be said of economics.

INTRODUCTION

Nicholas Kaldor's place in the history of economic thought is assured, as one of the most profound and influential economic thinkers of the twentieth century. His influence on both economic theory and economic policy was pervasive. From the bibliography at the end of the book, it is evident that hardly a branch of economics escaped his pen from his first published paper in 1932. The theory of the firm, welfare economics, public finance, growth and distribution theory, trade cycle theory, the theory of economic development, the applied economics of growth, and many other subjects were all touched by his fertile mind. While no obvious opportunity existed for a fundamental revolution of thought (as it did for Keynes), Kaldor can justifiably lay claim to have been one of the most original economists of his generation, as well as one of the most provocative and controversial. The combination of ingenuity and challenge to orthodoxy, together with his involvement in policy-making at the highest level in the United Kingdom and in several other countries, makes him a fascinating and challenging character to study. There is a Kaldorian economics, and an interesting story to tell.

Life began in Hungary in 1908, and he attended schools in Budapest until 1925 when he went to the University of Berlin for a year and a half to study economics. To pursue his studies further he then came to London to enrol as a student at the London School of Economics (LSE), a decision that was to have a profound impact on his life. He blossomed at the LSE; graduated with first class honours in 1930, and became the favourite pupil of the influential Lionel Robbins. Robbins persuaded the Director of the LSE, William Beveridge, to award Kaldor a two-year research studentship and eventually to appoint him to the staff as an Assistant in Economics in 1932. Kaldor made an immediate impression, producing a flood of papers of high quality in such diverse fields as

1

the theory of the firm, capital theory, trade cycle theory, welfare economics and monetary theory. In the early years his dominant mentors were Robbins and Hayek, but he gradually broke from their narrow Austrian approach to economics and their libertarian philosophy with the help of John Hicks, Abba Lerner and the Keynesian revolution. Kaldor was holding a Rockefeller Research Fellowship in America when Keynes' *General Theory* was published, but he was prepared for it and he was one of the first converts from the LSE to the Keynesian way of thinking. His early years in Hungary, and at the LSE before the war, are the subject matter of Chapters 1 and 2.

When the war broke out, he was evacuated with the LSE to Cambridge and came into much closer contact with the Cambridge economists, particularly Joan Robinson, Richard Kahn, Piero Sraffa and Keynes himself. Stimulated by Keynes and the exigencies of war, he also became much more concerned with policy issues. National income accounting was one preoccupation and he wrote regular reviews of the National Income White Papers (on War Finance) as they appeared. Another involvement was working out the financial implications of the Beveridge Report on Social Insurance (1942), and the quantitative aspects of full employment for the second Beveridge Report on *Full Employment in a Free Society* (1944). During the war period, Kaldor established a reputation for himself as a painstaking and incisive applied economist. He built up national and international connections with people impressed not only by his powerful theoretical brain, but also by his ability to handle and organise complex statistical material in a coherent and meaningful way. This reputation led to several requests on his time after the war. The French Commissariat du Plan hired him to examine the requirements for the financial stabilisation of France. The Hungarian government used him to advise on their three-year Plan, and he was appointed Chief of the Economic Planning Staff of the United States Strategic Bombing Survey to enquire into the effects of the US bombing campaign on the German war economy. There followed, at the invitation of Gunnar Myrdal, his appointment as Director of the Research and Planning Division of the newly established Economic Commission for Europe in Geneva originally created to administer Marshall Aid. He was responsible for initiating, and largely writing, the masterly annual *Economic Survey(s) of Europe* which were widely acclaimed for their penetrating analyses of the economies of both Eastern and Western Europe. The two and a half years spent in Geneva were among the happiest and busiest of his life. I describe his war and post-war work in Chapter 3.

Not long after he arrived in Geneva, the invitation came from King's College, Cambridge, to become a Fellow and to join the Faculty of Economics. Although he had been made a Reader in Economics at the LSE in 1945, he had resigned from the School before he left for Geneva owing to a clash with Robbins who had refused him leave of absence. The offer from King's was too good to refuse, especially with no permanent academic base, but he managed to delay his arrival in Cambridge until the end of 1949. Before leaving Geneva, he strengthened his international connections by serving on the Berlin Currency and Trade Committee (1948) and on a United Nations Expert Committee charged with the responsibility of writing a report on *National and International Measures for Full Employment* (1949). This report, and Kaldor's influential role on the committee, impressed the British Chancellor of the Exchequer, Hugh Gaitskell, and led later to Kaldor's appointment to the Royal Commission on the Taxation of Profits and Income heralding another important phase of his life.

He sat part-time for four years on the Commission during which he crystallised his views on the structure of an equitable and efficient tax system. He dissented (with two others) from the majority opinion of the Commission and authored a lengthy Memorandum of Dissent which immediately established him as one of the foremost thinkers on tax matters in the world. His later book, *An Expenditure Tax* (1955), which outlined the case for substituting expenditure for income as the basis of taxation, became a minor classic. His recognised expertise in the tax field led soon after to a request from the Indian government to undertake a comprehensive survey of the Indian tax system and to recommend reforms. This was followed by similar requests from Ceylon (Sri Lanka), Turkey, Mexico, Ghana, British Guiana (Guyana), Iran and Venezuela, all of which he accepted. His views on taxation and the results of his various tax missions are outlined in Chapters 4 and 5.

Meanwhile, back in Cambridge, he was elevated in 1952 to a Readership in Economics, and once again turned his attention to economic theory focusing on the theory of equilibrium growth, stimulated by the publication of Harrod's book, *Towards a Dynamic Economics* (1949). The theory of distributive shares also held a fascination for him, having lectured on the subject in Cambridge during the war and having written a major survey article on the 'Theory of Distribution' for the *Chambers Encyclopaedia* in 1948. Both the prevailing (orthodox) theory of distribution and equilibrium growth relied on the concept of an aggregate production function with constant returns to scale, diminishing returns to individual factors of production, marginal productivity pricing, neutral technical progress and smooth instantaneous substitutability between factors. The dubious notion of an aggregate production function with its implicit and explicit (unrealistic) neoclassical assumptions deeply disturbed the Cambridge school of economists. What Kaldor did, along with others, was to provide a completely new way of viewing the determinants of growth and distribution within a macroeconomic Keynesian framework. The first breakthrough in 1956 was to show that the distribution of income between wages and profits in a capitalist economy can be explained by the outcome of macroeconomic forces, drawing inspiration from the widow's cruse in Keynes' *Treatise on Money* (1930), and without invoking marginal productivity theory. This insight was followed a year later with his invention of the technical progress function to replace the production function with its artificial (and empirically dubious) distinction between movements along a production function (due to capital accumulation) and shifts in the whole function (due to technical progress). In practice, capital accumulation and technical progress are inseparably bound up, with the one impossible without the other. These new ideas and concepts, together with a Keynes–Harrod investment function, enabled Kaldor to formulate a combined growth and distribution model fully determinate with an equilibrium solution for the growth rate of output, the capital : output ratio, distributive shares, and the rate of profit. So it was that Kaldor became one of the founders of what is now referred to as neo-Keynesian growth theory, and of the school of post-Keynesian economics, providing an alternative explanation to neoclassical theory of the observed stylised facts of mature capitalist economies. This phase of intellectual endeavour, interspersed with all his tax work, lasted for nearly a decade, and is surveyed in Chapter 6.

The theory of equilibrium growth was not specifically addressed, however, to the applied economics of growth, or to the question why growth rates differ over time and between countries. Along with many others, Kaldor became interested in this subject in the 1960s particularly as the resident of a country with the slowest rate of growth in the industrialised world. His distinctive contribution to the debate was to take a sectoral approach distinguishing between manufacturing (or secondary) activities on the one hand and primary and tertiary activities on the other. The basic explanation of differences in growth rates between countries lay, he believed, in different rates of growth of the manufacturing sector. Manufacturing is special. It is the sector where the major labour-saving advances in technology take place.

It is the sector subject to increasing returns (both static and dynamic), while other activities tend to be subject to constant or diminishing returns. This accounts for the strong observed relation in manufacturing between output growth and productivity growth (Verdoorn's Law); a relation not generally observed in other activities. Moreover, because of disguised unemployment in agriculture and many service trades, there exists a strong relation between the growth of manufacturing and the growth of productivity outside manufacturing. Kaldor's growth laws, as they are now called, which were first articulated in lectures at Cornell University and Cambridge in 1966, have generated an enormous secondary literature, as did his growth and distribution theory before. These growth laws are the subject of Chapter 7.

The distinction between secondary and primary production also becomes important in his theory of the fundamental determinants of the growth of the world economy as a closed system. In neoclassical theory, equilibrium long-run growth is determined by the exogenously given rate of growth of labour supply in efficiency units. In Kaldor's theory, by contrast, long-run equilibrium growth is determined by the rate of growth of land-saving innovations in the primary goods sector. The basic underlying hypothesis is the Keynesian one that industrial growth is demand-determined, and in a closed economy the only source of autonomous demand for industrial goods must come from agriculture. Since agriculture is subject to diminishing returns, however, successive investments in agriculture will reduce the productivity of investment and reduce the growth rate of agricultural output. Thus the demand for industrial goods will slow down unless land-saving innovations offset diminishing returns. Kaldor lectured on this model in Cambridge and elsewhere for many years but was never able to bring it to fruition in published form. My own attempt to do so first appeared in the *Oxford Economic Papers* and is reproduced here in Chapter 8.[1]

As time passed, Kaldor became the recipient of various honours for his distinguished and multifarious contributions to economics. He had been elected a Fellow of the Econometric Society as early as 1941. In 1955 he became an Honorary Member of the Royal Economic Society of Belgium, and in 1962 an honorary doctorate was bestowed on him by the University of Dijon. In 1963 he was elected a Fellow of the prestigious British Academy. He also held several visiting positions, including Economic Adviser to the Economic Commission for Latin America (1956), visiting Ford Research Professor at the University of California (1959), and Visiting Economist at the Reserve Bank of Australia in Sydney

(1963). In 1969, the first year of the Nobel Prize in Economics, the *Financial Times* (8 August) reported that he was on a short-list of ten candidates for the honour, including Milton Friedman, Paul Samuelson, James Meade, François Perroux and the Russian, Leonid Kantorovich, but he was never to receive it. By his challenge to neoclassical orthodoxy he upset too many influential people in the economics establishment, including, presumably, the Swedish Nobel Committee.

Throughout his life Kaldor was also closely involved in politics, on the left of the political spectrum, and from the 1950s on he became particularly influential in Labour Party circles. Many of his proposals for tax reform in particular, relating to equity and the allocation of resources, found their way into Labour Party policy, and he was used by the Party as both a sounding-board and a think-tank over a wide range of economic policy issues. When the Labour Party assumed power in 1964 he was the natural choice for appointment as a Special Adviser to the Chancellor of the Exchequer. During the period of the Labour government 1964–70, Kaldor probably exerted more influence on economic policy-making in the United Kingdom, directly and indirectly, than any other economist this century, bar Keynes. During this period he was promoted to a Chair of Economics at Cambridge, and in 1970 he was chosen as President of the Economics Section (Section F) of the British Association for the Advancement of Science. In 1970, he was also made an Honorary Fellow of his *alma mater*, The London School of Economics. This political interlude, together with his period as Special Adviser to the Chancellor from 1974–76, is described in Chapter 9.

Outside of economics and politics, Kaldor also had a strong professional and personal interest in the financial markets which absorbed a lot of his time. His father-in-law, Henry Goldschmidt, had been a partner of Cecil Vickers in the stockbroking firm of Vickers da Costa, and when he died shortly after the war, Kaldor formed an active association with Ralph Vickers, the son. Both realised that when the war-time excess profits tax was eventually abolished, company earnings would rise dramatically. The firm published a book, *Investing in Success*, and in 1959 the Investment Trust, Investing in Success Equities, was formed, with Kaldor as one of the founder directors. He was largely responsible for pinpointing Japan as a growth area, which led to the creation of a separate Anglo-Nippon Trust. This was followed by the establishment of two further trusts, of which Kaldor was also a director: Acorn Securities in 1959 and Investing in Foreign Growth Stocks in 1961. Ironically, both Anglo-Nippon and Investing in Foreign

Growth Stocks were effectively killed by Kaldor's own hand, as one of the architects of capital gains and corporation tax introduced by the Labour government in 1965, when he was Special Adviser to the Chancellor.

As a government adviser he was prevented from speaking publicly on topical issues of the day. In the 1960s there was a mounting campaign for Britain to enter the European Economic Community (EEC). Kaldor was strongly opposed on the proposed terms, fearing that without the ability to protect itself, Britain could become the Northern Ireland of Europe. After the Labour government was defeated in 1970, and Kaldor left office, he became the most prominent and vociferous critic among economists of Britain's stance, firing all the intellectual ammunition he could muster against the claim that Britain would derive dynamic gains from entry to a larger market. He used the occasion of his address to the Scottish Economic Society in 1970 to develop his circular and cumulative causation model of regional growth rate differences to argue that if a region or country starts weak in the growth race, it will tend to suffer a perpetual growth disadvantage through low productivity growth, growing uncompetitiveness and poor export performance – exactly the position, he believed, in which Britain would find itself in the European Community if it entered on the 'wrong terms'. A great deal of his time and energy, up to Britain's eventual entry into the EEC in 1973, was spent in arguing this case. Kaldor's involvement in the Common Market debate is outlined in Chapter 10.

With a new Labour government in 1974, he returned to the Treasury as a Special Adviser to the Chancellor of the Exchequer but, disillusioned over the direction of economic policy and by his own impotence, he resigned in 1976. In 1974, however, he had been made a life peer, and he took refuge in the House of Lords, a platform which he used to great effect during both Labour and subsequent Conservative administrations. His photograph appeared in the National Portrait Gallery for the first time. Also in 1974 he had the honour to be elected President of the Royal Economic Society for two years, an accolade much treasured by the British economics establishment. In 1975 the American Economic Association made him an honorary member, one of only fifteen living at the time. Kenneth Arrow, the President of the Association, in a letter of congratulation to Kaldor, referred to his election as 'a small tribute to your great contribution to economics.' Later in 1979 it was a source of pride and satisfaction to be made an Honorary Member of the Academy of Sciences of his native country, Hungary.

Other important economic policy issues that actively concerned him throughout his academic life were international monetary reform and the techniques of balance of payments adjustment. He predicted the collapse of the Bretton Woods system, and in the 1960s he was in the forefront of designing proposals for a new international commodity-backed reserve asset to replace the dollar. Until the early 1970s he also favoured floating exchange rates as the most sensible exchange rate system, but then lost faith as it became apparent by the mid-1970s that nominal exchange rate changes were not acting as an efficient balance of payments adjustment mechanism. Kaldor was instrumental in reviving the concept of the foreign trade multiplier (which Harrod had introduced in 1933) which predicts in its dynamic form that, if relative prices in international trade are sticky, income will act as the adjustment mechanism such that long-run economic growth is fundamentally determined by the rate of growth of export volume relative to the income elasticity of demand for imports. International economic policy is discussed in Chapter 11.

The 1960s and 1970s witnessed a strong revival in classical modes of economic thinking, no more so than in the field of monetary economics with the recrudescence of the quantity theory of money, popularised by Milton Friedman in the maxim, 'inflation is always and everywhere a monetary phenomenon', in a *causal* sense. Kaldor had been a prominent witness for the Radcliffe Committee of Inquiry on the Working of the Monetary System (1959), and its conclusions largely reflected his evidence that money is just one asset in a spectrum of liquidity, and neither money nor monetary expenditure is easy to control by conventional techniques of monetary management, the latter because of the instability of the velocity of circulation of money. Monetarism was viewed by Kaldor as an attack on the role of the state in economic affairs and a euphemism for deflation. He likened the doctrine of monetarism to the practice of witchcraft, based on equally suspect scientific foundations. Friedman hinged his causal theory of the relation between money and prices, and his anti-Keynesian stance, mainly on the alleged stability of the demand for money function; and yet, as Kaldor pointed out, a stable velocity of money, far from refuting the Keynesian income-expenditure model, supports the notion that the money supply in a credit economy adjusts passively to demand and that is why it is so difficult to control. Through a series of lectures, papers and a magnificent polemic, *The Scourge of Monetarism* (1982), Kaldor led the anti-monetarist attack world-wide. He lost the policy battle in the United Kingdom, but history will show, I believe, that he won the theoretical war, as I describe in Chapter 12.

Lastly, Kaldor will be remembered for his challenge to equilibrium theory as part of his attack on neoclassical orthodoxy and his attempt to put the study of economic forces and phenomena on a realistic footing. Virtually the whole of neoclassical economics in general, and general equilibrium theory in particular, relies on the assumption that all activities are subject to constant or decreasing returns to scale (with diminishing returns to individual factors), that perfect competition prevails, that factors get paid according to the value of their marginal product, that agents maximise, that markets eventually clear, and so on. As soon as these assumptions are relaxed the house of neoclassical economics and general equilibrium theory appears to rest on very shaky foundations. Market clearing and full employment cannot be guaranteed; product and factor prices may not tend to equilibrium; 'regional' growth rate differences may diverge; balance of payments disequilibrium may persist and so on. Kaldor demonstrated in his work that economics can be written without resort to equilibrium assumptions, and that it is likely to be a good deal more realistic, and therefore interesting. *A priori* modelling may be more intellectually satisfying, but what is the point of the deductive method if it is based on a series of totally unrealistic assumptions? In his 'Recollections of an Economist' (Kaldor, 1986a), he gave a reminder of what he said in 1966: 'it is the hallmark of the neoclassical economist to believe that however severe the abstraction from which he is forced to start, he will win through by the end of the day – bit by bit, if he only carried the analysis far enough, the scaffolding can be removed, leaving the basic structure intact' (1966a). He went on,

I should, perhaps, have added that it is also the hallmark of the neo-classical economist – when he takes off his hat as a pure theorist and puts on his hat as a policy adviser or as an interpreter of current events – to behave as if the scaffolding *had been* removed already, and the basic structure had been *shown* to remain intact. When it comes to judging the effects of particular policy measures – whether it relates to unemployment, foreign trade, the incidence of taxation, exchange rates, etc. – he applies conclusions derived from the theory of general equilibrium to the real world without hesitation: that is to say without investigating how far his results are dependent on implied or explicit assumptions that are manifestly contrary to experience.

That, it might be said, is the problem with so much of modern economics.

In thinking and writing about Kaldor's life and work as an economist, it is impossible not to detect certain similarities with

Keynes. It is not only that Kaldor was one of the first converts to the Keynesian revolution outside of Cambridge, and then followed in Keynes' footsteps to King's College. The two men shared several characteristics in common, and in many respects Kaldor took on, consciously or unconsciously, the mantle shed by Keynes. First there was their urge to protest, combined with rational argument and persuasion. Keynes attributed his own presumption of rationality and his approach to the influence on policy to his early beliefs as an Apostle and as a member of the Bloomsbury Group. In his Essay to the Memoir Club in 1938[2] he talks of 'the impulse to protest, to write a letter to *The Times*, call a meeting in the Guildhall etc. etc. I behave as if there really existed some authority or standard to which I can successfully appeal if I shout loud enough.' Kaldor was an inveterate writer to *The Times* (and to many other newspapers) for over half a century, the most prolific of any economist this century, and an ardent campaigner for many causes, e.g. land nationalisation, tax reform, nuclear disarmament, and the anti-Common Market campaign, to name but a few.

Secondly, Keynes and Kaldor shared the belief that economics is and should be a moral science. Keynes regarded economics as a branch of ethics in the Cambridge tradition of Marshall, Pigou, Sidgwick and his father, Neville Keynes. Kaldor carried on the tradition. Only in his early years did he sometimes pursue economic theory for its own sake. For most of his life he used theory as a vehicle for elucidating complex economic phenomena and for understanding and ameliorating pressing contemporary economic difficulties. Throughout his writings there is an overriding concern for policy. He was a firm believer in the inductive method of economic analysis and a stern critic of deductive models which substitute elegance for relevance. In his recipe for the master economist, Keynes noted that good economists are scarce because the gift for using vigilant observations to choose appropriate models, although it does not require specialist skills of an unusually high order, appears to be a very rare one.[3] The explanation, he argued, lies in the fact that the master economist must possess a rare combination of gifts.

He must be mathematician, historian, statesman, philosopher – in some degree. He must contemplate the particular in terms of the general, and touch abstract and concrete in the same flight of thought. He must study the present in the light of the past for the purposes of the future. No part of man's nature or his institutions must be entirely outside his guard. He must be purposeful and disinterested in a simultaneous mood; as aloof and incorruptible as an artist, yet sometimes as near the earth as a politician.[4]

Kaldor never claimed to be a mathematician, but several of the other 'Keynesian' ingredients of a successful economist he acquired in good measure. Above all, like Keynes, he possessed that strong intuition and insight that enables people to distinguish the important from the unimportant, to understand complex (economic) relationships in a simple way, and which ultimately separate the great from the ordinary. What Keynes said of Marshall could also serve as an appropriate epitaph for Kaldor:

But it was an essential truth to which he held firmly that those individuals who are endowed with a special genius for the subject of economics and have a powerful economic intuition will often be more right in their conclusions and implicit presumptions than in their explanations and explicit statements. That is to say their intuitions will be in advance of their analysis and their terminology. Great respect, therefore, is due to that general scheme of thought, and it is a poor thing to pester their memories with criticism which is purely verbal.[5]

Much of Kaldor's work on disequilibrium growth and the theory of economic development falls, I believe, into this category.

Keynes and Kaldor were not only primarily interested in policy first and theory second, but both were actively involved in policy making at the highest level. Keynes' advisory career in the Treasury, in both an official and unofficial capacity, spanned more than thirty years, from the age of 29, when he was a member of the Royal Commission on Indian Currency and Finance in 1913, until his death in 1946. Kaldor had the ear of politicians from an early age; sat on one Royal Commission; gave evidence to numerous Select Committees, and crowned his domestic advisory role by acting as Special Adviser to three Labour Chancellors of the Exchequer. Both men had supreme faith in the power of intelligence and believed that through clear thought and appropriate action any problem could be solved.

To a certain extent, the two men also thought alike, politically and philosophically. It is true that Keynes was active in the Liberal Party, while Kaldor was a life-long socialist, but by his own admission Keynes lay on the 'liberal socialist' section of the political spectrum; more or less the position of Kaldor. Practically and philosophically what this amounts to is an espousal of the good life, and personal freedom to enjoy it, coupled with a desire to see a greater equality of opportunity to spread prosperity as widely as possible. Kaldor, though, was more of an egalatarian socialist than Keynes, and believed in a more *dirigiste* approach to policy-making.

Finally, both men suffered misinterpretation and misunderstanding in their lifetime. Every society and every profession needs its live heroes and whipping boys. In the economics profession, Keynes took on this dual role from World War I to his death. He was clever, articulate, urbane, a man of the world, and fundamentally revolutionised the way economists thought about economic behaviour at the macro-level. By many he was deeply admired; for others, he was a dangerous subversive who, by the use of the phrase 'the socialisation of investment', apparently declared his intention to undermine the prevailing organisation of free enterprise capitalism. In fact, of course, the very opposite was true. Keynes wished to save liberal capitalism, and by the practical application of his theories he helped to do so.

Kaldor is also a hero to many, in particular to those who find it difficult to accept an orthodox neoclassical view of the world. During his life this gave him a strong band of disciples throughout the world, especially in continental Europe and parts of Asia. At the same time he had many intellectual and political adversaries. The intellectual hostility came from asking awkward questions about neoclassical economics in general and equilibrium theory in particular, and was understandably most prevalent in the United States where his following was slight and his supporters were scattered. The political hostility and suspicion may have had something to do with his Hungarian background and with the facile association sometimes conjured up, particularly by the media, between the political systems of countries and the politics of people who have been born there. Needless to say, the idea of Kaldor as a subversive – a revolutionary rather than a reformer – could not have been further from the truth and could have had nothing to do with what he either said or wrote. He was not enamoured with capitalism and the power conferred by the possession of wealth, but equally he distrusted the centralisation of power which is an inherent feature of state socialism. In a paper delivered at a Conference in Mexico City in 1978 on the theme of 'Public Enterprise in Mixed Economies' he wrote:

'The greatest problem of the socialist countries which has not so far been resolved is connected with the centralisation of power which appears to be an inevitable adjunct of universal state ownership.... I do not think many people would dissent from the view that centralisation of power is undesirable in human society, as it generally leads to both moral and material corruption of those who exercise power. (1980d)

Above all, he was a democrat and in the last resort would probably have agreed with Keynes 'that it is better that a man should tyrannise over his bank balance than over his fellow citizens'.[6]

NOTES

1. 'A General Model of Growth and Development on Kaldorian Lines', *Oxford Economic Papers*, July 1986.
2. *The Collected Writings of J. M. Keynes*. Vol. X: *Essays in Biography* (London: Macmillan, 1972), p. 448.
3. *The Collected Writings of J. M. Keynes*. Vol. XIV: *The General Theory and After: Part II Defence and Development* (London: Macmillan, 1973), pp. 296–7, 300.
4. 'Alfred Marshall', in *Collected Writings of J. M. Keynes*. Vol. X, *op. cit.*, pp. 173–4.
5. Ibid., p. 211.
6. J. M. Keynes, *The General Theory of Employment, Interest and Money* (London: Macmillan, 1936), p. 374.

1   Early Life, 1908 To 1939

Nicholas (Nicky) Kaldor – or, in Hungarian, Káldor Miklós (Miki) – was born in Budapest on 12 May 1908 into a comfortable middle-class Jewish family.[1] Their home was a spacious apartment at 7 Géza Street near the Houses of Parliament, and still stands today. His father, Julius (Gyula), was of relatively humble origins, from a small Jewish community in the village of Kereny near Zombor, the capital of Bacska district, lying between the Danube and Tisza rivers about 150 miles south of Budapest. Julius, born in 1870, was the brightest son of a large family and received the best education possible at the local *Gymnasium*. From there he went to the University of Budapest to study law, living with his sister's family. He first came to prominence as a young lawyer in a famous and well-publicised trial in which he defended a young girl whose illegitimate child had been murdered and disposed of by her family to avoid disgrace. The defence was that the girl had no knowledge of what the family had done, and largely as a result of Julius's moving and eloquent speech at the jury trial (itself a novelty at that time in Hungary) she was acquitted. The trial caused a great stir and assured the father notoriety as well as success. Later on, he was to become legal adviser to the German Legation in Budapest as a result of another famous trial, this time involving fraud. In 1918 a number of German investors were swindled by a group of Hungarian stockbrokers who fabricated share price data. Julius first acted on behalf of his own clients, and then, as the German Legation received more complaints, it was suggested that he handle the whole business. This he did and secured the conviction of the swindlers. He was then formally appointed as the Legation's legal adviser. This was a lucrative post, improving the family finances which in turn were instrumental in financing Nicky's university education both in Berlin and London. The father suffered the misfortune of a nervous breakdown in the late

1920s and died in 1932, but not before feeling the pride of his son's appointment as an Assistant on the teaching staff at the London School of Economics (LSE).

Nicky's mother, Joan (Jamba), was twelve years younger than his father and came from a higher class Jewish family resident in Budapest, with interests in banking and the wholesale trade. She was educated at the Queen Elizabeth High School, the leading school for girls in Budapest at the time, and was particularly well versed in languages, including English, which proved to be useful to Nicky later. Joan and Julius married in 1901 and Nicky was their fourth child. There had been two previous sons and a daughter, but the two sons died in infancy, one at six months and the other at the age of two from scarlet fever. Nicky, as the only son in a Jewish family, was guaranteed a special place. The family was superstitious, and there was some concern that he would be born on the 'unlucky' 13 May but, so the story goes, this was avoided with the help of doctors and he arrived with fifteen minutes to spare.

Nicky first attended school at the age of six, at the outbreak of war in Europe. He remembers very well the news of the assassination of the Archduke Ferdinand at Sarajevo, but has no special memories of his early schooling. At the age of ten he transferred to Budapest's *Minta* (or Model) *Gymnasium*, sometimes referred to as 'the Winchester of Hungary'. It was no ordinary school. It was managed directly under the auspices of the University of Budapest rather than the Ministry of Education, and was held to be a 'model' school for prospective teachers. It was famous for its Socratic method of teaching. The classes were relatively large, up to 40 pupils, and the boys came from a wide cross-section of Hungarian society, from counts to artisans, Jews and Gentiles. Nicky's education was squarely in the classical tradition with an emphasis on languages and history. In English he received occasional private lessons at home, as well as some instruction from his mother. He developed his own interest in politics and also in freelance journalism which became a passion, and which he continued to practise during his student days in Berlin and London. The Minta school produced a long line of distinguished academics in those early years of the twentieth century, including Michael Polanyi, Edward Teller, Leo Szillard, Theo von Karman, Nicholas Kurti, Thomas Balogh, as well as Kaldor himself. John von Neumann, the brilliant mathematician-cum-polymath, was also a contemporary but attended the Evangelical School. Nicky was to become friendly with him in the early 1930s when they took summer walks together in the Buda Hills.

They renewed their acquaintance in Princeton in 1935–36 while Nicky was in the United States on a Rockefeller Scholarship and von Neumann was based at the Institute for Advanced Study.

Nicky's most cherished school friend was Robert ('Lolo') Vambery, grandson of the Orientalist, Arminius Vambery, a talented boy who subsequently became a playwright and emigrated to America in 1938. It was at the instigation of Vambery's father, a well-known criminal lawyer, that Nicky took his final examinations (Matura) at the Minta early (coached by Louis Erdos the father of the brilliant Hungarian mathematician, Paul Erdos). Both Robert Vambery and Nicky went to Berlin: Vambery in 1927 to work with Berthold Brecht on a production of the *Threepenny Opera*; Nicky in 1925 to enrol at the University of Berlin to study economics. Berlin was chosen as one of the leading European universities at the time, and Nicky spoke German fluently. At the same time he also enrolled in the Law Faculty at the University of Budapest, as a sort of insurance policy, taking preliminary oral exams on his return from Berlin (and later from London) in vacations, but he chose not to complete the degree. He was not exposed to economics at school and the major impetus behind his desire to study economics in Berlin seems to have come partly from his wider interest in politics and partly from his fascination with the German inflation of 1923 which he had witnessed and experienced first hand while on vacation in Garmisch-Partenkirchen in the Bavarian Alps. In January 1919 the mark quotation for the dollar was 8.9; in July 1922, 493.2; in October 1923, 25,260 million, and in the following month, 4200 billion! It was the same inflation, incidentally, that caused Richard Kahn, Nicky's later colleague at King's College, Cambridge, to lose faith in the Quantity Theory of Money, when he observed that although the German banknote printers were on strike, and money was severely rationed, prices still doubled every twenty-four hours.[2] Later, Nicky was given by his father a copy of Keynes' *Economic Consequences of the Peace* which further whetted his appetite for economics.

His eighteen months in Berlin from October 1925 to the spring of 1927 were not particularly fruitful. The Humboldt University was chaotic, the courses were unstructured, and none of his teachers (including Werner Sombart and Hermann Schumacher, the father of E. F. Schumacher) made an impression on him. He spent more time as an accredited foreign correspondent to a Hungarian newspaper, with official access to the Reichstag and a regular appointment with the Foreign Secretary, Stressmann, every Friday. He came into contact, however, with several

Germans who had studied in England and who spoke highly of the London School of Economics. The Vambery family were also strong anglophiles and received a constant stream of visitors from England which engendered in Nicky a curiosity and fascination for the country.

Kaldor arrived in London in April 1927 intending initially to spend only one term at the LSE, and accordingly registered as a general student, not for a degree. The object was to improve his English, which was still rudimentary, and to sample a variety of lectures and the atmosphere of the School. On his own admission, he did not take the term particularly seriously, and spent as much time on journalism as anything, which he continued during his undergraduate days. He wrote for the Hungarian newspaper *Magyar Hirlap* and was the London correspondent of *Pester Lloyd*, with his own personalised headed notepaper. He also worked for the London General Press which syndicated his articles in several countries. He specialised in conducting interviews with prominent personalities. In Europe, where he spent the summers, his interviewees were mainly political figures; in England he approached mainly literary figures, including Hilaire Belloc, G.K. Chesterton, Arnold Bennett, John Galsworthy, H. G. Wells, Sir Arthur Conan Doyle, Rebecca West, and others. Not all cooperated, but many did. The fees ranged from two to twelve guineas depending on the prominence of the person and the length of the article. A Central European theatrical agency also employed him to buy the playing rights of new plays in London, enabling him to attend many 'first nights'. The income from these sources, which amounted to well over £100 per annum, was a useful supplement to the allowance given by his father. Although he was rather casual in this first term at the School, his interest in study and economics grew sufficiently for him to enrol for the B.Sc. (Econ.) degree from October 1927. He lodged first in South Hampstead and then in various rooms in the Bloomsbury area.

He appears to have made no special friends as an undergraduate, except for Honor Scott (later Croome) who was the niece of C. P. Scott, editor of the *Manchester Guardian*, with whom he later collaborated in the translation from the German of von Hayek's *Monetary Theory and the Trade Cycle*. His first year supervisor, whom he held in high regard, was the economic historian Eileen Power who later married Michael Postan, also appointed to the staff of the School in the 1930s. Other members of the teaching staff covering statistics, commerce, economic history and banking, as well as economics, included: Professor A. L. Bowley (Mathematics and Statistics); Hugh Dalton (Reader in Economics); R. B. Forrester

(Reader in Foreign Trade); Professor T. E. Gregory (Banking and Currency); J. R. Hicks (Assistant in Economics); Professor A. J. Sargent (Commerce); R. H. Tawney (Reader in Economic History); P. Barrett Whale (Lecturer in Commerce), and Professor A. A. Young (Political Economy). The first year teaching consisted of 26 lectures on the Elements of Economics given by Dalton using as texts Cannan's *Wealth* and Henderson's *Supply and Demand;* fourteen lectures on Money, Banking and International Exchange given by Barrett Whale, and fourteen lectures on Trade and Industry given by Hicks.

Nicky's first year performance in economics was not particularly distinguished. He was also weak in mathematics and had to take private tuition before taking his exam a second time. After passing he wrote with apparent relief to his private tutor that he could 'now enjoy the glorious prospect that I have nothing to do with mathematics in the future'. In the second and third years there was a dramatic improvement in his work as he began to take his studies more seriously and as his interest in economics deepened. A few of his undergraduate essays still survive, including one on Malthus and a sophisticated exposition of Spiethoff's 'disproportionality' theory of the trade cycle.

The Head of Economics at the time was Professor Allyn Young, an American from Harvard who had been appointed in 1927 following the retirement in 1926 of Professor Edwin Cannan who had combined his appointment at the School with teaching in Oxford. At the time of Cannan's retirement there was a general consensus in the School that economics was in need of revitalisation with a view to expansion. At the part-two level there were several economic specialisms. Some were well staffed, others not. Economics: Analytical and Descriptive, in which Kaldor chose to specialise, was particularly weak. The Director of the School, William Beveridge, initiated the search for an economist of distinction to strengthen the theoretical side of economics and to spearhead the Department. Apparently no one suitable in the United Kingdom could be found or persuaded, and Young was invited to fill the post. To attract him, a special Chair was created with an above-average professorial salary. Although an erudite and eminent economist, who had been the chief American Treasury delegate to the Versailles Peace Conference in 1919, he turned out to be an indifferent lecturer and a poor administrator, and the original intention of rejuvenating economics and bringing some order to chaos was thwarted. He then suffered an untimely death from pneumonia in January 1929 at the age of 53, leaving the Economics Department where it was in 1926. Young

may have been an indifferent lecturer, but Kaldor found him an
inspiring teacher who sparked his interest in several fields. Kaldor,
in turn, impressed Young, particularly by some of the papers he
wrote including one on the nature of rent. Young himself wrote
very little, but one paper in particular was to leave a deep and
lasting impression on Kaldor (which he resurrected and popularised in later years), namely his 1928 address to the British
Association for the Advancement of Science entitled 'Increasing
Returns and Economic Progress' (*Economic Journal*, December
1928). Notwithstanding its serious implications for the whole
edifice of neoclassical economics, even Lionel Robbins described
this paper as 'one of the most important contributions to pure
economic analysis of that part of the century'.[3] The paper revived
the Smithian idea (expounded in the first chapters of Book One of
The Wealth of Nations and then forgotten) of economic progress as a
cumulative process in which, through increasing returns as a
macroeconomic phenomenon, the division of labour expands the
market and the expansion of the market leads to the further
division of labour. Just before his death, Young had hired Colin
Clark as his assistant to pursue research in the field. Increasing
returns has profound implications indeed for neoclassical equilibrium economics, and Young's insights formed part of Kaldor's
own challenge to equilibrium theory (see Chapters 7 and 13).

To fill the vacuum created by Young's death, Lionel Robbins was
appointed from New College, Oxford, at the age of thirty, making
him the youngest professor in the country. Because of his youth
and inexperience, a new ordinary Chair was created for him and
Young's Chair lapsed. Robbins was a graduate of the LSE in 1923
and had briefly held a lectureship there in the academic years
1925–27 when he shared the economics teaching with Hugh
Dalton. Prior to that he had been a temporary tutor of New
College in 1924–25, whence he returned in 1927. Robbins'
appointment at the School, supported by Dalton, caused heated
controversy and was bitterly opposed by some of the staff, notably
Harold Laski the Professor of Politics. The dust eventually settled,
however, and there began for Robbins an association with the
School that was to last for over fifty years, including the position
of Chairman of the Court of Governors from 1968 to 1974. With
precocious maturity he displayed all the characteristics that the
School had been looking for in Young – an inspirational teacher
and, above all, a flair for administration. As far as the teaching of
economics was concerned, there was no administrative apparatus
at the time for the coordination of the various specialisms in
economics such as Economics: Analytical and Descriptive; Bank-

ing, Currency and Finance of International Trade; Commerce; Organisation of Transport and International Trade; Statistics using Demography; Economic History, and so on. Each had its own Departmental Head, but there was no formal mechanism for consultation between the various Heads. Consequently, staffing and teaching arrangements for the various specialisms were not properly coordinated. Robbins initiated two forms of consultation: first, a weekly meeting over tea for any of the economics staff who wished to come along and air a problem; and secondly, periodic meetings of the Professorial Heads of the various specialisms.

In those first two years of his appointment, Robbins unquestionably made a major impact on the life of the School and on the teaching of economics, both by his own example, and through the staff that he gradually gathered around him. Among the younger economists at the time, later to become eminent, were R. G. D. Allen (in Statistics), John Hicks and Frederick Benham. Arnold Plant was recruited at Professorial level in 1930 to take charge of Business Administration, and Friedrich von Hayek joined in 1931 as the Tooke Professor of Economic Science and Statistics with shared responsibility with Robbins for Economics: Analytical and Descriptive. Other recruits at a junior level from 1929 on included: George Schwartz, Frank Paish, Jack Gilbert, Evan Durbin, Richard Sayers, Maurice Allen, Abba Lerner, Brinley Thomas, Ronald Coase, Ronald Edwards, Ursula Webb and Kaldor himself. Visitors and research students from abroad during the 1930s included: Haberler and Machlup from Vienna, Bresciani-Turroni from Rome, Lindahl, Ohlin and Frisch from Scandinavia, Schneider, Rothbarth and Emminger from Germany, Kalecki from Poland, Scitovsky from Hungary, and Marget, Knight and Viner from the USA. In this halcyon period the School moved to the centre of the economics stage even if its outlook was somewhat narrow, dominated by the economic liberalism of Robbins, and of Hayek, whom Robbins had deliberately enticed to London as a counterweight to the growing intellectual and political influence of Keynes and Cambridge. Hayek arrived in January 1931 and delivered four lectures, subsequently published as *Prices and Production*. They were enthusiastically received with a certain degree of awe, but not, by all accounts, with a great deal of understanding. When he gave the same lectures in Cambridge there was total incomprehension and embarrassing silence. Only Richard Kahn plucked up courage to ask a question. 'Is it true', he enquired, 'that if I went out tomorrow and bought an umbrella this would cause unemployment?' 'Yes', replied Hayek, 'but it would take a long mathematical argument to explain why.' Keynes was led to remark, 'it is an extraordinary example of how, starting with a mistake, a remorseless logician can end up in bedlam'.[4]

In his third year at the School, Kaldor learnt most of his economic theory from Robbins and from Maurice Allen, a young lecturer of the same age who had just graduated the year before. Allen later became a Fellow of Balliol College, Oxford, and a distinguished public servant in the Bank of England and the IMF. Both teachers made their impact in different ways: Robbins for his enthusiasm, erudition and mastery of the subject; Allen for his theoretical and technical virtuosity. Kaldor probably learnt more of his economics from Allen than anyone else. The theoretical emphasis was primarily in the field of microeconomics, with special emphasis on the theory of the firm and the cost controversy starting with Clapham's 'On Empty Economic Boxes' (*Economic Journal*, September 1922), followed by Sraffa's paper on 'The Laws of Returns Under Competitive Conditions' (*Economic Journal*, December 1926). There was relatively little exposure to, or discussion of, macroeconomic issues based, for example, on the writings of Dennis Robertson or Keynes. This was due partly to the neglect of Gregory who taught Principles of Currency, and who was hopelessly out of date in his reading, and never seriously considered Keynes' work. As a research student, however, Kaldor took an early interest in the *Treatise*, taking the trouble to write to Keynes soon after publication asking for clarification over his exchange with Dennis Robertson in the *Economic Journal* of 1931.[5] This is one of the first public signs of the intricacies of his agile mind and of his amazing command of the English language for a foreign student resident in England for only four years. The standard reading at the School were the books of Cannan on *Wealth, Money*, and the *History of Economic Doctrine*. Also some of the Cambridge Economic Handbooks, written under the general editorship of Keynes, were widely used, such as Henderson's *Supply and Demand* (1922) and Robertson's *Money* (1922) and *Control of Industry* (1923). Graduating students at that time took four examination papers in their special subject; three compulsory papers in Principles of Economics, Banking and Currency, and Economic History since 1815; Statistics and Scientific Method (for those specialising in economics); an essay paper, and one other. In the final examinations of 1930, only two first class degrees were awarded, one to Honor Scott, the other to Kaldor. Out of the ten finals papers, he obtained five clear alphas, his worst paper being Statistics and Scientific Method. The external examiner was the Cambridge economist, Maurice Dobb, who was even more impressed by Kaldor than the internal examiners and marked him up.

Robbins wrote personally to congratulate him on his achievement. Kaldor became Robbins' favourite pupil and he owed much to Robbins for his early advancement at the School. It was Robbins' influence with Beveridge that secured for him the only research studentship available in the School that year, worth £200 per annum, and his first taste of teaching came with taking supervisions for Robbins of second and third year theory students.

Kaldor's chosen research project was the Problems of the Danubian Succession States of Austria, Hungary, Czechoslovakia, Romania and Yugoslavia. One term of his two-year research studentship he spent at the University of Vienna in 1931. The main fruits were four anonymous articles on the subject in *The Economist* newspaper (14, 21 and 28 May and 4 June 1932); an article on 'The Economic Situation of Austria' in the *Harvard Business Review* (October 1932), and his first published letter in *The Times* on the dominance of farming in the Danubian States (31 March 1932). The states were experiencing several economic difficulties at the time, among them: the disintegration of trade between the states resulting from the break-up of the Austro-Hungarian monarchy, falling commodity prices and problems in servicing international debt – all of which led to the imposition of exchange restrictions. Kaldor was highly critical of this policy response and of the institution of bilateral trade deals, favouring instead devaluation to reduce the distortion between domestic and international prices and to expand trade. His argument against exchange restrictions elicited a letter of support from Hayek.

Hayek, as well as Robbins, was a dominant influence on Kaldor's thinking. In 1930 he had already embarked on an English translation of Hayek's *Monetary Theory and the Trade Cycle* assisted by his undergraduate companion Honor Croome (nee Scott) who helped to improve the English. Hayek welcomed the translation, and by the time the book was published in 1933, Hayek was already resident in England. Kaldor also translated from the German a paper by Hayek on 'The Paradox of Saving' which he published in *Economica* (May 1931). It was over this paper that Kaldor first started to lose respect for Hayek and his work which was to culminate in devastating critiques of his trade cycle theories and other contributions. There were many aspects of the 'Paradox of Saving' article that Kaldor did not fully understand. When he later had the opportunity to question Hayek about his doubts, no satisfactory explanation was forthcoming. From that point on he increasingly began to question Hayek's standing as a serious economist.

Hayek's early intellectual influence on Kaldor is clearly visible in his 1932 article on 'The Economic Situation of Austria' (1932b) which is almost pure Hayek in its analysis of the over-commitment of Austrian industry (see Chapter 2). There was more to the slump, he argued, than simply protectionism and the collapse of commodity prices. Factors inherent in the economic system itself must be understood arising from the 'wrong' response to the need to adjust living standards downwards. The movements in production, prices, costs, the value of industrial capital, savings and the volume of consumption were all examined for Austria over the years 1925–29. Industry was demonstrably working at a loss, eating into its capital, and once started the process had become cumulative. The banks, which owned large sections of industry, financed the losses to prevent enterprises closing, thus perpetuating a loss-making regime. Keynes was originally going to take the article for the June 1932 issue of the *Economic Journal*, but then declined it on receipt of the revised version.

During the tenure of his research studentship, Kaldor was busy in several other ways: widening his reading – although he was never an avid reader; cultivating academic friendships; translating economic literature from the German; practising his love of journalism, and taking an active interest in the weekly economic seminar run by Robbins and Hayek. This seminar has become as legendary in the folklore of the LSE as the Political Economy Club run by Keynes in Cambridge. Two special friends, later to become well-known economists, were Thomas Balogh and Paul Rosenstein-Rodan with whom Kaldor shared a flat in Gordon Square, Bloomsbury. Balogh, who had attended the same school as Kaldor in Hungary, came to England via America with a letter of recommendation from Schumpeter to Keynes. Keynes was initially attracted by him and secured for him a job in the City. Kaldor and Balogh (or Buddha and Pest as they were later called, sometimes affectionately and at other times disparagingly)[6] remained life-long friends, although they often disagreed, and both became influential thinkers in the British Labour Party, reaching high advisory office in the Labour government of 1964 (see Chapter 9). Rosenstein-Rodan came from a rich Polish family. He had travelled widely and knew the economics profession inside out, but neither he nor Balogh exerted any strong intellectual influence on Kaldor in those early years. His main source of ideas and intellectual companion was John Hicks, four years his senior, who came to the School from Oxford as an Assistant in Economics in 1926. Hicks gave lectures to graduate students on advanced economic theory which Kaldor attended. Just as Robbins had brought to the School the Austrian thought of Ludwig von Mises,

Carl Menger and Böhm-Bawerk, so Hicks introduced Walras and Pareto, comparing and contrasting their theories with the partial equilibrium approach of Marshall. Thus it was that Hicks helped Kaldor to escape from the narrow dogmatism of the Austrian School. Later Hicks was instrumental in exposing Kaldor to the Swedes, together with Brinley Thomas who had studied in Sweden and in 1934 gave a graduate course on Neo-Wicksellian Fluctuation Theory in Sweden which stimulated discussion. It was largely through Thomas that the *ex ante ex post* distinction was absorbed in London.[7] Hicks read Myrdal's essay on 'Monetary Equilibrium' which originally appeared in a collection of essays edited by Hayek (*Beiträge zur Geldtheorie*, Vienna, 1933). Kaldor borrowed Hicks' copy of the book and became influenced by Myrdal before Keynes. Thus Myrdal's essay prepared both Hicks and Kaldor for the Keynesian revolution to come. Intellectual discourse between Kaldor and Hicks was facilitated by the fact that they shared adjacent flats in Great Ormond Street and were constant companions, including taking holidays together, before their respective marriages – Kaldor to Clarisse Goldschmidt in December 1934, and Hicks to Ursula Webb in 1935. Kaldor also had the privilege of reading Hicks' *Value and Capital* (1939) almost chapter by chapter as it was written, consolidating his knowledge of money and general equilibrium theory.

It has already been mentioned that relatively little 'Keynesian' or Cambridge macroeconomics was taught at the LSE, at least while Kaldor was an undergraduate. Matters improved in 1930/31 when Dennis Robertson taught the Principles of Currency in place of Gregory but this was only for one year. At the end of 1930 an open clash developed between Robbins and Keynes representing, in a sense, the opposing Schools of London and Cambridge. Keynes had been asked by the Prime Minister, Ramsey MacDonald, to chair a Committee of Economists of the Economic Advisory Council. Included were Pigou, Josiah Stamp, Hubert Henderson and Robbins. Keynes had opposed the return to the gold standard in 1925 at the pre-war parity, but after the return he was against devaluation. The only real alternative was, therefore, protection (or, more precisely, a tariff-cum-bounty which would be formally equivalent to devaluation) which was bitterly opposed by Robbins. The clash highlighted a deeper intellectual and philosophical schism which was to become more pronounced as the 1930s progressed, with Robbins virtually denying that the inter-war depression had anything to do with a lack of effective demand and rejecting the diagnosis of the *General Theory* and the policy prescription of public works as a solution to unemployment. He believed, along with many of his hand-picked colleagues, in the orthodox Treasury view of resource crowding-out. Robbins admitted in later life that his stand against Keynes was the greatest intellectual mistake he ever made;[8] a repenter like Pigou.

Keynes was a not infrequent visitor to the LSE, and Kaldor first met him there. He occasionally addressed the graduate students, and read papers to the London Economics Club comprising Faculty members and selected graduate students. The Royal Economic Society, of which Keynes was Secretary, also held its annual meeting at the LSE. Kaldor became increasingly torn between Robbins and Keynes as mentors. In those early years of the 1930s his bread was still buttered by Robbins, but a metamorphosis was gradually taking place. After his appointment to the staff of the School in 1932 he began to feel a free spirit, and from then on relations with Robbins cooled, to a degree eventually bordering on hostility. Old allegiances die hard, however, and in 1933 Kaldor was still, if anything, in the Robbins camp at least as far as free trade was concerned. Keynes, by contrast, was campaigning for protection and the minimisation of international economic relations in the interests of peace. Kaldor took issue with Keynes' two articles on 'National Self-Sufficiency' published in the *New Statesman and Nation* (8 and 15 July). Keynes argued, firstly, that the advantages of the international division of labour had declined since the nineteenth century and no longer outweighed the political disadvantages, so that the economic cost of national self-sufficiency would not outweigh the other advantages of bringing the producer and consumer within the ambit of the same national economic and financial organisation; and secondly, that the free movement of capital leads to a much higher rate of interest than necessary for material prosperity at home. Thus 'let goods be homespun' and 'finance be primarily national' became his plea. Kaldor in reply (15 July) contended that there was nothing in modern industrial development which had reduced the advantages of the international division of labour and trade, and asked Keynes for evidence. Kaldor's stress was on the dynamic advantages of trade based on increasing returns from larger markets. In a further letter (5 August), replying to Austin Robinson, who had defended Keynes arguing that Kaldor had exaggerated scale economies, he made the Allyn Young point that the really significant economies of large scale do not depend so much on the output of the individual industry as on the output of industry as a whole. Even if there were no significant economies from the increase of output of a single commodity, a very considerable reduction in costs would occur if the size of all markets expanded simultaneously, and the extent to which these economies can be realised depends on the size of the free trade area. Kaldor, and others like Joan Robinson, were against protection on beggar-thy-neighbour grounds; having gone off gold in 1931 there appeared to be no further case for protection. To stimulate demand there were better, more desirable, alternatives. The argument for protection to promote industrialisation did not engage Kaldor at the time, Britain being already a highly industrialised country. With hindsight, he could not understand why he was a free-trader, and was later to attribute Britain's rapid industrial recovery in the 1930s to the protectionist measures that were taken. In retrospect he also believed Keynes to have been right on the need to control capital movements. Keynes refrained from responding to the comments on his articles.

As far as Kaldor's academic career is concerned, he was first appointed to a temporary lecturing post at the School in the summer term of 1931-32 to replace Frank Pakenham (later Lord Longford), and then to the permanent staff as an Assistant in October 1932 (afterwards renamed Assistant Lecturer). Such a post normally carried automatic promotion after four years, but owing to the antipathy that had grown up between himself and Robbins, he was denied a lectureship until 1938. Interestingly, Hicks was also held back at the School; in his case by Beveridge who was hostile to economic theory and to economic theoreticians. Kaldor's colleagues in economics and related subjects in those heady days of 1932 (apart from Professors Robbins, Hayek, Plant and Gregory) were: Hicks, Hugh Dalton, Frank Paish, George Schwartz, Richard Sayers, H. E. Batson, Evan Durbin, R. G. D. Allen, Brinley Thomas, Frederick Benham and P. Barrett Whale. The last named was often quoted with approval by Kaldor in later years for recognising that the foreign trade multiplier provides a far more convincing explanation of the workings of the nineteenth-century gold standard than the classical theory which relied on gold flows and on induced relative price changes.[9]

In the early years, Kaldor's teaching was not particularly arduous, although all lectures and classes at that time had to be repeated for the benefit of evening students. By all accounts, he was a superb teacher. Aubrey Jones, a student from 1929 to 1934, who got the top first in 1932, has described Kaldor as the most stimulating and helpful of all the tutors he had.[10] Another of Kaldor's star pupils who graduated with a top first in 1936 was Erwin Rothbarth, who later went to Cambridge as Statistical Assistant in the Faculty of Economics and collaborated with Kaldor on matters of war finance including the question of how to measure the cost of living in the presence of rationing (1941a). When Rothbarth was tragically killed in action in Holland in 1944, Kaldor with Champernowne wrote his obituary for the *Economic Journal* (1945a). Kaldor shared economic theory classes with Batson, Benham and Thomas. His lecturing consisted of eight lectures on the Theory of Costs in the Lent term and four lectures on the Danubian Problem in the summer term. The syllabus for the Theory of Costs reads as follows:

Classification of various cost concepts. Limitations in the concept of displacement costs. Cost analysis from the point of view of general and particular equilibrium. Short and long run analysis. The laws of returns and the problem of separating technical from psychological factors. Social costs and 'transfer expenditure'. Internal and external economies. The equilibrium firm. The compatibility of increasing returns with competitive equilibrium. Costs under a regime of imperfect competition. The present state of the theory of costs.[11]

The emphasis of the syllabus naturally changed from year to year, but he taught this course for nine years until 1941, with the title changed to the Theory of Production in 1934. The recommended reading was extensive, including literature in German and Italian for those who could read it. Books particularly recommended were Cannan's *Review of Economic Theory*, Marshall's *Principles*, Pigou's *Economics of Welfare*, and Knight's *Risk, Uncertainty and Profit*. Articles recommended included: Allyn Young's 'Increasing Returns and Economic Progress' (*Economic Journal*, 1928); D. H. Robertson, P. Sraffa and G. F. Shove, 'A Symposium on Increasing Returns' (*Economic Journal*, 1930), and Viner's 'Cost Curves and Supply Curves' (*Zeitschrift fur Nationalökomonie*, 1931).

At the same time as starting teaching, he published his first two papers in 1932. 'The Economic Situation of Austria' has already been mentioned. The other was a major review article entitled 'A Case Against Technical Progress' of the book *Technischer Fortschrift und Arbeitslosigkeit* by Emile Lederer (*Economica*, May). Lederer, a Professor at the University of Berlin, attacked the conventional view that technical progress will increase the demand for labour in the machine-making industries to the same extent as it diminishes the demand for labour in the machine using industries. More important, argued Lederer, is the effect that technical progress has on the direction of purchasing power resulting from increased productivity. In general, he was pessimistic about the effect of technical progress on the demand for labour and unemployment, maintaining that if technical progress reduced labour's share of income, and wages are sticky, unemployment must rise. Kaldor criticised many of Lederer's arguments and made the important point that inventions may not only be labour-saving but may be either neutral or even capital-saving. Content aside, one is struck above all in reading the review by the mastery of complex technical argument of a young man of 24 with only five years' economics training behind him. Kaldor reviewed another of Lederer's books in 1932, *Aufriss der Ökonomischen Theorie*, and also Landauer's *Planwirtschaft und Verkehrswirtschaft*. Although the latter review did not appear in the *Economic Journal* until June 1932, this was, in fact, the first journal paper he wrote in English.

By 1933 Kaldor might be said to have arrived on the academic scene, so to speak, and was beginning to make a name for himself. His lecturing was extended and diversified, with four lectures added on the International Aspects of the Trade Cycle, and he was starting to make his mark in several other ways. The year 1933 saw the launch of the journal *Review of Economic Studies* with the aim of publishing the more mathematical work of younger economists. The chief inspiration behind the new venture came from Paul Sweezy, with Abba Lerner and Ursula Webb, but Kaldor played an active part on the editorial board. He was made Chairman of the editorial committee from 1941 to 1962 and then became one of the editorial advisers. Keynes was sceptical of the new journal on the grounds that as Editor of the *Economic Journal* he had never turned down an article worth publishing, and Hayek predicted the demise of the venture within a year. Both were proved wrong. Kaldor's writing also took off in earnest in this year. He prepared three major papers that appeared in 1934: 'The Equilibrium of the Firm' (*Economic Journal*, March 1934); 'Mrs Robinson's "Economics of Imperfect Competition"' (*Economica*, August 1934), and 'A Classificatory Note on the Determinateness of Equilibrium' (*Review of Economic Studies*, February 1934). The last was a paper first prepared for the Robbins–Hayek seminar – in which he was playing an increasingly active part – and famous for its naming of the 'Cobweb' theorem (see Chapter 2).

In the academic year 1934–35, Kaldor took on further lecturing commitments: one series of five lectures on the Theory and Practice of Tariff-Making, and another series of eight lectures on Advanced Problems of International Trade, shared with John Hicks. In his course on the Theory of Costs, renamed the Theory of Production, he had the satisfaction of referring students to his own papers on the 'Equilibrium of the Firm' and the 'Determinateness of Equilibrium'. In December 1934 he married Clarisse Goldschmidt a history graduate of Somerville College, Oxford, who was working at the time for her uncle, Sir Osmond d'Avigdor-Goldsmid in the Central Fund for German-Jewish

Refugees. To borrow the words of what Mary Marshall (wife of Alfred) said of Maynard Keynes' marriage to Lydia Lopokova, 'it was the best thing Nicky ever did' as he often said to himself. Their home in London was 15, Mecklenburgh Square. Clarisse bore him four delightful and talented daughters – Katherine, Frances, Penelope and Mary – and provided the perfect blend of stimulus and stability conducive to scholarship and creativity, supported by a coterie of helpers: secretary, housemaids and gardener. The family was well-off and had homes in London and in the south of France at La Garde Freinet, Var, as well as in Cambridge. Undoubtedly part of the explanation of Kaldor's exceptional productivity as an economist was his complete single-mindedness and freedom from domestic chores. Early in 1935 his paper 'Market Imperfection and Excess Capacity' was published (*Economica*, February) which of all his early papers is probably the one still most widely quoted today.

Later in 1935, Kaldor was awarded a Rockefeller Research Fellowship for the study of 'the theory of production in relation to the problem of equilibrium of market demand' on a stipend of $200 per month, and took leave from the School for the academic year 1935–36. Abba Lerner, newly appointed to the School, took over his important course on the Theory of Production. Kaldor spent a term at Harvard University, where among others he met Schumpeter and Chamberlin (a former PhD student of Allyn Young), and then travelled extensively, working on research in Washington, and in the Universities of Columbia, Chicago and California. In New York in December 1935, he attended the meetings of the Econometric Society where he read a paper on 'Wage Subsidies as a Remedy for Unemployment'. Later, in Chicago, he showed the paper to Jacob Viner, the editor of the *Journal of Political Economy*, who accepted it for publication in the December 1936 issue. At the same New York meetings he also met Henry Simons and was impressed by a paper he gave on the measurement of income, which also showed how expenditure could easily be calculated to form the basis of an expenditure tax. Irving Fisher delivered a similar paper at the July 1936 meetings of the Econometric Society in Colorado Springs, which Kaldor also attended, and which considerably influenced his thinking.[12] He was to use these ideas later when the Labour Chancellor of the Exchequer, Hugh Gaitskell, invited him in 1950 to sit on the Royal Commission on the Taxation of Profits and Income. While in the United States, Keynes' *General Theory of Employment Interest and Money* was published on 6 February 1936, and Kaldor bought his first copy there. Some of his marginal notes are interesting. Although, unlike Roy Harrod, Dennis Robertson, Richard Kahn, etc., he had not seen any of the proofs, he was prepared for the onslaught on classical employment and interest rate theory and had no difficulty in assimilating the main ideas. He had read Myrdal's 'Monetary Equilibrium'; he had had long discussions with Abba Lerner, the strongest 'Keynesian' at the School, and had participated in the London–Cambridge seminars on economic theory. He was a complete convert to the Keynesian revolution, and never deviated from the faith. After Keynes' death in 1946, Kaldor took on in many respects the mantle of Keynes. He was to spend much of his intellectual energy in the 1950s and early 1960s developing and extending Keynesian modes of thinking to issues of growth and distribution (see Chapter 6), which made him a leader, and one of the foremost architects, of the post-Keynesian school of economists.

On his return from the United States for the academic year 1936–37, he started a new course at the School on the Problems of the Theory of Economic Dynamics covering such topics as: the assumptions underlying static theory, the problem of 'determinateness', the place of money in pure theory, the prerequisites of a dynamic theory, equilibrium relating to a point in time versus equilibrium as a time continuum (a subject very germane to Harrod's instability problem), and the conditions of stability under static and dynamic assumptions. He drew heavily on the works of Walras, Knight, Hicks and Myrdal, as well as his own paper 'The Determinateness of Equilibrium'. In 1937 the course was expanded, and changed its title to Advanced Problems of Economic Theory (Statics and Dynamics) with references to Keynes' *General Theory* and more material on the Swedish theory of savings and investment. Roughly the same course was given to graduate students in 1939, with the important new addition of Harrod's 'An Essay in Dynamic Theory' (*Economic Journal*, March).

Kaldor's research continued to flourish, details of which are discussed in the next chapter. There was his major survey of capital theory (*Econometrica*, July 1937); his attack on Pigou's theory of how wage cuts affect unemployment (*Economic Journal*, December 1937), and his critique of Chamberlin and the distinction between monopolistic and imperfect competition (*Quarterly Journal of Economics*, May 1938). On the teaching front in the academic year 1937–38, Kaldor had added to his lecture load ten lectures to graduate students on Capital and Interest covering such topics as: the Austrian theory of capital and the concept of the investment period, the nature of capital, the maintenance and renewal of capital goods, the process of saving and investment, the classical theory of the rate of interest, the liquidity preference theory of interest, and the relation of interest and prices. He used as references his own difficult survey of capital theory recently published, together with the works of Knight, Fisher, Hayek and Böhm-Bawerk. The course was considerably expanded in 1939 to include his own debate with Hayek over capital intensity and the trade cycle (*Economica*, February 1939). Such was his academic distinction that in 1938 he was approached by the University of Lausanne, on the recommendation of John Hicks, to accept a Chair there, but he was reluctant to leave London and declined the offer.

The research output from Kaldor's pen continued apace. The year 1938–39 saw four additional major research papers: 'Mr Hawtrey on Short- and Long-Term Investment' (*Economica*, November 1938); 'Stability and Full Employment' (*Economic Journal*, December 1938); 'Welfare Propositions in Economics and Inter-personal Comparisons of Utility' (*Economic Journal*, September 1939), and 'Speculation and Economic Stability' (*Review of Economic Studies*, October 1939). On top of this prodigious output he experienced that academic year his heaviest lecturing load with five sets of lectures plus regular classes in Economic Theory. As well as existing courses on the Theory of Production, Capital and Interest, Advanced Problems of Economic Theory, and the Theory of Tariff-Making, he gave five new lectures to graduate students on Public Finance and the Trade Cycle dealing with recent theories of the trade cycle and the role of public finance as a stabiliser, including discussion of the state stimulation of employment by budgetary deficits; the creation of public works and the use of subsidies; the economic effects of different types of taxation, and the short- and long-run consequences of government borrowing. Out of this course came his famous 'A Model of the Trade Cycle' (*Economic Journal*, March 1940). It was his expertise in trade cycle theory that attracted his first research student, Tom Wilson from Belfast, who was later Adam Smith Professor of Political Economy at Glasgow University. It was the first time in the history of the LSE that a prospective graduate student had asked for a lecturer as supervisor. Wilson's interest was in applying prevailing trade cycle theories to the United States' experience between the wars. He found Kaldor's advice and guidance invaluable, particularly on the theoretical side, and the thesis was later published as a book.[13]

At the outbreak of war, the LSE was evacuated to Peterhouse, Cambridge and teaching carried on there. Before continuing the story, however, let us pause and review some of the major contributions that Kaldor made to theoretical discussions during those formative years of the 1930s.

NOTES

1. In the first few pages I shall refer to my subject as Nicky to distinguish him from his father, and thereafter as Kaldor.
2. Richard F. Kahn, *The Making of Keynes' General Theory* (Cambridge University Press, 1984).
3. L. Robbins, *Autobiography of an Economist* (London: Macmillan, 1971).
4. Kahn, *op. cit.*
5. D. Moggridge (ed.), *The Collected Writings of John Maynard Keynes: the General Theory and After.* Part I: *Preparation* (London: Macmillan, 1973).
6. This quip first arose at a meeting of the Labour Party's XYZ Club in London in the 1940's when Balogh was proposed as a member, to which Dalton replied: 'We already have Buddha, why do we need pest?' Balogh was never admitted to the club because he couldn't keep secrets. Dalton continually accused Kaldor of talking too much.
7. See G. L. S. Shackle, 'News from Sweden', in H. Richards (ed.), *Population, Factor Movements and Economic Development: Studies Presented to Brinley Thomas* (Cardiff: University of Wales Press 1976).
8. Robbins, *op. cit.*
9. P. Barrett Whale, 'The Workings of the Pre-War Gold Standard', *Economica*, February 1937.
10. From J. Abse (ed.), *My LSE* (London: Robson Books, 1977).
11. *The Calendar of the London School of Economics and Politcal Science.*
12. Later published as 'Income in Theory and Income Taxation in Practice', *Econometrica*, January 1937.
13. T. Wilson, *Fluctuations in Income and Employment* (London: Pitman, 1942).

2 EARLY CONTRIBUTIONS TO PURE THEORY

In his pre-war days at the LSE, Kaldor concentrated his attention almost exclusively on pure theory, using his fertile mind to make lasting and original contributions to such diverse areas as the theory of the firm, trade cycle theory, welfare economics and Keynesian theory, clarifying the debates between Keynes and the classical economists and making his own extensions to Keynesian economics. His early theoretical contributions to economics will be discussed under these heads.

THEORY OF THE FIRM

Professor Shackle has called the interwar years 'The Years of High Theory',[1] referring not only to the Keynesian revolution in macroeconomics, but also to the revolution in microeconomics inspired first by Piero Sraffa[2] and then by Joan Robinson[3] and Edward Chamberlin.[4] Both Robinson and Chamberlin independently managed to release the theory of firm behaviour from the straitjacket of perfect competition with its implications for prices, output and the welfare of society. Kaldor (1934c) reviewed Robinson's book *The Economics of Imperfect Competition* and later (1938b) helped to clarify in debate with Chamberlin the difference between the theory of imperfect competition put forward by Robinson and theory of monopolistic competition put forward by Chamberlin. In addition, Kaldor made contributions of his own in papers on 'The Equilibrium of the Firm' (1934b); 'Market Imperfection and Excess Capacity' (1935a); and 'A Classificatory Note on the Determinateness of Equilibrium' (1934a).

His review of Mrs Robinson's path-breaking book was a mixture of praise and criticism. The book itself is described as a 'brilliant intellectual achievement', notwithstanding its misleading title since it is more about monopoly than imperfect competition as such. His major criticism concerned the excessive formalism of the theory built on notions of questionable validity, particularly the notion of a well-defined demand curve confronting each individual firm. Kaldor was clear that the market demand curve for a product cannot be the same as the demand curve upon which the individual producer reacts, and invented the notion of the 'imagined demand curve' based on how a firm perceives its rivals will react to a change in its own price. This curve may easily be discontinuous. The 'imagined demand curve' and the market demand curve will only coincide if there is perfect competition in the sense of perfect knowledge. A second point of contention was over Robinson's definition of an industry as the products of different firms each with the same sensitivity of demand to changes in the price of other firms. Kaldor made the reasonable point that the boundary of the gap in the chain of substitution is not likely to be the same for each producer. For example, the demand for cigarettes in a village shop may be more sensitive to the price of beer in the local pub than to the price of cigarettes in the nearest town. Which of the two products should be lumped together in 'one industry'? Space is another dimension of imperfect competition.

Chamberlin described deviations from perfect competition not as imperfect competition but as monopolistic competition. He admitted in the Preface to his book, however, that 'the title of this book is apt to be misleading, since I have given to the phrase "monopolistic competition" a meaning slightly different from that given it by other writers. Professor Young [Chamberlin's PhD supervisor] once suggested "The Theory of Imperfect Competition", and this, although it had to be discarded as inaccurate, comes close to describing the scope of the subject.' In a paper in 1937, Chamberlin outlined in general and specific terms what he thought the essential differences to be between his own concept of monopolistic competition and Joan Robinson's notion of imperfect competition.[5] In general, monopolistic competition is a blending between competition and monopoly whereas imperfect competition suggests that monopoly and competition are mutually exclusive. In Kaldor's view, what Chamberlin had shown was not that monopoly and competition are not mutually exclusive alternatives, but that the distinction between monopoly and competition is no longer valid. Monopolistic competition is not a case along the spectrum from pure monopoly to perfect competition, but the old theory of monopoly in a new guise. Kaldor made what he thought to be a constructive suggestion of using both concepts of imperfect and monopolistic competition side by side, but confining the term imperfect competition to cases where there is full freedom of entry to the industry and where the limitation on entry is due to scale economies, while monopolistic competition would refer to cases where limitation is due to monopoly elements (e.g. restrictions on entry). This distinction would coincide with the factors that the authors saw mainly as causing the phenomena they describe. Chamberlin, in response to Kaldor,[6] was broadly sympathetic to this suggestion, although he found it difficult to believe that Joan Robinson would agree with confining the term imperfect competition to situations which are free from monopoly elements altogether; that is, which rest on scale economies alone.

The major point of specific disagreement between Kaldor and Chamberlin concerned the question of the compatibility of free entry with the existence of monopolistic (or imperfect) competition and whether an increase in the number of firms necessarily leads an industry closer to pure competition in the sense of price being equal to marginal cost. Kaldor interpreted Chamberlin as denying that the degree of market imperfection depends on the number of firms competing and that if new firms enter an industry, and the average revenue curve shifts leftwards, this increases the elasticity of demand and brings price closer to marginal cost. Kaldor also interpreted Chamberlin as denying that if there is full divisibility of all factors of production and constant returns to scale this would necessarily establish perfect competition. Kaldor lost the argument although he helped to clarify the issues involved. In the first place it is not necessarily true that as a flat (linear) demand curve shifts inwards the gap between price and marginal cost narrows at the new equilibrium point. If marginal cost rises faster than the rate of output, the movement inwards of a straight-line demand curve, through the multiplication of firms, will decrease the elasticity of demand at the equilibrium point and increase the difference between price and marginal cost. Secondly, Chamberlin was not concerned with market imperfections as such but with product differentiation. Chamberlin remained adamant that where products are differentiated broad generalisations as to the effect of numbers on the slope of the demand curves for individual producers cannot be made. Kaldor himself seemed to accept this position. Thirdly, perfect divisibility of factors of production will not lead to perfect competition if the new firms produce different products. Monopolistic competition would remain. Kaldor was presumably thinking in terms of a definite number of products each characterised by an imperfectly competitive structure, and in this case free entry under constant returns would produce a competitive solution. The

distinguishing characteristic of monopolistic competition, however, is the infinite range (or differentiation) of products. Kaldor
agreed that with respect to a particular product there cannot be
freedom of entry because no one else can produce an identical
product. There can only be freedom of entry to produce substitutes, which leaves the structure of monopolistic competition
intact. The great achievement of monopolistic competition theory,
as distinct from imperfect competition, was to show the compatibility of monopoloid situations with full freedom of entry, and that
monopoly has an economic basis and is not simply the product of
natural or artificial barriers to entry.

Kaldor's attempt to unravel the essential differences between
imperfect and monopolistic competition, and his debate with
Chamberlin over the matter, followed his own original contributions, first to the debate (started by Sraffa) over the incompatibility of the assumption of long period static equilibrium and
perfect competition if there is a tendency for the size of a firm to
grow relative to the size of the industry, and secondly, to the
important notion of excess capacity under imperfect competition.
In 'The Equilibrium of the Firm' (1934b) the question posed was:
can a determinate cost schedule (and supply curve) be derived
from the premises on which static analysis is based? In Marshall,
the supply curve is based on the assumption of perfect competition
and the existence of a precise relation between the scale of output
and costs incurred. Kaldor argued that under imperfect competition and increasing returns, the optimum quantities of factors to
be used can only be known if the supply of one of the factors to the
firm is fixed. Coordinating ability was picked out as the only true
fixed factor. The supply of coordinating ability by its very nature
cannot be increased commensurately with other factors since the
essence of coordination is that every single decision should be
made in relation to all other decisions and must therefore pass
through a single brain. Differences in firm size are the natural
outcome of this limitation. But the optimum size is not determinate because change means that more coordinating ability is
required, and the more that is required the greater are the
diseconomies and the greater are the barriers to expansion. Apart
from demonstrating the incompatibility of the assumptions of
long period static equilibrium with perfect competition, this was a
novel theory of differences in firm size, although not dissimilar to
Marshall's theory of managerial diseconomies. It is not a theory,
however, that Kaldor later attached much importance to. Closer
to his later thinking on the size of firms was Kalecki's theory of the
principle of increasing risk based on the gearing ratio of firms.[7]

The higher is the ratio of own funds to borrowed funds, the greater is the ability of the firm to borrow for expansion and herein lies the importance of ploughed-back profits for the expansion of firms and for the economy as a whole.

'Market Imperfection and Excess Capacity' (1935a) was an important paper for several reasons, and one which is still widely used and quoted today. It had two main purposes. The first was to show that free entry into an industry will only lead to a state of perfect competition if there is constant returns to scale (constant average costs) over the whole range of output. Otherwise free entry will raise costs per unit of output which will ultimately halt the entry of new firms. Each firm will operate near its break-even point, not where costs per unit of output are at a minimum. Excess capacity will exist in the sense that the amount actually produced and sold is less than firms would prefer to sell at the ruling price. This has two important corollaries. First, an increase in the supply of resources to an industry (pushing profits to normal) can actually raise prices. Traditional laws of economics had never admitted this. Free competition need not lead to economic efficiency, but can create excess capacity and high costs. Secondly, if at the margin of production productivity increases and costs decrease, this has profound implications for neoclassical price, distribution and employment theory which assumes diminishing returns to labour and rising costs. Marshall recognised that the theory of long-period 'normal value' ceases to apply in the case of increasing returns, and Hicks later admitted in *Value and Capital* (1939) that if the assumption of increasing marginal costs is abandoned, 'the basis on which economic laws can be constructed is shorn away' causing 'wreckage of the greater part of economic theory'.

In the new classical macroeconomics, increasing returns completely undermines the concept of a natural rate of unemployment which presupposes an inverse relationship between employment and the real wage. With increasing returns and decreasing costs, real wages and employment are positively not negatively related. This early paper of Kaldor's has recently been used by Weitzman[8] to support the contention that a sufficient condition for involuntary unemployment is imperfect competition and excess capacity because in a perfectly competitive world each unemployed person could become self-employed without spoiling the market. While it is true that under imperfect competition firms may be reluctant to expand output individually, the state of competition is not the ultimate source of involuntary unemployment in Keynesian theory.

Keynes in the *General Theory* could have adopted the assumption of imperfect competition, which might have strengthened his case, but he claimed it was not necessary for his purpose.[9] The ultimate source of involuntary unemployment in a monetary economy is saving in the form of monetary assets combined with uncertainty in the minds of investors as to when the saving will be translated into consumption, and the pattern of consumption expenditure which will obtain.

Kaldor's second main purpose was to argue that if economies of scale exist, freedom of entry will not necessarily lead to a tangency of the demand curve and the average cost curve because the minimum size of new entry may reduce the demand for each product so much that the demand curve lies below the cost curve and all the firms would be involved in losses. Equally, the threat of this happening may also prevent the elimination of profit, so invalidating the Walrasian proposition that 'pure profit' cannot exist in a state of equilibrium.

Under constant costs, profits will never be eliminated as long as the elasticity of demand for output is less than infinite. That is why constant costs leads to perfect competition in Kaldor's model. He remarked:

mathematical economists in taking perfect competition as their starting point weren't such fools after all. For they assumed perfect divisibility of everything; and when everything is perfectly divisible, and consequently economies of scale are completely absent, perfect competition must necessarily establish itself solely as a result of the free play of economic forces. No degree of product differentiation and no possibility of further and further product variation will be sufficient to prevent this result, so long as all kinds of institutional monopolies and all kinds of indivisibilities are completely absent. (p. 71)

As we saw above, however, Kaldor later conceded in debate with Chamberlin that strictly speaking free entry and product differentiation are incompatible. Each product producer is his own monopolist. Free entry produces substitutes, but monopolistic competition remains without standardised products.

Kaldor admitted that it is difficult to draw any welfare conclusions from his own analysis or that of Chamberlin. There could be compulsory standardisation requirements of products or cartel arrangements and entry restrictions to stop costs rising with entry, but then the public would be offered a smaller number of products. What is the trade-off between quantity and diversity? To say that excess capacity is the 'price' of consumer choice, however, would not be correct because consumers are not given the choice of having either a smaller range of commodities at lower prices or a large range at higher prices. They are offered either one or the other but never both.

Finally in this section, mention may be made of his paper 'A Classificatory Note on the Determinateness of Equilibrium' (1934a). This was essentially a pedagogic exercise in the Walrasian tradition designed to clarify the assumptions of static theory necessary to make equilibrium determinate, and to classify the various causes of 'indeterminateness' under the headings of existence, uniqueness and stability. The paper is noteworthy not only for its clarity of exposition but also for the invention of the term 'cobweb' theorem (although not the invention of the theorem itself)[10] to describe oscillatory movements to and from equilibrium when adjustment in completely discontinous. He had previously presented the paper at the Robbins–Hayek seminar at the LSE where the felicitous description occurred to him.

TRADE CYCLE THEORY

Trade cycle theory was another major preoccupation in the 1930s. Hayek and the Austrian school provided the targets for attack by propounding a purely monetary theory of the trade cycle, not dissimilar in its initial causes to the theory of Wicksell. The theory was that credit expansion forces the money rate of interest below the natural rate of interest (at which the supply and demand for real savings are in balance) which leads to more roundabout methods of production (or a lengthening of the period of production) which can only remain profitable as long as credit expansion continues and the rate of interest is stable. If credit is contracted and the interest rate rises again, attempts will be made to revert to less capitalistic methods of production which then causes problems of adjustment. The real cause of depression and unemployment is not overproduction, but that the instruments of capital can only produce goods in an unwanted way.

Hayek's two influential books outlining this theory were *Monetary Theory and the Trade Cycle* and *Prices and Production*. The former was published first in German in 1929 and then in English in 1933, translated by Kaldor and Honor Croome. *Prices and Production*, based on four lectures given at the LSE, and subsequently in Cambridge where they were not well received, appeared in 1931. The two books complement each other. In the former, Hayek emphasised the monetary causes which initiate cyclical fluctuations; in the latter he concentrated on the successive changes in the real structure of production which constitute those fluctuations. In

Monetary Theory and the Trade Cycle 'real' or non-monetary theories of the trade cycle are dismissed ostensibly on the classical argument that the rate of interest must be an effective regulator of the supply and demand for saving (at least in the absence of money) so that if disequilibrium does occur it must be the result of money; in particular the elasticity of credit which affects the extent and duration of the cyclical fluctuations. The main reason for the necessity of a monetary approach to the trade cycle, he maintained, 'arises from the circumstance that the automatic adjustment of supply and demand can only be disturbed when money is introduced into the economic system.' As far as the 1930s recession is concerned, he believed, 'there is no reason to assume that the crisis was started by a deliberate deflationary action on the part of the monetary authorities, or that the deflation itself is anything but a secondary phenomenon, a process induced by the maladjustments of industry left over from the boom.' Moreover, there was no reason to suppose that the difficulties would be overcome by forcing more money into circulation because this would merely perpetuate the rigidities and maladjustments.

To combat the depression by a forced credit expansion is to attempt to cure the evil by the very means which brought it about; because we are suffering from a misdirection of production, we want to create further misdirection – a procedure which can only lead to a much more severe crisis as soon as the credit expansion comes to an end.

Kaldor was to absorb this theory and finally to demolish it in a powerful paper entitled 'Capital Intensity and the Trade Cycle' (1939a). Significantly, Hayek later changed his mind concerning the seeds of cyclical crisis during the upswing. Having earlier argued that the capital intensity of production increased on the upswing, which then caused adjustment problems as credit expansion was curtailed, he argued in *Profits, Interest and Investment* (1939) the exact opposite, that employers would seek more labour-intensive methods of production owing to the operation of what is called the Ricardo effect. Kaldor also launched into this *volte face*, for which he was partly responsible in the first place, in a paper entitled 'Professor Hayek and the Concertina Effect' (1942d).

Turning first, however, to Hayek's original theory, Kaldor started by examining the concept of the 'investment period' (its meaning and determination) which plays such a crucial role in Hayek's theory; and secondly, investigated the behaviour of the capital intensity during the cycle and how far the actual methods of production adopted are consistent with those required for a steady rate of progress. He concluded: 'we shall find that the changes in the degree of roundaboutness are by no means causally unrelated to cyclical fluctuations; but that insofar as there is malinvestment during a boom, it is of a very different character from that contemplated in the theories of the Austrian school.

The concept of the investment period of Austrian theory was debated in *Econometrica* with Kaldor (1937b) as a contributor.[11] The upshot of that debate was that the investment period concept is really nothing more than one way of measuring the ratio of capital to labour. But there is no unique measure of capital and therefore no unique measure of the capital : labour ratio. It is possible, however, to construct *ordinal* measures of the ratio to indicate whether it is moving up or down. Such measures include the ratio of the value of annual output to annual input; the ratio of interest costs to wage costs (per unit of output), and the ratio of initial cost to the value of annual output. Kaldor objected to these measures because they are all affected by a change in the relative price of inputs and outputs without any change in the real structure of production necessarily having taken place. He took instead an index of the ratio of 'initial cost' to 'annual cost' in the production of output. The higher the initial size of investment per unit of output the lower the corresponding stream of expenditures per unit of output to be deducted from gross receipts to obtain prospective yields. Hence the relation between initial outlay and annual outlay can be regarded as a measure of the proportion in which capital and other factors of production are combined. Kaldor's index is not sensitive to changes in the ratio of final goods' prices to wages or the rate of interest, but does assume that the price of newly produced equipment goods in terms of labour is given. In defining the concept and its application the normal rate of expenditure associated with the rate of output corresponding to the normal capacity of the equipment is assumed, and he borrowed the Marshallian concept of the 'representative firm' arguing that what happens to the behaviour of the 'typical' firm will be applicable, *mutatis mutandis*, to the system as a whole.[12] An increase in the degree of (normal) capital intensity could come about in two ways: either by the use of more durable equipment requiring lower amortisation per unit of output or by the installation of more 'automatic' equipment requiring less labour per unit of output – the latter being the most likely. The question then is what determines the optimum degree of capital intensity? Does capital intensity increase or decrease in the boom? To analyse these questions, Kaldor used the Keynesian construct of the marginal efficiency of capital combined with the supply curve of investible funds. With imperfect competition in the product and capital market, the marginal efficiency curve will be falling and the supply curve of investible funds will be rising. For each method of production there will be a different marginal efficiency curve. A profit-maximising entrepreneur will choose that technique which maximises the area between the marginal efficiency curve and the supply schedule of funds. Whether the marginal efficiency or rate of interest is dominant in determining the technique will depend on the relative elasticities of the two curves.[13] This discussion refers to the determination of the capital intensity of *new* investments. *Actual* capital intensity will depend on the relation between selling price and costs. This leads on to the question of variations in capital intensity over the trade cycle. *Actual* capital intensity must *fall* during the upswing and rise during the downswing since if capital is fixed in the short run, the only way output can increase is to employ more labour with it. But what happens to *normal* capital intensity? Kaldor argued that quite probably this also varies inversely with the trade cycle because real wages will fall during the boom and the rate of interest will rise, contrary to the Austrian view that techniques will become more capital-intensive. This 'opposite result' also has profound implications for trade cycle theory. Thus Kaldor praised the Austrians for 'getting hold of a stick' but mocked them for getting hold of the wrong end! Investments undertaken during booms are doomed to failure not because they involve excessively roundabout methods of production but because capital intensity falls and investments are not sufficiently capital intensive. What accounts for this Kaldor paradox? The explanation is akin to Harrod's paradox of investment. Obviously, the greater the capital intensity the smaller the increase in potential output for any *given* volume of investment. Hence if capital intensity falls during the boom and rises during depression, this implies that newly created productive capacity increases faster than the rate of investment during the boom and falls faster than the rate of investment during depression. The high rate of increase in productive capacity during the boom, because capital intensity falls, sows the seeds of the boom's destruction, bringing the high rate of investment and the boom to an end. First, consumption may not rise with the capacity to produce consumption goods because the desire to save increases as real income increases. In order to maintain full employment of equipment in the consumption good industries, the level of investment must rise to match the increase in saving. Hence the 'paradoxical' situation that investment activity must increase in order to prevent a reduction in investment activity – and the more so, the less the degree of capital intensity of new investment.

Secondly, even if this force is not operative, investment activity could not go on rising indefinitely, unless the degree of capital intensity increased, because of the scarcity of labour. To avoid cyclical fluctuations, investments must become more capital-intensive in the boom; the capital intensity of production must increase steadily and continuously. In a smoothly functioning economy, of course, there would be a switching from capital widening to capital deepening as the need arises, but in the real world this does not happen, at least not without some interruption of investment activity in the first place.

Hawtrey subsequently debated this issue with Kaldor without resolution. In his book *Capital and Employment* (1937), Hawtrey recognised like Kaldor that investment during the boom need not involve the adoption of more capital-intensive processes but believed that it is relatively easy to move from capital widening to capital deepening as the situation warrants. Kaldor reviewed Hawtrey's book in *Economica* (1938c). Hawtrey's distinctive theory of the trade cycle, to which he adhered all his life, was that it is fluctuations in the amounts of stocks of manufactured goods held that are responsible for cyclical fluctuations and it is the behaviour of the short-term rate of interest which is responsible for these fluctuations. He dismissed the importance of fluctuations in long-term investment, arguing that when capital outlays fall off, the surplus of unused savings will be absorbed by the investment market with consumption apparently unchanged. In other words, he continued to believe in the classical adjustment mechanism. Kaldor's position on the long term was entirely Keynesian. On the short term, he viewed the amount of traders' stock in relation to turnover as an empirical matter, and doubted on theoretical grounds whether the ratio depends on the short-term rate of interest. He thus remained unconvinced by Hawtrey's theory, although he expressed admiration for the book: 'Capital and Employment is a very valuable book of a very distinguished author. It contains a host of excellent ideas which makes it essential reading for ever student of the trade cycle.'

Hawtrey, in a formal reply to Kaldor's 1939 paper, whilst taking Kaldor's side against the Austrians, contended none the less that the contrast between Kaldor and Hayek was not so sharp as Kaldor maintained because both agreed that at full employment there is an excessive volume of resources being made available for the deepening process. In Kaldor's view it is the failure of the system to adopt more capital-intensive methods that is the source of the problem because this requires a fall in the rate of interest which will only occur if there is a fall in the rate of profit. Hayek assumed that the system does respond, and then when the rate of interest rises again, there are dislocations and structural problems. On the question of labour shortage, Hawtrey did not see why there should not be capital deepening when capital widening becomes impossible. Kaldor's reply (1940a) was that a scarcity of labour, which slows up supply, will also slow up demand and will therefore discourage both capital widening and deepening. The installation of labour-saving machinery would only be profitable if all producers acted simultaneously, otherwise the demand would not be forthcoming. Kaldor presumed that Hawtrey must have been assuming that while production ceases to expand, the expansion of demand nevertheless continues being fed from some source other than current production.[14]

Hayek's book, *Profits, Interest and Investment*, appeared in 1939 and took a radically different stance from that of *Prices and Production*. Kaldor wrote a long critical review (1942d). The gist of Hayek's new view was as follows: An expansion of credit expands the demand for consumer goods and raises the rate of profit in the consumer goods industries. The price of consumption goods rises and real wages fall. This has two effects: first, to increase investment demand; and secondly, to encourage the adoption of *less* capital-intensive techniques which Hayek labelled the Ricardo effect. According to Hayek the second effect always outweighs the first, leading to a fall in the total demand for loanable funds and to depression in the capital goods industries. This must be the case, he argued, because so long as investment rises the rate of profit will continue to rise, and the more the rate of profit rises (the lower the real wage) the stronger the latter tendency compared with the former. This is the only way an investment boom comes to an end: 'Once the cumulative process has been entered upon the end must always come through a *rise* in profits in the late stages and can *never come* from a fall in profits or an exhaustion of investment.' As Kaldor pointed out, this discussion of the trade cycle differed radically from Hayek's earlier theory and also from all other current theories on the subject. In *Prices and Production* Hayek believed that investment depended on the rate of profit relative to the rate of interest. Kaldor remarked: 'if he now succeeded in overthrowing this principle, its ramifications would be far wider than the theory of the trade cycle. Few branches of economic theory would escape unscathed this more than "Jevonian" revolution.' The rise in the rate of profit is not the only difference between Hayek's new and old theory. Techniques of production also become more labour-intensive which causes investment to fall. Kaldor was led to remark of the new theory:

if they [the capitalists] had curbed their greed, and contented themselves with the profits they could get on the usual methods, or if the choice of still-higher profits through the use of 'inferior machinery' had not been open to them, then, as far as Professor Hayek's present analysis goes, the boom would have been made permanent: high profits, high investment, high employment, could have gone on indefinitely. Thus, on this theory, a 100% excess profits tax is sufficient to eliminate the trade cycle and stabilise prosperity. For it would suspend the operation of the 'Ricardo effect'—there would be no point in trying to make profits still higher by making production less roundabout, if none of these profits could be retained.

There were two respects, however, in which Hayek's views remained unchanged. First, in both theories it is variations in the *technique* of production, rather than changes in the total stock of capital, which are causally significant in the explanation of the cycle. Secondly, the belief that it is always overconsumption, not underconsumption, which causes the boom to end. In the first theory it is excessive consumption and inflation which causes interest rates to rise, which makes more capital-intensive methods adopted in the boom unprofitable. In the new theory, it is excessive consumption and inflation which causes real wages to fall, producing the 'Ricardo effect' with less capital-intensive techniques and a fall in investment.

Hayek's new theory centred on the Ricardo effect, and it is this that Kaldor set out to undermine by arguing that (1) it 'presupposes certain special conditions as to the position of individual firms which are clearly inapplicable to the major field of modern industry'; (2) even where the effect does operate, its quantitative significance must be small; and (3) apart from points (1) and (2), under no circumstances can total investment demand become smaller as a result of a rise in the rate of profit. First, Kaldor rightly claimed that Hayek's use of the term 'Ricardo effect' is a misnomer in the context used. Ricardo's argument concerning the relative use of labour and machinery depended on the relative price of labour and machinery, whereas in Hayek the inducement mechanism is the rise in the price of consumption goods which is independent of any change in the relative prices of labour and machinery. Only if there is a rise in the rate of interest will there be a tendency for the capital intensity of new investments to be reduced. In a paper in *Economica* Hayek seemed to concede this point, saying that it is a truism that 'so long as the rate of interest remains constant, a change in real wages cannot alter the relative costs of different methods of production'.[15] Kaldor remarked that it is odd that Hayek should call this proposition a truism, having asserted the opposite in his previous writings. Kaldor went on to show the special conditions that must pertain for the Ricardo effect to work; and that if it does work, its quantitative effect would be small. But in any case it can never lead to *less* investment. The reason is that a rise in the rate of interest, which is a precondition for capital intensity to fall, can only come about as a result of the increase in investment. If there were no increase in investment there would be no rise in the rate of interest to bring about a fall in capital intensity. 'This is the fundamental point which knocks the bottom out of Professor Hayek's new theory of the trade cycle, quite apart from any arbitrariness or unreality of the assumptions on which it is based.'

Kaldor then turned to the question of the *existence* of the so-called 'concertina effect', that is, the change in capital intensity over the cycle. Does the concertina move cyclically or counter-cyclically? In Hayek's new theory the concertina was supposed to move counter-cyclically. What was the evidence? Taking US data from 1929 to 1941, Kaldor found no evidence of a rise in profit margins leading to a fall in investment, or of output per head falling in the boom through a fall in capital intensity; on the contrary. Does this mean we should revert to Hayek's original position? Kaldor joked; 'I think the evidence rather suggests that the concertina, whichever way it goes, makes a relatively small noise – it is drowned by the cymbals of technical progress.' Innovations are constantly occurring inducing increases in both capital and output per head. The investment cycle, as Hawtrey stressed, is essentially a matter of capital widening not deepening. Kaldor accused Hayek of wanting to demonstrate at all costs (including *volte faces* if necessary) that the scarcity of capital is the great cause of economic crisis and unemployment. But scarcity of capital can only mean insufficient saving and this can only cause inflation in a state of full employment, never depression and unemployment. Hayek never answered these arguments, or why the rate of profit in his model never falls bringing the boom to an end. Kaldor sent Keynes an offprint of his paper on Hayek, to which Keynes replied 'your attack on poor Hayek is not merely using a sledge hammer to crack a nut, but on a nut which is already decorticated... yours is a brilliant theory, but too much so, perhaps for this subject.' Kaldor defended his attack on Hayek by reminding Keynes that Hayek had spent the whole of the summer term (in Cambridge) discussing his latest paper on the Ricardo effect, creating an unwholesome muddle in the minds of the young.

KALDOR'S CONTRIBUTION TO TRADE CYCLE THEORY

Kaldor's first contribution to trade cycle theory came in his paper 'Stability and Full Employment' (1938d). He had sent Keynes both this paper and 'Capital Intensity and the Trade Cycle', with the idea of publishing the latter in the *Economic Journal*, with the former as a complementary paper. Keynes expressed the wish that 'it had been the other way round'.[16] He liked 'Stability and Full Employment', but had reservations about the paper on Hayek. The latter he described as 'half-baked' and not likely to be intelligible to more than a very small number of readers. He admitted that he did not fully understand the paper, claiming to have lost the thread of the argument on page 8 and never recovering it!

Kaldor's central thesis was that instability is inherent in the economic system itself because of the complementarity and specificity of the factors of production. There is no problem of attaining full employment, but it is bound to be unstable. In the short run, at the point of full employment, there will be a certain ratio of investment to consumption, and given the distribution of income there will be a certain division of real income between consumption and saving. Following Keynes there is no reason why this division of income should be in the same proportion as the division of output. At the position of full employment, investment will either exceed or fall short of saving and in either case forces will come into operation which are likely to cause, sooner or later, a reduction in the level of activity. This insight represents Kaldor's first contribution to the extension of static Keynesian analysis. If saving exceeds investment, full employment in the investment goods industries will not be sufficient to secure full employment in the consumption goods industries. The demand for new investment is thus bound to decline. If investment exceeds saving, the maintenance of full employment will be associated with a cumulative inflation of prices. If the money rate of interest is held constant, there is a Wicksellian-type situation in which the money rate of interest is below the natural rate of interest which equates real saving and investment. If labour and equipment are specific, however, the Wicksellian equality of saving and investment need not be compatible with full employment. A cumulative Wicksellian process presupposes that money wages rise in line with prices because if they do not there would be a redistribution of income to profits and saving would rise to match investment. We have here the early seeds of Kaldor's macro-theory of distribution, and a statement of the mechanism by which the warranted and natural rates of growth may be brought into equality with each other. Kaldor seemed to suggest that any excess investment situation will sooner or later convert itself into a situation of excess saving. In either case, however, maladjustment between saving and investment could be remedied, he argued, by measures to regulate the propensity to save via the distribution of income; for example, by lowering or raising taxes (subsidies) on wages through the variation of unemployment and health insurance contributions. Full employment *and stability* cannot be achieved by interest rate policy and public expenditure alone; 'the propensity to consume function has to be regulated as well.'[17] In the long run, when labour becomes scarce, current production cannot be further increased by adding more machines if labour and capital are complementary. Thus excess capacity in equipment will occur and the demand for investment will fall. Labour-saving technical progress could ease the problem provided that the labour required to work on the new equipment is no greater than the labour simultaneously released through depreciation and scrapping. But there is nothing to guarantee this, and the scope would diminish through time because the amount of labour released through the scrapping of obsolete equipment would fall so that labour-saving technical progress would have to accelerate. If the scarcity of labour caused wages to rise faster than prices, profits would fall and this would also discourage further investment. Thus, in the long run, a boom cannot be maintained because the economy ultimately comes up against a labour constraint which gives rise to excess capacity in the investment goods industries, and depression in the investment goods industries then spreads to the consumption goods industries.

Kaldor shared the same thesis as Dennis Robertson that the trade cycle is the price to be paid for a high rate of economic progress. Robertson wrote in private correspondence 'that the doctrine that unemployment is the result of the scarcity of labour is going to be a hard one to put across to the plain man.' Kaldor himself described the dilemma as a question of 'progress versus stability', but argued that it is not clear 'that the first ought to be sacrificed for the second'. Summarising, starting from a position of full employment, booms may come to an end for four main reasons: a check to investment through credit restriction; rising interest rates which put a stop to the process of cumulative inflation: the demand for consumption goods failing to expand as fast as the capacity to produce them (excess saving); and lastly, a scarcity of labour causing excess capacity in the investment goods industries. These four causes are likely to appear successively in time; the first two in the early stages, the last two in the later stages: 'Thus the boom is like a peculiar steeplechase, where the horse is bound to fall at one of four obstacles. If it survives the first, it might be checked on the second, the third or the fourth. It is probably a rare horse which survives until the last hurdle.' Governments can remove the first hurdle by monetary policy, and the second and third obstacles by appropriate taxation, but there is little they can do to alleviate a labour shortage.

This first foray by Kaldor into trade cycle theory was essentially a verbal model with almost exclusive emphasis on why a boom should end. The formal mechanics of the model are obscure; there is no explicit investment function, and there is virtually no discussion of the cyclical upturn. He had first started thinking about trade cycle theory when he gave four lectures on the International Trade Cycle at the LSE in 1933–34. He then gave a further course in 1936/37 on return from his year in America. He realised that the task was to explain oscillations between a low and high level equilibrium and this could not be done using a linear accelerator. The idea of an S-shaped investment curve then occurred to him which was incorporated into a formal model of the trade cycle published in 1940, after much discussion and correspondence with Keynes. At low levels of output, increased output will not call forth more investment because there is excess capacity, and at high levels of output there will be no inducement to investment if increases in output are impossible. Hence the nonlinear investment curve, capable of producing cyclical oscillations. Kaldor sent the paper to Keynes at the end of May 1939. Keynes replied that he liked it, but because he had recently given Kaldor a lot of space in the *Economic Journal* he would sit on it to see what else came forward for the September issue. Keynes did not like papers to pile up and usually only accepted papers if he could publish them immediately. Keynes' comments on the paper were somewhat confused. He seemed to interpret Kaldor as putting forward a multiplier-accelerator explanation of the trade cycle and yet it is clear in the paper, and stated explicitly in a footnote, that investment is a function of the level of output in relation to capacity *not* of the change of output – which would be an accelerator-type mechanism. Keynes expressed surprise that Kaldor meant investment is a function of the level of output,[18] but none the less promised publication in December. It is the novel investment function which makes Kaldor's model a distinct theory of the trade cycle. He was highly critical of the notion of an accelerator theory of investment, as we shall see later in his review of Hicks' book, *A Contribution to the Theory of the Trade Cycle* (1950).

Kaldor's theory of investment demand was based on the much simpler assumption that an increase in the current level of profits increases investment demand, and the demand for capital goods will be greater the greater is the level of production. Thus, both investment and saving are functions of output. If investment changes more than saving as output changes, any equilibrium between saving and investment will be unstable. Any increase in output would send the economy into hyper-inflation and any decrease in output would send the economy into depression. If, on the other hand, saving changes more than investment as output changes, there will a position of stable equilibrium and any departure from equilibrium will induce a return to equilibrium. Since we observe in practice neither the first case, nor the extreme stability of the second case, Kaldor conjectured that probably neither investment nor savings are linear functions of output. Investment will probably be insensitive to output changes at both low and high levels of activity, because of excess capacity in the first case and of the rising costs of investment in the second case. Saving, by contrast, will probably be sensitive at both high and low levels of activity compared to its normal level. He anticipated Duesenberry's idea of a 'customary' standard of living, below which people cut down drastically on saving and above which they save a lot.[19] If these functions are assumed, and if it is also assumed that *normally* investment changes more than saving as output changes, then there would be a situation of multiple equilibria, as shown by points A and B in Figure 2.1. Hence the economic system can reach stability either at high or low levels of activity. But both curves are short-run functions. Through time they will shift, and herein lies the source of instability. To quote Kaldor: 'the key to the explanation of the trade cycle is to be found in the fact that each of the two positions is stable only in the short period: that as activity continues at either one of these levels forces gradually accumulate which sooner or later will render that particular position unstable.' For example, at a high level of activity at point B, when the level of investment is high, the savings schedule will shift up, but the investment schedule will tend to fall because the accumulation of capital restricts the range of investment opportunities. Thus point B gradually shifts leftwards and point C rightwards, reducing the level of activity and ultimately bringing B and C together. At this point equilibrium becomes unstable in a downward direction and the level of activity falls rapidly to point A. By contrast, at a low level of activity at point A, the curves will tend to shift in the opposite direction. If investment is not sufficient to cover depreciation, net investment will be negative

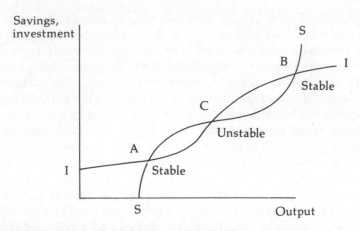

Figure 2.1

and investment opportunities will gradually accumulate shifting the investment curve upwards. Likewise, if there is capital consumption and real income is falling, the savings curve will tend to shift downwards. These two tendencies shift point A to the right and point C to the left, until where A and C meet the situation becomes unstable in an upward direction and the level of activity expands to point B. Kaldor was not entirely convinced, however, that the forces operative at low levels of activity will be sufficiently strong for the investment and saving curves not to get stuck before point C is reached so that there is no cumulative expansion:

the forces making for expansion when we start from a state of depression are not so certain in their operation as the forces making for a downturn when we start from prosperity: the danger of chronic stagnation is greater than the danger of chronic boom. A boom if left to itself is certain to come to an end; but the depression might get into a position of stationariness, and remain there until external changes (the discovery of new inventions or the opening up of new markets) come to the rescue.

The period of the cycle depends on two time rates of movement: first, on the rate at which the S and I curves shift; and secondly, on the time required for the system to move from B = C to A or from A = C to B. The rate at which the S and I curves shift depends on the construction period, and the durability, of capital goods. The shorter the construction period and the shorter the lifetime, the faster the rate of shift at any given rate of investment and the shorter the length of the trade cycle. If the capital intensity of investment varied inversely with the rate of investment, this would tend to reduce the period of the cycle, and if it varied directly, this would lengthen the period. If capital intensity increased steadily through time this would lengthen the boom periods and shorten the depression periods. The amplitude of the cycle depends on the shapes of the I and S curves which determine the distance between A and B at their normal position.

The appeal of the Kaldor model is that it appears to generate self-sustaining ('limit') cycles without the need for time lags, shocks or the rigid specification of parameters which characterise so many other trade cycle models. The main technical criticism of the model has come from Chang and Smyth,[20] who show that to establish a 'limit' cycle it is also necessary that, in addition to the other conditions of the model, a movement *along* the I or S curve proceeds more quickly in time than the rate of shift of these curves as a result of capital accumulation. In other words, it takes less time to adjust output to a change in investment than it takes to change investment (at a given level of output) on account of the change in the stock capital. Kaldor (1971b) conceded the point, regarding it as implicit in the model, as it is implicit in all Keynesian short-period equilibrium models. That is, the Keynesian short period treats the stock of capital as given. It ignores the change in capital due to past investment on the grounds that such changes are slow relative to changes in output associated with changes in the degree of capacity utilisation and the associated changes in the level of employment. If adjustments to the rate of investment due to changes in the stock of capital were more important in a given time interval than the changes in output in response to changes in investment, or of investment in response to changes in output, the whole Keynesian model of 'an equilibrium level' of output would collapse. There would be no such point other than a stationary state with zero net investment.

Kaldor's doubts about models of the trade cycle based on an accelerator theory of investment were well voiced in a penetrating and a lengthy review (1951a) of Hicks' book on the trade cycle mentioned earlier. The acceleration principle is described as 'a crude and highly unsuitable tool for analysis and also an obsolete one, that an economist of Mr. Hicks's subtlety should have long ago discarded'. Kalecki in *Essays in the Theory of Economic Fluctuations* (1939), and Tinbergen in his paper 'Statistical Evidence on the Acceleration Principle' (*Economica*, 1938) had previously raised doubts about its use. In what sense, asked Kaldor, can it be assumed that investment is a simple (and linear) function of the change in the level of output? In long-run equilibrium it may be supposed that there is a particular quantity of capital appropriate to a given rate of output and that an increase in output will raise profits sufficiently to justify an ultimate increase in the stock of capital that is proportionate to the increase in output, but it is not legitimate to suppose that positions of long-run equilibrium are sufficiently closely attained over the cycle as to make the accelerator or capital:output ratio serve as a guide to investment behaviour. This could only be the case if the time lag between adjusting the stock of capital to demand was the same as the output-demand lag, but these two lags are entirely different, in order of magnitude, and are the essence of the Marshallian distinction between the short and long run. The accelerator principle seems to regard the capital:output ratio as determined by technical factors which cannot undergo alteration in the short period. Yet, cyclically, the relation may change dramatically. Also the accelerator coefficient is assumed to remain the same irrespective of the absolute size of the change in output, yet firms cannot take advantage of large investment opportunities as quickly as small ones because they are constrained by their financial resources. In addition, expectations are likely to be far less elastic with respect to large changes in the demand for output than to small changes. All these points undermine the notion of a fixed incremental capital:output ratio.

Kaldor agreed with Hicks, however, that a theory of the trade cycle needs to be built around a rising trend in output, but objected to his assumption that the rate of autonomous investment will just be such as to give a rate of growth of output equal to the full employment rate. There is nothing to guarantee such a rate. In fact, Hicks' assumption is even more extreme than this. It amounts to the assumption that a given amount of autonomous investment will generate enough output to make, at a given growth, the sum of autonomous and induced investment bear the same relation to output as the ratio of saving to income. Hicks' investment is not only autonomous, therefore, it is extraneous of the type that generates no output capacity (e.g. digging holes, building houses and pyramids, etc.). If it were anything else, its relation to output at any given growth rate would still be determined by technical factors and would not be flexible enough to fit in with the requirements dictated by the savings functions. Kaldor claimed, therefore, that Hicks' argument is nothing more than the proposition that the government authority could, in principle, ensure that the economy expands at the full employment rate by expanding non-productive investment at the same rate. But this leaves unanswered the questions of the determinants of long-run growth, and of whether the growth in investment is the cause or the consequence of the growth in the economy. Kaldor by contrast brought to the fore the role of expectations in the Keynesian tradition and questioned the distinction between autonomous and induced investment. The most plausible explanation for the growth of investment is the expectation of a growth in demand, so that an economy is likely to grow at a rate at which businessmen expect it to grow. This has the implication that autonomous and induced investment are not really different animals; investment will be 'autonomous' or 'induced' according to whether the investment decisions of entrepreneurs are governed by expectation of long-term growth or by the actual growth in output in the recent past. Thus entrepreneurs' long-term expectations of growth have a major influence on the trend rate of growth, while the short-term volatility of these expectations is the prime cause of fluctuations around the trend: 'The solution to the problem should be sought, therefore, not in the device of postulating different kinds of investment, but in a theory of expectations that could account for both the autonomous and the induced element of entrepreneurial behaviour.'

Kaldor took up again the theme of the relation between economic growth and cyclical fluctuations in a lecture given at the Institut de Science Economique Appliquée, Paris, in May 1953, which was subsequently published in the *Economic Journal* (1954a). In many respects, this paper, together with the review of Hicks, provides the bridge between Kaldor's early interest in trade cycle theory, and his subsequent interest in growth theory which preoccupied him in the latter half of the 1950s (see Chapter 6). The lecture had three themes: first, that Keynesian static equilibrium theory becomes a model of the trade cycle by the introduction of the assumptions of his 1940 model; secondly, that the introduction of a trend into trade cycle theory does not alter the basic character of trendless models, contrary to the assertions by Hicks and Harrod; and thirdly, the importance of expectations in the determination of long-run growth. This third theme relates to the problem of explaining economic growth, which trade cycle theories typically do not explain since the trend rate of growth is assumed to be exogenously given outside the system, e.g. by technical progress and population growth. But technical progress and population growth are not like the weather or seasons that exist independently of human action. Rather they are themselves the product of social processes. The growth of population is as much a consequence of economic growth as a cause. Births and migration respond to labour shortage, as in the United States after the civil war and in England during the industrial revolution.

Similarly technical progress is largely endogenous – a product of the economic environment at the time. If technical invention and population are endogenous, where are we to look for the main-springs of growth? The classical economists stressed thrift but this itself is the outcome of capital accumulation and profit and must therefore be considered endogenous. Kaldor always believed that the most plausible answer to the question of why some human societies progress faster than others must lie in attitudes to risk-taking and money-making, not in fortuitous accidents like major discoveries or a favourable natural environment. It is the strength of the incentives to overcome physical limitations of capacity and labour that sets the long-run trend. A scarcity of labour in particular not only encourages population growth but also labour-saving invention. Thus, far from the trend rate of growth determining the strength and duration of the boom, as in trade cycle models, it is the strength and duration of booms which help to determine the trend rate of growth. Kaldor's thesis is in the Keynesian spirit giving a central role to the whims and dynamism of entrepreneurs and to the volatility of entrepreneurial expectations. It is also Schumpeterian, as Kaldor acknowledged: 'the same forces therefore which produce violent booms and slumps will also tend to produce a high trend rate of progress . . . and Schumpeter's hero, the innovating entrepreneur . . . [has] a key role in the drama. . . . He is a promoter, a speculator, a gambler, the purveyor of economic expansion generally and not just of the new techniques of production.' The caveat is added, however, that this does not imply that progress depends on there being fits and starts whatever the institutional arrangements of society. There is no reason why in theory progress should not be steady if investment is centrally planned and the consumption function is continually adjusted to secure full employment.

WELFARE ECONOMICS

In the broad area of welfare economics Kaldor made two significant contributions which spawned an enormous secondary literature. His seminal paper 'Welfare Propositions in Economics and Interpersonal Comparisons of Utility' (1939d) ushered in the New Welfare Economics, and a further short paper, 'A Note on Tariffs and the Terms of Trade' (1940f), revived the concept of the optimum tariff. Interestingly, he hardly participated in the subsequent debates that the first paper generated, correctly anticipating the subject matter of welfare criteria to be a dead end.

The short outburst on welfare propositions in economics was initially a reaction against the Paretian nihilism of his antagonist Robbins who argued that unless it is assumed that individuals have an equal capacity for satisfaction it is impossible to say anything scientific or positive about an economic change if it makes some people worse off at the same time as it makes others better off, because individual utilities cannot be compared.[21] Robbins frequently used the example of the repeal of the Corn Laws which, by reducing the value of land, caused a loss to the landowners but at the same time increased the real income of consumers. Unless everyone is treated as equal how can the loss be compared with the gain to decide whether society is better or worse off? Harrod seemed to endorse Robbins' position in his 1938 Presidential Address to Section F of the British Association.[22] According to Harrod, 'if the incomparability of utility of different individuals is strictly pressed, not only are the prescriptions of the welfare school ruled out, but all prescriptions whatsoever.' The economist as an adviser is made redundant.

Kaldor, and Hicks soon after, found it difficult to accept such a negative conclusion. The position of Robbins was interpreted by Kaldor as support for the laissez-faire approach to economic affairs. More generally such a stance becomes a recipe for economic paralysis. Kaldor's response was to introduce the idea of compensation tests, a concept first mooted, but not developed, by the Italian economist, Enrico Barone.[23] The approach was attractively, but deceptively, simple. If the gainers from a policy change could potentially compensate the losers and still be better off, the economist may prescribe on the policy change in the knowledge that physical productivity must have increased. The fact that utilities are not comparable is irrelevant since it is always possible to make everybody better off than before, or at least to make sure that no one is worse off. Kaldor acknowledged inspiration from Pigou's procedure in The Economics of Welfare (1920) of dividing welfare economics into two parts, that relating to output (efficiency) and that relating to the distribution of output. The compensation test would allow the economist to say something positive about output, although not about its distribution.

Kaldor had discussed this matter privately with Hicks who was quick into print in the next issue of the Economic Journal[24] supporting Kaldor's compensation test and the distinction between efficiency and distribution. According to Hicks, 'if measures making for efficiency are to have a fair chance, it is extremely desirable that they should be freed from distributive complications as much as possible.' He also noted (which Kaldor did not) that compensation may repercuss on efficiency which needs taking into account (and, as it turns out, can give ambiguous results in the application of welfare criteria, as later writers pointed out). Hicks used a reverse test for an increase in real social income, namely whether the loosers could bribe the gainers not to move to a new position. Scitovsky[25] was quick to show that if the Kaldor and Hicks criteria were taken separately, they could lead to contradictory results because of the different starting points for consideration. With the old output and distribution a change from situation A to B may be deemed desirable, but equally from the new output and distribution a change back from B to A may also pass the compensation test. This came to be called the Scitovsky paradox.

The paradox can be illustrated using community indifference curves and heuristically explained by the fact that the relative valuation of commodities (the marginal rate of substitution) differs with the quantities of goods produced and their distribution. Efficiency affects distribution and distribution affects efficiency. Maurice Dobb also made the same point to Kaldor in private correspondence in November 1940, after a Cambridge seminar on the matter. Kaldor agreed with Scitovsky that in order to be certain that a particular policy will potentially increase welfare, the test must be a double one. The new situation must not only show itself to be superior to the old one, in comparison with the old income distribution, but the old situation must also be inferior to the new one in comparison with the income distribution in the new situation. Scitovsky's insight did not invalidate compensation tests, but made them more rigorous, namely that the ranking of two positions should be the same whichever is used as the basis for comparison.[26]

The Kaldor, Hicks and Scitovsky criteria were developed in order to avoid interpersonal comparisons of utility, yet it is difficult not to concede that such comparisons are still needed if we are to talk unambiguously about welfare improvement, as opposed to increases in production. This opens up a whole Pandora's box. Before Little's critique of the New Welfare Economics,[27] Baumol had argued that while Kaldor's criterion is a necessary condition for an economic optimum, it is not a sufficient condition.[28] It is possible to conceive of situations which satisfy the Kaldor compensation test but which leave the community worse off than before because, for example, the income distribution is more 'undesirable' is some sense. In discussing hypothetical compensation, the prevailing distribution is being implicitly accepted, and it is implicitly assumed that everyone's capacity for satisfaction is equal. To revert to the example of the repeal of the Corn Laws, the application of the Kaldor test does not answer the question of *should* the Corn Laws have been repealed if, in practice, people cannot be treated equally. The real income of consumers may have increased by more than the real income loss of the landowners, but the compensation payment *satisfactory* to landowners might have exceeded the gain to the consumers. Thus whether the repeal increased welfare depends on relative utilities. Similarly we can say, in a general sense, that if the poor were to lose from an economic change and the rich gain, the rich may be able to compensate the poor in money terms and still be better off, but if at the margin the effect of a pound loss to the poor is greater (measured in 'utils') than a pound gain to the rich, total welfare may fall. Contrawise, over-compensation may not be possible but there may still be a welfare gain if the poor value a pound more highly than the rich. In the discussion of the relation between welfare and *hypothetical* compensation we are back to interpersonal comparisons of utility. If compensation is *actually* paid, we are back to the Pareto criterion for a welfare improvement that at least someone should be better off without anybody else worse off, but this still leaves the question of the altered distribution of income. There are an indefinite number of Pareto optima corresponding to different distributions of income. An objective criterion for the optimum distribution of income is still required.

Distributional considerations were the start, and at the heart, of Little's critique of the New Welfare Economics. What is welfare economics all about, if it is not about the distribution of income? In his own words, 'we do not believe that any definition of an increase in wealth, welfare, efficiency or real social income which excludes income distribution is acceptable.' Little strongly attacked the Kaldor-Hicks criterion on the grounds that if a policy change meets it, the presumption is that it should be made and yet the compensation is only hypothetical and the change could be consistent with making the poor poorer. In Little's view, Kaldor, by his compensation test, had merely defined 'efficiency' but not provided a measure of it. Little's criticism was essentially the same as Baumol's but outdated, and to that extent unfair, since Kaldor (1946a), in reply to Baumol, conceded that whether a new income distribution resulting from compensation is the most desirable one, or whether other distributions are even more desirable, is a question that cannot be answered without resort to normative (value) judgements (or what Baumol referred to as 'political postulates'). The natural outcome of Little's critique was a two-pronged criterion for an increase in welfare. State B is superior to State A if either the Kaldor-Hicks test *or* the Scitovsky reversal test is met, provided that the distribution of income is no worse in B than in A. Apart from the difficulty of how the income distribution should be measured, the application of this dual criterion of Little was also shown to yield contradictory rankings.[29] Kaldor's initial intuition seems to have been correct. Every proposition in welfare economics seems to be found wanting. It appears that nothing positive can be said on whether a policy change which causes some to benefit and others to lose is a welfare improvement unless a social welfare function is specified which makes explicit value judgements about the income distribution. But the social welfare function itself remains an abstraction. Who specifies the function and who decides the weights?

Here the matter must rest. Suffice it to say in conclusion that Kaldor did not repent over repeal of the Corn Laws or in rejecting Robbins' proposition that because it is impossible to make inter-personal comparisons of utility economics as a science cannot say anything by way of prescription. In concluding the Introduction to his *Collected Essays* (Vol. 1) he concluded, 'none of the strictures of Scitovsky, Samuelson, Arrow, Little et al., against the validity or sufficiency of compensation tests alters the fact that repealing the Corn Laws and compensating the landlords was in every way a preferable alternative to leaving the Corn Laws "in being".' This remains, of course, a value judgement outside the bounds of formal welfare theory.

Kaldor's other contribution to welfare economics on tariffs and the terms of trade was hardly controversial, although several others soon took up the same theme. He revived the concept of the optimum tariff showing with the aid of community indifference curves how the introduction of an import duty can reproduce exactly the same effects as the introduction of monopoly pricing. He showed that a tariff can always produce a higher level of real income up to a certain point provided the elasticity of foreign demand is less than infinite and there is no retaliation. There will, of course, be an indefinite number of optimum tariffs corresponding to different distributions of income.

WAGES AND EMPLOYMENT

From his early days at the LSE, Kaldor took a keen interest in employment theory and policies for the alleviation of unemployment. His first paper in the field on wage subsidies as a remedy for unemployment (1936a) reflects his neoclassical background and training. It was written, however, in a Keynesian spirit, and not long after he was to take up the attack against Pigou. Indeed, he did more to convert Pigou to Keynesian ways of thinking than any other economist. It is clear from the Keynes' correspondence that Pigou understood what Kaldor was saying more easily than he did Keynes.[30]

Wage Subsidies
Kaldor had become interested in the topic of wage subsidies in 1934, and before he sailed for the United States in the autumn of 1935 he had produced a Plan which he circulated privately to colleagues including Hugh Gaitskell at University College, London, Sraffa and Joan Robinson. The emerging 'Keynesian' consensus was against money wage cuts because this would simply reduce prices and not create extra employment in the aggregate. In seeking alternative remedies, subsidies to labour appeared to be another possibility, which would reduce the cost of employing labour while maintaining the purchasing power of the workers. When Kaldor wrote to Joan Robinson in Cambridge about his scheme she professed not to understand the argument unless it raised the propensity to consume through a redistribution of income to labour. It would, but this was not how Kaldor articulated the idea. He simply wanted to make a distinction between a shift in the labour demand curve to the left and a shift in the labour supply curve to the right. Robinson believed that subsidies would reduce prices, but Kaldor was adamant that the difference between subsidies and wage cuts is that subsidies do not reduce money demand and therefore do not affect prices. In exasperation, Kaldor declared at one point in correspondence: 'I fear that Cambridge economics is beyond me.'[31]

At this stage in his life, Kaldor still believed in diminishing returns to labour and that unemployment resulted from a discrepancy between the wage relative to the marginal product at full employment.

Given the revival of interest in recent years in subsidising labour in conditions of mass unemployment, it is interesting to follow Kaldor's argument in some detail. First the distinction is made between 'general' and partial (structural) unemployment. He was optimistic that partial unemployment would be self-correcting in time through market forces. For general unemployment, the remedy must lie either in an increase in the marginal product of labour or a reduction in the cost of labour (on the assumption of diminishing marginal productivity).There were three ways to increase the marginal product of labour, (1) through state employment; (ii) through tariffs or subsidies on goods; and (iii) by monetary measures to increase investment. There were two ways to reduce the cost of labour: a reduction in the wage level or wage subsidies. The relative merits of subsidies and wage cuts are compared, and the case is put for subsidies as superior from a theoretical point of view. At the level of the individual industry the effect of a wage cut and an equivalent labour subsidy can be expected to be identical. At the aggregate level, however, the effects will not be the same. A general reduction in wages will always cause, at least temporarily, some reduction in the demand for consumption goods and therefore prices, so that real wages will fall less than money wages and hence employment will not increase by as much as through the same reduction in real wages. To use Pigou's terminology, the elasticity of money demand for labour will be smaller than the elasticity of real demand for labour – for equal reductions in money and real wages. In the case of a wage subsidy, by contrast, the demand for consumption goods must rise. A subsidy, therefore, must lead to an equivalent or greater reduction in real labour costs, and the elasticity of money demand must be equal to or greater than the elasticity of the real demand for labour. Thus, a general wage subsidy will have a far greater effect on employment than an equivalent general reduction in money wages. Translated into Keynes' new terminology Kaldor concluded: 'it implies that a general subsidy on wages is capable of bringing about a shift in the aggregate supply function, relatively to the aggregate demand function which, on Mr. Keynes's assumptions, is not possible in the case of a general reduction of wages.' The question of how subsidies are financed is then considered. This is necessary, of course, for evaluating the relative merits of wage subsidies compared with other methods of state expenditure to alleviate unemployment. Assuming the subsidy is financed by taxation, there is first the net cost to the state to consider, and then the ultimate cost to the taxpaying community. The net cost to the state may be negative or positive, but in either case, Kaldor argued, it will be smaller if it takes the form of removing existing taxes on labour than if it is given as a direct payment. This is so because of the difference in the volume of employment on which the tax or subsidy is paid in the two cases. The removal of existing insurance contributions paid by employers was therefore considered as the optimal way of administering the subsidy. The attempt is then made to prove mathematically that the cost to the state in this case would be negative as long as the elasticity of demand for labour is equal to or greater than the ratio of wages to unemployment benefit. Since empirical research suggested a real elasticity of demand for labour of at least two, and given that the wage : benefit ratio in most countries lay between two and three, Kaldor concluded that the cost to the state of a subsidy was likely to be virtually zero. Even if the cost of the wage-subsidy scheme to the state was large, however, requiring a considerable addition to general taxation, the cost of the subsidy would still be negative to the taxpaying community as a whole, since the wage subsidy would augment taxpayers' incomes by almost as much as the subsidy itself. With regard to that part of the subsidy which is paid on labour already in employment, the taxpaying community's income would be augmented by the same amount as the total amount of the subsidy, while on additionally employed labour the loss to the taxpaying community would be unlikely to be larger than half the rate of subsidy per additionally employed worker, without allowing for the saving of unemployment benefits.[32] The net burden on the taxpayers as a whole would therefore be negative as long as the rate of subsidy per worker was less than twice the cost of maintaining the unemployment, which would certainly be the case. This conclusion is independent of the elasticity of demand for labour, provided it is greater than zero.

If the rate of investment remains the same, the increase in employment created by a wage subsidy and financed by taxation would be the same as that which would be brought about by an equivalent reduction in *real* wages. This is no longer necessarily true, however, if monetary effects are taken into account, since one of the effects of reducing real labour costs is the enlargement of investment opportunities at given rates of interest and the consequent increase in the volume of funds seeking investment. This expansion will be larger, the greater the increase in prospective yields in general. Because of this, Kaldor concluded that there was a *prima facie* case for financing the initial expenditure on wage subsidies by borrowing rather than by taxation to avoid reducing net yields. Although there would be future tax liabilities, individual investors would not think in this way in calculating future yields.

Compared to alternative methods of creating employment, such as public works and monetary expansion, Kaldor saw several advantages in subsidising wages, such as the relatively low cost to the community and the fact that they can be more easily varied. To be effective as an unemployment relief measure, however, the government should attempt to maintain somehow a steady level of money wages, otherwise wage subsidies would simply be a device for income redistribution. Whatever happened, however, Kaldor's argument would remain unaffected, that there can be no feasible case for taxing wages or payrolls while unemployment prevails.

The Debate with Pigou on Wages and Employment

Following the publication of Keynes' *General Theory* in 1936, Pigou was quick to defend the classical view of the relation between money wage cuts and employment in a controversial paper 'Real and Money Wage Rates in Relation to Unemployment' (*Economic Journal*, September 1937). Because Keynes had been ill, Dennis Robertson was acting-editor of the *Economic Journal* and had accepted the paper for publication. The paper turned out to be wrong, which Kaldor was quick to point out, and which Pigou later conceded. In a strongly worded letter, Keynes castigated Robertson for publishing the paper: 'the Prof's article I have recently considered thoroughly; and I think you've committed an unforgiveable sin in letting him print it. It is outrageous rubbish beyond all possibility of redemption....'[33]

The debate that ensued concerned the question of whether at the macro-level a cut in money wages could increase employment independently of a fall in the rate of interest. Pigou's vision of the macro economy was as follows: Price is defined as the ratio of money income to the quantity of output. What happens to price depends on what happens to money income which depends on banking policy. Money income is the stock of money (M) multiplied by its velocity of circulation (V). Pigou defined normal banking policy as the money supply responding positively to interest rate changes so that as interest rates rise the money supply expands, and as interest rates fall the money supply contracts. The rate of interest must equilibrate the supply of and demand for money and must also equal the rate of time preference in long-run equilibrium. Now suppose that there is a cut in money wages. If output does not change the rate of time preference will not change and so the rate of interest will not change. If the rate of interest does not change, the money supply will remain unchanged and also the velocity of circulation, so that MV remains unchanged. Therefore, when wages are reduced and output is fixed, prices cannot fall. But marginal prime cost is reduced, and therefore the new situation after the wage cut cannot be an equilibrium one. Entrepreneurs will be making abnormal profits and will be induced to take on new men. Thus, argued Pigou, 'the fall in money wage rates always carries with it, and, in a sense, may be said to act on employment through, a fall in the real wage rate.' Pigou went on

precisely how many men will be called into work in the new situation, and what will happen to the rate of interest and the volume of money income depend, of course, on detailed circumstances. These matters cannot be discussed here. One point, however, should be made. It may well be that immediately after a wage cut the rate of interest falls alike below its original level and below the level proper to it when the new (short-period) equilibrium situation is obtained. This may seem at first sight to confirm the view sometimes put forward, that a cut in money wage rates can only increase employment if and insofar as it causes a reduction in the money rate of interest; so that the same result could be secured more simply by reducing the money rate of interest leaving the money rate of wages alone.

Pigou rejected this however, arguing that if money wages are not reduced, then when bankers return to their original practice, employment will also return to where it was, whereas, 'if the money rate of wages is reduced, after a temporary fall in the money rate of interest, we shall have employment standing permanently above the original level. Thus the two processes are entirely different.' Pigou denied any causal relation between a cut in wages and the interest rate and denied that the new equilibrium must imply a lower rate of interest. He concluded, 'it is enough for my purpose to show that a money wage cut is not simply a piece of ritual that enables the real cause of employment expansion – a fall in the rate of money interest – to take effect.' It was this proposition that Kaldor objected to. Keynes' objection was more direct. Pigou had written to Keynes putting his argument in a nutshell:[34] if a cut in wages leaves employment unchanged, money income has no ground for change. Therefore we cannot conclude that a wage cut leaves employment unchanged without becoming involved in a contradication about money income. Keynes' reply to Pigou was quite simple: 'I maintain that, if there is a cut in wages, unemployment being unchanged, there *is* a ground for a change in money income.'[35]

There had, in fact, been considerable discussion of Pigou's paper before it was published, and after its appearance the discussion started again in earnest. Kaldor submitted his reply to the *Economic Journal* in September, writing to Keynes, 'I am sure there must be several people in Cambridge who could point out the same thing yet I am sending it along in the hope that I get in first!'[36] Kaldor's supposition was correct and Kahn was hostile to Kaldor's article for that reason. Kahn wrote to Keynes: 'I have not seen Kaldor's article but I am sure that publication of it will darken counsel. After all, we could all of us write replies to Pigou if you wanted them and I do not see why Kaldor should be thus favoured.'[37] Kahn also communicated to Keynes the general feeling in Cambridge about Pigou's paper: 'Gerald [Shove] says that without exception this is the worst article he has ever read... also Piero Sraffa is studying this [Pigou's article] with his research students. He agrees with Gerald's verdict.'[38] Sraffa also apparently thought that Kaldor was thoroughly muddled and 'fogs the issue' (Kahn's words). Keynes replied to Kaldor that he had written a reply to Pigou himself with the merit 'that it is immensely briefer', but that he would see how the matter is best treated when he had his own reply in final form.[39] Kaldor responded that he was not surprised that someone would write a reply, but 'I didn't realise you would write one yourself.'[40] As it turned out, Kaldor's response was much more cogent than Keynes', and it was his argument that ultimately persuaded Pigou of his error.

Both Keynes and Kaldor (unlike Kahn and Sraffa) accepted Pigou's position that if saving is regarded as purely a function of the rate of interest, then in long-run equilibrium (where saving is assumed to be zero) the rate of interest must equal the rate of time preference. The basis of Kaldor's attack (1937c) was to modify Pigou's model to make saving also depend on the level of real income. By doing so, it was then easily shown that there is no way in which a reduction in money wages can increase employment independently of a reduction in the rate of interest. Kaldor remarked in his paper, 'it is interesting to note that the assumption that savings are largely a function of real income has not been questioned by any of Mr. Keynes's critics. Yet in the present writer's view, it is this assumption, more than any other, which is responsible for the revolutionary innovations of Mr. Keynes's system'. In Kaldor's model an increase in real income would increase saving; increased saving leads to a fall in prices and an increase in the size of idle balances and thus a fall in the rate of interest. In terms of Pigou's model, an increase in real income would imply a reduction in the rate of time preference and hence, in equilibrium, a reduction in the money rate of interest. Kaldor concluded, in fact, that in a Keynesian framework, there is no way in which a change in money wages by itself could affect either the savings function or the investment function, and therefore no way in which it could alter the level of real output which secures equality between savings and investment at a given rate of interest. Hence if the rate of interest is given, the equilibrium level of employment is also given irrespective of the level of money wages. Thus wage cuts must affect employment through a reduction in the rate of interest brought about by an increase in idle money balances. Kaldor may be thought of as responsible for improving Hicks' IS-LM curve analysis by working in *real* terms.

Keynes had criticised Hicks for making saving a function of *money* income.[41] In this sense, Kaldor was the first economist (after Keynes) to use rigorously what later came to be called the 'Keynes effect', i.e. the effect of falling wages and prices on the real money supply. Kaldor stated explicitly that a reduction in money wages 'is exactly the same as that of an increase in the quantity of money or a reduction in liquidity preference' (1937c, p.752). Keynes' reply to Pigou was much shorter than Kaldor's, and Pigou claimed not to understand it. When Pigou answered his critics (*Economic Journal*, March 1938) he addressed his paper to Kaldor. Pigou's original reply was some 10,000 words long. Having shown the paper to Champernowne, however, who pointed out two major fallacies, it was reduced to some five journal pages and conceded Kaldor's main contention that the increase in employment must also entail (except in the special case of infinite liquidity preference) a fall in the rate of interest – the lesson being that an increase in employment and output will reduce time preference and hence the equilibrium rate of interest: 'if we assume that this is so it follows that, as between different equilibrium positions in our model, employment cannot increase unless the rate of interest is reduced; but whatever happens to anything else, *must* increase if it *is* reduced.' Pigou went on, 'given then that employment rises as interest falls, we can determine how a cut in money wage rates will affect employment if we can determine how it will affect the rate of interest', and 'in the sense that [a cut in money wages] would not entail an increase in employment *unless* it entailed a reduction in the rate of interest, we may properly say that it acts on the volume of employment *through* the rate of interest'. Pigou paid Kaldor the compliment of saying 'that the theory of the relation between money wages and employment, via the rate of interest, was invented by Kaldor'. He had forgotten Chapter 19 of the *General Theory* and its Appendix! As Keynes described it to Kahn, Pigou's reply was

in effect a complete and frank withdrawal of the whole of the previous argument. He now holds that, subject to his various assumptions, a cut in money wages does no good whatever except through and because of its effect on the rate of interest. On his special assumption, he now says, there is no means whatever of increasing employment except by reducing the rate of interest.[42]

Keynes mentioned to Kahn that there were really only two

remaining differences between himself and Pigou, 'the first arising out of [Pigou's] conviction that the theory of the relation between money wages and employment, via the rate of interest, was invented by Kaldor; and secondly he is still believing (I think) that a rise in the rate of interest increases aggregate savings which he still confuses with its increasing savings out of a given income'.[43] Keynes was understandably aggrieved that Pigou attributed to Kaldor the discovery of the 'Keynes effect', and reminded Pigou that 'Kaldor is mainly a restatement of my *General Theory* with reference to your special assumptions.'[44]

It is important to re-emphasise that although Pigou approved of Kaldor's modification of his simple model, he did not concede Kaldor's argument on grounds of liquidity preference but on the basis of the declining rate of time preference. For Pigou still maintained that *if* time preference was independent of aggregate real income a cut in money wages would increase employment while leaving the rate of interest unchanged. This led to some discussion in the literature afterwards[45] because it was contended that a Keynesian conclusion had, in effect, been accepted by a non-Keynesian route. This was an understandable reaction, but Kaldor (1939b) cleared up the confusion. As he pointed out, there was no need for Pigou to invoke liquidity preference for the simple reason that in the absence of liquidity preference the rate of interest would be entirely governed by the savings and investment functions – in this case by the rate of time preference – and would fall automatically with any reduction in the time preference rate. Liquidity preference considerations need only be introduced to explain why a reduction in time preference *fails* to elicit a corresponding reduction in the rate of interest. A reduction in the interest rate comes about automatically with a reduction in money wages and an increase in employment because the marginal propensity to consume is less than unity, so that, using Pigou's own terminology, 'the rate of time preference is a decreasing function of the level of employment.' Kaldor based his own belief in the liquidity preference theory of interest on the purely empirical facts that in the market for long-term bonds, the influence of the speculative element is dominant over other influences, and that the elasticity of savings with respect to the rate of interest is small. But if the speculative factor was small or the elasticity of savings with respect to the interest rate was large, he would cease to believe it. Although Kaldor used the 'Keynes effect', he none the less concluded: 'Mr. Keynes's propositions relating to money wages are, therefore, quite independent of liquidity preference: and if any particular function is to be held responsible, it is the propensity to consume function and not liquidity preference which is relevant.'

Pigou was a shy and retiring man and Kaldor had few dealings with him, not even when they were both Fellows in King's together. But they had great mutual respect for each other. Pigou was undoubtedly impressed by Kaldor; and Kaldor, in turn, could detect Pigou's anguish at the onslaught of the Keynesian revolution, and had some sympathy with him. He wrote a full length review (1941c) of Pigou's book, *Employment and Equilibrium* (1941), and wrote very generously about it nineteen years later in his *Collected Essays* (Vol. 2):

Pigou's book on *Employment and Equilibrium*, published at an inauspicious moment, did not receive the attention it deserved. For it contains an elegant macro-economic model built with neo-classical, rather than Keynesian, tools which demonstrate that if one starts from the same basic assumptions, it is possible to arrive at the same results by the old techniques just as by the new. It is questionable, however, as Pigou himself concedes in the Preface to his book, whether the neo-classical tools could ever have been wielded skilfully enough to produce these results if Keynes's new techniques had not provided the challenge. Once the challenge was there, it was possible to exhibit the Keynesian theory in terms of a more general framework which allows for a wider range of possibilities.

In the review itself Kaldor concluded,

it is hoped that the fact that this review is so largely taken up by detailed criticism will not have concealed from its reader the admiration which the reviewer feels towards the volume as a whole. Its well-planned logical construction, the subtlety of its analysis and the avenues it opens for further research on the same pattern are bound to place *Employment and Equilibrium* among the best things the author has written. The fact that this is the sixth major treatise on economic theory the author has produced bears witness to a record of achievement that must surely be unique among economists.

In a letter to *The Times* (6 June 1979) Kaldor was the first to come to Pigou's defence against the scurrilous accusation by Richard Deacon in his book *The British Connection* that Pigou was a Russian agent. With a touch of sarcasm, Kaldor offered himself as a more credible communist infiltrator of the Treasury.

OTHER EXTENSIONS OF KEYNESIAN THEORY

The paper that gave Kaldor most intellectual satisfaction during this vintage period of his theoretical writing was 'Speculation and Economic Stability' (1939e),[46] supplemented by the essay 'Keynes'

Theory of the Own-Rates of Interest' (1960f). The latter paper started as an Appendix to the first, but Ursula Hicks, editor of the *Review of Economic Studies*, declined to publish it because the main body of the paper was already far too long. It remained unfinished and unpublished until 1960. When Ursula Hicks received the main paper she wrote: 'John [Hicks] and I are quite agreed that it is one of your most important works.' In these two contributions Kaldor was concerned with three important 'Keynesian' questions. First, why is it that an increase in the propensity to save is not in itself capable of generating more investment contrary to the classical position – or, in other words, what are the general necessary, if not sufficient, conditions for the workings of the income multiplier? Secondly, what determines the structure of interest rates? Thirdly, what asset sets the ultimate limit on employment by limiting the willingness to invest in physical assets, and why?

The short answer given to the first question is that it is the stabilising influence of speculators in the bond market which causes the rate of interest to remain unchanged. If we think of 'goods' in general that are bought out of current income, if there were no speculation, movements in the price level would do all the adjustment in response to changes in demand and supply and there would be no change in income or output. The greater the price-stabilising influence of speculation, the greater the destabilisation of income. In the extreme, if the influence of speculation is infinite, so that price is constant, the whole of the adjustment is done by quantities to balance supply and demand. Kaldor believed that in the real world the most important type of asset whose price is stabilised through speculation is long-term bonds bought with savings.

It will be remembered that Keynes, in his discussion of liquidity preference, worked with the concept of a 'normal price' with inelastic expectations. Clearly, the more firmly speculators believe in a 'normal price', and the less the uncertainty about the future, the less price will fluctuate and the stronger is Keynes' theoretical conclusion that savings and investment will be equated by changes in the level of income rather than by the rate of interest. Keynes read Kaldor's paper soon after publication and in conversation apparently agreed with him that the explanation that he had given (rather than the concept of a liquidity premium) was the major theoretical explanation of the income multiplier (see 1986a). In practice, of course, balance in markets is likely to be brought about by a change in both prices and income, and stocks must also be replenished if the multiplier is to operate in the upward direction.

In the process of generalising Keynes' theory of the multiplier,

Kaldor gave one of the most lucid expositions ever written of speculation and price stability, and the circumstances under which speculation may be destabilising, challenging the traditional theory that speculation must always be stabilising otherwise speculators would make a loss and be eliminated. He showed how speculation can be destabilising with the losses of an ever-changing population of unsuccessful speculators sufficient to maintain permanently a small group of successful speculators. If the expected price is given there is no dispute that speculation must be stabilising. For speculation to be destabilising, *either a* change in the current price must lead to a more than proportionate change in the expected price (what Hicks originally called the elasticity of expectations), *or* there must be some spontaneous change in the expected price which itself is speculative (e.g. related to changes in stocks – what Kaldor called the elasticity of speculative stocks). The degree of price-stabilising influence is thus determined by the elasticities of expectations and speculative stocks. In any market there is likely to be a range of price fluctuations within which speculation will be stabilising, and outside of which speculation is destabilising. The range of price fluctuation in some markets will be wider than in others according to differences between markets in the conception of 'normal price'. Because of inelastic price expectations (held by everybody), the bond market is stable, and this was Keynes' position. The question remains, however, what determines the 'normal price' of bonds? Dennis Robertson accused Keynes of leaving the long-term interest rate 'hanging by its own bootstraps'.

Kaldor addressed this question of the structure of interest rates and provided what might be called a 'bottom-up' theory of interest rates in which the whole interest rate structure is determined by the convenience yield on money plus a risk premium on assets of different maturities. The short rate is determined in the money market, and it is this rate which anchors the edifice. He strongly opposed the view that expectations of the future rate of interest affect the current short rate with the corollary that the rate will be independent of changes in liquidity preference. Robertson and Kahn, amongst others, were highly critical, but Kaldor remained largely unrepentant. Indeed, writing in 1960, after the Radcliffe Committee Report on the Working of the Monetary System (see Chapter 12) and his evidence to it, he reasserted his original position: 'one cannot conceive of the short rate being "determined" in any other way than through the rediscount rate, or the open market policy of the Central Bank. Indeed, it is only through their power to control the whole range of short term interest rates that the monetary authorities can be said to "control" the supply of money in its broader sense' (*Collected Essays*, Vol. 2, p. 6).

We are led finally to Kaldor's masterly dissection of Keynes' complex and tortuous Chapter 17 of the *General Theory*, on the 'Essential Properties of Interest and Money', which considers the peculiar properties of money and poses two important questions: first, how do we know it is the long-term money rate of interest which sets the rate to which all other rates conform; and secondly, which asset, and its return, sets the limit to the profitable use of funds for investment in physical assets? To understand the answers that Keynes and Kaldor gave, the concepts of the own rate of own-interest and the own rate of money interest need to be understood. The former is the return to a commodity measured in terms of itself, which is the same thing as the amount of the commodity which can be bought for forward delivery in terms of a given amount of the same commodity for spot delivery. For example, if 100 tons of wheat for spot delivery can buy 102 tons of wheat for forward delivery, the wheat rate of wheat interest is 2 per cent. The own rate of money interest is the own rate of own-interest plus appreciation of the commodity in terms of money. For example, if the value of wheat appreciated by 5 per cent in terms of money, the wheat rate of money interest would be 2 per cent plus 5 per cent equals 7 per cent. Clearly, since money cannot appreciate or depreciate in terms of itself, the own rate of own-interest on money is necessarily equal to the own rate of money interest. This is a significant point because the general level of the own money interest (to which the own rate of money interest on each asset will conform by variation in the asset's price) will be determined by the highest of the own rates of own-interest among those assets whose own rate of money interest cannot vary relatively to their own rates of own-interest. The only asset for which this can be true (at least with inelastic expectations) is money. Thus by virtue of the fact that money is the standard of value, it is necessarily the case that it is the own rate of interest of money that sets the standard for other rates and not the other way round. If wheat was the standard of value the own rate of interest of wheat would set the standard.

It also follows from the property of money as the standard of value that it cannot be other assets that keep interest rates generally high because if the own rate of own-interest on an asset is high relative to others, its price will rise relative to others reducing the own rate of money interest in line with the own rates of interest of other assets. This has the important implication, which Keynes overlooked, that it must always be money (or whatever is the unit of account) that ultimately limits employment (rather than the rate of interest on any other asset) because only the money rate of interest cannot be negative whereas the own rates of interest on other assets can be.[47] In other words, it is the excess of the own rate of money interest over the own rate of own interest which is responsible for involuntary unemployment.

NOTES

1. G. L. S. Shackle, *The Years of High Theory: Invention and Tradition in Economic Thought* 1928–1939 (Cambridge University Press, 1967).
2. P. Sraffa, 'The Laws of Returns Under Competitive Conditions', *Economic Journal*, December 1926.
3. J. Robinson, *The Economics of Imperfect Competition* (London: Macmillan, 1933).
4. E. Chamberlin, *The Theory of Monopolistic Competition* (Cambridge, Mass.: Harvard University Press, 1933).
5. E. Chamberlin, 'Monopolistic or Imperfect Competition', *Quarterly Journal of Economics*, August 1937.
6. *Quarterly Journal of Economics*, May 1938.
7. M. Kalecki, 'The Principle of Increasing Risk', *Economica*, November 1937.
8. M. Weitzman, 'Increasing Returns and the Foundations of Unemployment Theory', *Economic Journal*, December 1982.
9. See the discussion by J. Kregel, 'Harrod and Keynes: Increasing Returns, the Theory of Employment and Dynamic Economics', in G. C. Harcourt (ed.), *Keynes and his Contemporaries* (London: Macmillan, 1985).
10. The theorem itself he attributes to H. Schultz, *Der Sinn de Statistischen Nackfragekurven* (Bonn: K. Schroeder, 1930); and U. Ricci, 'Die Synthetische Ökonomie von Henry Ludwell Moore', *Zeitschrift für Nationalökonomie*, April 1930.
11. It was in this paper that Kaldor anticipated von Neumann's famous result that the rate of interest represents the highest potential rate of growth which would obtain if nothing were withdrawn from the system for unproductive consumption. See J. von Neumann, 'A Model of General Economic Equilibrium', *Review of Economic Studies*, No. 1, 1945.
12. Kaldor expressed doubts about whether one can measure the capital intensity of production for society as a whole.
13. If there was perfect competition in the product market (but imperfect competition in the capital market) the marginal efficiency curves would all be horizontal, and the technique chosen would be that with the highest marginal efficiency. The rate of interest would not be important. In the opposite case of perfect competition in the capital market and imperfect competition in the product market, the technique chosen would depend entirely on the rate of interest. Kaldor (1940a) later agreed with Hawtrey that since selling power is a much more important limitation on the size of business than borrowing power, capital intensity in most cases is probably quite independent of real wages and depends solely on the rate of interest.
14. The Hawtrey papers in the Archives of Churchill College, Cambridge,

contain voluminous correspondence between Kaldor and Hawtrey on these matters.

15. F. von Hayek, 'Ricardo Effect', *Economica*, May 1942, p. 145.
16. Unpublished letter, 19 September 1938.
17. This, in fact, was also Keynes' position (*General Theory*, p. 378).
18. Letter 14 August 1939. Kaldor's model may be thought of as the precursor of the capital stock adjustment principle. See R. C. O. Matthews, *The Trade Cycle* (Cambridge: James Nisbet, 1959).
19. J. Duesenberry, *Income, Saving and the Theory of Consumer Behaviour* (Harvard University Press, 1967).
20. 'The Existence and Persistence of Cycles in a Non-Linear Model: Kaldor's 1940 Model Re-Examined', *Review of Economic Studies*, January, 1971.
21. See L. Robbins, *An Essay on the Nature and Significance of Economic Science*, (London: Macmillan, 1932); and 'Interpersonal Comparisons of Utility: A Comment', *Economic Journal*, December 1938.
22. R. F. Harrod, 'Scope and Method of Economics', *Economic Journal*, September 1938.
23. In an article entitled 'The Ministry of Production in the Collectivist State' (1908, translated into English 1935).
24. J. R. Hicks, 'The Foundations of Welfare Economics', *Economic Journal*, December 1939.
25. T. Scitovsky, 'A Note on Welfare Propositions in Economics', *Review of Economic Studies*, November 1941.
26. Samuelson later pointed out (*Foundations of Economics*, 1947) that even the Scitovsky test was unsatisfactory. Because efficiency loci may intersect, he showed rigorously that for a potential increase in real income (in terms of compensation tests), the Kaldor and Hicks test (and therefore the Scitovsky double test) must be satisfied for every possible distribution of income both before and after the change in question occurs. If situations are excluded in which there is more of every good, it is not possible to rank alternative states by compensation tests. (P.A. Samuelson, 'Evaluation of Real National Income', *Oxford Economic Papers*, March 1950.)
27. I.M.D. Little, *A Critique of Welfare Economics* (Oxford: Clarendon Press, 1st edition, 1950; 2nd edition, 1957).
28. W. Baumol, 'Community Indifference', *Review of Economic Studies*, No. 1, 1946.
29. A movement from state A to B might meet both criteria, but this result might also be consistent with a subsequent movement back from B to A also meeting the Kaldor–Hicks test in which the distribution of income in A appeared better than in B. See C. Kennedy, 'The Economic Welfare Function and Dr. Little's Criterion', *Review of Economic Studies*, No. 2, 1953.
30. D. Moggridge (ed.), *The Collected Writings of J. M. Keynes. Vol. XIV: The General Theory and After Part II Defence and Development*, (London: Macmillan, 1973).
31. Unpublished letter to Joan Robinson, 3 June 1935, King's College Library, Cambridge.
32. Kaldor proves this.
33. Moggridge, (ed.), *op. cit.*, p. 250.
34. Ibid., p. 256.
35. Ibid., p. 257.
36. Ibid., p. 240.
37. Ibid., p. 260.
38. Ibid., p. 258.
39. Ibid., p. 240.
40. Ibid., p. 241.

41. Ibid., p. 80.
42. Ibid., p. 266.
43. Ibid., p. 267.
44. Ibid., p. 267.
45. e.g. H. Somers, 'Money Wage Cuts in Relation to Unemployment', *Review of Economic Studies*, February 1939.
46. Some of the points of criticism of this paper from Hawtrey, Dow and Streeten were met in Kaldor (1940e; 1958d). The paper was relatively neglected, perhaps because it coincided with the publication of Hicks' *Value and Capital*. On re-reading the paper in 1986, Hicks wrote to Kaldor: 'I think that your paper was the culmination of the Keynesian revolution in *theory*. You ought to have had more honour for it.'
47. Kaldor was reacting against Keynes' suggestion (*General Theory*, p. 241) that the desire in the past to hold land might have kept the interest rate too high and that the desire to hold gold might do so in the future.

3 WAR AND THE RECONSTRUCTION OF EUROPE: 1940–1949

At the outbreak of war, Kaldor was considering seriously the possibility of going to Australia. He was approached by several universities, but eventually turned the offers down. Although he became a naturalised British subject in 1934, his foreign extraction precluded him from any important official civil service position during the war years. At one stage he expressed interest in working as a research assistant in the BBC which was a reserved occupation, but found the stipend too low. There was also the possibility that he might be given a part-time job at the Ministry of Fuel and Power, but he was turned down. He struggled with his conscience over whether to fight in the Jewish cause, and largely under the influence of his life-long friend, Piero Sraffa, eventually opted to have his call-up deferred. He settled for the academic life in England with the LSE evacuated to Peterhouse, Cambridge. After temporary accommodation at 2 Hedgerly Close and 1 Silvester Road, the Kaldor family settled in a cottage in Burnt Close, Grantchester for two years, and then moved to 50 Lensfield Road which became the family home for the duration of the war, and was retained until after the family's return from Geneva in 1949. In 1950, 2 Adams Road was bought, a commodious three-storey Edwardian property on the north-western outskirts of Cambridge, not far from the Robinsons at 62 Grange Road and the University Library. This remained the family base and the nerve centre of Kaldor's multifarious academic and political activities. Politicians were frequent visitors, and academics from all over the world would descend, invited and uninvited. But above all it was a family home to which Kaldor always looked forward to returning after long and tiring trips abroad. The spacious rooms provided ample space for a rapidly expanding family. Katherine, the oldest daughter, was born in 1937; Frances, who followed her father as an economist, was born in 1940; and Penelope and Mary came two and six years later, respectively.

The war, and the evacuation of the LSE to Cambridge, heralded a second major phase in Kaldor's working life. Exempted from military duties, and excluded from civilian war work, he not only continued to pursue pure academic research, including new projects on the economics of taxation (1942a) and advertising (1949a),[1] but also became actively involved in the economic aspects of the war in three important fields: the finance of the war effort; national income accounting, and the problems of post-war reconstruction particularly in relation to Beveridge's proposals on Social Insurance (1942) and Full Employment (1944). He also took a keen interest in the war effort of Germany and followed closely the economies of the Allied countries. From being a pure theorist for the previous seven years, he rapidly turned himself into one of the most respected applied economists of his generation. When the war ended he was employed extensively in an advisory capacity on various projects in various countries, and eventually became an international civil servant for two years in the Economic Commission for Europe (ECE) in Geneva, involved in the daunting and challenging task of the economic reconstruction of Europe.

Throughout the war teaching continued, and the burden was heavy with the LSE staff very much depleted. Key economists such as Roy Allen, Evan Durbin, Ronald Edwards, Brinley Thomas, Lionel Robbins and Dennis Robertson (the newly elected Sir Ernest Cassel Professor of Money and Banking) all took leave to join the war effort in various capacities, leaving only a handful of staff including Frederick Benham, Ronald Coase, Friedrich von Hayek, Frank Paish, Arnold Plant, George Schwartz, and the newly appointed Arthur Lewis. John Hicks had already departed to a Chair in Manchester. Kaldor continued to give twenty lectures on the Theory of Production; twenty lectures on Capital and Interest; ten lectures on International Trade and Foreign Exchange and six lectures on Outlines of Economic Dynamics. His course on Public Finance and the Trade Cycle was suspended temporarily, but then commenced again in 1941, together with a new course on the Problems of War Economics, which Keynes originally taught as part of the Cambridge syllabus and which, in effect, Kaldor took over for the duration of the war. Keynes also invited him late in 1939 to give a course of lectures to the Cambridge students on the Theory of Distribution for which he would be paid. But for the pettiness of Robbins, he would have been paid directly, but Robbins objected to the idea that, as a member of the LSE staff, he should be paid by another institution. In the end the money was paid to the Director of the LSE, who

then passed it on to Kaldor! Robbins had departed to Whitehall by
then. The lectures on Distribution started in 1941 and were
continued throughout the war, although under the title of Value
and Distribution from 1943. The lectures formed the basis of his
first article on income distribution written for the *Chambers
Encyclopedia* in 1948. Despite some complaints over the difficulty of
his lectures, he was very popular among the Cambridge students.
As a mark of their esteem he was the first non-Cambridge faculty
member to be elected as Chairman of the Marshall Society, the
students' economics club. He integrated totally with the Cambridge
economists, at least with those of his persuasion. Together with
Joan Robinson, Richard Kahn, and Piero Sraffa he formed what
was called the 'war circus', which afterwards became the 'secret
seminar', although everyone knew of its existence! Group walks in
the Lake District, visiting Pigou at his cottage in Buttermere,
became a favourite pastime. On one occasion in 1943 at the height
of rationing, Kaldor committed the crime of eating the whole of
Pigou's weekly butter ration at tea. To make amends, he and his
companions agreed that they would club together and give a jar of
marmalade in return. Sraffa saved up his marmalade ration and
accumulated a whole jar himself which he then used to appease
Pigou when he later suffered stage fright at the prospect of giving
a promised lecture on Ricardo. To Pigou's relief, Kaldor agreed to
step in at short notice, borrowing Sraffa's notes. Kaldor's greed in
Buttermere was forgiven, and such was his impression on Pigou in
those wartime years that it was no surprise that in 1949 the
Economics Faculty, dominated by Pigou, was to offer Kaldor a
university lectureship. Regular Sunday walks were also a feature
of the group, on one of which they walked into an RAF
ammunition dump and were promptly arrested. Out of this
'Seminar' came much of Joan Robinson's early writing on capital
theory. Relations with some of his LSE colleagues were not so
cordial. There was friction with Hayek, who accused Kaldor of
neglecting the supervision of his London students. Whatever the
truth in the allegations, and they were never substantiated
publicly, Hayek excluded him from the list of internal examiners
for the BSc degree for the duration of the war. Among his research
students at this time was Tibor Barna, also Hungarian, working on
the redistributive effects of public finance. He later assisted
Kaldor with work on Beveridge's *Full Employment in a Free Society*, and
then in 1948 joined him in Geneva. Another Hungarian friend was
Laszlo Rostas, renowned for his work on productivity, whom
Kaldor helped to bring to England in 1939 to join the National
Institute of Economic and Social Research to assist with research

on war taxation, and who then joined the Cambridge Faculty in 1951. When he died in 1954 at the young age of 45, Kaldor wrote his obituary for *The Times* (4 October).

In 1942 Kaldor added to his lecture commitments a new course of eight lectures on the Theory of Employment, which forced him to read again *The General Theory* even more carefully, but other courses were dropped and from 1942 to 1946 he settled into a regular teaching routine of the same courses: Problems of War Economics; International Trade and Foreign Exchange; The Theory of Distribution (Value and Distribution), and the Theory of Employment.

WAR FINANCE AND NATIONAL INCOME ACCOUNTING

Kaldor laid down the conditions which he believed should govern the principles of war finance in an early paper in *The Banker* (1939c). Ursula Hicks described it in correspondence as 'top notch'. (She was writing continually to Kaldor throughout the war in her capacity as editor of the *Review of Economic Studies*, with him as her major adviser.) Two important principles, he believed, should govern war finance; first, that the aggregate real burden should be kept as small as possible; and secondly, that the distribution of the burden should be equitable. As long as unemployed resources existed, the government should borrow rather than tax to finance expenditure; indeed, if aggregate production can be expanded the real burden will be negative. How far aggregate production could be expanded would largely depend on labour availability. Kaldor did not believe that the existing level of borrowing was excessive and reckoned that borrowing of some £1000 million a year would be justified for the war effort. He took the opportunity to expose the myth of the national debt as a burden on the economy in any real sense. Taxation, he declared, should be 'screwed up only to the extent necessary to avoid an inflationary spiral'. To stop excess profiteering from increased government expenditure, however, he argued the case for an excess profits tax (as during the First World War), and not just on the armaments industry as was being proposed by the government. If necessary, such a tax could also be applied to wage and salary incomes as well. Later in preparing some estimates on war finance for his lectures on The Problems of War Economics, Kaldor also wrote an article for the *Economic Journal*, only to discover that the Treasury had attempted the same estimates and published them. None the less he sent Keynes a copy of the paper, and Keynes gave in reply his classic statement of what he meant by an inflationary gap: 'I measure an inflationary gap by the amount of purchasing power which has to be withdrawn, either by taxation or primary savings, in order that the remaining purchasing power should be equal to the available supplies on the market at the existing level of prices.'

From the onset of the war, Kaldor was communicating with Keynes on a regular basis over a variety of matters connected with war finance and national income accounting. He made several practical suggestions in 1939 on how Keynes' compulsory saving scheme might be made operational, and helped to clarify and improve the papers Keynes wrote on the estimation of national income. Keynes also used him as a regular referee for the *Economic Journal*. Sometimes the Kaldors were the guests of Maynard and Lydia at the Cambridge Arts Theatre to see the ballet and for supper afterwards. On one such occasion in early 1940, a long discussion took place on the subject of national income accounting and the relationship between gross and net income. Keynes was preparing a Note for the March issue of the *Economic Journal*, and Kaldor had reservations about the concept of gross income. In correspondence, Keynes expressed gratitude to Kaldor for clarifying his mind on certain matters, but confessed he did not like the concept of Gross National Income. Kaldor defended the concept of gross income as analytically and statistically prior to net income because net income can only be arrived at by deducting depreciation from gross income. Since depreciation is arbitrary, net income must be a vaguer concept than gross income. Kaldor's claim was that using figures for net income and net investment may considerably understate the resources available for alternative (war) uses since depreciation conceals a considerable amount of net saving, e.g. if expected obsolescence is taken into account. Kaldor also insisted that calculations should be net of indirect taxation. His preferred measure of resource availability to measure war potential was: national output plus stocks that could be depleted, minus depreciation not available, minus indirect taxation, minus monopoly earnings and minus rents on specific factors. Keynes had the highest regard for Kaldor, both intellectually and personally. This is no more evident than in a letter Keynes wrote to Jesus College in 1943 mentioning Kaldor's name as a possible Economics Fellow:

I put him very high among the younger economists in the country. Only his alien origin has prevented him from having a government job. I should expect, though I have not had the opportunity to consult anyone, that the Economic Faculty would gladly co-operate with the College in making joint arrangements for him to leave the London School to join us. He is of the calibre which would justify the immediate election to a Readership (as a Faculty we consider that we have a Readership vacant, since no successor was appointed before the war to Dennis Robertson when Dennis accepted a Professorship in London). Kaldor would be an exceptionally delightful and acceptable member of the High Table, a brilliant talker and one of the most attractive people about the place. He has a particularly nice English wife and a family. The very best type of cultivated, civilised, learned Central European.

Keynes was the inspiration behind national income accounting inside the Treasury, and pressed for general circulation of the estimates. In the budget speech of April 1941, the Chancellor of the Exchequer, Kingsley Wood, announced that he would issue, along with the customary annual Financial Statement, an *Analysis of the Sources of War Finance and Estimates of the National Income and Expenditure in 1938 and 1940*.[2] Kaldor's growing reputation as an expert on war finance was enhanced by his detailed dissection and analysis of the first three *White Papers on National Income and Expenditure* which became regular features in the *Economic Journal* (1941b; 1942b; 1943c). At the end of 1942, his friend Tibor Scitovsky wrote from America: 'your articles on the two British White Papers on War Finance are regarded as classics in this country ... everybody regards them as a model on which the corresponding estimates in this country are being based.'

The first White Paper was divided into two parts: the first part dealing with the sources of war finance, and the second with estimates of the money national income and its distribution in 1938 and 1940. In his review, Kaldor pointed to certain deficiencies in the presentation of the accounts, some of which were subsequently remedied, and others of which Kaldor himself made a bold attempt to rectify. One problem was that the data relating to war finance did not cover the same period as the data for national income, making it difficult to calculate the *real* sources of war finance. Secondly, the government expenditure figures included subsidies and other wartime transfer payments. Thirdly, Kaldor suggested that estimates should be given of the distribution of the tax burden among different classes of the population. Finally, the estimates for 1938 and 1940 were at current prices, combining price and quantity changes. Kaldor himself made attempts to convert current values into real terms. What was clear from the estimates, however, was the remarkable way in which the domestic expenditure on the war effort was being covered out of income, and how little was being met by running down capital. Between 1938 and 1940, Kaldor estimated an increase in real output of 10 per cent and a reduction in real consumption by 10 per cent, both of which helped to provide resources for government war expenditure. The fall in real consumption of 10 per cent was much more than could be accounted for by increases in direct taxation, thus indicating a fairly dramatic increase in the community's propensity to save. Kaldor maintained, however, that both figures could be improved on, and that a 25 per cent drop in real consumption compared with 1938 would not be unreasonable. In total, he reckoned that about £2700 million might be made available out of current income plus, say, £300 million disinvestment, giving £3000 million per annum at 1938 prices as the maximum home-financed government expenditure which could be maintained for any length of time. Kaldor concluded by congratulating the government on their wisdom and courage in revealing the secrets of war finance which made possible intelligent discussion and criticism and 'provides a solid foundation for the confidence of the nation in its own tremendous strength'.

In the second White Paper, the data relating to war finance and the national income now covered the same period; subsidies and transfer payments were deducted from government expenditure, and estimates were given of the tax burden among different classes of the population. In addition there were separate tables analysing the accounts of the public authorities, separating the accounts of the central government, the extra-budgetary funds and local authorities. There was still no attempt, however, to calculate income in real terms (at constant prices). On the financial side, it was apparent that taxation was keeping pace with expenditure. While in 1940, 37.5 per cent of total expenditure was covered by taxation, in 1941 it was 40 per cent and was estimated to rise to 45 per cent in 1942–43. To estimate the real sources of war finance, Kaldor again had to make his own independent estimates. He calculated that approximately one half of increased government expenditure in 1941 came from increased output and decreased consumption – involving no burden in the future – compared with one-third of the increased expenditure in 1940. So there was improvement in this respect too. A major problem in all the calculations was still the uncertainty over the figure for home disinvestment, which in the government figures was simply calculated as a residual between income and expenditure. When this figure is properly calculated, he remarked, 'it will be possible to analyse the real sources of war finance on a more solid foundation.'

By 1943, the economics profession, the press, and no doubt the government too, all eagerly awaited Kaldor's review of the annual

National Income White Paper. The *Manchester Guardian* (2 October 1943) described Kaldor's exposition as a 'welcome annual habit'. The review of the 1943 White Paper was done with Tibor Barna. For the first time an attempt was made to estimate the change in the retail market price of goods and services entering consumption in order to make estimates of changes in real consumption. Information on the composition of personal expenditure was also given. Kaldor continued to view the organisation of war finances as highly satisfactory and expressed optimism for the future. An increasing proportion of government expenditure continued to be financed by revenue, and an increasing proportion of revenue was being financed by taxation. The attempt was again made to estimate the increase in real national income to gauge the real sources of war finance. By 1942, the real increase in government expenditure since 1938 was estimated to have been £2655 million of which £1140 million came from increased output; £665 million from reduced consumption; £285 million from an increase in the excess of imports over exports, and £565 million from disinvestment. Foreign disinvestment to finance balance of payments deficits since the beginning of the war was estimated at £2350 million compared with a market value of overseas assets in 1939 of £5000 million. The income loss from abroad was not reckoned to be dramatic, falling from £200 million in 1938 to £140 million in 1942. Viewing the overall economic situation, Kaldor and Barna remarked: 'the performance greatly exceeded the promise: there are few economists (if any) who would have dared to predict in 1939 that the war time increase in the national income could be so large, or that the war time capital consumption or the degree of price inflation could be kept so small. The latent reserves of our peacetime economic system have proved to be greater than even the most optimistically (or pessimistically) minded observer could have expected.' Rationing was one factor that helped to control the cost of living, and in one of his theoretical papers during the war, Kaldor (1941a) devised an ingenious method for estimating the 'true' cost of living increase in the presence of rationing. As far as output was concerned, there was a 30 per cent increase between 1938 and 1942 and Kaldor was optimistic about living standards on the return to peace – an optimism that was fully vindicated. With wartime hours reduced to their 1938 level and with 50 per cent of the increase in wartime employment remaining in industry, it was estimated that output would be 18 per cent higher after the war than before. The financial press seemed surprised by Kaldor's optimism, but the post-war record was indeed remarkable, particularly in comparison with other countries.

THE BEVERIDGE REPORT ON SOCIAL INSURANCE, 1942

Kaldor's understanding of national income accounting and his attempts at forecasting stood him in good stead in the arguments that arose over the financial burden of the Beveridge Report on Social Insurance and Allied Services published on 1 December 1942.[3] This 'first' Beveridge Report was an official report to government, unlike its sequel *Full Employment in a Free Society* published in 1944 which was written in a private capacity, although Beveridge had initially expected it also to bear the government's own imprimatur. The theme of the first Report was Freedom from Want; the theme of the second was Freedom from Idleness. The maintenance of employment was one of the underlying assumptions of the plan for social security proposed in the first Report but there were no detailed policy recommendations. Two other major assumptions of the Social Security Report were a comprehensive health and rehabilitation service and a system of child allowances.

The terms of reference of the first Beveridge Report were 'to undertake, with special reference to the interrelation of the schemes, a survey of the existing national schemes of social insurance and allied services, including workmen's compensation, and to make recommendations'. The fundamental objective of the Beveridge Plan (as it appeared) was to remove some of the worst evils of poverty and insecurity through an improvement in the system of social security to provide adequate old age pensions, sickness and unemployment benefits. Existing schemes had grown up piecemeal starting (apart from the Poor Law) with the Workmen's Compensation Act in 1897. Compulsory health insurance began in 1912. Unemployment insurance was made general in 1920. The first Pensions Act was passed in 1908 which gave non-contributory pensions subject to a means test at the age of 70. Contributory pensions for the aged, widows and orphans started in 1925. In addition, there was a huge growth of voluntary provision. The result was a vast complexity of provision against want, but little coordination.

Beveridge laid down three fundamental principles underlying his recommendations. First, that any proposals for the future should not be restricted by consideration of sectional interests. Second, that the organisation of social insurance should be treated as only one part of a comprehensive policy of social progress, as an attack on want: 'Want is only one of five giants on the road of reconstruction ... the others are Disease, Ignorance, Squalor and

Idleness.' Thirdly, social security must be achieved by cooperation between the state and the individual, the state providing the minimum without stifling incentive, opportunity and responsibility. The Plan of compulsory social insurance was to improve existing schemes in three directions: by extension of scope to cover persons excluded; by extension of purpose to cover risks excluded, and by raising the rates of benefit and relating income compensation to family size. Under the proposed scheme, everyone would be covered for all needs by a single weekly contribution on one insurance document. All the principal cash benefits for unemployment and disability; medical treatment, and retirement would continue as long as the need lasted, without a means test, and would be paid from a Social Insurance Fund built up by contributions from the insured persons, from their employers and from the state. The underlying principle was that benefit should be in return for contributions and not be free allowances from the state, and that whatever money was required for the provision of insurance benefits should come from the Fund to which the recipients had contributed (and to which they might be required to make larger contributions if the Fund proved inadequate). Also, premiums should not be related to individual risks, but be based on the principle of pooling risks. To oversee the Plan there would be a new Ministry of Social Security. In the first year of operation (assumed to be from 1 July 1944) the total additional cost of implementing the Plan was estimated at £256 million to be met by additional employees' contributions of £125 million, employers' contributions of £54 million and an Exchequer contribution of £86 million. For the employee the proposal was for a weekly increase in the insurance stamp of 2s 5d to 4s 3d, compared with existing schemes (approximately 12 and 21 new pence respectively), and an employer contribution of 3s 3d (approximately 16 new pence). The proposed minimum weekly income was £2.

The immediate political response to the Plan was that it could not be afforded; that it would impose a burden on the community. There was undoubtedly political prevarication over the Plan; so much so that Beveridge himself found it necessary to tour the country to marshall support. Some saw the Plan as the thin end of the wedge of socialism. Beveridge insisted in one of his speeches: 'It is wanted under any economic system; it is a plan; not a pipedream; it is figures, not fantasy; insurance, not charity.' The Parliamentary Secretary to the Ministry of Home Security, Mr Osbert Peake, argued that want could never be removed by social security because the poor would squander their weekly payments: 'Want can be abolished only by a system of regimentation such as that in the armed forces or in internment camps.' On the other hand, the scheme had a certain popular appeal. There were adverts on the buses which read 'Beveridges not Beverages!'

Kaldor played no part in formulating the Plan but was prominent in attacking the view that implementation of the Plan would impose any substantial burden on the community. In a contribution to a pamphlet *Planning for Abundance*, written for the National Peace Council in 1943, he stressed that expenditure under the Plan would involve merely transfer payments and therefore impose no real resource burden. As far as the individual was concerned, a large part of the income redistribution involved would be an intertemporal one and such a transfer could only be a burden if the individual was compulsorily made to save *more* for old age, unemployment and sickness than he would have done voluntarily. Beveridge himself reported that on average each man already spent 3s 1d (approximately 15½ new pence) per week voluntarily on such things as life and financial insurance, which would now be covered by his scheme, so the net additional cost would be negligible if a large proportion of the 3s 1d would be saved.

The major fuss was about the Exchequer contribution of £86 million in the first year, and about the increased employers' contribution which, it was argued, would increase manufacturers' costs so much as to price them out of export markets. One Member of Parliament claimed that income tax would have to be raised to 15 shillings in the pound to meet the Exchequer cost! Kaldor's major contribution to the discussion of the Beveridge Plan was his detailed assessment of the financial burden in the *Economic Journal* (1943a), written at the request of Austin Robinson, the Assistant Editor of the *Journal*, which he had already summarised in two popular articles in the *Manchester Guardian* (10 and 11) February) under the title of 'Beveridge Plan's Real Cost'. He attempted to show that, contrary to the widely held view, the burden on various groups in the community would be trivial and would not affect the post-war levels of taxation or disposable real income to any great extent. The estimate of 6d on income tax and 1d on a pint of beer was the calculation the press latched on to, which no one subsequently seriously disputed. Kaldor must take credit, therefore, for putting the Plan into financial perspective. To estimate the financial burden of the Plan along with other post-war commitments, it was first necessary to estimate post-war national income and expenditure, post-war government expenditure, and the necessary levels of taxation.

The estimate of post-war national income and expenditure was a conservative one based on the following assumptions: the same weekly hours as in 1938; unemployment of 1.5 million (or 10 per cent); the same terms of trade as in 1938; labour productivity 12.5 per cent higher than in 1938, and a net increase in the working population of 0.5 million. With a few other minor adjustments, national income was predicted to be £600 million (or 13.1 per cent) higher in real terms compared with 1938, or 38 per cent higher in money terms assuming 25 per cent price inflation. With transfer payments added to national income, the level of taxable income was obtained. Kaldor then estimated that as far as tax revenue was concerned, even if the excess profits tax and National Defence Contribution[4] were abolished, and pre-war levels of income tax allowances were restored, tax revenue would be £2,400 million at current rates of tax or £680 million in excess of estimated expenditure (including the full initial cost of the Beveridge Plan). This meant that it would be possible to cut all taxes by about 30 per cent; or to reduce the standard rate of income tax of 10 shillings to, say, 6s 6d in the pound. In fact, the Plan itself would add only 5 per cent to total government expenditure so that without the scheme, if all the saving came from income tax, income tax could be 10d lower at, say, 5s 8d compared to 6s 6d – or, in Kaldor's words, 'to put it another way, the cost of Beveridge is 10d on income tax or 6d on income tax and a penny a pint on beer'. He concluded: 'the argument that the Beveridge Plan would make the financial burden on the taxpayer unbearably heavy is just nonsense – for neither is the aggregate tax burden excessively large, nor does the Beveridge scheme make any appreciable difference to the size of the burden'. The estimated cost would amount to less than 1.2 per cent of average incomes of all classes of the community and just under 1.6 per cent of the average disposable income – 'a very moderate sacrifice indeed for the abolition of want'. It is true that the Plan provided for a gradual increase in expenditure over the following twenty years owing to the gradual increase in old age pensions and the number of people of pensionable age.[5] While expenditure would be 10 per cent more, however, tax revenue would be at least 25–30 per cent more. In addition, if there were to be full employment after the war (defined as 0.5 million unemployed) Kaldor estimated an annual saving on the proposed social security budget of £101 million – more than the Exchequer contribution of £86 million under the Beveridge Plan – and £100 million additional tax revenue.

Kaldor then turned to the question of the level of consumption and private investment consistent with the estimated levels of national income and government expenditure. Having estimated government expenditure on real goods and services to be about

£1150 million at factor cost, and assuming private consumption to be restored to its pre-war level in real terms, and that exports pay for imports, resources available for home capital investment were estimated at £816 million at 1938 prices or double the level of investment in 1938. This should be sufficient, he argued, to cover all the needs of post-war reconstruction – housing, shipbuilding and the country's contribution to reconstruction in Europe, as well as the necessary capital investment in industry, transport and agriculture.

Overall, therefore, he reached the optimistic conclusion that

we could 'afford' to keep about one million in the army, another 1.5 million in unemployment, restore aggregate real consumption to its pre-war level, spend on capital improvements about double the pre-war amounts (in real terms), export a sufficient amount to pay for our imports, adopt the Beveridge scheme in full all at the same time, and with income tax only 6/6d in the £.

Kaldor seemed surprised by his own optimistic forecasts, and felt it necessary to go back over the important assumptions in the analysis, the three main ones being the 12.5 per cent rise in labour productivity; defence expenditure of £500 million, and an unchanged terms of trade. If anything, he regarded the first assumption as an underestimate, but admitted the second assumption to be a shot in the dark which could easily turn out to be £1000 million. The weakest assumption, he thought, might be that the terms of trade remain unchanged. There was no suggestion at the time that import prices would rise, but export prices might have to fall to increase export volume sufficient to meet import requirements. An extra 50 per cent volume of exports might require a 25 per cent deterioration in the terms of trade, or a loss of £300 million real income. Alternatively, a 25 per cent cut in imports by import substitution would also reduce national income by £300 million assuming the excess cost of import substitution to be double that of domestic production. Thus, at the very worst, the available resources might be reduced by £300 million through a deterioration in the terms of trade and £500 million more on extra defence spending, or £800 million in all. On the other side of the coin, if unemployment was 0.5 million rather than 1.5 million this would add £350 million to the national income, and if consumption was only 90 per cent of its pre-war level this would release £400 million.

The discussion of exports and the terms of trade raised the question of the burden of the employers' contribution and the criticism of the Beveridge Plan that it would endanger the country's export performance. From the employers' point of view, the employers' contribution would be a tax on wages, and prices would rise by the proportion of total prime costs in output. Thus employees would ultimately bear the burden in the form of higher prices, an amount equal to 1.5 per cent of wages. Kaldor conceded that there might be some effect on export prices, but when the price levels of the various countries settled down, the foreign exchange value of the pound would have to be adjusted in any case. The employers' contribution however was the one aspect of the Beveridge Plan that Kaldor opposed on the grounds that if it was intended to be a charge on employers, it should have been imposed on profits, not on wages (by raising prices) and employment.

Taking additional taxes and contributions together, therefore, Kaldor's overall estimate of the cost of the Beveridge Plan amounted to 3 per cent of the incomes of wage-earners (and 1.5–2.0 per cent of the incomes of non-wage-earners). Kaldor's challenge to the opponents of the Plan was to show that this was not an excessive price to pay for the alleviation of the misery and poverty of the marginal 10 per cent of the population and of the undernourishment of a much higher proportion of children.

The question of the effect of the Beveridge Plan on the cost of exports continued to be raised in the press, however, and Kaldor continued to be prominent in the rebuttal of the argument that the cost would be substantial and that measures, other than exchange rate depreciation, would be necessary. He was prompted to write a major article for *The Banker* (1943b) in response to an article and subsequent correspondence in *The Times* which suggested that to aid the export effort manufacturers should sell abroad, if not at the social cost of production, at least at the marginal cost of production, rather than at average cost. Now it is perfectly true that if there are unemployed resources, the marginal social cost of production is zero or even negative when multiplier effects on output are taken into account. Kaldor accepted the argument but claimed that the general adoption of a discriminatory export pricing policy would be nothing short of disastrous. A private manufacturer would not sell below his own marginal cost since he is not able to reap the social gain. To sell exports at social cost would require that the government give subsidies to exporters. It would not, however, be difficult for manufacturers to price exports at marginal cost, by simply distributing overheads over domestic sales. The reason manufacturers do not do this are the difficulties involved in a policy of price discrimination and the fear of retaliation.

But even if the policy was feasible, would it be desirable? If the object of stimulating exports is to help to create more employment, export dumping, he argued, is an obnoxious way to do it because it creates unemployment abroad and, moreover, home prices would be higher than they need be. When there is generalised unemployment, there are easier, less costly and more internationally acceptable ways of achieving full employment and creating more employment in *all* industries. If the objective of stimulating exports is to pay for imports, is dumping in this case the appropriate policy? Selling exports at marginal prime costs and charging overheads to home consumers worsens the terms of trade. As such it is similar to devaluation. But compared with devaluation and other expenditure switching policies it suffers drawbacks. First, it does not discourage imports and therefore the change in the terms of trade needs to be greater with export subsidies than with a devaluation. Secondly, it is worse than a protective tariff which improves the terms of trade. Thirdly, there is the much greater danger of retaliation. There could be a massive slump in the price of manufactured goods in world markets, turning the terms of trade sharply against manufacturers without a rectification of the balance of payments. As a policy to boost post-war exports, therefore, Kaldor argued strongly against export subsidies. The *Manchester Guardian* praised the argument, saying, 'Mr. Kaldor has rendered a useful service by letting some common sense into confused councils.'

Throughout 1943 Kaldor continued to press for the implementation of the Beveridge Plan. He wrote several letters to the press, and early in October 1943 he delivered one of the talks in a BBC series 'The World We Want', edited by Joan Robinson, on the theme of 'The Cost of Social Security' (*The Listener*, 4 November). Keynes also participated in the series with a talk on 'Will the War Make Us Poorer?'.

THE BEVERIDGE REPORT ON FULL EMPLOYMENT 1944[6]

Beveridge regarded his 1944 *Report on Full Employment* as a sequel to his 1942 Report on Social Insurance but it was written under different circumstances. While the latter was written at the request of the government, there was no such request for the *Report on Full Employment*. Beveridge was disappointed by this and felt that the quality and scope of the Report was adversely affected as a result. Nevertheless, although written in a private capacity, the Report benefited from a considerable amount of expert help. Beveridge took advantage of policy seminars organised by G.D.H.

Cole at Nuffield College, Oxford, and received statistical help from the Oxford Institute of Statistics.

The Report took as its theme: Freedom from Idleness. One of the assumptions of the Social Insurance Report was that full employment would be maintained, not simply to make the Plan workable but also for its own sake. Full employment was defined by Beveridge as the minimum level of frictional unemployment:

Full employment means that unemployment is reduced to short intervals of standing by, with the certainty that very soon one will be wanted in one's old job again or will be wanted in a new job that is within one's powers.

Full employment also implies, therefore, 'more vacant jobs than unemployed men, not slightly fewer jobs.' Full employment also meant for Beveridge that the jobs should be 'at fair wages, of such a kind, and so located that the unemployed men can reasonably be expected to take them'. Great emphasis was placed on minimising the duration of unemployment: 'Full employment, in any real sense, means that unemployment in the individual case need not last for a length of time exceeding that which can be covered by unemployment insurance without risk of demoralisation. Those who lose jobs must be able to find new jobs at fair wages within their capacity, without delay.' The target for unemployment was a maximum of 3 per cent. The full employment policy had three main components: the maintenance of total expenditure; the control of the location of industry, and securing the organised mobility of labour – with by far the greatest emphasis on the maintenance of total expenditure.

Kaldor's contribution to the Report (1944a), contained in Appendix C, was the examination of the revenue and expenditure implications for the public authorities assuming that the government pursued a fiscal policy to maintain full employment. The statistical foundations of the estimates were based on work by Tibor Barna.

First, the alternative methods of securing full employment by fiscal policy were discussed, and then quantitative estimates were made of the implications of full employment policies in 1938, establishing the methodology for the later quantitative estimates for 1948 of the implications of implementing the Report. Four main fiscal methods of securing full employment were identified: (a) increased public expenditure covered by loans; (b) increased public expenditure covered by taxation; (c) increased private spending through tax reductions; and (d) increased private spending either by changing the incidence of taxation or by a system of taxes and subsidies. Methods (a) and (c) would involve deficit spending. Method (b) would be expansionary according to the 'balanced' budget multiplier, but for the same degree of expansion the change in expenditure and taxation would have to be greater for (b) than for (a) and (c). Likewise with method (d). Kaldor argued that in the pre-war conditions of 1938, (b) and (d) would have been impracticable. On the other hand, in post-war conditions, budget deficits would probably not be necessary to secure full employment, although in the longer term the conditions of the 1930s might re-emerge. In both predictions he was right.

To make quantitative fiscal estimates of the implications of full employment policies in 1938 required estimates of (1) how the value of the national output would have changed as a result of the change in employment and the reduction in unemployment; (2) how various types of income would have changed as a result of changes in the value of output; (3) how various elements of national expenditure – consumption, taxation, imports, private saving and investment and so on – would have changed with changes in national output and private incomes. Likewise, the same calculations had to be made for the fiscal predictions of full employment after the war.

For the post-Beveridge calculations, it was assumed that the war would end sometime in the middle of 1945 and that the 'transition to peace' would take some 2½ years. Thus the year 1948 was used as the basis for the full employment calculation of national income, government expenditure and tax revenue. The assumptions underlying the calculation of national income in 1948 were as follows: unemployment of 3 per cent; the same number of man-hours as in 1938; a 13 per cent increase in labour productivity compared to 1938; an unchanged terms of trade; income from foreign investment down to 40 per cent of its 1938 level, and prices 33.3 per cent higher than in 1938 (for income calculations in money terms). On these assumptions, net national income in 1948 was estimated at £7450 million at 1948 prices or £5600 million at 1938 prices – a real increase of nearly 20 per cent compared to 1938 when the national income was estimated at £4675 million. The next step was to estimate factor income shares in 1948 and then the levels of tax revenue and public expenditure implied. Making full allowance for the additional government commitments in the field of social security, and for higher expenditure due to higher prices, it was estimated that the government would need tax revenue of £1655 million to balance the budget of the public authorities as a whole. Applying 1938 tax rates to the 1948 full employment level of income gave an estimated tax revenue of

£1590 million, or a projected tax shortfall of £65 million. Such a deficit would require a 6 per cent rise in tax rates, or a standard rate of income tax of 5s 10d in the pound compared to 5s 6d in 1938 (and 10s during the war).

The question was then posed, what rate of investment would assure full employment in 1948? On the assumptions that government taxation was just sufficient to cover ordinary expenditure; that exports pay for imports, and that the proportion of income consumed in 1948 was the same as in 1938, Kaldor assumed the rate of net investment consistent with full employment to be £765 million or £575 million at 1938 prices. There was no suggestion that he regarded this figure as desirable. Indeed, he recognised that planned investment might be higher than this, and post-war reconstruction might require it. If so, the government would have to restrict real consumption, by some means or other, below the level it would reach with a balanced budget, and thereby release the resources for higher investment. He suggested, in fact, the creation of a surplus on the ordinary budget in the form of a sinking fund to be covered out of taxation. For illustration, net investment of £1000 at 1938 prices would require a sinking fund of £800 million and income tax at 8s 8d in the pound instead of the previously estimated 5s 10d.

Finally Kaldor recognised that continuous full employment in a growing economy would require an ever-increasing level of net investment outlay, and he discussed the long-run consequences of continuous public borrowing. He was concerned to show that the standard objection to deficit expenditure of a growing national debt carried little weight. It is not the absolute size of debt that matters, but the ratio of interest payments to national income which may affect incentives. Further borrowing can actually reduce this ratio if loan expenditure augments the yield of taxation by more than it increases the interest charge.

Kaldor's contribution to *Full Employment in a Free Society* received high praise from all quarters, including academic colleagues and the financial press. From across the Atlantic, Alvin Hansen, the American Keynesian, wrote: 'I think you did a wonderful job on Appendix C', and Colin Clark, an early pioneer in the field of national income accounting, wrote from Brisbane: 'I should like to congratulate you on a most effective piece of work'. John Hicks reviewed the book for the *Manchester Guardian* (17 November 1944) and described Kaldor's Appendix as one of the most important and fascinating chapters of the book. Mr David Worswick, writing in the paper *Socialist Commentary*, described Kaldor's contribution as 'a brilliant essay in applied economics'. The most serious questioning of the arithmetic came from *The Economist*.[7] First, it questioned whether national income would be 20 per cent higher in real terms in 1948 than in 1938. Suppose hours of work fell, or productivity increased by less than 13 per cent, or unemployment was higher than 3 per cent. Secondly, suppose government expenditure on real goods and services turned out to be higher than assumed and the share of consumption higher. Investment would then be lower in real terms in 1948 than in 1938 – a totally unacceptable state of affairs given Britain's industrial performance in the inter-war years and the needs of post-war reconstruction. *The Economist* not only criticised Kaldor for leaving investment as the 'residuary legatee' in his calculations, but argued that even if his assumptions proved to be correct, the provision for capital was far too small. *The Economist* suggested that annual investment of £1200 million may be needed post-war, and argued the case for a 'Plan for Capital'. It saw little alternative to keeping consumption down by taxation, casting doubt, therefore, on Kaldor's estimate of a tax rate of 5s 10d. Other papers also commented on Kaldor's optimism over the required levels of taxation necessary for post-war reconstruction.

Kaldor replied (3 March 1944) and agreed that capital formation must not be allowed to be the 'residuary legatee' from the national dividend, but defended himself on the grounds that his figures for investment were not put forward as an estimate of what was desirable, 'but were introduced for the very purpose of demonstrating how inadequate capital investment would be *if* it were treated merely as a "residuary item" '. He pointed out that two other alternative higher investment plans had been made both involving some control over consumption, though both consistent with a higher level of actual consumption than in 1938. He did not believe, however, that his estimate of a 20 per cent real increase in national income was too high; on the contrary he thought it might prove to be too low. In this he proved to be wrong. Even on *The Economist's* assumption of a 10 per cent increase, however, which proved to be nearer the mark, Kaldor claimed it would still be possible to *double* the rate of net investment in fixed capital without restricting real consumption below its pre-war level – while increasing private consumption by 25 per cent over its current level. 'The conclusion to be drawn from such estimates', he remarked, 'is not that we "can't afford" major schemes of national improvement without a drastic curtailment of consumption, but that we cannot afford to do without planning. Provided that the idea of budgeting the use of national resources in accordance with a scheme of priorities is carried over into peace-time, and the necessary controls are retained, there is little danger of the post-war reconstruction plans having to be curtailed for lack of means.'

Kaldor himself made two retrospective appraisals of his work for Beveridge: one in two unsigned articles in *The Times* in 1959,[8] the other in the Introduction to his Collected Essays (Vol. 1). Compared with the estimated tax rate of 5s 10d, the standard rate was still 9s in the pound in 1949 and 8s 6d in 1959. What went wrong? Kaldor admitted that his calculations assumed too rapid a rate of recovery after the war, and made no allowance for two factors hardly then predictable – first, the international tension precipitated by the Korean War and the nuclear arms race; and second, the inflation of public spending for purposes neither social or military. The productivity trend did not re-establish itself until 1951 and the pre-war savings ratios were not re-established until 1955/56. Also the terms of trade were worse in 1948 than in 1938. These 'errors' largely explain the discrepancy between the 20 per cent rise in real national income that was forecast and what actually occurred, and account for the erroneous conclusions concerning taxation. Despite the errors, the value of the exercise lay more in the method used than in the precise forecasts. It was the first attempt to make comprehensive estimates of income, taxation and other variables from a large number of separate forecasts and assumptions within the framework of a consistent 'econometric' model.[9]

ASPECTS OF POST-WAR RECONSTRUCTION

Apart from his work for Beveridge, Kaldor was engaged in a whole miscellany of activities and writing relating not only to the war effort but also to the conditions for a smooth transition to normality when peace was restored.

At the international level he gave a qualified welcome to the plan for a new international monetary system endorsed at Bretton Woods. In two articles in the *Manchester Guardian* (21 and 22 June 1944) entitled 'The New Monetary Plan' he praised the plan for making provision for the orderly adjustment of exchange rates through international agreement and for avoiding the spread of contractionary tendencies throughout the economic system. On the other hand, he believed it to be a weakness that currency adjustment was left to individual countries to decide and that there was no provision for blocs of countries to promote trade amongst themselves if some countries fail to maintain full employment or fail to revalue their currencies in the event of a surplus on the balance of payments. The scarce currency clause was no substitute for currency appreciation. He would have preferred the International Monetary Fund to have been a superstructure binding together a number of regional currency groupings each with its own subsidiary monetary fund. Thomas Balogh, his Hungarian compatriot, was highly sceptical of the implicit assumption in the new plan that exchange rate changes alone could reconcile full employment at home with fluctuations abroad. He wanted the option of managed trade left open and was strongly opposed to the principle of non-discriminatory trade insisted on by the Americans. Acceptance of this principle was one of the conditions of the American loan agreement of 1945 negotiated by Keynes on behalf of the British government. Kaldor also wrote two articles for the *Manchester Guardian* (11 and 12 December 1945) on the loan agreement entitled 'The Washington Settlement', generally approving the terms, although expressing concern that the move towards multilateralism and tariff reductions was bound to make the stability of one nation more dependent on the stability of others. There should thus be greater provision for the planned stabilisation of trade if necessary, particularly if some countries fail to maintain full employment and the volume of trade shrinks below potential. Keynes was very sensitive to this criticism and in a letter to Lord Halifax at the beginning of 1946 made some unseemly anti-Jewish remarks directed primarily, it must be assumed, at the outright hostility of Balogh to the conditions of the loan agreement. Keynes writes:

A section of the Socialists thought they had detected too definite a smell of *laissez-faire*, at any rate of anti-planning, in the American conception of international affairs. This is only half true; but the doctrine of non-discrimination does commit us to abjure Schachtian methods which their Jewish economic advisers (who like so many Jews are either Nazi or Communist at heart and have no notion how the British Commonwealth was founded or is sustained) were hankering after.[10]

The cost of the war to Britain was heavy. In the first of his articles on 'The Washington Settlement', Kaldor estimated the 'external' cost of the war effort to be of the order of £10,700 million financed by the sale of foreign investments (£1100 million); the depletion of gold and dollar reserves (£200 million); the accumulation of new sterling debt (£3300 million); lend-lease (£500 million), and the new American loan (£1100 million). He criticised the sudden cancellation of lend-lease just because hostilities had ceased, but welcomed the loan itself. The purely financial burden would be an annual payment (in dollars) equivalent to £33 million over 50 years. Existing debt interest obligations amounted to another £70 million a year. Kaldor was optimistic that in conditions of expanding trade and domestic prosperity such a burden could easily be borne without undue pressure on living standards, but not, of course, if the world was to slump as after the First World War.

In retrospect there was a consensus that after the First World War, war-time controls in Britain were abolished far too quickly. Reorganisation and readjustment was left to private enterprise. The result was a short-lived boom in 1920 and then a collapse of the heavy industries. Kaldor campaigned for the retention of controls to prevent this happening again and to ease the transition from war to peace in all the important areas of national economic life. In a pamphlet with M.F.W. Joseph (later Mrs Hemming) published in 1942[11] he directed attention to what he regarded as the three major objectives of economic reconstruction: full employment, the elimination of poverty and the elimination of inefficiency. As far as poverty was concerned, the Beveridge ideas on social security were naturally very much in the background. To eliminate inefficiency Kaldor proposed that the government should fix maximum prices for commodities sufficiently low that only the most efficient firms could survive. At the same time this would help to avoid monopolistic exploitation of the consumer. The continuation of utility production was strongly urged (see later). For the return to full employment, he believed controls would be needed on consumption, production and international trade. Consumer rationing and price control should continue. Raw materials should be allocated according to the urgency of needs, and production in civilian industries should be expanded in accordance with the availability of labour and raw materials. Control of capital movements abroad should continue, and import controls should be imposed if necessary in order to secure the most essential imports. On the problem of wage inflation, there was a prophetic statement:

There is a great danger... that with the present system of sectional wage bargaining, in a state of full employment, a tug-of-war will ensue between the workers of different industries for larger slices of the national cake, in the course of which wages and prices will continually rise. This senseless chase between wages and prices leaves no one ultimately better-off, but must, sooner or later, shake the confidence in the currency and endanger the stability of the whole system.

A national system of wage determination was recommended.

At this time Kaldor also turned to the question of budgeting for full employment. He contributed two (anonymous) articles to *The Times* in a series of ten articles on the theme of full employment.[12]

In these he argued the case on Keynesian lines for using the budget not simply as a balance-sheet, or as a barometer of the state of the nation, but as an instrument for full employment without inflation, and suggested at the same time that there should be two separate budgets: a current budget including all running expenditures covered out of ordinary revenue, and a capital budget to be covered by loan expenditure. This is what Keynes also wanted. The articles greatly impressed Keynes who, without knowing their authorship, wrote a private letter to the Editor of *The Times* expressing 'great satisfaction' with their content.

This deep concern with the state of employment after the war was all a prelude to Beveridge's Report on Full Employment, as was the series of private conferences held at Nuffield College organised by G.D.H. Cole, in which Kaldor participated along with industrialists, politicians, trade unionists and other academics including Evan Durbin, Hugh Meredith, Joan Robinson and Thomas Balogh. These deliberations led to a statement on 'Employment Policy and Organisation after the War',[13] outlining a programme similar to the Kaldor–Joseph plan of 1942, but with additional suggestions. One was the establishment of a National Development Board and the appointment of a Minister of National Development. Another, and more radical, proposal was that certain key industries should be taken into public ownership; a proposal that Kaldor endorsed.

In the quest for efficiency, the idea of utility production was a major subject of debate. Kaldor was very keen that utility production should be continued after the war in an effort both to save resources and to stimulate efficiency in order to encourage exports and to bring a wide range of consumer goods within the purse of the ordinary working man. In the early months of 1945 there was a lengthy correspondence in *The Times* over the matter and also a radio debate in which Kaldor participated. Kaldor's exchanges with Sir Miles Thomas of the Nuffield Organisation on the British car industry are particularly revealing in the light of the subsequent fortunes of the industry.

Kaldor's scheme for utility production in peacetime was for the bulk purchase of a wide range of consumer goods by a bulk wholesaling organisation, with product specification laid down by the government and a guarantee of quality. This would lower the price to the consumer by eliminating the unnecessary multiplication of brands; by eliminating the unnecessary features on standard models; by enabling full advantage to be taken of the economies of large-scale production; by relieving manufacturers of selling costs, and by reducing the wholesale and retail margins of distribution. He believed that the cumulative effect of these economies would be considerable. Kaldor claimed, in fact, that for a wide range of durable consumer goods, like furniture, heating and cooking appliances, vacuum cleaners, radio sets, refrigerators and even motor cars, pre-war prices were in many cases two or three times higher than they need have been if they had been marketed efficiently and full advantage had been taken of the potentialities of mass production. Critics maintained that the stimulus to bulk manufacture already existed through the buying power of modern large-scale retail organisations. Kaldor maintained that this was not so in the case of more expensive durable goods where the retail price was, in some cases, ten times the manufacturer's production costs and where the cost of production was raised by splitting up production among a great variety of models and by the addition of unnecessary frills for the purpose of differentiation. Other critics maintained that utility production would restrict consumer choice, and that consumer welfare would be reduced by the drabness and austerity of utility production. In his correspondence with Sir Miles Thomas, Kaldor emphasised that the nature and purposes of utility production should not be confused with the war time austerity regulations that served quite different ends. The poor quality of utility goods was not the result of the utility scheme as such but of the war time conditions. Restrictions on the make-up of goods were imposed by the Board of Trade on the utility and non-utility goods alike, partly to secure maximum war-time economy of materials, and partly to make goods deliberately unattractive to reduce consumption. This would not be the purpose of utility production in peacetime. On the contrary, it would be to enlarge consumer choice, and to bring within the range of the ordinary household mass-produced goods that otherwise would be beyond their financial reach. Kaldor used the example of the car industry and pointed to the American car industry where, as a result of mass production, output per man was three to four times higher than in Britain in the inter-war period. In America in 1939 the ten leading car manufacturers, accounting for 88 per cent of sales, produced altogether only fifteen engine types. In Britain, the eight leading makers, also accounting for 88 per cent of sales, produced 39 engine types.In America, three leading models alone accounted for 54 per cent of home sales, compared to 27 per cent in Britain.

Another objection raised against utility production was the issue of who should decide what the public wants. Kaldor pointed out that the consumer is not king in any case. The manufacturer initiates, not the public, as Galbraith was to argue more forcefully in his book the *New Industrial State* (1967). The utility scheme would not limit the freedom of manufacturers; it would simply ensure that the public has the choice of obtaining mass-produced utility models made out on the specification of the government.

Kaldor, in his correspondence with Sir Miles Thomas, also revealed his concern over exports in the inter-war period. He believed that the declining trend of British exports in the inter-war period could only be partially attributed to the shrinkage of world trade in the old staple industries like coal and cotton. It was equally due to the failure to capture an adequate share of world exports in the newer industries where trade was expanding rapidly. In the newer industries, including motor cars, not only was the comparative efficiency of Britain already inferior to that of her main competitors, but the annual rate of increase in productivity was lower so that comparative efficiency was deteriorating. Without a radical change in the performance of these industries, Britain's long-run export problem would not be solved, and he warned that in the more distant future, Britain would face the competition of new industrial powers. Standardised mass production achieved by bulk orders from government specifications would afford one means of assisting in the task of raising the productivity of Britain's industries and restoring Britain's competitive power.

POST-WAR ACTIVITIES AT HOME AND ABROAD

When the war ended in 1945, the LSE returned to London, but Kaldor stayed in Cambridge and commuted to give his lectures and classes. Robbins gave him an arduous new course of 40 lectures on the General Principles of Economic Analysis for second year 'final' economists and postgraduates. The course covered the general principles of the theory of value and distribution, money, employment and fluctuations using as texts Keynes's *General Theory*, Ricardo's *Principles*, Marshall's *Principles*, Wicksell's *Lectures on Political Economy*, Boulding's new book *Economic Analysis*, and Stigler's *Theory of Price*. This was a formidable undertaking, although synthesising much of the material in his earlier shorter courses. The teaching did not bother him but he was becoming increasingly unhappy and disenchanted with the School. There were constant petty rows with Robbins, with whom he disagreed philosophically, and he disliked the general right-wing atmosphere of the institution. He was more than receptive to invitations to go elsewhere,[14] notwithstanding his promotion to a Readership. The promotion, in fact, was not instigated by Robbins but by Harold Laski, much to Robbins' annoyance who on this occasion was in a powerless minority on the Appointments Committee.

There was no time for academic despondency, however. With his war-time reputation for incisive applied economic analysis, he was inundated with requests from newspapers and various organisations both at home and abroad to write commentaries, and to undertake research, on a whole variety of post-war economic problems. At home, for a short time in 1946 he was engaged by the Air Ministry and Ministry of Supply as an economic adviser (with the equivalent rank of Brigadier-General) to assist the British Bombing Survey Unit with the construction and comparison of the output series of the British and German armaments industries. He was a regular contributor to the *Manchester Guardian*, writing articles on aspects of post-war economic recovery. In 1946 he was paid by the paper to visit Hungary to write a series of articles on the economic and political situation there (including the surrounding Danubian states), with particular reference to the Hungarian hyper-inflation. This he did in a five-part series under the headings 'Hungary's Place in Europe'[15] and 'A Study of Inflation'.[16] The Treasury's Economic Survey for 1947 was also sent to him for detailed review.[17]

These annual Treasury surveys were to become important statements of the economic health of the nation. It was apparent that three major economic problems were emerging: a shortage of manpower, a shortage of foreign exchange, and insufficiencies in specific industries, particularly a shortage of fuels and building materials. Kaldor urged more direction of labour as in war-time, plus production targets for exports. He was attracted by Hawtrey's plan[18] for a state monopoly of wholesale trading whereby the wholesale dealers in the various trades would be made agents of the state, which would confer on the state the power of regulating the productive activity of every industry and the prices to be paid to producers. This would solve the problem of ensuring the maintenance of sufficient stocks and also of preventing an undue absorption of labour in the consumer goods industries and in distribution. The plea for more and better planning was repeated in a series of letters to *The Times* in early 1947[19] in which he warned, 'if we are to avoid unexpected breakdowns of the kind experienced at present [viz. the fuel crisis] it would seem essential that a comprehensive plan... showing the production targets of all major industries... their manpower, fuel and raw material requirements – should be worked out and published'. He severely criticised the Labour government for attempting to run a planned economy without a plan. Needless to say, his plea met with strong opposition from the economists of *laissez-faire* persuasion, among them John Jewkes, Eli Devons and Stanley Dennison, who responded with equally passionate letters expressing the virtues of the price system and the market mechanism. Dennison went so far as to suggest that mistaken central decisions during the war had led to wastes which made the inefficiencies of the market system and uncoordinated planning pale into insignificance. The efficiency of planning and the post-war reconstruction effort improved considerably after 1947 when Stafford Cripps became Chancellor of the Exchequer, but Kaldor still felt that not enough attention was being paid to the foreign balance, even after devaluation in 1949. In a BBC broadcast following the 1950 budget (*The Listener*, 11 May), he criticised the budget for not being austere enough to meet the external challenge to make Britain's foreign position secure and to become independent of American aid.

Abroad, Kaldor undertook three important missions: to act as Chief of the Planning Staff of the United States Strategic Bombing Survey in Germany (1945); to serve as an adviser to the Hungarian government (1946); and to assist Jean Monnet at the French Commissariat du Plan in preparing a plan for the financial stabilisation of France (1947).

The purpose of the US Strategic Bombing Survey was to investigate the military and economic effect on Germany of the strategic bombing by the Allied forces. Owing to a shortage of American economists, Tibor Scitovsky originally put forward Kaldor's name as someone who might head the investigation, but it was then decided that an American should take overall responsibility and J.K. (Ken) Galbraith was appointed, with Kaldor made Chief of the Planning Staff. Galbraith recruited what he later described as 'one of the more diversely talented groups of scholars ever brought together for a single research task'[20] – including E.F. Schumacher, Paul Baran, Tibor Scitovsky and E. Denison. The team was based in Bad Nauheim, 20 miles north of Frankfurt, and each person was put in charge of analysing a particular sector of the German economy. Kaldor interviewed many of the generals, including Halder, who was Chief of the General Staff of the German army in 1938. Halder told him that Germany's military leaders were unanimous in the view that their economy and army were totally unprepared for war in September 1938. Halder also confided that there was a *putsch* planned to arrest Hitler in Berlin on the very day that Chamberlain's journey to Munich was announced. Had Hitler not remained in Berchtesgaden to receive him, the Second World War might not have taken place.[21] The generals also exposed the myth of a ruthless German war machine imposing savage sacrifices on the German people for the sake of victory. In reality, production was never pushed to the point of bottlenecks (except for a brief period in the summer of 1944), nor was the German war organisation particularly efficient. There were too many controlling agencies with no clear demarcation between them. The working week was hardly lengthened; most industries continued to work a single-shift system, and no attempt was made to increase workforce participation. Nor was there any radical redistribution of the labour force. The proportion of the civilian labour force employed in the war industries was 5 per cent lower in Germany than in the United Kingdom. The official Report of the Survey was published in October 1945 after some disagreement between Galbraith and the Survey Secretariat. The US Air Force wanted to show that their bombers won the war, whereas the Survey team concluded otherwise. It was the ground troops that proved decisive, and German war production continued to expand despite US bombing, reaching a peak in 1944. Kaldor himself elaborated the findings of the Survey in a lecture to the Manchester Statistical Society in May 1946 (1945b), raising the interesting question of why Germany did not make a more concerted war effort. The basic reason, he believed, was the failure to plan for expansion and total mobilisation in the earlier years. The army and industrialists were behind the Nazi leaders in their desire for rearmament, but Hitler and the army differed over the manner in which rearmament should be carried out. The army wanted rearmament in depth, while Hitler wanted emphasis on speed and the maximum concentration on finished munitions. The 1936 Four Year Plan was an uneasy compromise between the two positions, with provision, as Kaldor put it, for a quick 'blitz' but not enough for a lasting war.[22] The successful campaigns in Poland, Norway and France appeared to vindicate Hitler's policy but the pressures from 1942, with difficulties on the Russian front, and America's entry into the war, exposed its weakness. The factors which limited war production in those crucial years lay in those elements of inertia in an economic system which set a limit to the rate at which adjustment and expansion can proceed, rather than in any absolute shortages of manpower, equipment or raw materials. The failures were due to the absence of planning and coordinated control: 'a monument to the inefficiency of a system of personal dictatorship', as Kaldor graphically described it.

In Hungary, a new coalition government was elected after the war, including communists and socialists. The communists had produced a new Three Year Plan under the direction of Eugene

Varga. The socialists, not to be outdone, employed Kaldor to produce an alternative Plan. This he did with the help of 30 staff in the space of six weeks, using the planning technique of material balances (which impressed the communists).

The request in 1947 to prepare a Plan for the financial stabilisation of France came from Robert Marjolin, whom he had got to know and like in London before the war, and who was Jean Monnet's right-hand man at the Commissariat General du Plan. The basic problem posed was how to ensure monetary stability without sacrificing the level of real investment envisaged in the new Five Year Plan. Kaldor saw the answer in reductions in potential consumption, either through compulsory loans or additional taxation. The existing French tax system was both regressive and inefficient, and because of evasion and avoidance, tax revenue as a proportion of national income was only 20 per cent compared to over 40 per cent in the United Kingdom. A whole new series of tax measures were therefore proposed, very similar to the reforms that he later advocated in developing countries (see Chapter 5) namely: a uniform income tax to replace various existing income taxes, an annual tax on capital, a tax on capital gains, a uniform value-added tax on businesses, a merger of tax administrations, and a strengthening of the system of controls and penalties (1947a). In the short term, special measures to discourage luxury consumption were recommended and a special levy on incomes as an explicit contribution to the finance of the investment plan. His research assistant on the project was Pierre Uri, with whom he later collaborated on other projects for the United Nations and the Atlantic Institute in Paris.

By far the most challenging and exciting offer at this time, however, came from Gunnar Myrdal to work in the newly established Economic Commission for Europe (ECE) in Geneva, a subsidiary body of the Economic and Social Council of the United Nations. Myrdal, then Minister of Commerce in the Swedish government, had been appointed as a 'neutral' Executive Director and was looking for recruits, particularly for someone to direct the Research and Planning Division. The post was initially offered to Robert Marjolin who declined. Rosenstein-Rodan mentioned Kaldor's name to Myrdal, who interviewed him in London in early 1947 and offered him the post. Previously Kaldor had already been offered a job with the International Monetary Fund and was given two years' leave by the LSE for this purpose, but he preferred the Geneva post. The creation of the ECE was one of the first attempts to organise Europe on a collaborative basis for the purposes of post-war reconstruction, bringing together both East and West.

The original intention was that the ECE should administer Marshall Aid to Europe. There was, however, a great deal of political intrigue and infighting surrounding the Marshall Plan. For one thing, Russia was sceptical about aid being distributed throughout the whole of Europe by the ECE, fearing 'western' influence in its satellites. On top of this, the British did not want the Russians to benefit. Kaldor learnt of some of the behind-the-scenes machinations from a diplomat friend and passed on the information to Myrdal. Myrdal's English assistant, Ronald Grierson, told the British Foreign Office of Kaldor's 'indiscretions', and the Foreign Office then exerted pressure on Robbins at the LSE to withdraw Kaldor's leave to work in Europe. Since this proved difficult to do, Robbins employed delaying tactics instead, insisting that Kaldor give nine months' notice. Tired of the School and of Robbins' attitude, Kaldor promptly resigned, ending an attachment of 20 years as a student and don.[23]

The result of the Russian refusal to participate in the Marshall Aid programme was the establishment of the Organisation for European Economic Cooperation (OEEC) in 1948 which took over the administration of the Plan. Although the role of the ECE was thereby diminished, Kaldor had no regrets in joining the organisation. Indeed, his two years in Geneva were among the most stimulating and happiest of his life; living in style in an eighteenth-century villa on the shores of Lake Geneva with a supportive wife and four growing daughters, in charge of a talented staff. He had his own budget, and created the Research and Planning Division from scratch. Between fifteen and twenty economists and assistants were recruited with the specific task of preparing the *Economic Surveys of Europe*. All the staff were of the highest calibre and collaborated well together. Among the economists recruited were Robert Neild fresh from Sraffa's tutelage in Cambridge, Esther Boserup, Helen Makower, Albert Kervyn, Hans Staehle, Hal Lary, Tibor Barna and P.J. Verdoorn. The atmosphere was one of constant excitement and creativity, combined with great enthusiasm for the work to be done, inspired by Kaldor himself who was held in some awe particularly by the more junior members of staff.[24] It was the practice for each person to be put in charge of a different section of the Survey and then for Kaldor to bring everything together working long hours into the night as the deadline for publication approached. On publication, the Surveys attracted widespread international interest. They were treated as the authoritative account of the economic conditions and trends in Eastern and Western Europe, and were prominently discussed in the leader columns of the quality press. The first 1947

Survey published on the 30 March 1948 was even printed beforehand by the US Congress as an Official Document. Kaldor wrote single-handed both the 1947 and 1948 Surveys, and co-authored with Hal Lary the Survey for 1949. He resigned from the ECE in the autumn of 1949 to move to Cambridge, but continued to act as an Economic Adviser and kept in regular contact with both Lary and Myrdal.

The first Survey identified clearly the fundamental tasks facing Europe in the wake of war-time devastation and destruction; primarily, the recovery of production and trade, and the restoration of balance of payments equilibrium to reduce dependence on the United States. As far as production was concerned the recovery after the Second War was much quicker than after the First War. By the end of 1947, industrial production, in the fifteen European countries surveyed, had almost returned to its 1938 level. Agricultural production lagged, but investment goods industries performed better than average. The need for increased production was seen primarily as necessary to raise exports and reduce imports, and to eliminate bottlenecks. Steel output was a major bottleneck at the time. The Survey concluded:

[the] prospects of attaining the existing production targets for the early 1950s do not appear unpromising provided that intra-European trade and credit arrangements can be developed sufficiently to permit a more rational utilisation of European resources, and that financial difficulties will not force an interruption in the flow of overseas supplies in the intervening period.

On the balance of payments front, Europe's trade deficit in 1947 was $6900 million and its current account deficit $7500 million, of which $5400 was accounted for by a deficit with the USA. On top of this there were autonomous net capital outflows of nearly $2000 million, giving a figure of over $9000 million for accommodating finance of one form or another. There had already been major American and Canadian loans in 1946. There was now a severe dollar shortage, so acute that trade between European countries moved towards the strict bilateral financing of accounts. The 1947 Survey called for a massive expansion of exports to the United States to improve the trade balance and to rectify the dollar shortage. While production had recovered, trade was still depressed. Exports to non-European countries were 23 per cent below their 1938 level and the volume of intra-European trade was even more depressed. It was recognised that to reduce external disequilibrium, efforts must be made to restore intra-European trade. The contraction of trade was largely the result of difficulties confronting Germany. Before the war, the United Kingdom and

Germany accounted for two-thirds of intra-European trade. After the war, intra-European trade was conducted predominantly on a bilateral basis owing to the shortages of essential goods and foreign exchange. The Survey made two suggestions to ease the transition from bilateralism to multilateralism in trade and payments; first the development of a structure of trade under which each country might have both import and export surpluses with other European countries, the one being offset by the other; and secondly, allowing import surpluses in one year to be offset by export surpluses in later years.[25]

The tone of the second and third Surveys for 1948 and 1949 were far less grave than the first. They continued to portray in fine detail the progress and problems of the European economies emerging from war, identifying the balance of payments as the most threatening aspect of Europe's economic situation. The appearance of the Surveys became a regular part of the economics calendar, and continue to this day.

During his time as a UN official in Geneva, Kaldor became involved in several special assignments including acting as an adviser to the UN Technical Committee on Berlin Currency and Trade in the winter of 1948–49, and serving on an Expert Committee of the United Nations between October and December 1949 to prepare a Report on National and International Measures for Full Employment. The Berlin Currency Committee was set up by six non-aligned members of the UN Security Council to settle the question of restoring a common currency for Berlin which was the Soviet condition for lifting the blockade of Berlin. Myrdal was the UN Secretary General's representative, and Kaldor was a member of the Committee's Secretariat. The Committee's job was to arbitrate between the big four powers. Kaldor's role was to cross-examine each of the representatives of the 'big four' in turn, in the light of the evidence of each. Sidney Dell, also a member of the Secretariat and now a high UN official, recalls Kaldor's performance as 'brilliant' and 'one of the most fascinating experiences of my entire career'. Kaldor drafted the Report which recommended making the Soviet mark the sole currency for Berlin and withdrawing the Western mark from circulation. But the American stance hardened as the blockade was breached and the attempt to reach an agreement between all four powers was abandoned in February 1949. In March the Western Powers announced their intention to consolidate their position in Berlin and the Western mark became the sole legal currency in the Western Zone on 20 March. Stalin eventually lifted the blockade unconditionally.

The Report on National and International Measures for Full Employment marked a landmark in the international campaign for progress towards full employment in the post-war era, as significant as the Beveridge Report on Full Employment in the narrower context of the United Kingdom. Apart from Kaldor, other members of the Expert Committee were Professor J.M. Clark of Columbia University; Professor Arthur Smithies of Harvard; Pierre Uri, economic and financial adviser to the French Commissariat du Plan, and Ronald Walker, economic adviser to the Australian Department of External Affairs. It was Kaldor, however, who largely drafted the Report, and its adoption by the UN owed much to his verbal fluency. Sidney Dell wrote to him afterwards saying that his influence in uniting inter-governmental interests had been 'without parallel', and ventured the guess that 'it would have been a wishy-washy Report of no international consequence if you hadn't been there and worked like hell'. In the press, the Report was generally well received, although it attracted a hostile academic review from Jacob Viner, who criticised it for its indifference to the inflationary problems that the pursuit of full employment would involve.[26]

Article 55 of the UN Charter pledged that the United Nations shall promote 'higher standards of living; full employment, and conditions of economic and social progress and development'. Three types of unemployment were distinguished: unemployment arising from a lack of complementary factors of production; structural unemployment due to 'mismatch' in the labour market; and demand-deficient unemployment. The Report concentrated on the latter type, defining full employment rather loosely and imprecisely (without constraints) as a situation in which employment cannot be increased by an increase in effective demand. At the international level a good deal of attention was paid to the international propagation of changes in effective demand, and countries were urged to strive for balance of payments equilibrium to avoid the restriction of trade and the emergence of deflationary bias in the world economy. The Report also pointed to the necessity of stabilising the flow of international investment to facilitate structural balance of payments equilibrium and for the efficient development of the world's underutilised resources. In this respect, it identified an important role for the newly created World Bank if its borrowing capacity could be increased and if it was allowed to lend to governments as well as for projects. The crux of the problem continued to be the payments imbalance between America and the rest of the world: 'We can envisage', the Report said, 'no satisfactory solution to the world full employment problem and no real improvement in the world trading system unless the chronic dollar shortage is attacked at its root'. Kaldor estimated that $200 billion would have been needed to avoid the slump of the inter-war years. The Report now recommended that in the event of a US recession, the United States should deposit with the World Bank dollars equivalent to the drop in imports measured against the continuing high level of exports, which would then be lent back to countries in exchange for their own national currencies to allow them to continue to buy American goods. This role for the World Bank never materialised. At a meeting of the UN Economic and Social Council in 1950 to discuss the Report, at which Kaldor was present, spokesmen for both the Bank and the IMF were hostile to the proposals. So was the United States delegation. One delegate, Dr Isador Lubin, questioned the propriety of Kaldor speaking at the Council meeting given that the Committee of Experts that had prepared the Report under discussion had been disbanded. Kaldor had been invited in his personal capacity, however, by unanimous decision of the Council, and Lubin's objection was overruled. One sentiment expressed at the meeting was that any sort of endorsement of the Experts' Report by the Council would provide justification for the British Labour Party's resistance to the re-establishment of sterling convertibility and to the abandonment of the principle of discrimination in the conduct of foreign trade. None the less, the Report provoked widespread international interest, no more so than in Europe, and prompted the Committee on Economic Questions of the Council of Europe to request the Secretariat-General to prepare a study of how the measures recommended in the UN Report should be applied within the field of the Council of Europe. A Working Party was set up in December 1950 chaired by Kaldor. The result was a Report entitled *Full Employment Objectives in Relation to the Problem of European Co-operation* published in 1951 in which, among others, Robert Triffin and Anthony Crosland (later a Cabinet Minister in two Labour governments) also participated; the major recommendations being a European Advisory Board to oversee national efforts to secure full employment, a European Investment Bank to promote the development of underdeveloped regions of Europe, and import controls rather than deflation to achieve simultaneous internal and external equilibrium.

The 1949 UN Report, and Kaldor's contribution to it, impressed Labour's future Chancellor of the Exchequer, Hugh Gaitskell, and was instrumental in Gaitskell appointing Kaldor to the Royal Commission on the Taxation of Profits and Income in 1950, which ushered in another phase in his life and was later to open unexpected doors in high places in Britain and overseas. At this time, Kaldor was also influential in persuading Gaitskell that the pound should be devalued. Stafford Cripps, the Chancellor, was ill in hospital in Zurich. The decision had to be taken in his absence. Most ministers were against devaluation. Kaldor came to London from Geneva specifically to advise on the devaluation issue. He lunched with Gaitskell and Douglas Jay on 18 July and all had made up their mind that devaluation was the wisest course.[27] Kaldor elaborated the case more fully in a letter to *The Times* (15 July 1949), written under the pseudonym 'Exile', in which he pointed out that while the arguments for and against devaluation might be finely balanced, if the City had made up its mind that the sterling exchange rate with the dollar was overvalued, the most effective exchange controls in the world would not prevent a loss of confidence in sterling from having increasingly costly effects on Britain's foreign trade and financial reserves. The authorities must respond accordingly. The pound was devalued from $4.03 to $2.80 on 18 September.

Kaldor had not been long in Geneva when he was approached by King's College, Cambridge to accept a Fellowship there. King's were short of economists. Keynes had died of a heart attack in 1946, Gerald Shove had died of cancer earlier in 1947, and Richard Kahn was preoccupied as First Bursar and in disposing of Keynes' estate. Kahn put forward Kaldor's name, influenced to some extent by Joan Robinson who wanted him back in Cambridge. An informal college dinner was arranged with the Provost, John Sheppard, and other Fellows of the College. Kahn arranged the seating such that Kaldor could impress influential members of the College with his classical education. Quite coincidentally, he met (Sir) Dennis Proctor on the train going to the dinner, who gave him some friendly advice on how to 'behave'. He was duly elected but had to ask that the Fellowship be postponed until September 1949 in order to allow him to complete his work in Geneva. With some reluctance Kahn agreed; and then had little choice but to accede to a further request for postponement to allow Kaldor to serve on the UN Expert Committee on Full Employment. In the meantime a College Lectureship was also conferred on him. A profile of the ECE in the *New York Times Magazine*[28] interpreted Kaldor's decision to postpone his departure to Cambridge as a measure of loyalty to his staff, and went on to describe his new appointment as 'being one of such honour and prestige for an economist that there are not five posts in the world more coveted by a man of that profession'. The profile painted a not inappropriate portrait of Kaldor as resembling a jolly medieval monk but 'masking a powerful coordinating mind and a sharp eye for economic nonsense hidden behind official phraseology'. The King's Fellowship was formally conferred in July to take effect from 29 September 1949 but it was not until the beginning of the new year that he finally started college teaching. The induction ceremony, shared with Walt Rostow in King's magnificent Chapel, was not without incident. Kaldor's alarm watch inadvertently went off. He had confused a.m. and p.m. - a not uncommon occurrence in his future hectic life. Unlike Keynes, he was never to play a prominent part in College life, preferring to devote his time exclusively to research and writing and later to the role of economic adviser. Prior to his arrival at King's, the Economics Faculty, still presided over by Pigou, appointed him to a University Lectureship in Economics. In 1952 he was made a Reader, but had to wait another fourteen years for a Chair (having been over-looked in 1957 when James Meade was appointed to the Chair of Political Economy). In the early years his teaching consisted mainly of lectures on the Theory of Value and Distribution and Economic Dynamics and classes in Economic Theory and Current Economic Problems. From 1952 he switched to lecturing on the Economics of Growth, which he continued to do until his official retirement from Cambridge in 1975 at the age of 67. Sraffa was his closest academic friend. Before infirmity set in, Sraffa would cycle round to Kaldor's house from Trinity College every afternoon to discuss economics and political matters. Their mutual admiration was unbounded. On Sraffa's death in 1983, Kaldor paid many moving tributes to him, including an address at his memorial service in Trinity in which he described him as 'one of the most remarkable men I have known' (1984b; see also 1986c; 1986d; 1987a).

NOTES

1. Both projects were under the auspices of the National Institute of Economic and Social Research. The first was initiated with Joan Robinson in 1941. The second was started at the instigation of Austin Robinson in 1943, for which Kaldor was given part-time leave from the LSE. Progress was slow, however, and in the end the promised wide ranging survey of the economics of advertising, and the relation between advertising and welfare was never completed. The fruits of the statistical work were published in a book with his research assistant, Rodney Silverman, in 1948 (see bibliography).
2. Cmnd. 6261, HMSO, 1941.
3. Cmnd. 6404, HMSO, 1942.
4. This was a flat 5 per cent levy on all corporate profits.
5. There was to be deferment of the payment of full pensions for 20 years

because Keynes, as adviser to the Treasury, insisted on keeping the Exchequer cost to under £100 million in the first few years as a condition for supporting the Plan.

6. W. Beveridge, *Full Employment in a Free Society* (London: George, Allen and Unwin Ltd, 1944).

7. In an article entitled 'Post-war Arithmetic', 24 February 1945. Among distinguished economists, Hubert Henderson was a severe critic in his Oxford lectures.

8. 3 and 4 December.

9. Richard Stone and E.F. Jackson later attempted to formalise Kaldor's model to portray the structure more clearly. See 'Economic Models with Special Reference to Mr. Kaldor's System', *Economic Journal*, December 1941.

10. D. Moggridge (ed.), *The Collected Writings of J.M. Keynes: Activities 1944–1946* Vol. XXIV *The Transition to Peace* (London: Macmillan, 1979), p. 626.

11. N. Kaldor and M.F.W. Joseph, *Economic Reconstruction After the War*, Association for Education in Citizenship (English Universities Press, 1942).

12. 'National Income and State Finance' 25 March 1943; and 'Closing the Deflationary Gap', 26 March 1943.

13. Published by the Oxford University Press, July 1943.

14. Scitovsky wrote in 1946 to say that Paul Samuelson had enquired whether he might be tempted to a Chair in America, but there is no record of a formal offer having been made.

15. 29 and 30 October, and 1 November.

16. 21 and 22 November.

17. 10 and 11 March 1946.

18. R.G. Hawtrey, *Economic Rebirth* (London: Longman, 1946).

19. 25 February, 15 March and 3 April.

20. J.K. Galbraith, *A Life in Our Times* (Boston: Houghton Mifflin, 1981).

21. For a fascinating discussion of the credibility of the assassination plot and the effect of appeasement on the capitulation of Czechoslovakia, see the correspondence in *The Times* between Kaldor, Dr Otto John and Lord Boothby, 10 August, 21 August, 4 September and 8 September 1970.

22. The idea that the German economy was only organised for 'blitz' has been challenged by D.J. Overy who argues that Hitler was planning for a lengthy war, but did not foresee its outbreak so quickly: see 'Hitler's War and the German Economy', *Economic History Review*, May 1982.

23. An Honorary Fellowship was bestowed on him in 1970.

24. I am particularly indebted to Mrs Giselle Podbielsky for her vivid impressions of this period when she worked as a member of Kaldor's staff in a junior capacity (at that time).

25. The United Kingdom made attempts to induce a number of countries to agree to accept and hold sterling to facilitate multilateral trade. Sterling was for a short time made convertible for current transactions, but had to be suspended because of the pressure to convert sterling into dollars. A multilateral compensation agreement among several European countries then came into effect on 1st January 1948, under the auspices of the Bank for International Settlements. Later in 1948 a new OEEC Intra-European Payments and Compensations scheme was launched.

26. J. Viner, 'Full Employment at Whatever Cost', *Quarterly Journal of Economics*, August 1950.

27. See Philip Williams (ed.), *The Diary of Hugh Gaitskell 1945–1956* (London: Jonathen Cape, 1983), and also D. Jay, *Change and Fortune: A Political Record* (London: Hutchinson, 1980).

28. 12 September 1948.

4 TAXATION

Kaldor's appointment by Gaitskell to the Royal Commission on the Taxation of Profits and Income in 1951 proved to be another turning-point in his life. His immersion in tax matters for the next five years turned him into one of the world's recognised experts on tax theory and policy. The Memorandum of Dissent (hereafter, the Minority Report) of the Commission, which he drafted, and his book *An Expenditure Tax* (1955), became minor classics in the literature on taxation. The consequences of this recognition were a greater influence in Labour Party circles in the United Kingdom, culminating in his appointment in 1964 as a Special Adviser to the Chancellor of the Exchequer on the Social and Economic Aspects of Taxation, and a flood of invitations from developing countries to advise on budgetary policy and tax reforms, starting with India in 1956.

The Royal Commission, appointed on 2 January 1951, worked initially under the Chairmanship of Sir Lionel Cohen and then (from April 1952) for the majority of the time under Lord Radcliffe. John Hicks was the other academic economist on the Commission, although much more conservative in his approach to tax matters than Kaldor. The terms of reference of the Commission were to

inquire into the present system of taxation of profits and income, including its incidence and effects, with particular reference to the taxation of business profits and the taxation of salaries and wages: to consider whether for the purpose of the national economy the present system is the best way of raising the required revenue from the taxation of profits and income, due regard being paid to the points of view of the taxpayer and of the Exchequer; to consider the present system of personal allowances, reliefs and rates of tax as a means of distributing the tax burden fairly among the individual members of the community and to make recommendations consistent with maintaining the same total yield of the existing duties in relation to national income.

The terms were later extended to include the following direction:

to make recommendations bearing in mind that in the present financial situation it may be necessary to maintain the revenue from profits and income: and, in so far as they make recommendations which would on balance entail a substantial loss of revenue, to indicate an order of priority in which such recommendations should be taken into consideration.

There were two subsequent requests to extend the terms of reference to the consideration of first, capital gains taxation; and secondly, an expenditure tax. It was agreed that the taxation of capital gains could be legitimately considered within the existing terms of reference, but not an expenditure tax which would have implications for the system of indirect taxation which was not within the terms of reference. This was the topic that Kaldor later took up in a separate book.

The Commission divided itself into two sections, one dealing with personal taxation, the other with company taxation. Kaldor chose to be associated with the former and regarded the taxation of capital gains as the most important reform. The Commission met once a week in Somerset House, Kaldor travelling from Cambridge where he continued to teach full-time. Although there were disagreements, he worked particularly well with Radcliffe, and a strong mutual admiration developed which was renewed in the late 1950s with the Radcliffe Committee on the Workings of the Monetary System (see Chapter 12). Before the Final Report of the Commission there were two Interim Reports (the first produced at the request of the government and the second on the Commission's own initiative), both signed unanimously (although with specific reservations). In the second Interim Report, for example, Kaldor joined forces with George Woodcock, Mr H.L. Bullock and Mrs Vera Anstey in disagreement over such matters as the exemption limit for taxation and the size of personal allowances; the aggregation of children's and parents' income, and the differentiation between earned and investment income.

When it came to the Final Report, Kaldor found himself isolated from most other members of the Commission on major issues of principle relating to the taxation of capital gains; the treatment of expenses under Schedules D and E, and the taxation of company profits. His only support came from George Woodcock (later General Secretary of the TUC) and Bullock, who together signed a lengthy Memorandum of Dissent, largely written by Kaldor. It was a masterly exposition of inequities in the existing tax system which the Majority Report proposed to leave untouched. The equity of a tax system is to be judged by whether people with the same taxable capacity, or ability to pay, pay the same amount of tax. By this criterion, Kaldor viewed the UK tax system as 'absurdly inequitable' in the sense that the tax burden on some people was very heavy while on others it was very light according to how income was earned; whether or not they were property-owners, and other factors that ought to have nothing to do with the distribution of the burden of taxation. Inequity was further compounded by the general relationship between the way people were treated for tax purposes and their social rank.

If a tax system is to be fair between individuals according to ability to pay the first requirement is a just and comprehensive definition of income. The problem that preoccupied Kaldor was finding a definition of income which would be fair to all taxpayers. The essence of the problem is that however comprehensively income is defined for tax purposes, it remains an inadequate measure of ability to pay because it ignores taxable capacity that resides in property as such. This constitutes an argument for measuring ability to pay by spending power rather than by income. The question then becomes: is there a definition of income capable of approximating to an individual's spending power better than his actual expenditure, and would a tax based on expenditure be more equitable than one based on income, however income is defined? This question, however, was not within the Commission's terms of reference. The Minority Report therefore confined itself first to the question of how the present system might be reformed to reduce existing inequities, and secondly to the reform of company taxation. The major inequities dealt with concerned the exemption of capital gains from tax, and differences in the treatment of income receipts under Schedules D and E. The Majority Report did not propose widening the existing legal definition of taxable income and did not fully get to grips with the inequitable treatment of income as between Schedule D and E taxpayers. When the Majority and Minority Reports were published in 1955,[1] Hugh Gaitskell, the Leader of the Labour Party, (himself an economist of distinction) was strongly in favour of the reforms proposed by the Minority Report, and it was the result of his influence that two major recommendations for capital gains taxation and the separation of personal and company taxation were adopted as official Labour Party policy before the 1959 general election. The reforms were then introduced when the Labour Party assumed office under Harold Wilson in 1964. Further major tax reforms were proposed in the budget speech of 1965, including a wealth tax, but nothing subsequently happened. Kaldor once described the 1965 Finance Bill as the 'high point' reached towards an impartial and just system of taxation, after which progress had been backwards.

CAPITAL GAINS TAXATION

The equity argument for the taxation of capital gains is the obvious one that capital gains increase an individual's capacity to spend or save like any other form of income. The fact that capital gains accrue only to a small minority of property-owners also means that the exemption of capital gains from taxation probably widens the post-tax distribution of income, and in this sense is doubly inequitable. The traditional arguments against capital gains taxation were that gains tend to be irregular and therefore are not like other income; that only the taxation of realised gains is feasible and this would be inequitable *vis-à-vis* unrealised gains, and that capital gains are often 'illusory' resulting from inflation and falling interest rates. None of these arguments Kaldor found convincing and the Minority Report had no difficulty in undermining them. Gains from inflation may not be 'real', but if the proceeds of the gain are spent, the recipient derives the same benefit as spending taxed income. If the gains are saved, their 'illusory' character applies equally to all saving, the real value of which falls with inflation. Also, those with property yielding capital gains are generally much better off than those who own fixed income assets. Equity requires that the tax system recognises the relative changes in the taxable capacity of different property-owners. If capital gains arise because interest rates fall, the beneficiaries still gain relative to other savers and therefore should be taxed. In the mid-1950s the bulk of capital gains in practice did not arise through inflation or falling interest rates[2] but from higher profits which were anticipated by the purchaser. This is the motive for supplying risk capital and there is no reason why successful property-owners in this respect should be treated any differently from other successful people who, for example, have invested in themselves and earn income in the normal way. Even if gains were not anticipated, and represented an unforeseen windfall, this would still not constitute an argument against taxation in a system which taxes saving as well as spending.

Apart from being a source of inequity, the exemption of capital gains from taxation gives the opportunity to the owners of capital to avoid income tax by converting taxable income into capital appreciation by, for example, having the interest payable appear as capital appreciation, or by choosing securities with a low dividend yield but a high expected capital appreciation. The Majority Report made no reference to the scope for tax avoidance permitted by the exemption of capital gains from tax.

The difficulty of treating capital losses seemed to be one of the major reasons why the Majority rejected the idea of capital gains taxation. They said,

indeed no form of the tax that was based on realised gain and realised losses – and there is no alternative – would escape the serious objection to its foundation in equity that it would tax to the same extent a man who had realised a gain on one of his assets, though showing a net loss on others that he retained, as the man who had realised a similar gain without any current depreciation of his other assets to set against it.

The Minority view was that such concern was misplaced because there would be nothing to stop the sale of a depreciated asset and its repurchase; but even so, the case would only be a violation of equity if equity is so narrowly conceived as to require full equality of treatment between diferent taxpayers for each particular year. Under a flat-rate tax, a taxpayer's cumulative liability would be unaffected by any delay in realising a loss. The Minority Report therefore recommended a flat-rate capital gains tax on net realised gains (i.e. after the deduction of realised losses), with no distinction between short- and long-term gains. The Minority Report estimated a yield from such a tax of between £200 and £350 million per annum (at prevailing prices), compared to an estimate of only £50 million by the Majority Report.

SCHEDULE D AND SCHEDULE E INCOME

Another source of inequity in the existing tax system lay in the treatment of expenses of Schedule E income earners and Schedule D earners where much more liberal arrangements applied including allowances for depreciation, advertising, entertainment and so on. Under Schedule E, only 'unavoidable' expenses were allowable. The Majority recognised this inequity and wanted to relax the Schedule E expenses rule, but the Minority felt that this would lead to further abuses. It would be much more desirable, they argued, to bring Schedule D earners in line with Schedule E and to have a tax on trading receipts less unavoidable expenses (e.g. wages and salaries, etc.) which would be, in effect, a tax on net output. On the other hand, they recognised that a strong case existed on economic grounds for granting capital allowances, and the proposal would put traders in the UK at a disadvantage compared with foreigners. The best the Minority Report could do was to recommend the abolition of the upper income limit for earned income relief under Schedule E (equal to 2/9th of gross income). This was no solution at all for those not affected by the limit, and the inequities of treatment between Schedule D and E income remain to this day.

The Minority were also concerned with the ability of those taxed under Schedule D to offset losses against tax on other income. Apart from inequity, this was also a means of tax avoidance by allowing people to accumulate capital in loss-making business at the expense of the Revenue. The Minority recommended that at the most losses should only be allowable as offsets against income from the same source.

COMPANY TAXATION

The system of company taxation in operation at the time of the Royal Commission's deliberations was that profits were subject to the standard rate of income tax plus profits tax which discriminated between distributed and undistributed profits in favour of the latter. The degree of discrimination was varied periodically and in April 1955 distributed profits were taxed at 22.5 per cent and undistributed profits at 2.5 per cent. Both the Majority and Minority Reports agreed that subjecting companies to both income tax and profits tax was unsatisfactory. Separating the two would make it possible to vary the rate of company tax without varying personal taxation and vice versa. The Commission tried to work out a scheme for a uniform corporation tax but the idea was finally rejected by the Majority owing to certain technical difficulties relating to the desire to avoid the double taxation of dividends whereby the shareholder was subject to income tax on dividends when the profits of the company had already been taxed. The Minority believed this objection to be based on a misconception. Given that the company rate could vary from the personal rate, equity does not require that one tax be offset against another any more than in the case of other taxes. Neither did it follow that the shareholders would be any the worse off under a different system; this would depend on the new rates of tax chosen. The Majority Report made two major recommendations: first, that a corporation profits tax be levied independent of the personal income tax; and second, that companies should act as agents for the Inland Revenue deducting income tax on all interest and dividends paid out. On the question of tax discrimination against distributed profits, the Majority concluded that this was undesirable because it artificially depressed the market value of shares, making it more difficult for enterprises to raise new capital. Encouraging retention does not necessarily mean that consumption is reduced and investment encouraged. The Minority view was that the Majority case would have carried more weight if the taxation of capital gains had not been rejected. The Minority Report claimed a much stronger link between dividend growth and share values than between earnings growth and share values, and calculated that a doubling of dividend payments would double stock exchange values, adding some £12,000 million (at prevailing prices) to the (untaxed) disposable wealth of shareholders. If this were to happen, and part of the gain spent, this would add seriously to inflationary pressure. The Minority therefore dissented from the recommendation that discrimination against distributed profits should be ended, at least not before the introduction of a capital gains tax. Then a single corporation tax would be appropriate on all profits. To raise the same level of company tax as then prevailing, it was estimated that the flat rate corporation tax would have to be 40 per cent. With a capital gains tax, this could be reduced to 33.3 per cent, implying a 50 per cent tax on company saving if one half of net earnings were distributed.[3]

Kaldor gave a full resumé of his views on company taxation in an address to the Manchester Statistical Society in March 1955 (1954b), and examined the extent to which taxes on industry had raised costs and prices or deprived industry of investment funds, distinguishing between the short and long run. In the long run the taxation of business profits tends to get passed on in the form of higher profit margins and thus its true incidence is shifted from the shareholder to the general consumer. While, in equity, therefore, the case for taxing companies is to tax the owners of shares who experience capital appreciation from both retained profits and the payments of dividends, in the long run, company taxes cannot be a substitute for capital gains tax. If there was a capital gains tax, most of the equitable justification for levying taxes on companies as such would disappear. Kaldor found that in 1948, 1949 and 1950 compared with 1937 there was an increase in the margin of profit relative to turnover, and an even more pronounced rise in trading profits as a percentage of net output, which suggested to him that a considerable part of the increased burden of taxation during and after the war was offset by an increase in prices relative to costs. Company saving also rose. In 1951/53, undistributed profits were nine times higher than in 1938, and five times higher in real terms allowing for depreciation at current replacement cost. There was in fact a surplus of company saving over investment. Kaldor attributed this to the discriminatory profits tax against distributed profits and to dividend restraint, so that in the short run the burden of company tax must have fallen on the shareholder through lower dividends and lower capital appreciation than otherwise would have been the case. In fact, he noted that share values had failed to keep pace with the increase in the value of underlying assets, so much so that the market value of quoted shares had fallen below the current value of underlying assets leading to the highly unusual situation of the yields obtainable on shares being higher than the rates of profit earned by companies themselves on real capital employed. This made it more difficult for new expanding firms to compete for capital. He concluded, therefore, that in the short run company taxation exerted an unfavourable effect on economic efficiency, not so much through discouraging productive investment, but through a less efficient allocation of the community's savings. For one thing, it makes business more reliant on internal savings for expansion and makes it more difficult to use the facilities of the capital market. Secondly, the existence of the tax tends to discriminate against firms with high potential rates of expansion and in favour of more sedate firms, which tends to strengthen monopolistic tendencies and to slow down the speed of change and adaptation in the economy.

AN EXPENDITURE TAX

Kaldor ended his work with the Royal Commission on the Taxation of Profits and Income by writing an important book on the case for an expenditure tax (see bibliography), which was deemed to fall outside the Commission's terms of reference. The ideas contained must be regarded as complementtary to the ideas on other tax matters contained in the Minority Report of the Commission. When the book appeared in 1955, it received widespread press coverage and review. The Times (1 December) devoted a leader to its contents praising the argument but doubting the practicality of such a tax. The anonymous hostile reviewer in The Economist (10 December) was Ursula Hicks, much to Kaldor's surprise and annoyance. Arnold Plant gave a radio broadcast on the book, subsequently published in The Listener (15 December). Within ten years, the book sold 6000 copies and was translated into Spanish, Italian and Japanese.

　　The idea of an expenditure tax (or a tax on consumption) was not a new one, but no one before Kaldor had argued comprehensively on the same lines that the measurement of income as a measure of taxable capacity is inevitably ambiguous and is likely to be a bad proxy for the measurement of spending power so that the taxation of spending as such may be regarded as equally equitable, with other positive advantages. A case for an expenditure tax had been made by the political philosopher Hobbes in the seventeenth century on the grounds that people should be taxed according to the resources of the community they absorb not according to what they contribute. There was also the general concern with the discouragement of thrift, and the inequity of taxing those who had to save for emergencies, because their income was irregular, at the same rate as those with the same secure income derived from property. This was the argument put by J.S. Mill in his *Principles of Political Economy*, and before the Select Committee on Income and Property Tax in 1861. The case was later taken up by economists such as Marshall and Pigou. There seemed to be a general consensus, however, that such a tax was a practical impossibility. Keynes remarked in his evidence to the Colwyn Committee on National Debt and Taxation 1927 that although such a tax may be theoretically sound, 'it is practically impossible'. Kaldor was most influenced, however, by a paper by the American economist Irving Fisher, which he first heard while attending the July 1936 meetings of the Econometric Society at Colorado Springs, which indicated that such a tax would be feasible administratively since an individual's saving and dissaving could be computed on much the same lines as business saving.[4] At the time, however, Kaldor agreed with Keynes that the prevailing economic situation did not make it sensible to suggest reforms that might encourage saving, however desirable on other grounds. The circumstances of the 1950s, however, were entirely different.

The principle of progressive income taxation rests on the concept of taxable capacity or ability to pay. The fundamental question is, does 'income' approximate to this concept? This for Kaldor was a more important question than the degree of progression. There are three main worries: first, income is only one measure of taxable capacity; secondly, income by itself is not an unambiguous concept, and thirdly, the actual definition of income for tax purposes can introduce major inequities into the system by some receipts being treated as income and others not. Income is taken as a proxy for 'spending power', but there are other sources of spending power and it is not easy to express them all in a single measure of taxable capacity. Wealth confers spending power in addition to any income it may yield, but it is hard to assess in terms of an annual sum except on arbitrary assumptions. Similar problems arise with the treatment of irregular receipts such as gifts and windfalls of various kinds. Kaldor conceded that it would be possible to move towards a system of taxing spending power more closely if there existed a wealth tax; if all income were aggregated, and if spasmodic income could be averaged over the years, but there would still be the problem of capital gains (then untaxed). Some capital gains give rise to the same spending power as other types of earnings, while others do not. For example, in times of inflation, adding capital appreciation to the measure of taxable capacity would be inequitable between those who own property and those who work, but excluding capital appreciation would be inequitable between those who hold assets, the money value of which is fixed, and those who do not. Thus, in Kaldor's view, the fundamental case for an expenditure tax did not rest particularly on inequities in the way that existing tax systems operated (some of which could be easily rectified) but on the fact that no objective definition of income exists suitable for tax purposes.[5] The sources of spending power are numerous and cannot be reduced to an objective common denominator. Since there is no objective definition of income that would provide a true measure of spending power, there can be no presumption that any income tax system would be superior from an equity point of view to an expenditure tax. The attempt to compensate by taxing richer people at higher rates merely discourages saving, risk taking and work effort. All this would be avoided by a tax on expenditure itself. The problems created by the non-comparability of different forms of income, capital gains and wealth would resolve themselves. The individual himself would declare his spending power when he spends. Kaldor also believed that an expenditure tax would be a more efficient instrument for controlling the economy, so that there need be no necessary conflict between an egalitarian system of taxation, efficiency and growth.

Kaldor discussed at length the likely effects that a switch to an expenditure tax might have on risk bearing, the supply of effort, saving and economic progress. We may briefly discuss his main conclusions, some of which must still, even today, be regarded as tentative.[6] On the question of risk-bearing, does income tax discriminate against risky investments compared with alternative taxes yielding the same revenue, such as an annual tax on capital, a tax on accrued income, or an expenditure tax? Kaldor attempted to show that with a given yield structure of assets, a proportional income tax will favour less risky investments because the yields after tax will narrow. Thus if short-term bonds earn 2 per cent and long-term bonds earn 4 per cent, the earnings differential is 2 per cent. A 50 per cent tax will reduce the yield on short-term bonds to 1 per cent and on long-term bonds to 2 per cent, giving a premium of only 1 per cent on the more 'risky' investment. Compare this with a 2.5 per cent tax on capital which would yield the same revenue as a 50 per cent income tax if the average return on capital is 5 per cent. This would leave the distribution between assets unchanged since the additional net income to be obtained by holding a more risky investment will be the same as it is without the tax. A tax on accrued income (i.e. income tax plus a tax on realised capital gains) would be even more injurious to risk-taking since it taxes the whole yield on capital and not just the part which compensated for 'capital risk'. This conclusion was challenged by Richard Musgrave in his review of Kaldor's book in the *American Economic Review*,[7] and the issue was formally taken up by Cary Brown in the *Review of Economic Studies*,[8] citing the work of Musgrave and Domar in 1944 who showed the contrary result that a comprehensive income tax, with allowance for capital losses, favours risk taking in comparison with an annual capital tax or lump sum levy. In response, Kaldor (1958i) conceded Brown's objection, and then became muddled over whether the prevailing British tax system was more or less likely to discourage risks than a tax on accrued income. He had concluded in his book that the effect of the non-taxation of capital gains is to reduce the discrimination against risk-bearing inherent in income tax. In his reply to Brown he also made the valid point that the taxation of capital gains may discourage risk-bearing by more than it is encouraged by the allowance for capital losses, so that a tax system which operates in this way is not necessarily less discriminatory against risk taking than an income tax which exempts gains and disallows losses. But he then concluded with two contradictory propositions: first, that the British-type income tax might be less discouraging to risk-bearing than a more comprehensive tax which includes realised taxable gains and losses; and second, a tax on accrued income might on balance be more favourable to risk-bearing than the British-type income tax, and no less favourable than the expenditure tax. The truth would seem to depend on whether there is asymmetry between attitudes to capital gains and losses, and on the assumptions made about the income elasticity of demand for risk-taking.

The comparison with the expenditure tax turns out to be just as uncertain. On the one hand, an expenditure tax is less discriminating against risk in so far as part of taxable income is saved, but on the other hand it is more discriminating in so far as a part of the capital gain is spent. Kaldor attempted to resolve what he called 'the apparent contradiction between the two approaches' with the conclusion that

an expenditure tax may be thus said to discriminate, not against the assumption of risks, but against the spending of income obtained through the assumption of risks. In comparison with a lump sum levy it will cause, not the income obtained on capital to be smaller, but the proportion of that income devoted to consumption. As far as the distribution of assets is concerned, this will be the same as under an equivalent property tax, or a lump sum levy: the difference will consist in that he will spend less and save more than under the other two alternatives.

As far as the incentive to work and the supply of effort are concerned, different conclusions can be reached depending on the assumptions made concerning the relative stability of income and consumption, and whether taxation is progressive or proportional. Kaldor concluded that a progressive expenditure tax would be less of a disincentive to work than a progressive income tax yielding the same revenue, the more so the greater the fluctuations in a person's earnings and the higher the marginal rate of income tax. But if earnings are reasonably steady, and income is not high enough to be taxed at a high marginal rate, there would be no particular advantages associated with an expenditure tax as far as the supply of effort is concerned. On the other hand, it can be shown[9] that with an equal yield proportional expenditure tax, the tax cost of current consumption will be greater under an expenditure tax than under an income tax so that in so far as the choice between work and leisure depends on the price of current consumption, work effort will diminish. It may also fall if the choice between work and leisure depends on the price of future consumption. Thus increased saving from taxing expenditure may be offset by a fall in saving from lower work effort. In the case where taxation is progressive, however, this seems highly unlikely especially if the degree of progression under the expenditure tax is less than under the income tax owing to less tax avoidance and evasion.

Kaldor did not pay much attention to the argument that an expenditure tax would avoid the double taxation of saving under income tax, and therefore avoid distortions and encourage saving. Musgrave in his Review expressed some surprise that Kaldor did not stress more forcefully the importance of saving and investment to achieve a higher rate of growth in Britain for the country to maintain its competitive position in world markets.

As far as enterprise and economic progress are concerned, an expenditure tax has other advantages. In the absence of a capital gains tax, income tax puts a premium on speculation (as distinct from enterprise) compared to an expenditure tax, where both yield and capital gains are equally taxed if spent, or equally exempt if saved. If capital values fluctuate more with speculation, yields must be higher and the valuation of securities will stand lower. An expenditure tax which discouraged speculation would therefore enhance the supply of risk capital. To regulate the economy, Kaldor believed it would make sense to have just two taxes: a tax on personal expenditure and a tax on capital expenditure. The latter would be far more desirable than trying to regulate investment through changes in taxes on profits or by variations in the rate of interest. Ian Little, the distinguished Oxford economist, who reviewed Kaldor's book in the *Economic Journal*[10], was impressed with the case made for the expenditure tax on grounds both of equity and economic progress. Little concluded:

it would, in my opinion, be foolish to dismiss the expenditure surtax in the belief that our present tax system can continue without any radical change. It seems to me that we shall either have a capital gains tax like most other advanced countries, pretty soon, or Mr Kaldor's tax; or even both.... But for practical reasons the choice may lie between the two, in which case there is little doubt to my mind that the expenditure tax could be used, if so desired, as a more effective instrument for restraining the consumption of the rich, that it would be more equitable as between individuals and more beneficial economically, than a capital gains tax.

Little proved to be right in his prognostication of a capital gains tax, but an expenditure tax has yet to find favour with any political party or the tax authorities in the United Kingdom. In more recent times, the Meade Committee endorsed the idea of an expenditure tax.[11] As well as mentioning the traditional arguments concerning the difficulty of defining income and measuring accruals, most emphasis was placed on the elimination of capital market distortions, particularly those associated with various concessions in the existing income tax system, which have differential and distorting effects on rates of return to different forms of saving, and with having to correct nominal capital gains and losses for inflation. Such problems automatically disappear with an expenditure tax.

Several theoretical objections have been raised against the tax, but none is particularly convincing. The major problem is at the level of administration. First, it is claimed that actual spending is not a good measure of spending power because the relation between the two is non-linear. This could be dealt with, however, by the progression of the expenditure tax rates. In practice, the rich would find themselves far worse off than under income tax because of the difficulty of avoidance and evasion. By reducing avoidance and evasion, actual spending would get closer to spending power than taxable income. Secondly, it has been argued, why should people be taxed differently simply because of tastes and temperament? Kaldor's response was that tax systems never have been, and never could be, so constructed as to take account of the peculiarities of individual temperaments. Thirdly, it is argued that some people need to spend more because of family size, unfortunate circumstances and so on, but these problems could be accommodated within the new system. So, also, could fluctuations in consumption from year to year (particularly with discrete expenditures on durable consumption goods) by some form of averaging.

The main difficulties concern the practical implementation of the tax. The common early view[12] was that an expenditure tax would be wholly impractical because of the difficulty of taxpayers keeping accurate records of personal expenditure and of checking returns. It was Irving Fisher who first showed that this would not be necessary since a person's expenditure is the difference between what he has available for spending and what he has left at the end of the accounting period. Thus, in theory, the only information required is the size of a person's bank balance at the beginning of the year plus income and other receipts, and from this is then deducted net investments, exempted expenditure and the size of the bank balance at the end of the year; the difference is chargeable expenditure. The major problems concern the definition of chargeable expenditure, and evasion through the avoidance of the use of bank accounts. The purchase of durable goods presents a problem because they represent 'lumpy' expenditure and have an investment content. If they are treated as consumption there would be inequity with a progressive tax if the whole outlay was reckoned as taxable expenditure in the year of purchase. If they are treated as investment (and exempt) there would be inequity if the flow of benefit was not taxed. Kaldor suggested that, except for houses, durable goods should be treated as consumption expenditure, with total expenditure spread out over a number of years. Gifts pose another difficulty because rich people subject to a high rate of expenditure tax could avoid tax by arranging for other people to do their expenditure for them. Gifts, therefore, except for certain transfers such as alimony, should be treated as expenditure, at least over a certain limit. To allow for differences in needs owing to differences in family size, the tax should be computed on a per capita basis. To cope with expenditures related to illness and other misfortunes, there would be exemption for those items that cannot be covered by insurance. For those contingencies that can be insured against, compensation from insurance companies would not then be treated as a receipt that had to be accounted for.

Kaldor recognised that it would be impossible to switch from an income tax system to an expenditure tax system overnight, however desirable. Moreover, because of the administrative complexities, it would never be a suitable tax extending down the income scale. In any case, most of the inequities and disincentives of income tax relate to the upper income groups which suggests it might first be introduced as a substitute for income tax at the highest rates. Kaldor not only made this suggestion for the United Kingdom, but also for India and Ceylon where he gave tax advice in 1956–58 (see Chapter 5). It was tried in India and Ceylon, and on the basis of this experience he later admitted that he underestimated the power of evasion and avoidance as well as the political objections to such a system (1978a). In his original exposition, perhaps it is fair to say that he exaggerated the objections to income tax and played down the objections to the expenditure tax. Conceptually, the dividing-line between what is consumption and what is saving may be said to be as arbitrary and fraught with difficulties as answering the question, when does income accrue? And from an administrative point of view, the difficulties of the expenditure tax were perhaps also understated; the conclusion which Prest also came to in his review of the Meade Committee Report.[13] There was a move in the 1960s towards a more comprehensive income tax system in the United Kingdom, but certainly not radical enough to satisfy Kaldor's objections. The United Kingdom still lacks a wealth tax and this remains a stumbling-block to an equitable tax system based on the concept of taxable capacity or ability to pay.

Whether an expenditure tax will ever become a permanent feature of the tax structure of the United Kingdom or elsewhere is impossible to forecast. Whether it does so or not, Kaldor's book will remain a classic reference. Alan Peacock, in a review in the *Manchester Guardian* (23 December 1955), described the book as 'one of the most stimulating post-war books on Public Finance'; Harberger[14] held it to be 'one of the best books of the decade in public finance, ranking with the classic works of Edgeworth, Pigou, Simons and Vickrey'; while Musgrave[15] remarked: 'the book, while small in size, excels in a high idea-to-page ratio. It makes a splendid contribution to rethinking of the traditional principles of taxation. Like the tracts of old, it may even have an effect on the actual course of legislation.'

Kaldor believed in the power of taxation to alter significantly the performance of an economy. Later in the 1960s he was to be the devisor of a variety of ingenious new tax schemes for the solution to particular problems, some of which were adopted and some not. Notable examples include the Selective Employment Tax introduced in 1966 to make service industries more productive and manufacturing industry more competitive; stock relief introduced in 1975 which saved many companies from bankruptcy (see Chapter 9); and the proposal for a levy on press advertising revenues, graduated according to circulation, to halt the growing monopolisation of the press, with the levy's proceeds redistributed to the smaller newspapers. This last idea was proposed in a memorandum submitted with Robert Neild to the Royal Commission on the Press in February 1962 (1962d), but was never adopted.

NOTES

1. Cmd 9474, London: HMSO, June 1955.
2. If interest rates on average are steady over time, changing interest rates are not a source of net capital gains.
3. The ratio of tax to company saving may be expressed as $\dfrac{rP}{U+T}$, where r is the rate of corporation tax; P is total profits; U is undistributed profits and T is tax paid. Undistributed profits may be expressed as q (P – T) where q is the retention ratio out of net profits (after tax). Hence: $\dfrac{rP}{U+T} = \dfrac{rP}{q\,(P-T)+T} = \dfrac{rP}{q\,(P-rP)+rP} = \dfrac{r}{q\,(1-r)+r}$. Therefore if r = 0.33 and q = 0.5, the effective tax rate on company saving is 0.5 or 50 per cent. With a retention ratio of 2/3rd, the tax on saving would be 43 per cent and with a retention ratio of 1/3rd, the tax would be 60 per cent.
4. 'Income in Theory and Income Taxation in Practice', *Econometrica*, January 1937. Fisher later published a book, *Constructive Income Taxation* (with H.W. Fisher) (New York: Harper Brothers, 1942), but it received virtually no attention.
5. Income is consumption plus net saving. The problem of defining 'income' is really the problem of defining 'net saving'.
6. A.B. Atkinson and A. Sandmo show, using optimal tax theory in an intertemporal context, that no firm conclusions can be reached on the relative efficiency of expeniture and income taxes from a welfare point of view: it all depends on the form of the social welfare function; what other instruments governments can use to achieve a desired intertemporal allocation of consumption, and on crucial parameters of the model such as the interest elasticity of labour supply. See 'Welfare Implications of the Taxation of Savings', *Economic Journal*, September 1980.
7. March 1957.

8. E. Cary Brown, 'Mr. Kaldor on Taxation and Risk Bearing', *Review of Economic Studies*, October 1957.

9. See A.R. Prest, 'The Expenditure Tax and Saving', *Economic Journal*, October 1959.

10. March 1956.

11. J. Meade, *The Structure and Reform of Direct Taxation* (London: George Allen and Unwin, 1978).

12. See A.C. Pigou, *Public Finance* (London: Macmillan, 1928).

13. A.R. Prest, 'The Structure and Reform of Direct Taxation', *Economic Journal*, June 1979.

14. *Journal of Political Economy*, February 1958.

15. *Op. cit.*

5 TAX ADVISER TO DEVELOPING COUNTRIES

Kaldor gave tax and budgetary advice to a variety of developing countries including India, Ceylon (now Sri Lanka), Mexico, Ghana, British Guiana (now Guyana), Turkey, Iran and Venezuela. His journeys around the world as a tax adviser started in India in 1956, and his classic Report on Indian Tax Reform is by far the most comprehensive. It is thorough and lucid in its exposure of the inadequacies of the tax structure in a typical developing country, and provides a framework of tax reform for the promotion of social justice, economic efficiency and growth. Many of the features and recommendations for tax reform in India are to be found later in his proposals for other countries, with modifications reflecting individual country circumstances. The Indian Report lays down the model, although that model itself follows closely the reforms that were suggested in his 'Plan for the Financial Stabilisation of France' (1947a) which was prepared for the French Commissariat Général du Plan in 1947 at the request of Jean Monnet (see Chapter 3). Many of his proposed tax reforms received a stormy reception from vested interests, and from workers and business alike, but he never wavered in his conviction that a fairer and broader-based tax structure in developing countries must be an integral part of any development programme.

Tax potential is rarely fully exploited in developing countries. Some measure of this is given by the fact that whereas in developed countries tax revenue as a proportion of national income averages approximately 30 per cent, in developing countries it averages about 15 per cent. Much income is not taxed at all; there is widespread avoidance and evasion; and the rich are allowed to consume heavily, particularly out of property income. Kaldor always recognised that the efficient utilisation of a country's tax potential would raise problems peculiar to each country, but he believed there were certain fundamental reforms in the tax systems of all developing countries which, if adopted, would make it possible to increase public revenue and to reduce inequities at the same time.

He accepted the classical canons of taxation: that taxation must be judged by the standards of equity, efficiency and administrative convenience. The greatest need is to use taxation to release resources for investment (without inflation) rather than to provide incentives. There are more direct ways to give incentives. Some of his proposals, however, clearly have the incentive consideration in mind. In most developing countries the tax system is neither equitable nor efficient, and is administratively cumbersome. Avoidance (legal) and evasion (illegal) are rife. Equity requires a comprehensive definition of income and non-discrimination between income sources. A major deficiency of tax systems all over the world, and particularly in developing countries, is that there is no single comprehensive tax on all income. Typically there is a 'cedular' system with separate taxes on different sources of income. Wage- and salary earners tend to be discriminated against *vis-à-vis* both owners of property and capital, and the self employed such as professional people and small traders. An equitable system should also be such that it discourages luxury consumption and makes it difficult to avoid and evade taxation. Relatively low marginal rates of taxation would discourage evasion, and also provide a greater incentive to work and invest at the same time.

Taxable capacity is not measured by income alone, but also by wealth. Equity therefore also requires the taxation of wealth. Another major deficiency of the tax system of many developing countries is anonymity in the ownership of wealth, which takes the form of bearer shares in the case of companies, or the system of *benami* in India. Gifts *inter vivos* should be taxed.

The taxation of business income should not be progressive which penalises companies just because they are large. The entire tax system should be self-reinforcing and self-checking and be based, as far as possible, on a comprehensive annual return.

These beliefs and common features of Kaldor's tax advice to developing countries led to five major recommendations for most countries. First, that *all* income (including capital gains) should be aggregated and taxed in the same way, at a progressive rate but not exceeding a maximum marginal rate of 50 per cent. Secondly, that there should be a progressive personal expenditure tax levied on rich individuals imposed where income tax leaves off. Thirdly, the institution of a wealth tax. Fourthly, the introduction of a gifts tax. And lastly, the simplification of corporation tax to be imposed at a single rate. Other miscellaneous tax reforms were recommended for individual countries.

Kaldor's first visit to India was in 1955 when he, Austin Robinson, Joan Robinson and others from Cambridge took part in a refresher course for University teachers of economics in Poona in the summer of that year at the invitation of the University of Bombay. After the seminar, he visited the Indian Planning Commission in Delhi and met the Minister of Finance, Chintaman Deshmukh who, in his capacity of Chairman of the Indian Statistical Institute, invited him to investigate the Indian tax system in the light of the revenue requirements of the second Five Year Plan. The Institute had been entrusted with the task of monitoring the long-term requirements of economic planning. Kaldor was due for sabbatical leave from Cambridge in 1956, and accepted the invitation as part of a world tour accompanied by his wife. As well as working in India, arrangements were made to give several lectures in Japan and to act as a consultant to the Economic Commission for Latin America in Santiago at the invitation of Raul Prebisch. While in Asia he was also to visit Burma, Thailand, Hong Kong, Singapore and Malaysia, giving lectures wherever he went (see 1956b; 1956c), and to pay his first visit to China. In Latin America he extended his visit to include Mexico and also Brazil, where he delivered a series of five lectures at the University of Rio de Janiero at the invitation of Roberto Campos on the theme of the Characteristics of Economic Development (1957a; see Chapter 8). What turned out to be a momentous year ended in the United States with visits to Michigan and Harvard Universities and teaching for a short while at Columbia University as the Seager Visiting Lecturer.

Work began on Indian taxation at the beginning of January 1956, based in the Indian Income Tax Office and assisted by I.S. Gulati of the Indian Statistical Institute who looked after the publication of the Tax Report when Kaldor left.[1] The 139-page document, which confined itself to personal and business taxation, was presented to the Finance Minister at the end of March. Kaldor was to return to India several times – a country he loved – including January 1984 when he gave the first Memorial Lecture inaugurated by the Reserve Bank of India in honour of his former friend the Finance Minister, Chintaman Deshmukh. His chosen theme on that occasion, however, was not taxation but the failure of monetarism (see Bibliography).

Total tax revenue in India in 1956 was only 7 per cent of national income, with very little built-in flexibility. The second Five Year

Plan envisaged additional tax revenue of Rs 450 crores,[2] while Kaldor reckoned that, given the limits to deficit finance, some Rs 1250 crores would be required. He was optimistic that such a target could be attained provided the extra burden imposed on the ordinary people was complemented by effective and progressive taxation of the very rich. The search was for a tax system appropriate for a country desiring to strike a middle road between western capitalism and eastern socialism. In launching his attack on the inadequacies of the Indian tax system, a number of pertinent observations were made on why progressive taxation had not attained its objectives in a variety of countries. First the absence of a clear and comprehensive notion of what constitutes income for tax purposes. The exclusion of certain receipts leads to the predictable result of the conversion of otherwise taxable income into such receipts. Secondly, the failure to recognise that the ownership of disposable assets confers a benefit on the owner over and above the income which the property yields. Thirdly, over-generous allowances for expenses and 'losses' to offset against taxable income. Fourthly, the failure to secure the full reporting of income; a particularly serious defect in the case of India. From a technical point of view it is quite feasible to tighten up any tax system; the problem is opposition from vested interests.

Not surprisingly, Kaldor found the Indian tax system riddled with inefficiency and inequity, with vested interests particularly powerful. To overcome the deficiencies, his proposals included broadening the tax base through the introduction of an annual tax on wealth; the taxation of capital gains; a general gifts tax; and a personal expenditure tax, combined with a comprehensive tax return and the introduction of a comprehensive reporting system on all property transfers and other capital transactions. The general object was to make the system self-enforcing and self-checking so that information provided by one taxpayer to prevent over-assessment would automatically bring to light tax evasion by others. One of the purposes of the personal expenditure and wealth tax proposals was also to reduce the need for high marginal rates of personal taxation which can act as a disincentive to work, saving and enterprise. It was an integrated package of reforms for implementation over a long period. The main detailed proposals for reform were as follows: (i) progressive income tax up to a maximum marginal rate of 45 per cent (to replace the existing highest marginal rate of 92 per cent); (ii) an annual wealth tax levied at 0.33 per cent on personal net worth (including real estate and land) over Rs 100,000 rising to 1.5 per cent over Rs 1,500,000;

(iii) capital gains chargeable to income tax, and taxed at the maximum rate when income plus realised gains exceeded Rs 25,000 (approximately £1875); (iv) a general gifts tax payable on gifts in excess of Rs 10,000, with tax levied on the recipient according to total net worth at a rate of 10 per cent up to Rs 100,000 and then at progressively higher rates up to a maximum of 80 per cent on total estates (including the value of the gift) in excess of Rs 2 million. The gifts tax was to replace the existing estate duty, once the wealth tax was in operation; and (v) a personal expenditure tax, levied on a per capita basis within the family, with children counting as one-half, at a rate of 25 per cent on personal outlay in excess of Rs 10,000 per annum, rising to 300 per cent on expenditure in excess of Rs 50,000 per adult per annum. Four of the five recommendations were accepted in principle by the government, although not in detail. The one not accepted was the reduction in the maximum rate of income tax to 45 per cent. Some of the tax proposals are worth considering individually.

The proposed wealth tax was interesting because it represented Kaldor's most detailed, yet succinct, written case for taxing wealth. The UK Royal Commission on the Taxation of Profits and Income did not consider it, and the discussion of the matter in his book on the expenditure tax was incidental to the case for taxing spending which was regarded as superior. The general case for an annual wealth tax is that income by itself is not a good measure of taxable capacity, or ability to pay. The ownership of disposable assets endows the property-owners with an inherent taxable capacity, irrespective of the money income which the asset yields. Kaldor used the example of the beggar who has nothing and the rich man who holds all his wealth in the form of jewellery and gold which yields no money income. Judged by income their capacity is the same (i.e. zero), but clearly their ability to pay is not equal and for tax purposes they should not be treated equally. Income tax is not only inequitable between those with property and those without, but also between property holders. For example, two property holders may derive the same income from property, but the value of their property may differ. One has a greater taxable capacity than the other. Because a mixture of income streams can be derived from a mixture of property values, only a combination of income and property taxes can achieve equity according to ability to pay. One counter argument is that property taxes are inequitable if property yields no income to pay the tax. This begs the whole question of what is meant by 'income'. If the property is not yielding an 'income' in some form, why is the property held and not sold for property which does yield income? It is also sometimes claimed that a property tax is administratively impossible because it is difficult to trace the ownership of property and because of valuation problems. But if property is concealed, so is income. If income is known, the wealth giving rise to the income flow should in principle be traceable. Thus income and property taxes should complement one another. Kaldor strongly recommended for India a tightening up of the methods of registration and control of property ownership. The valuation problem should be solved by taking the 'book value' of the property until it is sold. The problem of valuation then only arises with the introduction of the tax and with the transfer of property other than by sale. On introduction, valuation could rest with the taxpayer. If the Revenue Department was to dispute the value, the taxpayer should be able to specify a reserve price. If the Revenue Department still disputes, it should be able to buy up the property at the reserve price. This would discourage undervaluation or setting a reserve price above the market value which would run the risk of higher tax liability.

With a tax rate of 0.33 per cent on net worth over Rs 100,000 rising to 1.5 per cent over Rs 1.5 million, Kaldor estimated the yield from the introduction of a wealth tax of between Rs 17 and 25 crores. The Wealth Tax Act was passed by the Indian Parliament (Lok Sabha) on 29 August 1957. The actual yield averaged Rs 10 crores per annum up to 1966.

The proposal to tax capital gains was not new. India once had a capital gains tax but it was suspended in 1949 after only two years of operation before it really had time to work. Even so, it yielded Rs 6 crores on 1814 transactions. As we saw from Kaldor's Minority Report of the Royal Commission on the Taxation of Profits and Income, the exclusion of capital gains from income tax is indefensible on the grounds of equity, as well as permitting income tax avoidance by allowing income to be disguised as tax-exempt capital gains. With capital gains (including transfers on death) taxed at the same rate as ordinary income, Kaldor reckoned a long-term annual yield from the tax of between Rs 25 and 40 crores. A capital gains tax was introduced in November 1956 along with the Supplementary Budget for 1956–57.

Gifts were also to be taxed in Kaldor's Plan. He saw no logic in restricting the right to pass on property at death and not during life. Taxing one and not the other is not only illogical; it is inequitable and encourages avoidance of the former. Kaldor preferred the tax to be on the recipient rather than on the donor with the rate of tax progressive, related to the wealth of the recipient rather than to the size of the gift or the wealth of the donor. An exemption limit of Rs 10,000 was recommended for any single recipient, and gifts over this level should be taxed at 10 per cent if the net wealth of the recipient was less than Rs 100,000, and at progressively higher rates up to 80 per cent on recipients with net wealth over Rs 4 million. Taxpayers should have the option, however, of having gifts in any one year aggregated with income for income tax. The estimated yield of the tax was Rs 30 crores per annum, with an estimated loss of estate duty of only Rs 2 crores per annum. Because of loopholes and exemptions, the actual annual yield turned out to be Rs 1.5 crores up to 1966.

The proposal for a personal expenditure tax followed the argument of his book, and India became a testing ground for this new tax. Expenditure would be calculated by assessing income and deducting certain allowable expenses and expenditures. Personal consumption would exclude, for example, business expenses and all investment outlays, and only the annual benefit on capital expenditure for personal use would be taxed e.g. on houses, works of art, jewellery, and so on. Such expenditures as funeral and birth expenses, medical expenses and expenses resulting from disasters might also be exempted. Since family size differs, it was intended that the tax should be on a per capita basis, with children and 'other family' members counted as one-half of a full unit. To avoid excessive division, five adult units should be the maximum division of total expenditure on which tax is assessed. Thus the *minimum* liability to tax would be the per capita liability multiplied five times. The suggested rates of tax were 25 per cent on net expenditure per adult unit of Rs 10,000, rising to 300 per cent on net expenditure of Rs 50,000 per head per annum. The tax would replace the existing super-tax.

The expenditure tax bill was passed on 4 September 1957 and was levied for the first time during the assessment year 1958–59 on the basis of expenditure for the year ending 31 March 1958. In the first instance, it affected about 8000 assessees. Before its introduction there were many compromises leading to contradictions and loopholes. The per capita basis of assessment suggested by Kaldor was rejected, making it inequitable compared to income tax. The new Finance Minister, Mr T.T. Krishnamachari, who was persuaded by Kaldor's scheme, proposed that the tax be levied on the 'slab system on individuals and Hindu undivided families with income not less than Rs 60,000.' Persons who spent out of accumulated fortunes were not to be touched. The Select Committee of the Lok Sabha restricted the liability to tax to only those persons whose net income from all sources *after the payment of taxes* exceeded Rs 36,000, and this was accepted by Parliament. To tie the liability to expenditure tax to a minimum income limit was a serious defect and departure from the Kaldor Plan. It made it possible for people to keep income low in one year and spend heavily, while 'bringing forward' income into another year and spending little – thus effectively escaping the tax. In addition, very generous expenses and expenditures were allowable in calculating tax liability. Deductions were permitted for marriages, medical expenses, foreign education, legal fees, property, bullion, precious stones and jewellery, charitable and religious gifts, expenditure incurred by wives unless out of funds by the assessee, and so on. In addition assessees were able to make a gift of Rs 35,000 to a daughter and to claim exemption. The daughter was not liable to tax unless she spent more than Rs 36,000. These provisions invited evasion. With Members of Parliament pressing for even more concessions, the Finance Minister was quoted as saying, 'do not make the Bill more ridiculous'! Kaldor noted later how inequitable it was to allow certain 'unavoidable' expenses against expenditure tax payable by the rich but not for ordinary people against income tax. Notwithstanding the inequities, evasion and difficulties of administration, the tax stayed on the Statute Book until 1966 yielding Rs 4.3 crores. Kaldor clearly underestimated the practical difficulties of administering such a tax, and ignored some of the contradictions. On the question of evasion, if income can be concealed, expenditure is automatically concealed (unless it becomes in someone else's interest to declare it). This means that the possibilities of evasion under an expenditure tax are at least as great as under an income tax. Kaldor's idea was to have a self-enforcing system by inducing an opposition of interests between various parties so that one man's attempt to evade would lead to a higher tax liability for someone else. As one Indian economist pointed out, however, 'the average tax evader is likely to be rather cleverer than the average tax reformer; and the most skilful tax evader is certainly head and shoulders above the shrewdest tax reformer. Thus tax evasion even under the spendings tax may assume monstrous proportions.'[3] Kaldor conceded, in fact, that there was nothing to stop the production of bogus certificates pertaining to allowable expenses, and that a completely bogus set of accounts might be maintained for the purposes of evasion. If an expenditure tax is to encourage saving, there would also seem to be an inconsistency between such a tax and a wealth tax which would tax saving even before it was used for the purpose of expenditure. Indeed, in his book *An Expenditure Tax*, Kaldor argued that if an expenditure tax was introduced, the case for an annual tax on capital would be weak, and yet both taxes were recommended for India.

A substantial section of the Report on Indian Tax Reform was devoted to company taxation and the taxation of business profits. Company tax provisions in India were described as 'a perfect maze of unnecessary complications, the accretion of years of futile endeavour to reconcile fundamentally contradictory objectives'. The heavy taxation of private companies Kaldor found particularly worrying since industrialisation depends on the growth and multiplication of these companies before they are big enough to become public. Yet they find it difficult to plough back profits. If Indian legislation had been in force in the United States, 'Henry Ford might have been effectively prevented from growing beyond the stage at which he manufactured a 100 cars a year'! On the taxation of the profits of public companies, the inequity and resource misallocation involved in the more generous treatment of companies than employees over allowable expenses came in for strong criticism, although Kaldor appreciated that India could not easily move to a stricter definition independently of other countries without putting the country at a competitive disadvantage internationally. Indian companies could deduct any expenses related to maintaining the earning capacity of the enterprise whereas employees could only deduct expenses which are 'wholly, exclusively and necessarily incurred' in the performance of their job. It was recommended that deductible expenses for both companies and employees should be 'expenses that are wholly, exclusively and unavoidably incurred in earning profits of the year'. Tightening up on expenses would yield, he reckoned, about Rs 80 crores per annum, although less if the tightening up were coupled with a lower rate of tax. In general, he wanted a lower tax on a broader base than a high tax on a narrow and uncertain base. He also thought that the capital allowance provisions were too generous (and complicated). Depreciation allowances should be scrapped to be replaced by initial allowances.

A major preoccupation of the Report was how to deal with tax evasion. Kaldor's proposals must be seen as partly designed to reduce incentives to evasion and partly to erect greater obstacles. A comparison of assessable income from the national income accounts with assessed income from tax returns suggested that in manufacturing and commerce evasion represented between 50 and 60 per cent of tax income. In the professions, the ratio of assessable to assessed income was 4:1. Income tax lost through evasion was estimated to be of the order of Rs 200–300 crores.[4] Apart from reducing the incentives to evasion, Kaldor suggested a comprehensive, self-re-enforcing reporting system to cover personal income, based on code numbers and an annual statement of income from all sources. The taxpayer would be asked to supply annually seven statements, covering the whole of his transactions of a personal and business nature: (i) net wealth; (ii) income (including business accounts); (iii) gifts made and received; (iv) purchase and sale of capital assets including income yielding assets and assets for personal use; (v) borrowing and lending during the year; (vi) other capital and casual transactions; and (vii) personal expenditure less allowable deductions. Every taxpayer would have a code number and all property transfers would have to disclose the code numbers of transferer and transferee. By this system, attempts by a taxpayer to avoid one tax would increase his liability to another, and the attempt of one party to conceal a transfer would increase the tax liability of the other party if he did so. With approximately 1000 tax districts, and with not more than 2 million code numbers to be allotted, such a system should easily be manageable. A number of other attacks on the evasion of business income were suggested: (i) the compulsory auditing of the accounts of taxpayers whose income exceeded a certain minimum (ii) the extension of the use of prescribed vouchers to business transactions, (iii) increased powers of inspection and seizure of business books; and (iv) increased penalties and public exposure in the case of fraud. It was recognised however that the prevention of evasion is greatly dependent on the standards of administration in the Revenue Departments.

The Kaldor Report was praised by tax experts, but received a generally hostile press in India itself. Ursula Hicks, herself familiar with tax problems of developing countries, described the Report as 'an outstanding and remarkable achievement'.[5] From Indian economists, however, many of the reviews were highly critical.[6] Some argued that the whole set of proposals would simply encourage the hoarding of gold and other valuables. Others expressed doubts that the proposals for reform themselves would reduce tax evasion without better detection and stiffer penalties, evasion being deeply rooted in the Indian way of life. Yet others criticised Kaldor for recommending far-reaching reforms of the tax system based on such a hasty, imperfect and statistically deficient study. B.K. Nehru, a contemporary of Kaldor at the LSE from 1929 to 1933, and former Indian Ambassador to the USA and Indian High Commissioner in London, was later to say:

my distinguished contemporary Nicky Kaldor whose theoretically perfect system of direct taxation was modified by us in practice – as I warned him it would be – into an absurd monstrosity which has had the most disastrous effect on our economic development and in the dismantling of which we have not fully succeeded.[7]

Initially, most of the recommendations were implemented in one form or another. The two recommendations not acted on were a reduction in the rate of income tax to a maximum of 45 per cent, and a wealth tax on companies combined with a lower rate of profits tax which would favour those companies with a high rate of profit. The dilution of the expenditure tax and its eventual withdrawal have already been mentioned. The wealth tax excluded real estate and raised the exemption limit. The gifts tax introduced was also so riddled with loopholes and exemptions as to be virtually ineffective. The provisions of the Act made it possible, for example, for the donor to avoid tax by spreading gifts over time. The capital gains tax integrated capital gains with other forms of income but the maximum rate of tax was set at 27.5 per cent. Thus, there still existed a strong incentive to convert income into capital gains to avoid higher rates of tax on earned, and other 'unearned' income. Also, capital gains transferred *inter vivos* or on death were still exempt. When in 1959 Kaldor returned to India to give evidence to the Taxation Enquiry Commission, the need for far-reaching reforms to check tax evasion was still very apparent despite closure of some of the loopholes. His preferred scheme was for a *corps d'élite* of highly paid tax officials (on French lines), immune from the temptation of bribes, deriving instead pride and satisfaction from their social distinction as highly paid state officials.

CEYLON (SRI LANKA)

The thoroughness and incisiveness of the Report on Indian Tax Reform established Kaldor's reputation as one of the world's leading authorities on tax matters in developing countries. There followed a long line of requests from other countries for him to undertake similar diagnoses. One of the first came in 1958 from Mr Bandaranaike, the Prime Minister of Ceylon, on the recommendation of Pandit Nehru, to make recommendations for tax reform in that country (now Sri Lanka). A Report was made in 1958 on lines very similar to the proposals for India, which the government accepted, but it was not published until 1960.[8] Ironically it was published by the right-wing United National Party, after an election in March, in an attempt to show that the Bandaranaike government (and that of Dr Dahanayake who succeeded him after his assassination) did not fully implement the desirable recommendations relating to the extension of the tax base and the reduction of tax rates.

Kaldor described his suggestions for a comprehensive reform of direct taxation as 'a set of inter-related proposals designed to create a system of progressive direct taxation suited to the needs of a democratic socialist community. Their object is to provide incentives to progress at the same time as to bring about greater social and economic equality.' The proposals, as in the case of India, were aimed at eliminating both tax avoidance and tax evasion, and at bringing the taxes levied on individuals into a far closer relationship with capacity to pay, in the interests of equity and efficiency. The proposals also aimed to achieve the maximum simplicity of administration. With regard to income tax, a much tighter control of deductible business expenses was urged; and that capital gains should be aggregated with income for tax purposes. The family should be used as the basis of taxation, with tax levied on adult 'units' within the family up to a maximum of four units (with children counting as a half-unit). Each adult unit should be given a tax free allowance of Rs 2000 and then taxed according to a single schedule of rates up to a maximum of 45 per cent. Taxes on wealth, gifts and expenditure were also advocated. The suggested starting-point for the wealth tax was net family wealth of over Rs 100,000, which would be chargeable at 0.5 per cent up to Rs 500,000; then at 1 per cent between Rs 500,000 and Rs 1 million, and at 2 per cent thereafter. With regard to gifts, it was thought that an *inter vivos* tax on the recipient might raise serious administrative difficulties. The retention of the existing Estate Duty was therefore recommended, supplemented by a cumulative gifts tax levied on the donor. The rate schedule for the cumulative gifts tax should be the same as for Estate Duty. Gifts up to Rs 2000 by any one donor would be exempt, although they would be subject to expenditure tax. The expenditure tax should start where income tax leaves off, and be assessed on the family 'unit' method. After the tax free allowance of different amounts according to the number of units in the family, the expenditure tax rates should start at 25 per cent on the first Rs 5000 of expenditure rising to 50 per cent; 100 per cent; 200 per cent, and a maximum of 300 per cent on successive Rs 5000 expenditure increments. Personal expenditure would exclude business expenses, investment outlays, capital investment for personal use and gifts over Rs 2000 (already subject to gifts tax), and there would also be exemptions including all direct taxes paid, funeral, birth and marriage expenses up to a certain figure, medical expenses and the education of children abroad up to a certain limit.

In order for the recommended system to be efficient, it was proposed that all the taxes should be administered jointly. There should be a single file relating to each taxpayer and to each of the taxes, and they should all be assessed at the same time on the basis of a comprehensive return, as proposed for India. Although such a comprehensive return might look formidable, for the vast majority of people only one or two sections would need filling out: the section relating to income (including capital gains), and perhaps occasionally the section relating to gifts. Part of the reform would also include an automatic reporting system on capital (including property) transactions.

Turning to business taxation, Kaldor found the existing income plus profits tax system an unnecessary complication, and argued that there was no case for a differential charge on business income if capital gains were taxed and allowable expenses against profits were reduced. A single corporation tax of 45 per cent was recommended plus a 33.3 per cent tax on gross dividends declared in the year. Depreciation allowances should be replaced by initial allowances, and there should be a special development subsidy of 20 percent on the acquisition of *new* assets to be added to the normal capital allowance. The government of Mr Bandaranaike was strong enough at the time for many of the tax proposals to be implemented, including the expenditure tax, but successive governments were not powerful enough to enforce them.

MEXICO

A second request for Kaldor's services came in July 1960 from the Finance Minister of Mexico, Señor Antonio Ortiz-Mena, to make a study of the 'Possibilities and Conveniences of Modifying the Structure and Organisation of the Mexican Tax System'.[9] He was happy to accept the challenge, but the mission was a very sensitive one, so much so that for a whole month he remained *incognito*, locked away in a hotel in the hills outside Mexico City. He was fearful, and so were the politicians, that any attempts at major reforms of Mexico's inefficient and inequitable tax structure would cause a ferment, little short of social revolution comparable to that caused by land reform following the revolution in 1910. The Report was prepared in the course of September 1960 with the help of Mexican economists and other experts, and was submitted at the end of the month. The recommendations followed broadly the same pattern as those for India and Ceylon, but with an expenditure tax omitted on 'political grounds'. The experience of India and Ceylon had led him to the conclusion that the opposition of the property-owning classes might be so violent that other important reforms would be jeopardised. He was far from sanguine, in general, that Mexico was politically ready for a progressive reform of the tax system, but the Finance Minister insisted and promised freedom to publish the Report. In the event, it was never published, but was given instead to a series of committees for consideration. The proposals were then blocked by President Mateos and his Cabinet. Only in later years were some of the recommendations for a simplified system of income tax carried out.

Four compelling reasons for tax reform were given. First there was the simple need to raise more revenue for development purposes. Tax revenue at the time was only 9 per cent of national income. Low tax revenue was not only restricting expenditure in important areas such as health and education, but also by making the budget deficit larger it was forcing the Central Bank to pursue more restrictive monetary policies than otherwise would be the case, impairing growth and development. Secondly, Kaldor wanted to counter the regressive nature of the tax structure and the growing inequality in the distribution of income and wealth which threatened to undermine the existing social order. Five per cent of families received 40 per cent of national income in 1957. Thirdly, there was the need to reduce inefficiency and injustices in the tax system. Evasion was rife and income from the ownership of capital was favoured compared with income from work. Income from capital was hardly taxed at all. Income from land and houses was not taxed nationally; dividends were not taxed in the hands of the recipients; many types of interest payments escaped taxation, and capital gains were exempt. Moreover, wealth-holding in Mexico could be anonymous through the ownership of physical assets being transferred to legal entities, the titles to which were held in the form of bearer shares. The final motive for tax reform was to reduce luxury consumption resulting from the tax immunity of the wealthy, which Kaldor saw as an impediment to development and contributing to balance of payments difficulties.

The major recommendation in the field of income taxation was the replacement of the existing 'cedular' taxes on income with a single comprehensive tax on individuals. The maximum rate of tax, however, would be set at 40 per cent on taxable income over 84,000 pesos, to replace the existing higher marginal rates at much higher ceilings of 500,000 and 2 million pesos depending on the source of income. The anonymity in the holding of mobile property should be abolished as a precondition for a wealth tax. The suggested rates of wealth tax were 0.5 per cent on net wealth between 500,000 and 1,500,000 pesos, rising by 0.25 per cent per additional 1,000,000 pesos to 1 per cent of net wealth over 4,500,000 pesos. In the field of company taxation, the proposal was for a single rate of corporation tax on total profits to replace the existing progressive tax on distributed profits and the excess profits tax, with no exemption for new industries. To promote industrial growth, direct subsidies should be used. Depreciation allowances should be replaced by initial allowances and special development allowances might be given on newly created capital assets which could be varied between industries according to their importance in the national economy.

Mexico already possessed a gift and inheritance tax administered nationally and by the various states, levied on the recipient according to the size of the gift and discriminating between gifts to close relatives and to others. Kaldor recommended that there should be a uniform gift tax encompassing both gifts and inheritance and administered by the Federal government on behalf of the states, with the tax dependent on the wealth of the recipient including the gift. At the same time, it was suggested that the existing rates of gift tax be reduced. The first gift of up to 10,000 pesos, and further gifts of under 20,000 pesos given to persons who do not possess more than 50,000 pesos of net wealth, should be exempt altogether. Above that there should be a 10 per cent tax on gifts to individuals with wealth between 50,000 pesos and 500,000 pesos, with progressively higher rates reaching 65 per cent on gifts to those with wealth of over 3 million pesos. Had all the reforms been implemented, some extra 6000 million pesos might have been raised for the development effort, compared with actual tax revenues in 1959 of half that figure. Some reforms were introduced in early l962 following a study group that split into two camps: economists wanting a single consolidated personal income tax and lawyers wanting to proceed much more cautiously. Ortiz-Mena was in favour of a single consolidated income tax but was not in favour of Kaldor's Report being published (despite the written promise of freedom to publish) for fear that continuing reform might be jeopardised.

GHANA

Kaldor's next stop as an itinerant tax adviser was Ghana in 1961. This too was a sensitive mission, fraught with political overtones. Ghana was heading for an economic crisis as a result of the reckless and extravagant policies of the government of Dr Nkrumah, based on the (temporarily) high price of cocoa. Kaldor described the ambience of Nkrumah's government as that of a medieval court: 'Flamboyant, extravagant and corrupt'. Nkrumah himself was a charming, charismatic man, but had inflicted terrible harm on the Ghanian economy by wasteful expenditure. He also lacked the will (and the power) to deal with corrupt ministers and to take the necessary actions. The invitation to Kaldor to sort out the mess came from the Ghana High Commission at the end of April 1961. The letter read: 'I am requested by tbe President of Ghana to extend to you his personal invitation to visit him in Ghana as soon as possible. There are a number of economic, financial and budgetary questions on which my President might like to consult you.'[10] Kaldor went immediately, returning on two further occasions in June and October. By the force of his personality and expertise he made a deep impression on Nkrumah. His hold over the President was likened, by some, to the captivating powers of the ju-ju magicians!

The immediate task was to advise on the forthcoming budget in the light of the financial crisis facing the country. There was the prospect in the coming financial year of a budget deficit of over G£ 20 million and a balance of payments deficit of G£ 50 million. There was thus an urgent need to control imports and to increase the amount of taxation, as well as to reform the tax structure in various aspects. At the time, income tax yielded only G£ 5 million from companies and less than G£ 1 million from individuals. Kaldor wanted to widen the net, and particularly to shift the burden of taxation from the agricultural community to the industrial population. A whole series of measures, on Kaldor's advice, were introduced by Mr Goka, the Finance Minister, in the July budget. A new single progressive income tax was proposed on all persons in receipt of more than G£ 480 per annum; and to avoid evasion, taxation would be deducted at source. The self-employed and professional people would be taxed on 'presumptive' income and businesses would be liable at the rate of 7.5 per cent of turnover. There were also proposals to reform company taxation to prevent foreign subsidiaries escaping tax through transfer-pricing. Henceforth, companies would pay tax on profits assumed to be in the same proportion to turnover as global profits to global turnover. But the most revolutionary tax proposal of all, which precipitated a workers' strike, was for a compulsory saving scheme to aid the development effort, rather like the system of post-war credits introduced in the United Kingdom to help finance the Second World War, as Keynes had recommended (with advice from Kaldor) in his How to Pay for the War (1940). All wage- and salary-earners would be obliged to contribute 5 per cent of current income to the purchase of National Development Bonds repayable at the end of ten years and carrying tax-free interest of 4 per cent per annum payable in the form of lottery draws. For the self-employed, professional persons, individual businesses and private companies, the contribution would be 10 per cent of income assessed for income tax. Farmers would subscribe 10 per cent of the cocoa producer price of 60 shillings (i.e. 6 shillings per load). The new scheme was designed to raise G£ 11 million, in addition to the G£ 20 million extra tax revenue from the tax reforms (including increased import duties to reduce the luxury consumption of imports).

The whole package of proposals united both employees and employers against the government. The result of the tax policies and compulsory saving scheme, combined with rising food prices, was to reduce workers' real income by some 20 per cent. Port and railway workers went on strike, which was illegal in Ghana, and there was a call for a general strike to force the government to change its policies. The whole presentation of the package was badly handled, and the administration of the compulsory saving scheme ran into difficulties from the start. Sometimes there were not enough savings bonds printed, and workers found deductions from their wages very irregular. Storage also became a problem. The Minister of Finance himself, for example, received 82 5-shilling bonds a month! Eventually the scheme was withdrawn. The General Secretary of Ghana's Trade Union Council berated the workers as 'frightened by measures taken by the government to streamline the nation's pattern of expenditure, demonstrate the soundness of our finances and gear both to a programme of industrialisation.'[11]

Despite the initial hostility and setbacks to the proposals for tax reform, they proved to be a sound basis for further improvement of tax policy in the future. It would also be too facile to blame the strikes on Kaldor, as the popular press delighted in doing (particularly later at the time of his appointment as Special Adviser to the British Chancellor of the Exchequer in 1964). Reginald Green, a leading expert on the Ghanian economy (and later economic adviser to Julius Nyerere of Tanzania), absolves him of all responsibility. Writing to Kaldor in March 1965,[12] he pinpointed two 'errors' which caused the mass dissatisfaction and quasi-insurrectionary activity, neither of which were Kaldor's fault. The first was a 66.5 per cent purchase tax on lorries which had a major effect on food prices; the second was the failure by the government to explain the compulsory savings proposals to the public as a form of pension scheme as had been envisaged.

Neither the budgetary situation nor the balance of payments showed signs of improving in 1961 and when Kaldor returned later in the year three further emergency measures were urged: a drastic reduction of government spending particularly on items with a high import content; a prohibition of all luxury imports, and new loans to buy imports (e.g. use of the American PL480 programme for grain imports from the United States). He was also involved with the President and the Principal Secretary of the Budget Secretariat in the establishment of a State Planning Commission and State Control Commission. The functions of the former body were to examine and evaluate all existing development projects in accordance with a system of priorities laid down by it; to direct and supervise the formulation of a new comprehensive economic plan, and to recommend new projects. The functions of the latter body were to keep under review the financial position of the state and the general economic position of the country; to recommend necessary adjustments in expenditure and taxation, and to keep under review the organisation of the State Administration (e.g. public Boards and Corporations) to economise on expenditure and scarce administrative resources.

In the ensuing years, he continued to advise Nkrumah by correspondence from Cambridge, and then in 1963 he returned to Ghana again to participate in a conference on Ghana's first Seven Year Development Plan. In 1963, the foreign exchange situation was still acute with reserves equal to only five months' import supply and forecast to fall still further. In a letter on the Foreign Exchange Position in April[13] he urged a further tightening of import licences; import procurement at more favourable prices, and an international campaign to secure higher prices for cocoa, manganese and bauxite. Control of the terms of trade was the major theme of his contribution to the discussion of Ghana's Seven Year Plan, and he urged Ghana to take control of the world cocoa market using an export quota system in collaboration with the small number of other producers.

BRITISH GUIANA (GUYANA)

No sooner had Kaldor returned from Ghana in 1961 than an urgent request came to undertake a similar overview of the financial and economic situation in British Guiana. The Finance Minister, Charles Jacob, on behalf of the Prime Minister, Dr Cheddi Jagan, wrote saying: 'an expert is needed to make a comprehensive examination of our tax structure and to recommend changes thought desirable for the purpose not only of increasing revenue but also distributing the tax burden more equitably.'[14] Financial assistance for the mission was sought and received under the Technical Assistance Programme of the United Nations. The country's finances were in a parlous state. There was a prospective budget deficit of $7 million, and the international reserve position was extremely weak due to a deficit on current account and heavy capital outflows. There was both an external and internal loss of confidence in economic management. Domestic depositors were withdrawing money from post office savings accounts and the new building societies, and restrictions on capital flight added to the sense of insecurity. The country also lacked a Central Bank to operate an effective monetary policy.

Kaldor arrived in the country on the 11th December; he stayed ten days, and his Report was presented to the Finance Minister on the 30th. It was prepared with extraordinary speed by any standards. The immediate object was to protect the balance of payments, by a combination of exchange controls and an increase in import and excise duties, and to increase tax revenue by some $10 million to cover the budget deficit and to provide a surplus on the government revenue account of $3 million for development purposes. Exchange controls ran into trouble right from the start. First, they were largely ineffective because the currency was shared with other territories participating in the Eastern Caribbean Currency Board. Secondly, the IMF objected to the request for the bank notes to be overprinted for control to be exercised. On the tax front detailed recommendations were made relating to personal and company taxation, and for new taxes on capital gains, property and gifts, as well as proposals for a compulsory savings scheme on the lines introduced in Ghana. Virtually all the proposals were accepted by the government and were contained in the budget statement of 31st January 1962. Most outside observers thought that the budget was a realistic attempt to grapple with the economic problems of the country, and was certainly not confiscatory. Inside the country, however, the mood was very different. Such was the public hostility, incited by the press and the two Opposition Leaders, Mr Forbes Burnham and Mr Peter D'Aguiar, that the budget debate was delayed for twelve days and then further postponed owing to a general strike called for 13 February. The strike lasted six days during which time there were serious anti-government riots. Sixty thousand demonstrators stormed the Parliament building; the Finance Minister's house was stoned; one policeman and four rioters were killed; there was massive destruction of property, and 500 British troops were called in to assist the police in restoring calm. There had developed an unholy alliance between the middle class, the civil service, private capital and the Georgetown working class against the Jagan government, and the new budget proposals provided one of the sparks to ignite an already smouldering (partly racial) political powder-keg.[15] Various elements in society were concerned about Jagan flirting with communism, and that this might become the country's political complexion on independence. The budget measures were portrayed in the press as the thin end of the wedge of communism.

The civil service was unhappy because the extra pay recommended by the Guillebaud Report had not been paid. Big business was even more unhappy because of the proposals to force companies (mainly foreign) to pay tax. Tax avoidance and evasion through transfer-pricing was commonplace. An amendment to the law was proposed which would deem the profits of a subsidiary company to be no lower as a proportion of the parent company's total profits than the subsidiary's share of total turnover, unless the subsidiary company could prove that it transacted no business with the parent company. It was also proposed that any person carrying on business should be required to make a minimum annual contribution to the government based on the turnover of business to ensure that no business carried on year after year showing continual losses and paying no tax. This would not alter the provision for losses to be offset against profits for tax purposes, but only against profits from the *same source*. There was the further intention to exercise tighter control of business expenses (including advertising) and directors' emoluments offsettable against tax. Kaldor was also against the system of giving a five-year tax holiday to newly-established industries in the country as a means of promoting industrial development, maintaining that foreign companies would come in any case if the political climate was right and the opportunities for making profits were sufficiently lucrative. Instead, a write-off of 70 per cent of any new capital expenditure incurred in the first five years of operation was proposed.

The personal tax proposals antagonised both the middle and working classes. With the existing personal allowances only a small minority of employees paid tax. Kaldor thought it desirable in a democracy that everyone should make some tax contribution above a certain minimum income, however small. A drastic reduction in personal allowances was therefore proposed, estimated to save $1 million, together with the introduction of the PAYE system with a full range of progressive tax rates. The middle class were incensed by the new range of taxes outlined – on capital gains, property and gifts – and by the rise in import duties and excise tax on consumption goods including cars, fabrics, durable consumer goods, alcohol and tobacco. The duty increase was to be just over 50 per cent and expected to yield $5.4 billion additional revenue, and another $1.1 million would come from parallel increases in excise duties on spirits and beer. To administer the new taxes there was to be a new statistics and intelligence department within the Inland Revenue, and a new investigation and valuation section.

Undoubtedly the most contentious proposal, however, which inflamed the trade unions, and companies as well, was the compulsory saving scheme, the purpose of which was never fully conveyed to the public. The scheme was to operate in the same way as in Ghana with monthly deductions of 5 per cent of wages and salaries for workers earning more than $100 dollars per month (and 10 per cent of taxable income of companies) in return for government bonds repayable with accrued interest after seven years. There would be two types of bonds: straight interest bearing bonds or lottery bonds with large cash prizes paid. The straight interest bearing bonds would be repayable after seven years at 130 per cent of the face value of the bond equal to a compound interest rate of 3.65 per cent. The lottery bonds would be repayable at 110 per cent of face value with 2 per cent of the face value of bonds given away as prizes each year. The scheme was estimated to yield over $5 million from companies and individuals, which would have been a substantial release of resources for the development effort, but the scheme was uniformly opposed. Huge placards in the streets of Georgetown equated 'saving', and 'slaving'. After the general strike had been called, the removal of the compulsory savings scheme was one of the major conditions listed by the Trade Union Congress for a return to work. In addition there should be no change in income tax; not more than 5 cents added to the price of soft drinks and rum; no increase in company taxation, and no more talk of nationalisation. The unions in British Guiana were largely company unions and sided with big business. Indeed the general strike was supported by the companies who continued to pay the workers.

The strike did have some effect. Many of the budget proposals were modified, including the compulsory savings scheme, which was renamed 'The National Development Savings Scheme', with workers earning less than $300 a month exempt.[16] Advising the government at the time was Sidney Dell. He had been released by the United Nations in early February 1962, under pressure from

Kaldor, and became, *faute de mieux*, embroiled in the budgetary exercise. Dell was anxious that the principles laid down in the Kaldor plan should be adhered to, but was in favour of taking a much softer approach, particularly with respect to the treatment of foreign companies and exchange control. Kaldor, now remote from the scene of action, did not at first agree with Dell's caution and there were several impetuous exchanges between Georgetown and Cambridge but later he came to accept the wisdom of Dell's position. The press reports emanating from British Guiana referred to Kaldor's proposals as communist-inspired, which the British press latched on to and revelled in exposing him as a trouble-maker in developing countries. Kaldor defended himself against the charges in letters to *The Times*.[17] In view of the precarious financial situation of the country he wondered whether any responsible adviser could, or would, have tendered any very different advice either as to the amount or the kind of taxes raised. It is worth noting too that the Commonwealth Commission,[18] appointed in early March to enquire into the origins of the disturbances, reached the anodyne conclusion that the 1962 budget was not responsible. Kaldor himself explained the happenings as a political conspiracy to oust Dr Jagan and his government.[19] The Commission of Inquiry, however, found no evidence of a plot to overthrow the government by force. It was a case of spontaneous combustion fermented by a number of forces.

After Kaldor returned to England, he continued to correspond with Charles Jacob, the Finance Minister, on a range of political and economic matters. He expressed concern over the continued presence of British troops in the country and urged the formation of a coalition government with Forbes Burnham. He also advised on the modified budgetary proposals which were gradually introduced between 1962 and 1964, and on drafts of the Bank of Guyana and Currency Bill containing proposals for a Central Bank and a separate currency.

TURKEY

Later in 1962, Kaldor was asked by the State Planning Organisation of Turkey, under the auspices of the British technical assistance programme, to prepare a memorandum on the problems of fiscal reform in Turkey for the confidential use of the Prime Minister, Mr Ismet Inönü, and his advisers. This was against the background of a Report of the Tax Reform Commission, which Kaldor believed, having read the summary in German, was totally misguided, giving more concessions to income tax-payers who were already favourably treated and which recommended that the family cease to be the unit for taxation. Kaldor's Report on the Turkish System presented to the Prime Minister on 21 April integrated much more fully than hitherto his thinking on tax reform with the development difficulties of less developed countries. For example, there was specific reference to the important role of agriculture and the need to induce a faster rate of growth of agricultural productivity. The target for tax revenue in Turkey in 1963 was put at 10,000 million Turkish lire (TL) or 3500 million more than in 1961. An extra TL 1000 million was expected to accrue naturally, leaving tax reform to raise the extra TL 2500 million. To achieve the target growth rate of 7 per cent per annum, a required investment ratio of 18 per cent was estimated implying a cut in current consumption of at least 3 per cent of GNP. Taxing the rich to reduce luxury consumption would be necessary but not sufficient to achieve the growth target. More investment requires more labour, and more labour requires more wage goods from the agricultural sector. Equally, it is the supply of foodstuffs and other land-based products which determines the autonomous demand for the products of industry and other sectors of the economy (see Chapter 8). Thus Kaldor argued that tax reform must give the highest priority to raising the level and growth of agricultural productivity. The Turkish agricultural sector was hardly taxed at all. Agriculture accounted for 42.5 per cent of net domestic product, yet contributed only 0.8 per cent to total direct taxation. Because a lot of agricultural income was directly consumed, it also bore a less than proportionate share of indirect taxation. Kaldor reckoned that agriculture ought to yield at least TL 1000 million in taxation which would still amount to only 5 per cent of agricultural income. He argued against a conventional income tax on agriculture, however, on the grounds that it would be clumsy and inefficient, and in any case the accountancy required would be alien to the agricultural sector. Instead, a new land tax was proposed based on the *potential* output of land (i.e. the output that land would yield if managed with average efficiency), which would be progressive based on the size of the owner's land-holding and wealth. The idea of taxing the *potential* output of the land was designed to encourage the most efficient and fullest use of the land since the tax liability would be incurred whether the land was used or not. And making the tax progressive would act as a potent instrument for land reform, encouraging the redistribution of land to smaller and more efficient farmers. It was reckoned that the burden of the tax would not fall on more than 17 per cent of families with relatively large land holdings, and would not exceed 15 per cent of the net product of the land. These proposals were strongly supported by agricultural experts in Turkey, including officials from the United Nations Food and Agricultural Organisation.

In addition to the major proposal for the taxation of agriculture, Kaldor made various proposals for the taxation of business profits and capital, and for a whole series of miscellaneous 'taxes' designed to deal with specific difficulties including the taxation of road users; a building tax; fees for import licences; and a rise in the prices of goods of state enterprises. Most of the proposals, however, including the land tax, sank without trace. The State Planning Organisation adopted the Report enthusiastically, and it was supported by the Planning Minister; but it was opposed by the Cabinet who represented the landed interest, which led in turn to the collective resignation of four of the leading officials of the State Planning Organisation.

IRAN

Kaldor's appointment in 1964 as Special Adviser on Taxation to the British Chancellor of the Exchequer curtailed his activities abroad, but in 1966 he took time off to advise the Prime Minister of Iran, Mr Hoveyda, on issues relating to tax policy and economic policy in general. The letter of invitation read: 'during your stay . . . the Iranian government would wish to benefit from your wisdom, expertise and recommendations with regard to certain fiscal and monetary questions.'[20] The invitation was largely on the recommendation of the Shadow Chancellor of the Exchequer, Reginald Maudling, who had been on a fact-finding mission to the country. When Kaldor remarked to Maudling that he thought it odd that he should have suggested a Labour man as adviser, Maudling's response was that he thought it was a convenient way of getting him out of the Treasury! The specific brief was to advise on the best way to defer the consumption effects of increases in the pay of civil servants.

His Report was submitted after eight days of work, with the conclusion that the only practical method of deferring consumption was some form of compulsory saving. Three schemes were outlined. First the deferment of consumption for a fixed period. Secondly, deferment for an indefinite period, like post-war credits in the UK during the Second World War. Thirdly, deferment until retiring age. This last scheme would be analogous to a compulsory endowment policy in favour of the employees which could, if desired, be combined with an element of life insurance. Kaldor favoured the last scheme because it would be more popular and acceptable from an economic point of view. Such a scheme could come into effect immediately, which would give confidence, and the bunching of payments would be avoided. A continuing scheme of this type, moreover, would be more than self-financing because if the number of government employees grew, payments into the scheme would always exceed payments out, and the size of the fund would grow indefinitely. The scheme would therefore secure not just a temporary deferment of consumption but a permanent deferment. It was suggested, in fact, that the scheme might be extended to the private sector. The only drawback to the scheme would be the administrative apparatus necessary to keep records.

In his observations on economic policy, Kaldor expressed approval of the progress towards land reform if this resulted in a steadily rising surplus of food production over rural self-consumption. As in Turkey, he regarded this as the key to faster growth of the industrial sector without inflation. A number of measures and policies were suggested to make land reform a success: the extension of credit to farmers, the better organisation of marketing, an efficient agricultural extension service for the training of farmers and the introduction of improved seeds, rural education, irrigation, and improved communications between rural and urban areas. Agriculture he believed should have priority over industry for at least five to ten years. With increases in marketable food supplies, industrial activities would follow automatically, while the reverse is not true, and industrialisation would be retarded. Industrialisation, in turn, should be export-oriented to pay for imports, not import-substitution-oriented which would impair growth and development in the long run.

Kaldor also argued the case for a more elastic tax system to meet the growing demand for more public expenditure. Several critical observations were made on the new Income Tax Bill that was before Parliament at the time: 'it is a most unsatisfactory piece of legislation that seems quite unsuited to Iran.' He noted particularly the inequity in the tax system whereby wage- and salary-earners paid 7–8 per cent of their income in tax while tax revenue from income on capital amounted to only 1.5 per cent. Several specific amendments to the new tax bill were suggested. Particularly he proposed scrapping existing business taxes in favour of a flat rate 'value added tax' – say 5 to 10 per cent on profits, interest, rent and wages and salaries. This would give greater certainty and could be collected at a fraction of the existing cost and effort. Two new taxes were also proposed to boost revenue: a production tax, and an annual tax on the value of urban properties. The production tax would be a sales tax on consumption goods levied at the factory stage. This would reduce excessive protection given to domestic industries and raise revenue at the same time. The tax on urban properties would be the easiest way to levy tax on property owners.

A tangible expression of gratitude for Kaldor's help and advice was the gift to his wife from the Prime Minister of a fine Persian carpet chosen by Clarisse herself.

VENEZUELA

The request for Kaldor's services as a fiscal adviser in Venezuela in 1976 came through the Foreign Office from Mr Gumersindo Rodriguez, the Minister of Coordination and Planning, who had met Kaldor earlier in the year in London. A Tax Bill had been put before Congress early in November and the Minister wanted his suggestions and recommendations for revision, as well as advice on broader issues of public finance. Having resigned from the Treasury earlier in the year, and retired from the University, he was free and keen to offer his services to another developing country after a ten-year lapse. His Report was presented on 10 December. In Venezuela's case more importance was attached to the structural aspects of fiscal reform than to the revenue raising aspects. He questioned whether additional tax revenue was needed given the small size of the projected budget deficit and the anticipation that the balance of payments would continue to be in surplus. He regarded the growth target of 13 per cent per annum for the manufacturing sector as extremely ambitious in view of sectoral bottlenecks. The lack of managerial talent and skilled labour were mentioned specifically; and he doubted whether reduced consumption through increased taxation would ease such bottlenecks. In these circumstances physical controls over the allocation of resources would be required.

A number of specific comments were made on the tax situation. The smooth progression of the income tax structure was praised, but he saw no justification for exempting the first 30 per cent of income. He also criticised the fact that the maximum rate of tax did not bite until a very high level of income had been reached (in excess of Bs 2 million).[21] The idea of taxing business people on 'presumed' income was also praised. This would tackle evasion and be a way of taxing expenditure and reducing luxury consumption.

He had doubts, however, about certain features of the company tax structure, particularly its progressive nature and the high marginal rate of 55 per cent. Companies should not be discriminated against merely on account of their size. On the other hand he supported the removal of the 40 per cent credit on dividends, and the proposal for a 10 per cent surcharge on retained profits if not reinvested in the enterprise after three years. At the time, company taxation was only 4.6 per cent of the total profits and rents suggesting widespread avoidance and evasion. To plug loopholes Kaldor proposed the abolition of all 'exoneracione' (exonerations) and the use of direct subsidies to investment instead. Bribery and corruption should be tackled by raising the status and remuneration of tax officials creating a corps d'élite similar to the French 'Inspecteurs des Finances'. This was a common feature of his tax advice to all developing countries. His Report was published in Revista Haciende, the official journal of the Ministry of Finance, and was widely quoted in the press with such headlines as 'Kaldor against the fiscal reform'.

CONCLUSIONS

Two major themes recur throughout Kaldor's writings and proposals for tax reform in developing countries. The first is the desirability of broadening the tax base and reducing tax rates in the interests of equity and efficiency. The second is the necessity of a comprehensive reporting system to reduce evasion and avoidance. In most of the countries he was privileged to visit, the politicians accepted the advice and in some cases tried hard to effect reform, but as Kaldor said in his own retrospective reflections on his role as a tax adviser,[22] it became clear that the power behind the scenes of the wealthy property-owning classes was very much greater than the political leaders suspected. In India there was bitter opposition in Cabinet and Parliament and the reforms were considerably diluted; the same was true in Ceylon. In Mexico and Turkey, the proposals were blocked even before the legislative stage. In Ghana and British Guiana, the proposals before Parliament led to attempts to overthrow the governments through strike action. Through subtle misrepresentation of the issues and measures involved, the monied interests recruited the workers to their cause. The workers in British Guiana, for example, demanded the withdrawal of the anti-avoidance provisions relating to the taxation of business profits. Similarly in Ghana, the railway unions insisted on the withdrawal of the new tax provisions on foreign companies and of the new property tax and purchase tax on luxury goods, none of which affected the workers. As Kaldor later remarked, 'the moneyed interest is capable of exerting its influence in peculiar ways!

Vested interests, of course, are not confined to developing countries. The City columnists of many British newspapers were later to use the events in developing countries where Kaldor had visited to cast doubt on his suitability and desirability as a tax adviser to Mr Callaghan. John Chown of the *Sunday Telegraph*, recalling the events in British Guiana, wrote an article 'The Kaldor System in Operation'[23] including the cryptic rhetorical question: 'It couldn't happen here – or could it?' And James Macmillan of the *Daily Express* reminded his readers in 1966 in even more sensational terms, 'wherever [Kaldor] has proferred advice from India to Ghana, from Turkey to Ceylon, it has been followed by revolution, inflation and toppling governments'.[24]

Despite the setbacks and disappointments (not to mention misrepresentation), Kaldor was unapologetic: 'Progressive taxation is, in the end, the only alternative to complete expropriation through violent revolution.' He believed firmly that the economic adviser must stick with his brief of advising, to the best of his technical knowledge and competence, on the best means of achieving economic and social aims within the democratic framework.

NOTES

1. *Indian Tax Reform: Report of a Survey by Nicholas Kaldor* (Delhi: Dept. of Economic Affairs, Ministry of Finance, 1956).
2. One crore is equal to 10 million rupees, and in 1956 the exchange rate was 13.3 rupees to the pound.
3. O. Prakash, 'An Indian View of the Expenditure Tax', *Manchester School*, January 1958.
4. The Indian tax authorities would only admit to one-tenth of this figure.
5. U. Hicks, 'Mr Kaldor's Plan for the Reform of Indian Taxes', *Economic Journal*, March 1958.
6. e.g. G.C. Mandal, 'Kaldor on Indian Tax Reform', *Indian Journal of Economics*, January 1957; book review by R.N. Bhargava, in *British Tax Review*, June 1957; O. Prakash, 'An Indian View of the Expenditure Tax', *Manchester School*, January 1958.
7. From J. Abse (ed.), *In My LSE* (London: Robson Books, 1977).
8. *Suggestions for a Comprehensive Reform of Direct Taxation*, Sessional paper IV—1960 (Colombo: Ceylon Government Publications Bureau, 9 April 1960). The decision not to publish was related to the racial and other disturbances in the country at the time.

9. Letter of 6 July 1960.

10. Letter of 24 April 1961.

11. Quoted in T. Killick, *Development Economics in Action: A Study of Economic Policies in Ghana* (Heinemann, 1978).

12. Letter dated 30 March 1965.

13. Letter to Nkrumah dated 8 April 1963.

14. Letter dated 12 October 1962.

15. Kaldor got into trouble for implying in an interview with Tom Stacey of the *Sunday Times* that the negroes were partly behind the trouble, being more susceptible to bribes from businessmen. See *Sunday Times*, 18 February 1962, and Kaldor's reply, 25 February.

16. The savings levy was eventually declared illegal by the Courts.

17. 20 February; 1 March.

18. *Report of the Commission of Inquiry into Disturbances in British Guiana in February 1962*, Colonial White Paper No. 354 (London: HMSO 1962).

19. Letter to *The Times*, 18 February 1962.

20. Letter dated 12 April 1966.

21. Bs 7.14 = £1.

22. *Introduction to Collected Essays* (Volume 3), 1964.

23. 6 December 1964.

24. 24 May 1966.

1. As a small boy, with Mother (Mimi), Father (Julius) and sister in Budapest.

2. On graduation from the London School of Economics, 1930.

3. John Hicks (left) and Kaldor walking in the Austrian Alps, 1933.

4. Kaldor and his wife Clarisse, 1935.

5. As Director of Research at the ECE, Geneva, 1948.

6. The Kaldor children with Clarisse, 1950. From left to right: Frances; Penny; Mary; Katherine.

"Balogh and Kaldor, you can take the day off—I'm embarrassingly rich in foreign advisers"

PUPPET SHOW *by WIJESOMA*

7. Kaldor as adviser to the Wilson Labour Government; and 'pulling the strings' in the Ceylon Parliament, 1958.

8. Induction to the House of Lords, 1974.

9. Receiving (from Professor B. Schefold) an Honorary Degree from the University of Frankfurt, 1982.

10. In front of his old elementary school in Budapest.

6 GROWTH AND
DISTRIBUTION THEORY

In the economics profession Kaldor is perhaps best known for his profound and sustained contributions to the theory of growth and distribution, the first of which (1956a) was written in the interval between his work for the Royal Commission on the Taxation of Profits and Income and his departure for India in 1956, and which occupied his mind into his period of office as Special Adviser to the Chancellor of the Exchequer (see 1956c; 1957c; 1961a; 1962b; 1962e; 1963b; 1966a). This was the second great theoretical epoch in Kaldor's academic life. The task he embarked on in these exciting years (while continuing to advise developing countries on tax matters) was no less than to explain the dynamics of the capitalist system in the Keynesian tradition in order to provide an alternative to the neoclassical theory of growth and distribution, and to undermine the pessimism of classical theory (particularly of Ricardo and Marx) at the same time. Neoclassical distribution theory had gripped the economics profession for over half a century, and neoclassical growth theory looked like doing likewise in response to the disequilibrium theory of Harrod:[1] while classical growth and distribution theory was clearly at variance with the facts. The outcome of his thinking was a revolution in thought significant enough to form a distinct school of economists with disciples throughout the world, variously called neo- or post-Keynesians.

He was not alone in this intellectual assault on prevailing orthodoxy. He had powerful allies in Joan Robinson, Richard Kahn and Luigi Pasinetti, who in their various ways contributed to the intellectual revolution. By the sheer volume of her writing and missionary zeal, Joan Robinson in particular must be singled out as co-founder and co-leader of the School. Both of them raised awkward questions relating to the neoclassical paradigm, and both became *bêtes noires* of large sections of the orthodox economics

159

establishment, particularly in the United States. During Kaldor's tenure as Visiting Ford Research Professor at the University of California in 1959–60, at the zenith of the neoclassical–Cambridge controversies, he became affectionately known in economics circles as the *'enfant terrible* of the Bay area'. Joan Robinson's approach, however, differed in some respects to Kaldor's. For one thing, she generally eschewed mathematics and formal model-building while Kaldor, with the help of Champernowne and Mirrlees, attempted to give his models greater precision. Robinson's excuse, particularly in American company, used to be that she knew no mathematics which forced her to think – intended as a jibe at the slick mathematics based on unreal assumptions of the neoclassical school. Robinson was also ada-mant that even in the long run steady growth with unemployment is possible – the bastard golden age – while in most of Kaldor's models the assumption of *long run* full employment is retained. To emphasise the point, Samuelson in an assessment of post-Keynesian economics, once made a jocular reference to the invisible hand of Jean-Baptiste Kaldor.[2]

While the Cambridge triumvirate of Kaldor, Robinson and Kahn were united against neoclassical orthodoxy, there was infighting and disagreement among themselves which frequently surfaced in private correspondence. Kahn disputed with Kaldor over whether Keynesian analysis can be applied as a distribution theory, and later there were acrimonious exchanges between Robinson and Kaldor over production functions and technical progress functions leading on one occasion to Kaldor accusing Robinson of being a neoclassicist! Personal rivalry and petty jealousy over intellectual property seems to have played a major part in the internecine strife, with Kahn accusing Kaldor, for example, of rushing into print with his distribution theory to deprive Robinson of priority.

At the same time as questioning and undermining the tenets of neoclassical theory as an adequate description of how economies actually behave, Kaldor also wanted to contrast his models with the pessimistic outlook of the classical economists: the gloom and doom stemming from the subsistence wage theory of Ricardo; undiluted diminishing returns, and the Marxian assertion of the falling rate of profit. In his pathbreaking paper on distribution (1956a), classical theory is taken to task, before outlining his own macroeconomic theory of distribution based on the idea of the 'widow's cruse' found in Keynes' *Treatise on Money*, Volume 1 (1930) and in the work of Kalecki.[3] For Ricardo, the laws that govern distributive shares were the 'principal problem in Political Economy'. Ricardo thought that relative shares would differ according to the stage of society, yet historically relative shares have altered very little. Kaldor argued,

no hypothesis as regards the forces determining distributive shares could be intellectually satisfying unless it succeeded in accounting for the relative stability of these shares in the advanced capitalist economies over the last 100 years or so, despite the phenomenal changes in the techniques of production, in the accumulation of capital relative to labour and in real income per head.

In Ricardo's theory rent is determined by the difference between the output of labour on 'average' and 'marginal' land, with the remainder of the product divided between wages and profits. Labour is paid a subsistence wage, and profits are a residual which determines the rate of capital accumulation. The demand for labour is determined by the rate of accumulation, not by labour's marginal product. Ricardo then predicted that as the intensity of land cultivation increased, rent would rise and profits would become squeezed between rent and wages, bringing capital accumulation to a halt and heralding the stationary state. In Ricardo's theory, profits determine investment, a relationship that Kaldor and the neo-Keynesians were later to reverse.

Marx's theory also predicts crisis due to falling profits, although by a different mechanism from the one suggested by Ricardo. Kaldor, like Keynes, never had much time for Marx. It is part of the Cambridge hearsay that Keynes never read *Das Kapital*, although he did read the correspondence between Marx and Engels, published in 1934. But he says in his famous letter to George Bernard Shaw (1 January 1935) – the same letter in which he confidently predicted that the *General Theory* would revolutionise the way the world thought about economic problems – 'I've made another shot at old K.M. [Karl Marx] last week without making much progress... if you tell me that they [Marx and Engels] have discovered a clue to the economic riddle, still I am beaten. I can discover nothing but out-of-date controversialising'.[4] Kaldor's first (public) assault on Marxist growth and distribution theory came in a lecture at the University of Peking in 1956. While in India as a tax adviser he mentioned to Prime Minister Nehru that he would be interested to visit China and this was arranged through Nehru's nephew who was Indian Ambassador to China. An added bonus was a meeting with Mao Tse-Tung. Ken Galbraith was also in India at the time and jealous of Kaldor's trip to China at a time when very few foreign visitors were permitted, least of all Americans. In his autobiography, Galbraith recalls the amusing, but quite typical, story that the Kaldors, having bade

farewell to their friends, were to return two hours later having
forgotten their passports![5] The visit elicited a considerable amount
of interest in the press. There was a leading article in The *Manchester
Guardian* and Kaldor gave a full-scale interview to Henry
Lieberman of the *New York Times*,[6] in which he related his
impressions of China and the contents of the Peking lecture.

His talk in a communist country was a bold and controversial
one, being devoted to a fundamental critique of the Marxist theory
of capitalist development. He took issue with the view that the
progress of capitalism must involve ever-widening economic
crises and that the capitalist system must finally collapse through
its own 'contradictions'. Unemployment, fluctuations and growing
concentration of economic power are not inevitable features of
capitalist evolution. 'Men can control the endogenous forces of
human society in much the same way as through science we can
control the forces of nature.' Since Marx's predictions have not
materialised, it is pertinent to ask, where did Marx go wrong?
There are three important strands to Marx's theory of capitalism.
First, that the wages of labour are determined by the necessary
minimum subsistence level, and profit is the difference between
output per man and minimum consumption per man. There is no
analytic distinction in Marx between profits and rent. Second, that
labour supply exceeds demand giving a reserve army of unemployed which is essential to the functioning of capitalism. Third,
that profits must be reinvested for capitalists to compete: 'Accumulate, accumulate, that is Moses and the Prophets.' The share of
profits in output (P/Y) is determined by surplus value: $SV = Y - CL$,
where Y is total money income, C is consumption per worker and L
is the number of workers. Therefore $P/Y = SV/(SV + CL)$, where CL
is the 'variable' capital of the economy. The problem Marx saw was
that as accumulation took place, the reserve army of unemployed
would disappear, driving wages up and profits down. In Kaldor's
view, Marx's fundamental error was to confuse money and real
wages. Money wages may rise, but what happens to profits also
depends on prices, and, in the growing economy, on what happens
to real wages relative to productivity. A rise in money wages does
not necessarily mean a reduction in profits if productivity and
prices are also rising. There is thus no basis for the presumption of
a falling rate of profit. Marx attempted to explain his prediction in
terms of a rise in the ratio of fixed to 'variable' capital (or what he
called the organic composition of capital) but this will not do
because with an increase in the amount of capital per head, output
per head will rise and thus the rate of profit could equally rise.[7]

Furthermore, if real wages are fixed at subsistence, every increase in output per head must be associated with a fall in labour's share of income and a rise in the share of profits.

Kaldor then proceeded to contrast Marx and Keynes, showing that in Keynesian theory money and real wages are determined by fundamentally different forces. The real wage must be such as to lead to a division between wages and profits which makes the aggregate supply and demand for goods equal. If the real wage leads to such a division as to cause excess demand, prices rise reducing the real wage and aggregate demand; contrawise, if there is excess supply prices fall, increasing the real wage and aggregate demand. Either way real wages may move quite differently from money wages.[8] Kaldor went on to outline his own neo-Keynesian distribution theory, based on his 1956 paper. Before presenting this in some detail, his critique of neoclassical distribution theory also needs considering.

He first voiced disquiet over neoclassical theory in his entry on 'The Theory of Distribution', in the *Chambers Encyclopedia* (1948a), and the criticisms are repeated in the 1956 paper. The basic proposition of neoclassical distribution theory is that any variable factor of production will be rewarded according to its marginal product and that relative shares of the national product will therefore be related to relative marginal products (that is, the marginal rate of substitution between factors) and the relative quantities of factors employed. There are a number of problems with this theory. First, the theory implies perfect competition, profit-maximisation and the absence of external economies and diseconomies. Secondly, the theory requires constant returns to scale because, as the clergyman economist, Philip Wicksteed, first showed in 1894,[9] if there are not constant returns there will be an 'adding up' problem. If there are increasing returns, and factors get paid their marginal products, the total product will be more than exhausted, and if there are decreasing returns to scale, the total product will be less than exhausted. Euler's theorem provides the formal proof. Thirdly, there is the problem of the meaning and measurement of capital as a factor of production. Capital, because of its heterogeneity, cannot be aggregated in physical units and therefore, in the first instance, must be measured in money units. But since the value of capital is the capitalised value of income streams this already assumes a certain rate of profit, or rate of interest, on the basis of which the services of capital accruing in different periods in the future, or the costs incurred at different dates in the past, are made equivalent. Thus to derive the marginal product of capital it is necessary to know its 'price' in the first place.

The theory of marginal productivity factor pricing and distribution is, according to Kaldor, circular. It is also circular in the sense that for distributive shares to be related to relative marginal products, through the elasticity of substitution, the rate of profit must be known and yet this is what needs to be determined. The possibility that the marginal product and rate of profit may be jointly determined is not entertained.

DISTRIBUTION THEORY

Kaldor's own macro-theory of distribution is based on the insight of Keynes that entrepreneurial incomes are the result of their expenditure decisions rather than the other way round, which Kaldor described as 'perhaps the most important difference between Keynesian and pre-Keynesian habits of thought'. The insight occurs in the *Treatise on Money* Vol. 1 (p. 139) where profits are likened to a 'widow's cruse':

If entrepreneurs chose to spend a portion of their profits on consumption (and there is, of course, nothing to prevent them from doing this), the effect is to increase the profits on the sale of liquid consumption goods by an amount exactly equal to the amount of profits which have been thus expended. ... Thus, however much of their profits entrepreneurs expend on consumption, the increment of wealth belonging to entrepreneurs remains the same as before. Thus profits, as a source of capital increment for entrepreneurs, are a widow's cruse which remains undepleted however much of them may be devoted to riotous living. When on the other hand entrepreneurs are making losses, and seek to recoup those losses by curtailing their normal expenditure on consumption i.e. by saving more, the cruse becomes a Danaid Jar which can never be filled up; for the effect of this reduced expenditure is to inflict on the producers of consumption goods a loss of equal amount. Thus the diminution of their wealth as a class is as great, in spite of their saving, as it was before.

Just as the Keynesian multiplier can be used to determine the level of income given the distribution of income, Kaldor saw the potential of using multiplier analysis to determine the distribution of income (that is, the relation between prices and wages) given the level of income. Kaldor first thought of using the multiplier technique for the purpose of a theory of distribution when as a member of the Royal Commission on the Taxation of Profits and Income he attempted to analyse the ultimate incidence of profits taxation under full employment. Kalecki's paper 'A Theory of Profits'[10] was also influential where, in effect, the same notion of the 'widow's cruse' is used for showing why the level and fluctuations of output are particularly dependent on entrepreneurial behaviour. Kalecki did not explicitly use the concept, however, for a theory of the share of profits in output, relying instead on the concept of the 'degree of monopoly.'[11] Above all, however, it was a meeting of the 'secret seminar' in Ruth Cohen's room in Newnham College in 1955 that triggered the 1956 paper.[12] Harry Johnson, then a Fellow of King's, who was a Keynesian at the time, attended the seminar. Johnson saw immediately that if investment determines saving, and the propensity to save out of profits is different from (higher than) the propensity to save out of wages, the investment ratio must be associated with a unique distribution of income between wages and profits. Kaldor wrote up his paper in less than a week and submitted it to the *Review of Economic Studies* at the end of December. It was launched on an unsuspecting world almost simultaneously with Joan Robinson's *Accumulation of Capital*, first published in June 1956.[13]

The Kaldor theory of distribution is beautiful in its simplicity, and has survived relatively unscathed from the various attacks made upon it. Let full employment income (Y) be divided between consumption (C) and investment (I), with consumption out of wages equal to $c_w W$, and consumption out of profits equal to $c_p P$ (where W is wages, P is profits, and c_w and c_p are the propensities to consume out of wages and profits, respectively). Therefore, $Y = c_w W + c_p P + I$. But $P = Y - W$. Therefore, $P = c_p P + I - s_w W$, where s_w is the propensity to save out of wages. This equation illustrates the 'widow's cruse' that capitalists 'get what they spend', but workers' saving reduces profits. The share of profits in income is equal to: $P/Y = (I/Y)/(s_p - s_w) - s_w/(s_p - s_w)$, where s_p is the propensity to save out of profits.[14] Profits are the dependent variable and investment is the independent variable because capitalists can decide what to invest but they cannot decide what they earn. The share of profits in income is determined by decisions to invest. At full employment, investment determines the relation between prices and wages and hence real wages and profits. The model is stable as long as prices (or profit margins) are flexible and the propensity to save out of profits is greater than the propensity to save out of wages, so that income redistribution from wages to profits as investment rises also raises the savings ratio. The model is exactly the opposite of Ricardo's because now it is wages (not profits) that are the residual factor income (unless workers can always defend themselves against reductions in real wages, or always receive real wage increases in line with productivity increases in the growing economy). If the share of investment in income, and the propensity to save out of profits, remain constant over time, the share of profits will also remain constant over time (assuming the relation between wages and prices remains unchanged, i.e. full employment is maintained).

Kaldor's theory of distribution not only provides an alternative to the neoclassical marginal productivity theory of distribution, but also provides an alternative equilibriating mechanism between the required rate of growth to absorb full employment saving (the so-called warranted role) and the natural rate of growth which does not rely on smooth adjustment of the capital to labour ratio along a neoclassical aggregate production function. Sir Roy Harrod, in his path-breaking 1939 essay,[15] had pointed to the consequences for an economy of the rate of growth desired by entrepreneurs (the warranted rate) diverging from the long-run capacity rate determined by labour force growth and productivity growth (the natural rate). If the warranted rate should exceed the natural rate, this would mean excess saving and long-run stagnation, and if the natural rate should exceed the warranted rate this would imply insufficient saving and inflationary pressure, combined with growing unemployment of the 'structural' variety through the effective labour force growing faster than capital accumulation to absorb it (as in many developing countries). From Harrod, the investment ratio (I/Y) is determined by the growth of output ($\Delta Y/Y = g$) and the required incremental capital-output ratio ($I/\Delta Y = c_r$), i.e. $I/Y = gc_r$. In continuous full employment, g must equal the natural rate of growth. Equilibrium requires that the investment and saving ratios should be equal ($I/Y = s$). From Kaldor's distribution equation, we know that the aggregate savings ratio is a function of the distribution of income: $s = s_p (P/Y)$, assuming all wages are consumed. Therefore $s_p (P/Y) = gc_r$, so that the warranted and natural growth rates are not independent of each other. There is an adjustment mechanism between s and gc_r working through the share of profits in income. If the warranted or desired rate of growth exceeds the natural rate, prices will fall relative to wages, reducing the share of profits in income, and therefore reducing the savings ratio and the desired rate of growth to keep capital fully employed. If the natural rate of growth exceeds the desired rate, prices will rise relative to wages, raising the share of profits in income, thereby raising the savings ratio and the desired rate closer to the natural rate.[16]

There are four major limitations to the workings of the model. First, real wages cannot fall below a certain minimum so there is a limit to which the wage share can fall and the profits' share can rise. Secondly, there is a limit to which the share of profits can fall given by the minimum rate of profit necessary to induce capitalists to invest. Thirdly, apart from the minimum rate of profit on capital there must be a certain minimum rate of profit on turnover due to imperfections in the market, which may be called the 'degree of monopoly' rate. Lastly, the investment ratio must be independent of the share of profits in income (and hence the rate of profit) if investment is to be treated as the autonomous variable in the system.

If the first condition is not satisfied, a Ricardian world would prevail. The wage share would be determined by subsistence needs, profits would be a residual, and growth would be limited by the ability to accumulate, at a rate which may no longer correspond to the natural rate. If, at the other extreme, the minimum rate of profit condition was not met there would be no investment, the full employment condition would break down, and the economy would lapse into stagnation. The fourth condition is not strictly necessary for the workings of the model, and in later papers the investment ratio was made a function of the profit share, so that the equilibrium level of the investment ratio and the share of profits are simultaneously determined. The stability of the model then requires that, out of equilibrium, the savings ratio is more sensitive than the investment ratio to changes in the profits' share. If all the conditions are satisfied, there will be an inherent tendency to full employment. A tendency to continued economic *growth* will only exist when the system is stable at a full employment equilibrium, when there is a continued incentive to invest.

The strength and beauty of the model lies in the fact that it dispenses with the dubious concept of an aggregate production function, and marginal productivity theory derived from it, which can only explain aggregate distributive shares on quite unrealistic assumptions. The model has survived the various attacks made upon it, particularly by neoclassical writers, and the elegant generalisation of the model by Pasinetti.[17] The fact that the savings propensities may not be fixed; that the capital:output ratio may vary with the share of profits, and that income may deviate from its full employment level, do not undermine the thrust and focus of the model derived from the basic insight of the 'widow's cruse' that for profits to exist expenditure must exceed business outlays, and thus the share of profits in equilibrium income must bear a fixed relation at any point in time to the propensity to invest relative to the propensity to save out of wages (which reduces profits).[18] Tobin[19] was particularly forcefully rebutted by Kaldor (1960b). Tobin asked rhetorically: if Kaldor wants to turn Keynes' *General Theory* into a theory of distribution, why not a general theory of distribution to more than two factors of production – like marginal productivity theory which can explain the division of the cake between 101 factors? Kaldor had no difficulty in responding that there are very good (and obvious) reasons for picking out investment and profits for an understanding of the capitalist system, but in any case, a narrow definition of factors would make nonsense of the whole marginal productivity approach since divisibility and substitutability can only be assumed to exist between broad categories.

The generalisation of the model by Pasinetti resulted from the recognition that if workers save they must receive profits and thus Kaldor's approach of relating saving propensities to wages and profits implicitly assumes that workers have the same propensity to save out of profits as capitalists. Pasinetti reworked the Kaldor model attaching saving propensities to classes of individuals – workers and capitalists – allowing the workers' propensity to save out of profits to be different to the capitalists' propensity to save out of profits. Assuming that the rate of interest received by workers on saving is equal to the rate of profit, and given that in the steady-state capital owned by workers must grow at the same rate as capital owned by capitalists, Pasinetti showed that the equilibrium share of profits in income and the rate of profit are the same as in the Kaldor model. The fact that workers save apparently makes no difference to the steady-state profit share and rate of profit, only to the distribution of income between workers and capitalists. This came to be known as the Pasinetti Paradox. But the explanation is clear. The steady-state condition that capital owned by workers and capitalists grow at the same rate requires that workers' saving out of wages (which reduces aggregate profits) be exactly matched by workers' extra consumption out of profits (vis-à-vis the level of consumption if capitalists had received the profits) leaving aggregate profit and the rate of profit unchanged.

Pasinetti's result did not challenge Kaldor's theory; it confirmed it. Notwithstanding this, Kaldor always maintained that it is the characteristic or nature of profit income as such that determines the propensity to save not who receives the profit. Profits are saved for investment and as a means of securing complementary external finance. Also, a large proportion of workers' saving is in the form of life insurance and pension funds, the returns from which are reinvested.[20] It is more sensible, therefore, and probably more accurate empirically (if a choice has to be made), to relate saving propensities to income type rather than to classes of individuals.

A major attempt to undermine the Kaldor–Pasinetti result that workers' saving does not affect the equilibrium factor shares, and to resurrect neoclassical marginal productivity theory, was made in 1966 by Samuelson and Modigliani (hereafter S–M).[21] Kaldor replied, along with Pasinetti and Joan Robinson, with his famous neo-Pasinetti theorem (1966a). S–M wrote a rejoinder to Pasinetti and Robinson, but Kaldor's neo-Pasinetti theorem was left unchallenged. S–M excused themselves by saying that they saw the Kaldor paper too late, and promised Kaldor in private correspondence that they would respond, but nothing to date has been forthcoming. Perhaps the ingenuity of Kaldor's defence of 'Pasinettiland' was too much, as to why the distribution of assets will approach a constant equilibrium value between workers and capitalists so that both classes continue to own capital. Geoffrey Harcourt has described Kaldor's rejoinder to S–M as 'a mighty performance by anyone's standards... all the more so as it was written while Kaldor was busily revolutionising the Inland Revenue'.[22]

The essence of the S–M argument was that the Pasinetti result highlighted only one of a pair of balanced growth possibilities in which the capital of workers and capitalists is growing at the same rate. But there is a 'dual' to the Pasinetti theorem where the capital owned by workers grows faster than that owned by capitalists so that in the long run all capital is owned by the workers and 'pure' capitalists cease to exist. In this case the steady-state conditions will be determined by the workers' propensity to save. S–M argue that there is no reason to believe that one case is any more general than the other. The condition for the Pasinetti case to hold is the same as in the basic Kaldor model that $s_w < I/Y$[23] (or $s_w < \pi_k s_c$, as S–M prefer to define it, where π_k is the share of capital in income and s_c is the capitalists' propensity to save out of profits). S–M argue that a relatively small s_w would violate the condition. For example, if $\pi_k = 1/4$ and $s_c = 1/5$, Pasinetti's theorem could not hold for s_w any higher than 0.05 which would be very low.

Kaldor's reply to S–M was not only designed as a rehabilitation of why the Pasinetti result should hold, but also represented a further attack on neoclassical modes of thinking. In fact, he started his defence by listing all the unreal assumptions that have to be made to make the neoclassical theory of distribution work: linear and homogeneous production functions; universal profit-maximisation, autonomous Harrod-neutral technical progress, etc. – abstractions that have to be made but which neoclassical economists use as if they were descriptions of the real world. 'It is the hallmark of the neoclassical economist', says Kaldor,

to believe that however severe the abstractions from which he is forced to start
he will win through by the end of the day – bit by bit, if only he carries the analysis
far enough, the scaffolding can be removed, leaving the basic structure intact. In
fact, these props are never removed; the removal of any one of a number of
them – as, for example, allowing for increasing returns or learning by doing – is
sufficient to cause the whole structure to collapse like a pack of cards.

S–M assert that macro-theories of distribution fare best if
production coefficients are fixed, because if they are variable 'one
would have no need for a genuinely alternative theory of
distribution'. But marginal productivity theory would still imply
constant returns in the long run; diminishing returns to labour in
the short run and so on, none of which is supported by the
empirical evidence. Kaldor showed impatience:

the whole antithesis that either marginal productivity must explain pricing or
else there must be fixed coefficients is neoclassical reasoning carried *in extremis* . . .
Can't they see that it is possible for a market economy to be 'competitive' without
satisfying the neo-classical equations? Can't they imagine a world in which
marginal productivities are not equal to factor prices, and are not in any definite
relation to factor prices?

Kaldor then directed his attention to S–M's anti-Pasinetti
theorem pointing out that if the basic inequality $s_w < I/Y$ is not
satisfied no Keynesian macroeconomic distribution theory could
survive for an instant let alone in Golden Age equilibrium. If the
equilibrium level of investment was less than workers' saving we
could not envisage investment as autonomous with saving
adapting. Either there would be less than full employment or
profits would be negative, and profits would not be determined by
the need to generate sufficient savings to finance investment. If
the Keynesian theory goes, something needs putting in its place
where there is just enough investment to finance full employment
saving. S–M are accused of conjuring up a world of Walrasian
purity in which all saving is invested without disturbing full
employment. Ultimately the validity of the Pasinetti inequality is
an empirical question, just as the matters of perfect competition,
constant returns to scale, etc. should be, and not simply assertions.
S–M claim that capital's share of income (π_k) of $1/4$ and the
propensity to save of capitalists out of profits (s_c) of $1/5$ (so that s_w
must be less than 0.05) 'are econometrically reasonable for a mixed
economy like the U.S., U.K. or Western Europe', thereby
invalidating the Pasinetti theorem since $s_w > 0.05$. Kaldor noted a
number of errors in their empirical reasoning. First, their estimate
of the profit share relates to gross profit while their low estimate
of the capitalists' propensity to save relates to saving out of net

profits after allowance for capital consumption. The empirical saving propensity out of gross profits after tax is closer to 0.7–0.8 in most advanced countries. From the point of view of the mechanics of a Keynesian model, it is gross saving and investment that are relevant. Secondly, the value of s_w may be above 0.05 but a large part of workers' saving goes to finance personal investment in consumer durable goods, and particularly housing, and thus is not saving available for business. The net acquisition of financial assets as a proportion of income in the personal sector is probably between 2 and 3 per cent. Thirdly, Kaldor noted that in the UK and US, the increase in life insurance and pension funds exceeded the net acquisition by the personal sector of financial assets, thus indicating a net diminution in other financial assets. This is probably a measure of the net consumption of property-owners out of capital or capital gains. There is nothing, in fact, in the Kaldor–Pasinetti model that requires s_w to be positive. The model works equally well if s_w is negative with the business sector as a net lender rather than a net borrower. S–M ignore the case of $s_w \leqslant 0$. With realistic values of s_w and s_c the Kaldor–Pasinetti condition will be satisfied empirically. Finally, it should be remembered that the government may also spend more than its income, which can be seen by looking at the figures for the net acquisition of financial assets of the whole of the private sector – personal and business. In the UK and the US, there have been many years in which the private corporate sector has been a net lender to the rest of the economy, not a net borrower. As far as the distribution of income is concerned, this amounts to the same thing as if $s_w < 0$. As far as profits are concerned, it makes no difference whether the net saving is due to the activities of the personal sector or the government. Kaldor's neo-Pasinetti theorem gives the same result as Pasinetti's, but by a different route. Workers save and also consume out of capital gains. Companies save out of profits and also issue new securities. Kaldor showed that given the workers' propensity to save and the coefficient of consumption out of capital gains, there is a certain valuation ratio (i.e. the market value of shares to capital employed) which will secure just enough saving by the personal sector to take up the securities issued by companies. Thus the personal sector's net saving depends not only on its saving propensity but also on the policy of companies towards new issues. In the absence of new issues, the level of security prices will be such that the purchase of securities by savers is just balanced by the sale of securities by dissavers, making the net saving of the personal sector zero. The equilibrium rate of profit can then be shown to be equal to the natural growth rate divided by the propensity to save of capitalists – the original Kaldor–Pasinetti result, independent of the workers' propensity to save.

Kaldor left at a loose end the question of the distribution of assets between 'workers' (pension funds) and capitalists. What is to stop the extermination of capitalists with all shares ending up in the hands of pension funds and insurance companies? It is argued that there will always be new firms coming along with the value of their shares rising faster than average, so that the rate of appreciation of shares in the hands of the capitalist group as a whole will be greater than the rate of appreciation in the hands of the pension funds, and there will be a long-run distribution of assets between capitalists and pension funds which will remain constant. The argument is ingenious but not proved rigorously. In the early 1970s, Kaldor supervised the pioneering research work of Adrian Wood who generalised the neo-Keynesian distribution theory showing that the household savings ratio, the firms' retention ratio, and the desired ratio of externally financed investment can 'explain' both the distribution of income and the level of output in both full employment and non-full employment situations.[24]

GROWTH THEORY

Kaldor used his distribution theory as an integral part of his model of long-run growth, which is designed to explain what he was first to call the 'stylised facts' of economic history. His growth theory also constitutes an integral part of the neo-Keynesian challenge to neoclassical growth theory.

There are several unsatisfactory features of neoclassical growth theory. First there is no independent investment demand function. Investment is assumed to adapt passively to saving. In this sense, the theory is profoundly anti-Keynesian, with the Keynesian problem of effective demand swept under the carpet. In the real world, it is decisions by entrepreneurs governing the rate of capital accumulation that drive the whole economic system. Secondly, neoclassical theory assumes the long run growth rate to be exogenously determined by labour supply growth and (Harrod-neutral) technical progress. In practice, technical progress is mainly induced by capital accumulation itself. It is difficult, if not impossible, to distinguish between movements along a production function and shifts in the whole function. The long-run growth rate will depend on the rate at which new ideas are infused in the economy by capital accumulation. Thirdly, in neoclassical theory, the institutional basis of saving is ignored. In effect, there is a single propensity to save assumed for the community as a whole. In Kaldor's models, and in neo-Keynesian theory generally, it is recognised explicitly that the bulk of saving comes from profits and that the share of profits in income may change. As the classical economists emphasised, it is in the very nature of profits that they should be devoted to investment rather than to consumption. All this has implications for distribution theory and the existence of growth equilibrium. Fourthly, neoclassical theory uses the concept of an aggregate production function, about which neo-Keynesians express grave reservations. Not only do they question whether it can be used for the purposes of the marginal productivity theory of distribution, but they also dispute the assumptions of malleable capital and the smooth, infinite substitutability of capital for labour which in neoclassical theory is the mechanism by which growth equilibrium is attained.[25] Underlying the use of the aggregate production function for distribution and growth theory is the assumption of competitive markets and optimising generally, which neo-Keynesians question in an imperfectly competitive, uncertain world. In fact, Joan Robinson denies that the neo-Keynesian/neoclassical debate in growth theory has anything to do with the valuation of capital as such. For her, it is concerned with reconstructing a pre-Keynesian equilibrium in which accumulation is governed by the desire of society as a whole to save and where full employment is guaranteed by real wages finding the level at which the existing stock of 'jelly' will be spread out or squeezed up to employ the available labour. Neoclassical theory is obsessed with equilibrium models, while neo-Keynesians believe it is important to emphasise uncertainty and disequilibrium as essential features of real life.

Kaldor's position was unequivocal. We need models which explain the facts. It is no good having models which lead to results contrary to the facts and then explaining the difference by omitted variables. Any theory must of necessity be based on abstractions but the type of abstraction cannot be decided in a vacuum. In choosing a particular approach, the theorist should start off with a summary of the 'stylised' facts relevant to the problem. 'Stylised' facts are broad tendencies, not necessarily historically accurate at every moment in time. The important 'stylised' facts that Kaldor attempted to explain in both his 1957 and 1961 papers (1957c; 1961a) are these: a steady trend rate of growth of labour productivity; a steady increase in the amount of capital used per worker; a steady rate of profit on capital; the relative constancy of the capital:output ratio; a steady share of wages and profits in national income; and finally, wide differences in the rate of growth of output and labour productivity between countries associated with differences in the level of investment, but none the less similar capital:output ratios and distributive shares. These tendencies or constancies are explained in neoclassical theory by unsupported assumptions such as neutral technical progress and a unitary elasticity of substitution between capital and labour. The main attraction of Kaldor's models is the introduction of greater realism, showing how the various tendencies and constancies are the consequence of endogenous forces operating in the system and not simply the result of chance and coincidence. The main deficiencies of the models are that they lack explicit consideration of microeconomic decision-making; they neglect the spatial aspects of development and they assume a closed economy. They are also highly aggregative and really only apply to the manufacturing sector of an economy. Kaldor later recognised this deficiency and from 1966 on adopted a sectoral approach to all his work relating to the comparative growth performance of countries and to the growth of the world economy.

The 1957 model possesses a number of interesting, novel and important features.[26] First, the model assumes full employment in the Keynesian sense. Only at full employment, Kaldor argued, will the relation between prices and wages be such as to give a profit and savings ratio consistent with steady growth. In other words, an equilibrium of steady growth is inconsistent with underemployment equilibrium because if there is underemployment the relationship between wages and prices will change in such a way as to produce a distribution of income that implies steady growth. In Kaldor's view, this was Harrod's mistake, to assume that the savings ratio is extraneously determined so that a dynamic equilibrium of growth is necessarily unstable. In the 1961 paper his full employment theorem is based on an examination of the stability of various possible positions of goods market equilibrium using supply and demand curves for Marshall's 'representative' firm. The validity of the theorem rests heavily on the investment function which because of induced investment makes the demand curve U-shaped. Investment here is related to the level of output – as in his early trade cycle work – in contrast to the change of output which is the assumption used in the growth models.

A second major and novel feature of the 1957 model is the introduction of the idea of a technical progress function relating the rate of growth of output per worker to the rate of growth of capital per worker (see Figure 6.1).

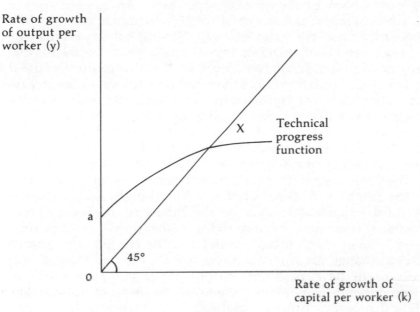

Figure 6.1

Kaldor rejected the notion that it is possible to distinguish, at least empirically, between movements along a production function (the substitution of capital for labour) and movements in the whole function due to technical progress. The one implies the other. There cannot be capital deepening without some technical progress embodied in the new capital, and most new ideas need capital accumulation for their embodiment. Society's ability to absorb new knowledge depends on capital accumulation.[27] The position of the new technical progress function, which replaces the production function, depends on the rate of progress taking place independently of capital accumulation, and the shape of the function depends on the degree to which capital accumulation embodies new techniques which improve labour productivity. A given curve relating output growth per worker to capital accumulation per worker assumes a constant flow in the rate of new ideas over time. A change in the rate of flow will shift the whole curve. Important new discoveries will tend to raise the curve for a considerable period of time if society has the capacity to absorb the ideas. Contrawise, a lull in the speed with which new ideas come forward will shift the curve downwards. Long waves in economic activity may be explicable in these terms, as well as the

long run stability of the capital:output ratio. An upward shift in
the technical progress function through a technological burst will
temporarily raise the ratio of output to capital (or reduce the
capital:output ratio), making inventions appear capital saving,
until capital accumulation has caught up. It will catch up, because if
the rate of accumulation is less than adequate to exploit the stream
of inventions, and the capital:output ratio falls, the profitability of
investment will rise and there will be an incentive to invest. The
economic system will tend, therefore, to approach an equality
between the rate of growth of output and the rate of capital
accumulation at point X in Figure 6.1, which then gives the long-
run equilibrium growth rate which depends on the parameters
(i.e. the height and slope) of the technical progress function.[28]

A third important feature of the model is the independent
investment function. The underlying mainspring of growth must
be the willingness to invest capital and the readiness to absorb
technical change. In order for there to be continued growth, it is
necessary to have not only output increasing as a result of
investment, but investment increasing as a result of output. The
technical progress function embodies the former relation; the
investment function is designed to capture the latter. Investment
in any period is made to be partly a function of the change in
output in the previous period (the acceleration principle) and
partly a function of the change in the rate of profit in that period. It
will be remembered (see Chapter 2) that in his early trade cycle
work, Kaldor had dismissed the acceleration principle with its
assumption of a constant capital:output ratio on the grounds that
the changing relation between capital and output is essential for
understanding the cyclical mechanism. On the other hand, he did
recognise the validity of the acceleration principle 'as between
alternative positions of long period equilibrium'.[29] Kaldor argued
that for long-run growth models, it is appropriate to define
periods long enough for the capital stock in any one period to be
fully adjusted to the output expected for that period at the
beginning of that period, so that the acceleration principle
provides the basis for an acceptable investment function. On the
influence of the rate of profit, if investment decisions are regarded
as being taken at the beginning of the period, the linking of
investment to the change in the rate of profit in the current period
implies perfect foresight of output and profits. Thus the one
period lag that Kaldor had in his original investment function is
unsatisfactory, which he later recognised and rectified in the 1961
paper.

A fourth feature of the model is that the influence of a change in the rate of profit, and the share of profit in income, on the choice of techniques is ignored. Kaldor considered it much more reasonable to assume that the choice of techniques is far more dependent on the price of different capital goods and the price of labour relative to productivity (the efficiency wage). For example, consider the use of bulldozers for building roads in developed countries compared with shovels in less developed countries which has nothing to do with the differences in the rate of profit or rate of interest, but with the price of bulldozers and labour. Superior techniques are substituted for inferior techniques as the relative price of superior techniques falls with technical progress in the capital goods industries.

In considering the workings of the model, the case is first taken where the population is static and then when it is growing. In the short-run equilibrium of the model, the savings equation, which depends on the distribution of income, and the investment equation, which depends partly on the rate of profit, simultaneously determine the distribution of income and the proportion of income saved and invested at time t. The level of profits must be such as to induce investment that is just equal to the rate of saving at that particular distribution of income. If profits are a lower proportion of income, investment plans will exceed savings, prices will rise in relation to wages, and the gap between investment and saving will be eliminated by a rise in profits. Stable equilibrium is possible if the function relating the savings ratio to the profit share is steeper than the function relating the investment ratio to the profit share, which is assumed. The other restrictions on the model were mentioned earlier: the profit share cannot rise above a certain level because there is a subsistence minimum below which wages cannot fall, and profits cannot fall below a certain level without the inducement to invest drying up.

Assuming all the above conditions are satisfied, the technical progress function gives the movement of the economy from a short period equilibrium to a long period equilibrium of steady growth. Long-run equilibrium must be where the growth of capital and output are equal. This rate is independent of the savings and investment functions and depends only on the coefficients of the technical progress function. With this result for the long-run equilibrium rate of growth, the equilibrium ratio of investment to income, the equilibrium share of profits in income, and the equilibrium rate of profit on capital[30] can all be derived. The model bears similarities to Harrod's growth model, but with important differences. The equilibrium growth rate determined by the technical progress function is like Harrod's natural rate of growth, but it is not exogenously given. Technical progress is not treated as a constant but as a function of investment. The equation determining the equilibrium investment ratio, along with the savings function, gives a variant of Harrod's warranted rate of growth, except that a given savings ratio is consistent with any number of warranted rates depending on the distribution of income. The system tends towards an equilibrium rate at which 'natural' and 'warranted' rates are equal since any divergence between the two will set up forces tending to eliminate them, the difference acting partly on the 'natural' rate and partly on the 'warranted' rate.

In the case of an economy in which the population is growing, the long-run equilibrium growth of income and capital is given by the parameters of the technical progress function and the rate of population growth. Positive population growth has implications for the position of the technical progress function and the stability of the model. Since the dependent variable of the technical progress function is the rate of growth of output per head, positive population growth reduces this rate. Only if autonomous productivity growth exceeds population growth will the rate of growth of output per head be positive and stable growth be assured.

Kaldor stressed that his model is a long-run one and therefore the conclusions from it cannot be applied directly to actual situations. Particularly the theory of distribution, which makes the share of profits in income entirely dependent on the investment ratio and the propensity to save out of profits and wages, is only acceptable as a long run theory. In the short run, if profit margins and real wages are sticky, variations in investment will not be offset by variations in consumption, and distributive shares will not change sufficiently for saving to match desired investment. Full employment is not guaranteed. If there are shifts in the technical progress function, the effect of short period rigidity of profit margins is to slow down the rate at which capital investment changes in response to such shifts. The system is liable to major breakdowns after the exploitation of major discoveries when the technical progress function shifts down again. The growth of income then lags behind the growth of capital and the capital:output ratio rises again.

Although Kaldor later modified the 1957 growth model, there were no further major innovations comparable to the distribution mechanism and the idea of the technical progress function. The modifications were of a more technical nature relating to the investment function and the form of the technical progress function. In the 1957 model it was assumed that investment depended not only on the rate of growth of output but also on the expected rate of profit, and the higher the rate of profit the more worthwhile it would be for entrepreneurs to adopt more labour-saving techniques requiring a higher amount of investment per unit of output capacity. For the model to be stable, however, the response of investment to changes in the rate of profit had to be below a certain critical level, as shown by Champernowne,[31] which in turn depended on the difference in savings propensities between wages and profits, respectively.

In the 1961 model, there are two changes in the investment function. First, instead of assuming that firms wish the capital stock to grow in line with actual output, the assumption is made that firms wish the capital stock to grow at such a rate as to keep capacity output growth in line with actual output growth. Secondly, the expected rate of profit is assumed to depend not on the currently prevailing rate but on an average of past rates. In other words, while decisions to change the capacity to produce are responsive to recent events, decisions to change the capital intensity of production, or investment per unit of output, are based on the experience of a whole range of past periods. The average profit rate is proxied by the existing output:capacity ratio, and it can be shown that the longer the period taken, the wider is the range over which the investment function is consistent with a stable solution. The direction of change of investment always goes in the direction of the steady-state path. If the growth of capital is below equilibrium, the output:capital ratio rises, profit expectations rise and the growth of capital increases. Contrawise, if the growth of capital is above equilibrium, the output:capital ratio falls, profit expectations fall and the growth of capital falls.

The 1962 model written with James Mirrlees (1962b) carried on from the previous ones, but both the investment function and the technical progress function are modified. As far as investment is concerned, the model recognised that once technology is embodied in capital, its profitability will diminish through increasing competition from superior vintages. The fact that obsolescence in this sense is anticipated leads to a new rule for determining the investment decision, namely a 'pay-off' period subject to a satisfactory return over the life of the asset. On the technical progress function, since technical progress is introduced into the economic system through new equipment which depends on gross investment, the technical progress function is redefined as a relationship between the rate of growth of output per worker on newly installed equipment and the rate of change of gross fixed investment per worker. Investment is primarily induced by the growth of production itself and the assumption that growth equilibrium can only occur in a state of full employment is maintained. Investment is independent of propensities to save, and remains Keynesian in this sense, but the scrapping rules for machinery and the determination of the real wage, and hence distributive shares, have decidedly neoclassical features. The model continues to assume a closed economy, with continuous technical progress and a steady growth of the working population. The model shows that with a limited number of parameters, the equilibrium values of all the important variables in the system can be uniquely determined i.e. the share of profits; the investment:output ratio; the life of equipment and the share of labour transferred to new equipment each year. Kaldor was impressed by the fact that realistic values for the parameters of the model produced sensible results for the United States economy.

The common feature of all the models is the prime role given to both exogenous and endogenous technical progress as the main engines of growth. But Kaldor ends with a policy message: raising the technical progress function is 'not only a matter of more scientific education and more expenditure on research, but of higher quality business management which is more alert in searching for technical improvements and less resistant to their introduction.'

Sir Dennis Robertson, in his 'valedictory' Marshall Lectures,[32] set the provocative sample examination question: 'Compare and contrast the growth models of Harrod, Domar, J. Robinson, Kaldor Mark I, Kaldor Mark II, Kaldor Mark III, Hahn, Matthews, Goodwin, Champernowne, Hicks, Little, Duesenberry, Tobin, Fellner, Solow and Swan. Which seems to you the biggest nonsense and why?' The question, no doubt set with tongue in cheek, none the less revealed a disdain for the construction of theoretical skeletons with little or no empirical flesh. The disdain and scepticism began to be shared by Kaldor himself, resulting from a combination of age and intellectual conviction. His 1962 paper with Mirrlees and his 1966 reply to Samuelson and Modigliani's anti-Pasinetti theorem were the last of his theoretical papers on growth (and distribution) theory. Instead, he became much more pragmatic, turning his attention to two important areas of empirical interest: first, the explanation of inter-regional and inter-country growth rate differences and the search for empirical regularities associated with these differences; and secondly, the limits to growth in a closed economy (including the world economy). These topics are the subject matter of the next two chapters.

NOTES

1. R.F. Harrod, 'An Essay in Dynamic Economics', *Economic Journal*, March 1939; and *Towards a Dynamic Economics* (London: Macmillan 1948). The original neoclassical response came from R.M. Solow, 'A Contribution to the Theory of Economic Growth', *Quarterly Journal of Economics*, February 1956; and T.W. Swan, 'Economic Growth and Capital Accumulation', *Economic Record*, November 1956.
2. P. Samuelson, 'A Brief Survey of Post-Keynesian Developments', in R. Leckachman (ed.), *Keynes' General Theory: Reports of Three Decades* (New York: St Martin's Press, 1964).
3. e.g. M. Kalecki, 'A Theory of Profits', *Economic Journal*, June–September 1942.
4. Quoted in R.F. Harrod, *The Life of John Maynard Keynes* (London: Macmillan 1951), p. 545.
5. J.K. Galbraith, *A Life in Our Times* (Boston: Houghton Mifflin, 1981).
6. 27 May 1956.
7. Mathematically, the rate of profit on capital (P/K) may be expressed as.
$$\frac{P}{K} = \frac{(Y/L - W/P)}{K/L}$$, where Y/L is labour productivity; W/P is the real wage, and K/L is the capital per head. What happens to the rate of profit depends on the relation betwen these three variables.
8. Twenty years later in a paper delivered at a conference in Madrid (18 October 1976), entitled 'The Political Implications of Different Phases of Economic Development' (unpublished), Kaldor took up cudgels against Marx again. He pointed out that Marx's predictions were never inductive anyway, based on empirical observations, and argued that the way capitalism has developed in different countries itself undermines the determinism of Marx's theory of history. He concluded the paper with a rebuttal of the Marxian view that particular techniques of production necessarily require, or necessarily bring about, a particular set of political or social institutions.
9. *An Essay on the Co-ordination of the Laws of Distribution* (London: Macmillan, 1894).
10. *Op.cit.*
11. Kaldor was a strong admirer of Kalecki (although not of his theory of distribution), but did not have a close academic relationship with him. They met periodically in London in the 1930s and then Kalecki went to Oxford in 1940 to join the Oxford Institute of Statistics. Kaldor wrote Kalecki's obituary for *The Times* (21 April 1970) and, before his death in 1970, recommended him (unsuccessfully) for the Nobel Prize in Economics (first awarded in 1969).
12. The origin of the 'secret seminar' is mentioned in Chapter 3. The seminar used to meet in Kahn's room in King's but after he retired as College Bursar he was given a magnificent French carpet which he didn't want spoilt!
13. The seeds of such a distribution theory were also in a dissertation published by the German economist Hanns Joachim Rüstow in 1926, and in his later book *Theorie der Volbeschäftigung in der Freien Markwirtschaft* (Tübingen: Mohr, 1951), where he shows that profits in the aggregate are determined by excess investment expenditure over savings out of wages and salaries, while the

level of employment is a monotonic function of the share of profits. Kaldor gives due recognition in (1983g). Frank Hahn also presented a model in 1951 which showed that the equilibrium share of wages (and profits) must be that which equates aggregate demand and supply. See 'The Share of Wages in the National Income', *Oxford Economic Papers*, June 1951.

14. An obvious condition for profits to be positive is that $I/Y > s_w$; in other words, investment outlays must exceed workers' saving which reduces profits. From this model was derived the famous 'Cambridge equation' that if all wages are consumed, the rate of profit (r) is equal to the growth rate (g) divided by the propensity to save out of profits i.e. multiplying both sides by Y/K gives $r = g/s_p$.

15. *Op. cit.*

16. There is an obvious link here with Robertson's theory of forced saving over the trade cycle and the increase in voluntary saving due to a shift in profits, reducing the long term instability of the economy. See T. Wilson, 'Robertson, Money and Monetarism', *Journal of Economic Literature*, December 1980.

17. L. Pasinetti, 'Rate of Profit and Income Distribution in Relation to the Rate of Economic Growth', *Review of Economic Studies*, October 1962.

18. Amartya Sen has shown that all the results of the neoclassical and neo-Keynesian distribution models based on full employment can be derived without contradiction in a full Keynesian model with unemployment: see 'Neo-Classical and Neo-Keynesian Theories of Distribution', *Economic Record*, March 1963.

19. J. Tobin, 'Towards a General Kaldorian Theory of Distribution', *Review of Economic Studies*, February 1960.

20. A compromise function between the Kaldor and Pasinetti saving functions would be: $S = s_{ww}.W + s_{pw}P_w + s_{pc}P_c$, where S is total saving; W is wages; P_w is profits received by workers; P_c is profits received by capitalists; s_{ww} is the propensity to save out of wages received by workers; s_{pw} is the propensity to save out of profits received by workers and s_{pc} is the propensity to save out of profits received by capitalists. The Kaldor and Pasinetti functions are special cases of this more general function. If $s_{pw} = s_{pc} > s_{ww}$, saving would depend on income source alone and the Kaldor function would obtain. If $s_{ww} = s_{pw} < s_{pc}$, saving would depend on income class alone and the Pasinetti function would obtain. See A.C. Chiang, 'A Simple Generalisation of the Kaldor–Pasinetti Theory of Profit Rate and Income Distribution', *Economica*, August 1973, for a model along these lines.

    One of the uses to which these functions can be put empirically is to estimate the effects of inflation on saving. See my paper 'Inflation and the Savings Ratio Across Countries', *Journal of Development Studies*, January 1974, and A. Woodfield and J. McDonald, 'On the Relation Between Savings, Distribution and Inflation', *Journal of Development Studies*, April 1978.

21. P. Samuelson and F. Modigliani, 'The Pasinetti Paradox in Neoclassical and More General Models', *Review of Economic Studies*, October 1966.

22. G. Harcourt, *Some Cambridge Controversies in the Theory of Capital* (Cambridge University Press, 1972).

23. Except that s_w is the propensity to save of workers not the propensity to save out of wages.

24. See A. Wood, *A Theory of Profits* (Cambridge University Press, 1975).

25. See Solow, *op. cit*; and Swan, *op. cit.*

26. The original model, partly inspired by Joan Robinson's book *The Accumulation of Capital*, originally started as a joint paper with Champernowne, but the outright rejection of neoclassicism was too much for his co-author

who withdrew into the background helping only with the mathematics.

27. There was some meeting of minds on this matter between Kaldor and some of the American neoclassicists, including Arrow (see 1962e), but they continued to employ neoclassical assumptions with respect to savings and investment. Kaldor and Joan Robinson concurred that this is the big difference between the neo-classical and Keynesian growth models. See also Kaldor (1963b).

28. In linear form, the technical progress function may be expressed as: $y = a + b(k)$. The capital:output ratio is constant when $y = k$. Therefore the equilibrium growth rate is: $a/(1 - b)$. Despite Kaldor's disclaimers, the model must be assuming a steady rate of Harrod neutral technical progress.

29. Kaldor (1951a).

30. If all profits are saved, the rate of profit is equal to the growth rate of output, as in classical theory.

31. D.G. Champernowne, 'The Stability of Kaldor's 1957 Model'. *Review of Economic Studies*, January 1971.

32. *Growth, Wages and Money* (Cambridge University Press, 1961).

7 THE APPLIED ECONOMICS OF GROWTH[1]

Why do growth rates between advanced capitalist countries differ at roughly similar stages of development? Kaldor's first serious attempt to answer this complex and intriguing question came in two sets of lectures delivered in 1966: the Frank Pierce Memorial Lectures delivered at Cornell University under the title of 'Strategic Factors in Economic Development' and his Inaugural Lecture at Cambridge University in November, entitled 'Causes of the Slow Rate of Growth of the United Kingdom'. In these lectures he presented a series of 'laws' which form the basis of a distinct model of the applied economics of growth. The interpretation and validity of these 'laws' have been the subject of considerable scrutiny and debate,[2] and Kaldor himself subsequently clarified and modified his own position. The basic thrust of the modified model consists of seven key propositions: First, the faster the rate of growth of the manufacturing sector of an economy the faster will be the rate of growth of total output (GDP), not simply in a definitional sense in that manufacturing output is a large component of total output, but for fundamental economic reasons connected with induced productivity growth inside and outside manufacturing. This is not a new idea. It is summed up in the maxim that the manufacturing sector of the economy is the 'engine of growth'.

Secondly, the faster the rate of growth of manufacturing output the faster will be the rate of growth of labour productivity in manufacturing owing to static and dynamic economies of scale, or increasing returns in the widest sense. Kaldor, in the spirit of Allyn Young,[3] his early teacher at the LSE, conceived of returns to scale as a macroeconomic phenomenon related to the interaction between the elasticity of demand for and supply of manufactured goods. It is this strong and powerful interaction which accounts for the positive relationship between the growth of manufacturing and productivity growth, otherwise known as Verdoorn's Law.[4]

Thirdly, the faster the rate of growth of manufacturing output, the faster the rate of transference of labour from other sectors of the economy where there may be either diminishing returns or where no relationship exists between employment growth and output growth. In either case, a reduction in the amount of labour in these sectors will raise productivity growth outside manufacturing. Thus, as a result of increasing returns in manufacturing on the one hand and induced productivity growth in non-manufacturing on the other, it is to be expected that the faster the rate of growth of manufacturing output, the faster the rate of growth of productivity in the economy as a *whole*.

Fourthly, as the scope for transferring labour from diminishing returns activities dries up, or as output comes to depend on employment in *all* sectors of the economy, the degree of overall productivity growth induced by manufacturing growth is likely to diminish, with the overall growth rate correspondingly reduced.

Fifthly, it is in this latter sense that Kaldor believed that countries at a high level of development, with little or no surplus in agriculture or non-manufacturing activities, suffer from a 'labour shortage' and will experience a deceleration of growth; not in the sense that manufacturing output is constrained by a shortage of labour, which he suggested in his Inaugural Lecture was the UK's problem but soon retracted (1968a) and later regretted.[5]

Sixthly, the growth of manufacturing output is *not* constrained by labour supply but is fundamentally determined by demand, and more particularly by the rate of growth of exports. Export demand is the major component of autonomous demand in an open economy which must match the leakage of income into imports. The level of industrial output will adjust to the level of export demand in relation to the propensity to import, through the working of the Harrod trade multiplier,[6] and the rate of growth of output will approximate to the rate of growth of exports divided by the income elasticity of demand for imports which is the dynamic version of the Harrod trade multiplier.[7] Within this framework, manufacturing output growth determines employment growth; not the other way round. A labour supply constraint could be a constraint on output before a balance of payments constraint becomes operative, but it is unlikely in the vast majority of countries.[8] A low rate of growth of exports could be due, however, to labour supply difficulties, particularly in a qualitative sense in certain key sectors of the economy.

Lastly, a fast rate of growth of exports and output will tend to set up a cumulative process, or virtuous circle of growth, through the link between output growth and productivity growth. The lower costs of production in fast-growing countries make it difficult for other (newly industrialising) countries to establish export activities with favourable growth characteristics, except through exceptional industrial enterprise.

This catalogue of propositions is more or less the full Kaldor model of why growth rates differ between advanced capitalist countries. Now let us trace its origins from 1966; examine the evidence adduced at various stages along the way, and consider the criticism to which the model has been subjected and how Kaldor reacted to it and subsequently modified his position.

KALDOR'S FIRST LAW: MANUFACTURING AS THE 'ENGINE OF GROWTH'

Kaldor's first law states that there exists a strong relation between the growth of manufacturing output (g_m) and the growth of total output (g_{GDP}). Manufacturing is the 'engine of growth' which in turn is a characteristic of the transition from 'immaturity' to 'maturity' where 'immaturity' is defined as a situation in which productivity is lower outside industry (particularly in agriculture) so that labour is available for use in industry in relatively unlimited quantities. Kaldor's early suggestion in his Inaugural Lecture was that the UK, with a comparatively poor growth record, suffered from 'premature maturity' in the sense of having reached the stage of roughly equal productivity in all sectors of the economy before attaining a particularly high level in manufacturing industry. Taking a cross section of twelve[9] developed countries over the period 1952/54 to 1963/64, Kaldor estimated a strong correlation between g_{GDP} and g_m:

$$g_{GDP} = 1.153 + 0.614 \, (g_m) \qquad r^2 = 0.959$$
$$(0.040)$$

The fact that the regression coefficient (0.614) is significantly less than unity implies that the greater the *excess* of the rate of growth of manufacturing output over the rate of growth of the economy as a whole, the faster the overall growth rate. Setting $g_{GDP} = g_m$ shows that rates of growth above 3 per cent are found only in cases where the rate of growth of manufacturing exceeds the overall growth of the economy; that is, where the share of the manufacturing sector in the total economy is increasing. In other words, the high correlation between the two variables is not simply the result of manufacturing output constituting a large proportion of total output. There must also be a positive association between the overall rate of economic growth and the *excess* of the rate of growth of manufacturing output over the rate of growth of non-manufacturing output (g_{nm}). This is confirmed by Kaldor's data:

$$g_{GDP} = 3.351 + 0.954 \ (g_m - g_{nm}) \qquad r^2 = 0.562$$
$$(0.267)$$

The contention that the strong correlation between g_{GDP} and g_m does not depend on manufacturing output constituting a large part of total output is also supported by the strong relation between the growth of non-manufacturing output and the growth of manufacturing:

$$g_{nm} = 1.142 + 0.550 \ (g_m) \qquad r^2 = 0.824$$
$$(0.080)$$

There is no correlation between the rate of growth of GDP and either the growth of agriculture or mining. There is a correlation between the growth of GDP and the growth of services, and the relation is virtually one to one, but Kaldor surmised that the direction of causation is almost certainly from the growth of GDP to service activity rather than the other way round. The demand for most services is derived from the demand for manufacturing output itself. The work of Cripps and Tarling[10] taking the same twelve countries over the longer period 1951 to 1970, breaking up the data into four sub-periods and pooling, supported Kaldor's first law, as does unpublished work of my own over a large sample of low and middle-income countries.

What accounts for the fact that the faster manufacturing output grows relatively to GDP, the faster GDP seems to grow? Since differences in growth rates are largely accounted for by differences in productivity growth, there must be some relationship between the growth of the manufacturing sector and productivity growth in the economy as a whole. This is to be expected for one of two main reasons, or both. The first is that wherever industrial production and employment expand, labour resources are drawn from other sectors which have open or disguised unemployment (that is, where there is no relation between employment and output), so that the labour transference to manufacturing will not cause a diminution of output in these sectors. In addition, the expansion of industry will automatically generate an increase in the stock of capital employed in industry.

A second reason is the existence of increasing returns, both static and dynamic. Static returns relate to the size and scale of production units and are a characteristic largely of manufacturing where in the process of doubling the linear dimensions of equipment, the surface increases by the square and the volume by the cube. Dynamic economies refer to increasing returns brought about by induced technical progress; learning by doing; external economies in production, and so on. Kaldor draws inspiration here from Allyn Young's pioneering paper[11] with its emphasis on increasing returns as a macroeconomic phenomenon. Because economies of scale result from increased product differentiation, new processes, new subsidiary industries and so on, it was Young's contention that they cannot be discerned adequately by observing the effects of variations in the size of an *individual* firm or of a *particular* industry. Economies of scale and increasing returns derive from general industrial expansion which should be seen as an interrelated whole, or as an interaction between activities. Young, in turn, derived his inspiration from Adam Smith, who recognised the importance of increasing returns over 200 years ago in *The Wealth of Nations* (1776). Productivity depends on the division of labour, which in turn depends on the size of the market. As the market expands, productivity expands, but the increase in productivity resulting from a larger market in turn enlarges the market for other things, and this causes productivity in other industries to rise. As Young observed:

Adam Smith's famous theorem amounts to saying that the division of labour depends in large part on the division of labour. [But] this is more than mere tautology. It means that the counter forces which are continually defeating the forces which make for equilibrium are more pervasive and more deep rooted than we commonly realise ... Change becomes progressive and propogates itself in a cumulative way.

Kaldor used to bemoan that it was from Chapter 4, Book One of *The Wealth of Nations* that economics went wrong, when Smith abandoned the assumption of increasing returns.

The empirical relation between productivity growth and output growth in manufacturing industry has come to be known as Verdoorn's Law following Verdoorn's 1949 paper[12] showing such an empirical relation for a cross-section of countries in the inter-war period. Kaldor was the first to use the term Verdoorn's Law in print, although he had heard Arrow use it in conversation in connection with models of learning-by-doing. Verdoorn worked in Kaldor's team in the Economic Commission for Europe after the War, and Kaldor was aware of the 1949 paper, but had neglected it (and its implications), like the rest of the profession, perhaps because of its publication in Italian. Although the Verdoorn coefficient can be derived from a static Cobb-Douglas production function, it is essentially a dynamic relationship dependent on the rate at which capital is growing relative to labour, and on the scale parameters which may include both static and dynamic returns.[13] This leads on to Kaldor's second law, which is Verdoorn's Law.

KALDOR'S SECOND LAW: VERDOORN'S LAW

Kaldor's second law states that there is a strong positive (causal) relation between the growth of manufacturing output as the independent variable and the growth of productivity in manufacturing industry (p_m). Kaldor's test of this relationship across countries yielded:

$$P_m = 1.035 + 0.484 \, (g_m) \qquad r^2 = 0.826$$
$$(0.070)$$

and

$$e_m = -1.028 + 0.516 \, (g_m) \qquad r^2 = 0.844$$
$$(0.070)$$

where e_m is employment growth in manufacturing. The two equations are two ways of looking at the same relationship since $g_m = p_m + e_m$. Only in construction and public utilities was a Verdoorn relation also found to exist. The primary sector, agriculture and mining, revealed no such relation. In both agriculture and mining, productivity growth showed a large trend factor independent of the growth of total output and the coefficient relating productivity growth and output growth was not significantly different from unity. Productivity growth exceeded output growth in every country. In the case of transport and communications, no correlation was found between productivity growth and output growth. In commerce, a high correlation was found, but with autonomous productivity growth *negative*.

Returning to the strong relationship between p_m and g_m, the question may be raised of what is cause and what is effect? It could be argued that the causation is from fast productivity growth to fast output growth because faster productivity growth causes demand to expand faster through relative price improvement. On this view, all productivity growth would be autonomous. But if this were so, how can large differences in productivity growth in the same industry over the same period in different countries be explained? The reverse causation argument would also be a denial of the existence of dynamic scale economies and increasing returns. Kaldor later conceded, however, that there is an inter-action process at work through cost and price changes, and this indeed is an integral part of his circular and cumulative causation model of regional growth rate differences (see later). It also means that a well-determined estimate of the Verdoorn coefficient requires simultaneous equation estimation.

The question then is, if productivity growth in manufacturing is faster the faster rate of growth of manufacturing output, and this is one of the explanations of the faster growth of GDP in countries whose share of manufacturing is rising, what determines the growth of manufacturing output? Kaldor was clear that the explanation lies partly in demand factors and partly in supply factors and both combine to make fast growth a characteristic of an intermediate stage of economic development. Following the arguments of Allyn Young, the more demand is focused on commodities with a large supply response, and the larger the demand response (direct and indirect) induced by increases in production, the higher the growth rate is likely to be. For there to be self-sustaining growth, two conditions must be present: returns must increase and the demand for commodities must be elastic in the sense that 'a small increase in [their] supply will be attended by an increase in the amounts of other commodities which can be held in exchange for [them]. Under such conditions, an increase in the supply of one commodity is an increase in the demand for other commodities and it must be supposed that every increase in demand will evoke an increase in supply'. The growth process is a complex interaction of supply and demand. The demand for industrial products is very elastic in the intermediate stage of development and continues to be so in maturity. There is no constraint on growth here. But whatever the demand for commodities, growth may be slowed down by supply constraints. There may be a labour constraint and/or a commodity constraint which is Kaldor's meaning of a balance of payments constraint. In the UK context he claimed in 1966 that it is difficult to prove that the balance of payments is the *effective* constraint on the rate of growth. 'This would only follow if it could also be shown that, with a faster rate of growth of exports, the country could have achieved a higher rate of growth of manufacturing production.' Would it have come up against other supply constraints? It was at this juncture in the Inaugural Lecture that he went on to say things in the context of the UK that he later disowned. Explicitly he stated: 'inelasticity in the supply of labour seems to me the main constraint limiting the growth potential of the UK in a way in which it is not true of any other advanced country with the possible exception of Germany in the last few years'. He claimed the UK to be almost alone in having reached a stage of 'maturity' with no low productivity sectors outside industry where labour can be tapped. The evidence, however, of unemployment, participation rates, part-time working etc. showed this not to be so. His view then changed dramatically to the proposition that manufacturing output growth is fundamentally determined by export growth and that employment would respond to higher output growth. The point made about a labour surplus outside industry is not irrelevant, however, because the faster the growth of output determined by (export) demand, the greater the rate of labour transference to manufacturing industry from other sectors of the economy where productivity is lower (or where there is no relation between output growth and employment growth), so that the faster the *overall* rate of productivity growth will be. In this sense the UK has been 'short of labour' because of its relatively small agricultural sector. The relationship between the rate of labour transfer to manufacturing and overall productivity growth is a part of Kaldor's third law which is considered in more detail below.

Since Kaldor retracted his view about the UK economy early in 1968 in reply to some niggling points of criticism made by Wolfe[14] it is a pity that there should have been subsequent criticism of the model as a whole based on a misunderstanding, which in turn, through the way tests of the model have been conducted, has led many to reject Verdoorn's Law. The trouble seems to have started with the work of Cripps and Tarling[15] who, although writing in 1973, and in close academic contact with Kaldor, continued to interpret him as believing that manufacturing output growth is *dependent* on employment growth (and not the other way round), and so set up the Verdoorn relation with productivity growth in manufacturing as a function of employment growth in manufacturing. They found that their version of the law held from 1951 to 1965, but broke down in the period 1965 to 1970. Rowthorn,[16] with no reference to Kaldor's (1968a) reply to Wolfe, also continued to interpret Kaldor as believing that manufacturing output growth is endogenous and employment growth exogenous, and used the same Verdoorn formulation as Cripps and Tarling.

Rowthorn claimed to show that Kaldor's results, as well as those of Cripps and Tarling, were heavily dependent on the inclusion of Japan in the sample of countries which, because of its deviant position on the scatter diagram, must be regarded as a special case.

Now it is perfeclty true, since $g_m = p_m + e_m$, that mathematically speaking there are four different specifications of the Verdoorn relation,[17] but only if the equations are exact will the estimates be the same. From an economic and econometric point of view, the specification is not a matter of indifference. Rowthorn criticised Kaldor for estimating the Verdoorn coefficient 'indirectly' using g_m as the independent variable rather than what he considered to be 'directly' using e_m as the independent variable. He contended that had Kaldor done so, his estimate of the Verdoorn coefficient would have been much lower. But if output growth is exogenous and employment growth is endogenous, the Cripps–Tarling and Rowthorn specification of the Verdoorn relation is not correct for well known statistical reasons. Moreover, Kaldor's original results using the correct specification of the Verdoorn relation, do not depend on the existence of Japan in the sample. The r^2 between p_m and g_m excluding Japan is 0.536 and between e_m and g_m is 0.685. Research by Vaciago[18] for 18 European countries over the period 1950–69 supported the existence of the traditional Verdoorn relation, as does the more recent extensive research by McCombie and de Ridder using United States regional data.[19]

Whether or not Verdoorn's Law holds, however, it is *not*, contrary to the popular view, an indispensable element of the complete Kaldor model by which it stands or falls. Even in the absence of increasing returns in manufacturing the growth of industry would still be the governing factor determining overall output growth as long as resources used by industry represent a *net* addition to the use of resources (a) because they would otherwise have been unused, (b) because of diminishing returns elsewhere, and/or (c) because industry generates its own resources. This leads on to Kaldor's third law.

KALDOR'S THIRD LAW

Kaldor's third law states that the faster the growth of manufacturing output, the faster the rate of labour transference from non-manufacturing to manufacturing so that overall productivity growth is positively related to the growth of output and employment in manufacturing and negatively associated with the growth of employment outside manufacturing. It is in this additional sense that fast manufacturing output growth is also important for overall productivity growth, and in this sense in which labour in the UK may have been in short supply. Kaldor's first test of this hypothesis (1968a) was to regress GDP growth on the rate of increase in employment in manufacturing:

$$g_{GDP} = 2.665 + 1.066 \ e_m \qquad r^2 = 0.828$$
$$(0.110)$$

The strong correlation is support for the hypothesis unless e_m is closely correlated with total employment growth. There is no relation at all, however, between g_{GDP} and the growth of total employment. These two results can only be reconciled if overall productivity growth is positively correlated with employment growth in manufacturing and negatively associated with the growth of employment outside manufacturing (e_{nm}). This is confirmed:

$$g_{GDP} = 2.899 + 0.821 \ e_m - 1.183 \ e_{nm} \qquad r^2 = 0.842$$
$$(0.169) \qquad (0.367)$$

Cripps and Tarling[20] supported the links in Kaldor's third law and the law itself. They found in their sample of countries that the supply of labour from the primary sector (agriculture and mining) is consistently higher in countries with a faster growth of output. Moreover, the association is much stronger than for total employment growth suggesting that the primary sector is consistently a more important source of labour in fast growing countries and periods. There is also a negative relationship between the growth of output and the absorption of labour by the tertiary sector. They found no relation between the growth of output and employment in the non-manufacturing sector. The implication is that growth can be accelerated by diverting labour to manufacturing where there is correlation, and this is a plank in Kaldor's argument. They confirm Kaldor's third law for both the period 1951–65 and the period 1965–70, notwithstanding their finding that the Verdoorn relationship apparently broke down in the latter period (although they used an incorrect specification). The importance of manufacturing growth for productivity growth outside the manufacturing sector is strongly confirmed.

THE ROLE OF DEMAND

The Economist journal (5 November 1966), reviewing Kaldor's Inaugural Lecture, expressed surprise that a Keynesian, and an advocate of export-led growth, should come to the conclusion that the major factor constraining the growth of UK manufacturing output had been a lack of labour. Their explanation was that Kaldor, being in the Treasury at the time, had to be careful about mentioning balance of payments difficulties and such unmentionables as an over-valued currency and export incentives! Another explanation would be that he was providing a theoretical justification for the selective employment tax, which had just been introduced, without at the time realising that the case for such a tax does not rest solely on the grounds that increasing returns exist in industry whose output growth may have been constrained by a shortage of labour (see Chapter 9). A tax would be fully justified to raise the overall rate of productivity growth if there is no correlation between output growth and employment growth in the service sector. It could also be, of course, that a balance of payments constraint on manufacturing output growth is related to labour supply difficulties in certain sectors of the economy.

Subsequent model specifications and results have confirmed the importance of demand factors as determinants of the growth of manufacturing output and that employment growth must be considered as endogenous. Cornwall[21] like Wolfe cast doubt on whether the statistical evidence on employment growth in different sectors; on unemployment and vacancies, and relative wage movements, showed that manufacturing output was constrained by a labour shortage. Service employment was rising faster than manufacturing employment in the 1950s and 1960s, and since 1966 labour has been shed from manufacturing. Cornwall sets up an alternative demand-oriented model, in which labour supply is assumed to adjust to demand, in which the determinants of the rate of growth of manufacturing output are a technological gap variable proxied by the reciprocal of a country's level of per capita income; the investment ratio; export growth, and population growth. Differences in European growth rates are readily explicable in terms of these demand determinants. None of this casts doubt, of course, on Kaldor's fundamental contention that the manufacturing sector is the engine of growth, which Cornwall accepts.

Parikh[22] also confirms, using a simultaneous equation approach, that it is demand that determines output growth and output growth which determines employment growth. In Parikh's simul-

taneous equation model, employment and output are both endogenous recognising that in practice there undoubtedly exists a
two-way interaction between output growth and productivity
growth. Employment growth is made a function of output
growth, the growth of the workforce, and investment, and output
growth is a function of employment growth and exports. Parikh
finds that it is output growth in manufacturing that determines
employment growth, and output growth depends primarily on
export growth not on employment growth. He concludes, 'it is the
rate of growth of industrial output that seems to be constraining
the growth in employment, and low growth in manufacturing
may be attributed to demand factors'. Parikh confirms the view to
which Kaldor was later converted, and for which there is a good
deal of other evidence[23], that the rate of growth of industrial
output and GDP are fundamentally determined by the rate of
growth of exports in relation to the income elasticity of demand
for imports. Through the benefits that faster manufacturing
growth then brings, countries become engaged in a cumulative
process of relative improvement, with the consequent relative
decline of other countries, because fast growing countries are able
to sustain their advantage in export activities which gave fast
growth in the first place, and slow growing countries find it
difficult to break out of the vicious circle working against them.

Kaldor's change of mind on the causes of slow growth of the
United Kingdom (if it was a genuine change of mind and not a
provocation!) does not undermine the significance of the complete
model for an understanding of the growth process in advanced
capitalist countries. In many ways, bringing in the foreign sector,
the richness of the model is enhanced. Moreover, a breakdown of
the Verdoorn relation (if it has broken down) does not undermine
the model either. Kaldor's final position may be summarised as
follows: Manufacturing growth is the engine of GDP growth. The
higher the rate of manufacturing growth the faster the overall
rate of productivity growth. Labour is necessary for growth to
take place, but manufacturing output is not constrained by it
because there are more fundamental demand constraints which
operate long before supply constraints bite. Labour is very
adaptable and elastic, and even in mature economies more labour
used in manufacturing need not be at the expense of growth
elsewhere. The fundamental demand constraint on the growth of
output in an open economy is the balance of payments.

EXPORT-LED GROWTH AND 'CUMULATIVE CAUSATION'[24]

Kaldor first propounded a verbal model of 'regional' export–led growth in the Fifth Annual Lecture to the Scottish Economic Society in February 1970 (1970d). He subsequently expounded the theory in several other places (e.g. see 1975d; 1981a; 1981f). The main thrust of the argument is Hicks'[25] view that the long-run growth of output is governed by the growth of autonomous demand to which other components of demand adjust via the 'super-multiplier'. In open economies, be they regions or countries, export demand is the major component of autonomous demand, so that the rate of growth of exports will govern the long-run rate of growth of output to which consumption and investment adapt. Thus we may write:

$$g_t = \gamma (x_t), \tag{7.1}$$

where g_t is the rate of growth of output at time t and x_t is the rate of growth of exports. Now let exports be a multiplicative function of relative prices measured in a common currency and income outside the 'region' so that the growth of exports may be expressed as:

$$x_t = \eta (p_{dt} - p_{ft}) + \epsilon (z_t) \tag{7.2}$$

where p_{dt} is the rate of change of the domestic price of exports; p_{ft} is the rate of change of foreign (competitors') prices measured in domestic currency; η is the price elasticity of demand for exports ($\eta < 0$); z_t is the growth of income outside the 'region', and ϵ is the income elasticity of demand for exports ($\epsilon > 0$). The growth of income outside the economy and foreign prices may be taken as exogenous, but the growth of domestic export prices is assumed to be endogenous derived from a 'markup' pricing equation in which prices are based on labour costs per unit of output plus a percentage mark-up:

$$P_{dt} = (W_t/R_t) (T_t), \tag{7.3}$$

where W_t is the level of money wages; R_t is the average product of labour, and T_t is 1 + % mark-up on unit labour costs. Thus:

$$P_{dt} = w_t - r_t + \tau_t, \tag{7.4}$$

where lower case letters represent rates of change of the variables. Productivity growth, however, is partly endogenous by Verdoorn's Law. Hence:

$$r_t = r_{at} + \lambda(g_t),$$
(7.5)

where r_{at} is the rate of autonomous productivity growth and λ is the Verdoorn coefficient. The Verdoorn relation opens up the possibility of a virtuous circle of export-led growth. The model becomes 'circular' since the faster the rate of growth of output the faster the rate of growth of productivity; and the faster the growth of productivity the slower the rate of increase in unit costs and hence the faster the rate of growth of exports and output. The model also implies that once a 'region' obtains a growth advantage it will tend to sustain it. Suppose, for example, that an economy acquires an advantage in the production of goods with a high income elasticity of demand in world markets, which raises its growth rate above that of other economies. Owing to the Verdoorn effect, productivity growth will then be higher and the economy will reinforce its competitive advantage in these goods making it difficult for other economies to produce the same commodities except through protection or exceptional industrial enterprise. In models of 'circular and cumulative causation', in which some economies produce goods which are expanding fast in demand while others produce goods which are sluggish in demand, it is the difference between the income elasticity characteristics of exports and imports which is the essence of the theory of divergence between 'centre' and 'periphery', and between industrial and agricultural economies. This is also the essence of Kaldor's view that the opening up of trade between (unequal) economies may create growth rate differences which are sustained or even widened by the process of trade, as was his prediction for the United Kingdom economy within the EEC (see Chapter 10).

The equilibrium solution to the model is given by combining equations (7.1), (7.2), (7.4) and (7.5) which gives:

$$g_t = \frac{\gamma\left[\eta(w_t - r_{at} + \tau_t - p_{ft}) + \epsilon(z_t)\right]}{1 + \gamma\eta\lambda}$$
(7.6)

Remembering that $\eta < 0$, the equilibrium growth rate is shown to vary positively with autonomous productivity growth; the rate of growth of foreign prices and 'world' income growth, and negatively with domestic wage growth and a rise in the 'markup'.

The Verdoorn coefficient (λ) serves to exaggerate growth rate differences between economies arising from differences in other parameters and variables. It is an interesting question whether 'regional' growth rates will tend to diverge through time. This depends on the behaviour of the model out of equilibrium. In a two-region model, a necessary condition for divergence is that the growth rate of one of the regions diverges from its equilibrium rate. In order to consider the growth rate in disequilibrium, a variety of lag structures could be introduced into the equations which constitute the model. If, for simplicity, we confine ourselves to a first-order system, a one-period lag in any of the equations gives the same stability condition namely that convergence to, or divergence from, equilibrium depends on whether $|\gamma\eta\lambda| \lessgtr 1$. If for the moment it is assumed that $\gamma = 1$, this would mean there would be cumulative divergence away from equilibrium if $(-\eta\lambda) > 1$ i.e. if the product of the Verdoorn coefficient and the price elasticity of demand for exports exceeds unity. Given a Verdoorn coefficient of 0.5, this would imply a price elasticity of demand for exports in excess of two. This is possible. In practice, however, it is not usual to observe *growth* rates between 'regions' diverging through time; growth rates differ because the equilibrium rates differ. In the context of the above model, the explanation for lack of divergence probably lies in the fact that in practice the parameter, γ, is likely to be substantially less than unity and therefore the price elasticity of demand for exports would have to be substantially in excess of two. Imports typically grow faster than output. For balance of payments equilibrium, exports must also therefore grow faster than output. If relative prices in 'regional' trade are sticky (so that income adjusts to preserve balance of payments equilibrium), γ in equation (7.1) will approximate to the reciprocal of the income elasticity of demand for imports. Hence if the income elasticity of demand for imports is typically two, then γ in equation (7.6) will be 0.5, and the price elasticity of demand for exports would have to be in excess of four for divergence from equilibrium growth to occur. Such a high elasticity is unlikely.

Out of this simple model sketched above, the dynamic Harrod trade multiplier can be derived which played such an important part in Kaldor's thinking about the determinants of the pace and rhythm of industrial growth. For balance of payments equilibrium, the growth of exports and imports must be equal (starting from balance). If the real terms of trade are assumed constant (which was Harrod's assumption), the condition for a moving equilibrium through time is:

$$\pi g_t = \epsilon(z_t), \tag{7.7}$$

where π is the income elasticity of demand for imports. Therefore:

$$g_t = \frac{\epsilon(z_t)}{\pi} = \frac{x_t}{\pi} \tag{7.8}$$

which is the dynamic Harrod trade multiplier result, that the growth of income is equal to the growth of export volume divided by the income elasticity of demand for imports. This result also implies that one 'region's' growth rate relative to all others will be equal to the ratio of the income elasticity of demand for its exports to its income elasticity of demand for imports: $(g/z) = \epsilon/\pi$. It is differences in the income elasticity of demand for exports and imports that lie at the heart of growth rate differences between regions within countries and between countries in the world economy.

NOTES

1. This chapter is taken from the author's article 'A Plain Man's Guide to Kaldor's Growth Laws', *Journal of Post-Keynesian Economics*, Spring 1983. I am grateful to the publishers, M. E. Sharpe, for allowing me to use it.
2. See, for example, the Symposium on Kaldor's Growth Laws in the *Journal of Post-Keynesian Economics*, Spring 1983, and the references cited therein.
3. 'Increasing Returns and Economic Progress', *Economic Journal*, December 1928.
4. P. J. Verdoorn, 'Fattori che Regolano lo Sviluppo della Produttivita del Lavoro', *L'Industria*, 1949.
5. *Collected Essays*, Vol. 5, Introduction.
6. For an exposition and elaboration of the Harrod trade multiplier see C. Kennedy and A.P. Thirlwall, 'Import Penetration, Export Performance and Harrod's Trade Multiplier', *Oxford Economic Papers*, July 1979; and A.P. Thirlwall, 'The Harrod Trade Multiplier and the Importance of Export Led Growth', *Pakistan Journal of Applied Economics*, March 1982.
7. See A.P. Thirlwall, 'The Balance of Payments Constraint as an Explanation of International Growth Rate Differences', *Banca Nazionale del Lavoro Quarterly Review*, March 1979.
8. It is true, of course, that the whole world cannot be balance of payments constrained in its growth, but it only requires one country not to be constrained for it to be possible for all the other countries to be so.
9. Japan, Italy, West Germany, Austria, France, Denmark, Netherlands, Belgium, Norway, Canada, UK and USA.
10. T. F. Cripps and R. T. Tarling, *Growth in Advanced Capitalist Economies 1950–1970* (Cambridge University Pres, 1973).
11. *Op. cit.*
12. *Op. cit.*
13. See A. P. Thirlwall, 'Rowthorn's Interpretation of Verdoorn's Law', *Economic Journal*, June 1980.

14. J. N. Wolfe, 'Productivity and Growth in Manufacturing Industry: Some Reflections on Professor Kaldor's Inaugural Lecture', *Economica*, May 1968.
15. *Op. cit.*
16. R. Rowthorn, 'What Remains of Kaldor's Law?', *Economic Journal*, March 1975.
17. $p_m = a + b\,(g_m)$, $0 < b < 1$; $e_m = -a + (1-b)g_m$;

$$g_m = \frac{a}{1-b} + \frac{1}{1-b}\,e_m; \text{ and } p_m = \frac{a}{1-b} + \frac{b}{1-b}\,e_m$$

18. G. Vaciago, 'Increasing Returns and Growth in Advanced Economies: A Re-Evaluation', *Oxford Economic Papers*, July 1975.
19. J. McCombie and J. de Ridder, 'Increasing Returns, Productivity and Output Growth: the Case of the United States', *Journal of Post-Keynesian Economics*, Spring 1983. See also, J. McCombie, 'Kaldor's Laws in Retrospect', ibid.
20. *Op. cit.*
21. J. Cornwall, 'Diffusion, Convergence and Kaldor's Laws', *Economic Journal*, June 1976.
22. A. Parikh, 'Differences in Growth Rates and Kaldor's Laws', *Economica*, February 1978.
23. See A.P. Thirlwall, 'The Balance of Payments of Constraint as an Explanation of International Growth Rate Differences', *op. cit.*
24. This section relies heavily on the author's papers with R.J. Dixon, 'A Model of Regional Growth Rate Differences on Kaldorian Lines', *Oxford Economic Papers*, July 1975; and 'A Model of Export-Led Growth with a Balance of Payments Constraint' in J. Bowers (ed.), *Inflation Development and Integration: Essays in Honour of A.J. Brown* (University of Leeds Press, 1979).
25. J. Hicks, *The Trade Cycle* (Oxford University Press, 1950).

8 THE THEORY AND PRACTICE OF ECONOMIC DEVELOPMENT

Kaldor never published a fully-fledged development model in the spirit, for example, of the early classical economists, or of Arthur Lewis in more modern times.[1] For many years he lectured in Cambridge on a two-sector model of the growth of a closed economy which integrates the growth of agriculture (primary production) and industry in an equilibrium framework, which can form the basis of a general model of growth and development (see later), but he never brought it to fruition.[2] His writings on the theory and practice of economic development are scattered, largely representing the product of invitations to visit developing countries to give advice or to give lectures. Serious involvement with development issues started in 1956 during his sabbatical year from Cambridge which took him to several countries in Asia and Latin America. His ambitions and provocative lecture in China on 'Capitalist Evolution in the Light of Keynesian Economics' (1956c) has already been mentioned in Chapter 6. In addition, while in India, Hong Kong, Singapore and elsewhere he lectured widely on the characteristics of economic development (see 1956b). On return visits to India, following his classic survey of the Indian tax system, the problems of Indian planning began to interest him, with particular reference to the third Five Year Plan (see 1958b). He was critical of planning which examined resource mobilisation in financial terms before an assessment of the actual (real) resources required for attaining the targets of the Plan. A major suggestion for India was that the targets of the Third Plan should be worked out primarily in terms of additional employment and what this would imply for food production, since the main problem of employment creation in developing countries is the generation of an agricultural surplus. In Ceylon in 1958, while acting as a tax adviser there, he was likewise concerned with the economic development of the country (see 1958a), arguing the case on rather unconventional lines for expanding plantation agriculture, in preference to import substitution, coupled with the development under public ownership of power intensive producer goods' industries (e.g. fertilisers, cement, rubber processing, etc.), which would also absorb labour. In December 1957 he attended an Eminent Persons Symposium organised by the United States Committee for Economic Development on the theme, 'What is the most important problem faced by the United States in the next twenty years?' A constantly recurring theme at the Symposium was the gap between rich and poor countries which could endanger world peace. According to press reports (e.g. *The Times*, 30 December) Kaldor's paper (1958c) was one of the most impressive in which he warned of the spread of communism if America did not help the Third World.

Following his initial visit to Asia in the first half of 1956, he journeyed to Latin America in the summer. He gave thirteen lectures in Chile on 'The Theory of Economic Development and Its Implications for Economic and Fiscal Policy', and five lectures in Brazil on 'The Characteristics of Economic Development' (1957a). The lectures in Chile, delivered in August, were wide-ranging, covering such topics as growth theory, the meaning of technical progress and full employment, the problems of accelerating growth, monetary and fiscal policy, inflation, taxation and development, and the problems of economic policy-making. These lectures, which were never published, are significant in containing Kaldor's first statement of the principle of circular and cumulative causation, and how increasing returns can lead to the concentration of industrial activities in selected favoured regions.[3] The inapplicability of Ricardo's theory of trade if there is unemployment on the land is also forcefully stressed. While at the Economic Commission for Latin America (ECLA) in Santiago he prepared a paper on the 'Economic Problems of Chile' (1959b) blaming the country's poor development performance mainly on political and social factors and emphasising the need to promote a vigorous entrepreneurial class in both industry and agriculture. The lectures in Brazil, delivered in October, were similar to those in Chile, but also mark the origin of the two-sector agriculture – industry model, in which the limits on industrial growth are attributed to the rate of land saving technical progress in agriculture. This idea came to dominate his thinking in the years ahead and resurfaced for the last time before his death in his 1985 Hicks Memorial Lecture 'Limits on Growth' (1986b).

He returned to Latin America on numerous occasions. In the summer of 1960 he delivered a series of lectures on economic development at the Centre of Latin American Studies in Mexico City, published in Spanish as *Ensayos sobre Desarrollo Economico* (1961), following broadly the pattern of the Brazilian lectures four years earlier, but with some differences in emphasis. Much more attention was paid to the financing of development, particularly the role of inflationary finance. Three years later, he visited Brazil and ECLA again preparing papers on the terms of trade and dual exchange rates, both of which subsequently appeared in the *Economic Bulletin for Latin America* (1964a, 1964e). The latter paper, 'Dual Exchange Rates and Economic Development', has become a classic reference in the literature on the case for separate exchange rates for agricultural and industrial goods traded by less developed countries. Visiting India in 1984 he personally presented and discussed such a plan for India with the Prime Minister, Indira Gandhi, which later was published in *Economic and Political Weekly* (1984a).

CHARACTERISTICS OF ECONOMIC DEVELOPMENT

In all his development writing, Kaldor starts with the fundamental proposition that the task of a true theory of economic growth and development must be to explain why some societies have experienced such rapid increases in living standards while others have lagged behind. Why has development not spread? The explanation in general must lie in the fact that at different stages of economic development, different kinds of constraints (or limitations) on progress operate and, although some of these factors are sociological or political in origin, the major constraints are likely to be economic. 'Basically it may be described in terms of the varying nature of the responses of supply to changes in demand and of the responses of demand that result from changes in supply.'[4] Kaldor regarded as deficient the classical, neoclassical and Harrod-type theories of why some societies experience more rapid growth than others and why their own growth may vary inter-temporally. All these theories of long run growth focus on the supply side of the economy: classical theory stressing thrift and capital accumulation; neoclassical theory stressing an exogeneously given rate of technical progress and population growth, and Harrod theory postulating a natural rate of growth determined by population and labour productivity growth as if both were exogenous and God-given. For Kaldor, by contrast, capital accumulation, technical progress and population growth are all manifestations of the process of development; they cannot explain why development occurs *where* it does and *when* it does. What drives an economic system, as in Keynes' theory of income determination, are decisions to invest. The greatly accelerated economic development of the last two centuries can only be explained in terms of changing human attitudes to risk-taking and profit-taking. The rate of development is the outcome of the strength of entre-preneurial pressures on the one hand and the elasticity of supply response on the other. Demand creates its own supply. We know from Keynes that investment generates its own saving; likewise strong demand will generate within limits a labour supply response and faster technical progress.

The question still remains why capitalist enterprise has not spread more quickly and widely throughout the world. The reason is that development requires a balanced expansion of the various sectors of the economy, and if a critical sector is slow to expand the others are retarded. In the context of industrialisation the critical sector is agriculture, its ability to feed an industrial population, and its willingness either to buy industrial output or to accumulate capital assets outside the agricultural sector. It is differences in this ability and willingness which is the major explanation of disparate levels of development across the world. Agriculture as well as industry must become possessed of the capitalist spirit because the strength of demand for industrial output from agriculture depends on the growth of income of the agricultural sector which, in turn, depends on the rate of land saving innovations. Kaldor was led to the policy conclusion that a vast effort is required at raising the general level of education in rural areas, since it is educational differences which largely account for the differences in outlook between urban and rural populations. Bringing to the fore the entrepreneur, the risk-taker and the profit-seeker has certain affinities with the development theories of Schumpeter[5] and Hirschman.[6] Moreover, in both Kaldor and Schumpeter, after the initial impetus has been made development will tend to gather its own momentum; in Schumpeter through the 'mechanisation of progress'; in Kaldor through the process of 'circular and cumulative causation'.

Some of Kaldor's development thinking arose from his con-sideration of the question of why modern capitalism first devel-oped in England (1975e); a phenomenon still not fully understood by economic historians but clearly associated with the process of industrialisation. Four important factors are identified as contri-buting to Britain's early start. The psychological attitudes asso-ciated with the Reformation and the protestant ethic. A socio-political framework conducive to market-oriented enterprise following Cromwell and the 'Glorious Revolution' of 1688/89. An agrarian revolution, unusual in character because it expropriated the peasants and not the feudal landlords as in France, leading to a dramatic increase in the agricultural surplus and labour available for work. Last, and most important, the development of the factory system which itself was the product of the social and political climate and the agrarian revolution. At the turn of the eighteenth century there arose a powerful class of merchant-capitalists originating from the development of overseas trade, following on the establishment of the American colonies. Up to about 1780 capitalist manufacturers put out work to cottage industries using the system of piecework. With the enclosure of land, the expropriation of the peasant class, and the emergence of surplus labour it became obvious that large numbers could be employed in large buildings for the production of many goods previously produced in cottage industries, with consequent reductions in the cost of handling and working raw materials. The factory system then initiated a cumulative process of technical change and capital accumulation out of growing profits.

But what are the limits to the growth of output in this system? According to the classical conventional wisdom of Ricardo and Mill, output growth is governed by the availability of labour and capital accumulation: supply creates its own demand. But not all income generated in the industrial sector is spent in that sector. Some will be spent on agricultural goods. According to classical theory, however, if the supply of industrial goods exceeds the demand, the prices of industrial goods will fall relative to the price of agricultural goods, and the improvement in agriculture's terms of trade will ultimately ensure that all industrial goods are bought. However, there is a limit to the degree to which the terms of trade can improve in favour of agriculture because there is a limit to which industrial wages and therefore prices can fall in terms of food, set by the subsistence wage.

Keynesian theory undermined Say's Law at the macro-level. Say's Law is equally invalid at the sectoral level in considering the relation between agriculture and industry. If there is a limit to which the terms of trade between the two sectors can alter, the ultimate constraint on the rate of growth of the industrial sector is the rate of growth of demand from outside the sector, or agricultural production in the closed economy. The same problem arises internationally in the open economy when a part of the income of the country is spent on imports, and exports fall short of imports. In this case, exchange rate changes are supposed to balance exports and imports to ensure full employment but there are also limits to the degree to which real exchange rates can be altered. In this case the ultimate constraint on the rate of growth of a country's output is the rate of growth of export volume.

The dependence of industrial output on agricultural output can be expressed as $Q_i = I_a/k$, where Q_i is industrial output, I_a is the demand for industrial output from agriculture dependent on the marketable surplus in agriculture and k is the industrial sector's propensity to import agricultural goods. The dependence of a country's output on export demand can be similarly expressed as $Y = X/m$, where Y is national income, X is the volume of exports and m is the propensity to import. These propositions are the antithesis of Say's Law and extend to the 'open' economy the fundamental propositions of Keynes relating to the closed economy that output depends not on supply but on 'effective demand'. For Kaldor, these 'trade' multipliers between sectors of an economy and between countries are much more significant than the Keynesian investment multiplier for explaining and understanding the pace and rhythm of industrial development within countries and in the world economy at large. Kaldor was critical of traditional development theory for the neglect of complementary demand. Therein lies the significance of his pioneering two-sector model.

A CRITIQUE OF EXISTING DEVELOPMENT THEORY

There can be little doubt from the empirical evidence that the pace of long-run growth and development is closely associated with the growth of industrial activities. The fundamental question is what determines the growth of industrial output? In the standard neoclassical two-sector model,[8] the answer to this question lies in the allocation or supply of scarce factor endowments, technology and tastes, all exogenously determined. The first objection to this approach is that neither labour nor capital are scarce in the manner envisaged by the model. It is very doubtful, particularly when considered in a growth context, whether less labour on the land means less agricultural output. All the evidence suggests an enormous 'dynamic' surplus of labour, with increasing food production going hand in hand with a declining agricultural workforce. And capital is not 'allocated', it is accumulated. There is no way of withdrawing capital from one sector for use in another. Rather the process of industrial production itself generates its own capital. Secondly, there is no treatment of the complementarity between the output of one sector and the output of the other within the framework of reciprocal demand. There is no recognition that the level of output in agriculture may itself determine the demand for the output of the industrial sector and vice versa, and there is no explicit role for the terms of trade as the mechanism for achieving balance between the supply of and demand for output in both sectors, so that growth is neither supply or demand constrained below its potential.

Lewis's classical model[9] is an improvement on neoclassical models in that labour is plentiful and capital is accumulated but it is still basically a supply-oriented model, with the demand for the output of the industrial sector side-stepped. Lewis's discussion of the relationship between the two sectors focuses only on checks to the expansion of the capitalist surplus, and particularly on how a deterioration in the industrial terms of trade chokes the rate of capital accumulation. There is no recognition of the fact that a worsening terms of trade for industry may be associated with faster industrial growth because of higher rural incomes which accompany a faster growth of agriculture. There is no analysis of trade between the sectors. Johnston and Mellor[10] recognised this worrying feature of the Lewis model many years ago when they perceptively remarked: 'one of the simplifying assumptions of the [Lewis] two-sector model is that expansion of the capitalist sector is limited *only* by a shortage of capital. Given this assumption, an increase in rural net cash income is not a stimulus to industrialisation but an obstacle to expansion of the capitalist sector'. Johnston and Mellor continue, 'there is clearly a conflict between emphasis on agriculture's essential contribution to the capital requirement for overall development and emphasis on increased farm purchasing power as a stimulus to industrialisation. Nor is there any easy reconciliation of the conflict.'

The challenge of reconciliation has never been taken up in a satisfactory way, not even by Lewis himself, who recognised the limitations of his 1954 model in his 1972 essay in honour of Prebisch,[11] where he distinguishes three models: (i) his original classical model with no trade between sectors and no foreign trade; (ii) a second version with a closed economy, but the capitalist (industrial) sector depending on trade with the non-capitalist sector for food and raw materials, and (iii) a third version with an open economy whose industrial sector trades either with the non-capitalist sector or with the outside world. The latter two versions are not well developed and in a sense Kaldor's model to be developed corresponds to them.[12] There is a resolution of the conflict in Lewis, referred to by Johnston and Mellor, if the complementarity between industry and agriculture is recognised from the outset, and it is remembered that there must be an equilibrium terms of trade that balances the supply of and demand for output in both sectors.

THE BASIC TWO-SECTOR MODEL OF AGRICULTURE AND INDUSTRY

The basic model to be developed and extended formally models the complementarity between industry and agriculture and explicitly derives the equilibrium terms of trade, showing at the same time the consequences of disequilibrium. In presenting the model informally, Kaldor (see 1975a; 1979a) originally discussed it in the context of the (closed) world economy divided between primary producing countries on the one hand, and industrial countries on the other. But clearly the model is equally applicable to an individual dual economy closed to trade. The basic model can then be extended in various directions by: (i) introducing technical progress in agriculture through a technical progress function; (ii) introducing the possibility of labour supply constraints in industry (in the sense of a higher real wage having to be paid for labour); and (iii) opening up the economy to trade. A number of interesting things can then be seen and done with the model. For example: (i) it can be subjected to autonomous shocks (such as harvest fluctuations), and the attempt by the industrial sector (capitalists) to force the pace of growth; (ii) it can be seen how industrial growth becomes supply or demand constrained if the terms of trade between the two sectors are not in equilibrium; (iii) Prebisch effects can be seen, *i.e.* the institutional mechanisms which may generate a long-run tendency for the agricultural terms of trade to deteriorate;[13] (iv) it can be seen how through time, the importance of export growth will come to dominate the growth process; and (v) the model is also versatile enough to incorporate the notion of circular and cumulative causation. Finally, the model helps to explain why some countries have industrialised and developed sooner than others, and points to a number of ways in which the smooth functioning of individual countries (and the world economy) could be enhanced. One of the fundamental conclusions of the closed economy model is that in the long run the growth of industry is fundamentally determined by the growth of land saving innovations in agriculture as an offset to diminishing returns. This contrasts with the standard neoclassical result that the long-run steady state growth of industry is determined by the exogenous rate of growth of labour supply in efficiency units.[14]

First   of all, assume a closed economy with two activities, industry and agriculture. Industry produces a capital good, say steel, by means of inputs of labour and capital goods, the latter being steel retained in previous production periods.[15] Agriculture produces wage goods, food or 'corn', by means of inputs of labour time, land and capital goods (steel). Industry sells steel to agriculture in exchange for food.

AGRICULTURE

There is a reservoir of surplus labour in agriculture. Disguised unemployment exists, which takes the form of work sharing – a ubiquitous feature of the agricultural sector of most developing countries. The marginal product of labour *time* in such circumstances is not necessarily zero but the marginal product of labour itself may be considered zero if the total number of hours worked on the land remains the same when a unit of labour is absorbed into industry. Thus changes in agricultural output are assumed to be independent of changes in the number of men. To begin with the level of technology in agriculture is also held constant. The price of agricultural goods is assumed to be determined competitively in free markets. Capital is obtained from the industrial sector in exchange for the agricultural surplus or saving. The lower the price of industrial output in terms of agricultural output, the faster will be the rate of increase in agricultural output and hence agriculture's purchasing power over industrial goods. This can be shown formally as follows: Let a proportion of agricultural output be consumed in agriculture itself and a constant proportion (s_a) saved to exchange for industrial goods. Agricultural saving may be expressed as:

$$S_a = s_a Q_a,$$ (8.1)

where Q_a agricultural output and S_a represents the agricultural surplus. Agricultural investment, I_a, is then equal to the amount of steel which can be obtained by the agricultural sector in exchange for the agricultural surplus. If p is the price of steel in terms of corn (or the industrial terms of trade) then:

$$I_a = S_a/p$$ (8.2)

Equation (8.2) is a market clearing equation.

Now the growth of agricultural output may be expressed as the product of the investment ratio in agriculture and the productivity of investment in agriculture (σ).

$$\Delta Q_a / Q_a = \sigma I_a / Q_a \qquad (8.3)$$

Substituting (8.1) into (8.2) and the result into (8.3), gives:

$$\Delta Q_a / Q_a = \sigma \, s_a (1/p) \qquad (8.4)$$

Equation (8.4) not only gives the rate of growth of agricultural output but also the rate of growth of purchasing power, or demand, over industrial goods (g_d). The equation traces out a hyperbola showing an inverse relation between the industrial terms of trade and the growth of agricultural demand for industrial goods. The more favourable the industrial terms of trade the lower the rate of growth of demand, and vice versa. The relation is shown in figure 8.1 with the terms of trade between industry and agriculture (p) measured on the vertical axis and growth (g) measured on the horizontal axis. A rise in agricultural productivity will shift the curve outwards, as will a rise in the agricultural savings ratio. If some agricultural saving was used to purchase a consumption good from industry this would lower the agricultural growth rate for any given terms of trade.

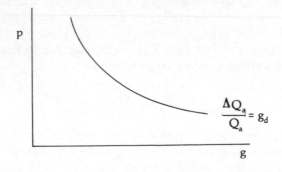

Figure 8.1

INDUSTRY

Industry produces steel by means of inputs of labour and capital, and fixed coefficients of production are assumed. The productivity of labour can be improved by technical progress, but for the moment the level of technology is held constant. Because of the existence of surplus labour in agriculture, the supply curve of labour to industry is infinitely elastic at some conventional real wage. The determinants of this real wage are considered later. All steel not sold to agriculture for food is invested. There are assumed to be profitable investment outlets for all saving.[16] The price of industrial goods is assumed to be determined by a fixed markup on unit labour costs. The consumption of workers in the industrial sector depends on the real wage and the level of output. It is assumed that all wages are spent on the consumption of food from agriculture. Therefore:

$$C_i = kQ_i, \tag{8.5}$$

where C_i is the consumption of food in industry; Q_i is industrial output, and $k = wl$ shows the food inputs per unit of steel output which must be paid in wages. w is the real wage (in terms of food) and l is labour input per unit of steel output (the reciprocal of labour productivity). For a given l, k is determined by the real wage, which for the present is exogenous.

The growth of industrial output can be expressed as the product of the investment ratio in industry and the productivity of investment:

$$\Delta Q_i / Q_i = \mu I_i / Q_i, \tag{8.6}$$

where μ is the productivity of investment. Now I_i is equal to the total output of steel less the steel sold to agriculture:

$$I_i = Q_i - I_a, \tag{8.7}$$

and from (8.2)

$$I_a = S_a / p$$

Since the agricultural surplus is sold to industry for workers' consumption, $S_a = C_i = kQ_i$. Therefore $I_a = kQ_i/p$.

Substituting for I_a in equation (8.7) and the result into (8.6) gives:

$$\Delta Q_i / Q_i = \mu [Q_i - kQ_i/p] / Q_i = \mu - \mu k(1/p). \tag{8.8}$$

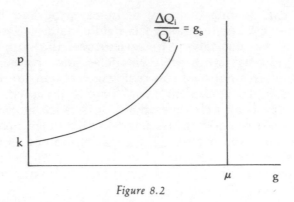

Figure 8.2

Equation (8.8) traces out a positive relation between the industrial terms of trade and the rate of growth of industrial output (g_s) as shown in Figure 8.2.

The growth of industrial output approaches asymptotically a maximum, μ, at which food would be 'free', and all industrial output (steel) could be retained and invested in the industrial sector itself. The point where the $\Delta Q_i / Q_i$ curve cuts the vertical axis gives the minimum price of steel in terms of food at which no steel can be retained by industry itself, which from equation (8.8) can be seen to be equal to k. A rise in the productivity of investment in industry will shift the asymptote, μ, outwards, and an improvement in labour productivity in industry, unmatched by an increase in the real wage, will shift the intercept (k) downwards. If industry produced a consumption good and workers spent only a portion of their wages on food, and the rest on industrial goods, this would make no difference to the industrial growth rate. The surplus for reinvestment is the same however wages are disposed of.

EQUILIBRIUM

The stationary equilibrium growth rate (g^*), and the equilibrium terms of trade (p^*), are found where the two curves (from Figures 8.1 and 8.2) cross in Figure 8.3.

Formally these values are found by solving the pair of equations (8.4) and (8.8). This gives:

$$p^* = k + \sigma s_a / \mu \qquad (8.9)$$

and

$$g^* = \frac{1}{k/\sigma s_a + 1/\mu}$$

(8.10)

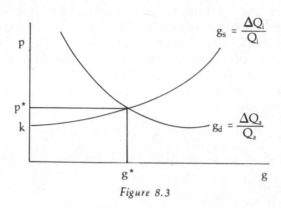

Figure 8.3

The equilibrium growth rate will be faster, the higher is the productivity of investment in industry and agriculture, μ, and σ, the higher is the agricultural savings ratio, s_a, and the lower are industrial wage costs per unit of output, k. The terms of trade move in favour of industry and against agriculture, the higher are k, σ and s_a, and the lower is μ.[17]

This equilibrium solution implies that steel output and corn output should be in a particular relationship to each other. We know that food demanded in exchange for steel is kQ_i, and that food offered (the agricultural surplus) is $s_a Q_a$. Thus in equilibrium the ratio of steel output to corn output must be:

$$Q_i /Q_a = s_a /k$$

(8.11)

or

$$Q_i = I_a /k \text{ (where } I_a = s_a Q_a /p)$$

(8.12)

This is the (Harrod) trade multiplier result that at a given terms of trade ($p = 1$) at which trade is balanced, industrial output is a linear multiple ($1/k$) of the export of industrial goods (to agriculture), where k is the propensity to import (agricultural goods).

STABILITY AND THE CONSEQUENCES OF A DISEQUILIBRIUM TERMS OF TRADE

Now suppose that equilibrium is disturbed. Is the model stable, and what are the consequences for growth of a disequilibrium terms of trade? Whether the model is stable or not depends on the nature of the adjustment process out of equilibrium. The stability conditions will not be derived here[18], but the consequences of a disequilibrium terms of trade are illustrated in Figure 8.4. At p_1 the industrial terms of trade are 'too high', and at p_2 the industrial terms of trade are 'too low'.

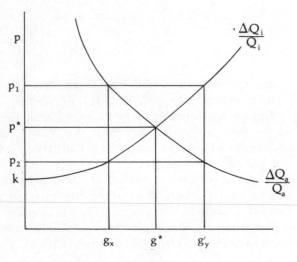

Figure 8.4

Suppose there had been an autonomous increase in agricultural productivity (a good harvest) which shifted upwards the agricultural growth curve to $\Delta Q_a/Q_a$ in Figure 8.4, but the terms of trade overshoots to p_1. In this case, industry would have the ability or capacity to grow at the rate g_y, but because agricultural prices are 'too low' agriculture's growth of demand for industrial goods is constrained to g_x. In these circumstances, the system cannot grow at its equilibrium rate, g^*, but is demand constrained to the lower rate, g_x. Conversely, suppose there is a bad harvest equivalent to an autonomous decrease in agricultural productivity and the terms of trade overshoots in the opposite direction, below its equilibrium level, to p_2. In this case, the agricultural sector has the capacity to grow and buy industrial goods at the rate g_y, but industry cannot invest enough to grow at that rate, and is constrained in its growth to the rate g_x. As Kaldor (1976b) wrote:

continued and stable economic progress requires the growth of output in these two sectors should be at the required relationship with each other – that is to say, the growth of the saleable output of agriculture and mining should be in line with the growth of demand, which in turn reflects the growth of the secondary (and tertiary) sectors. However, from a technical standpoint there can be no guarantee that the rate of growth of primary production, propelled by land saving innovations, proceeds at the precise rate warranted by growth of production and incomes in the secondary and tertiary sectors. To ensure that it does is the function of the price mechanism, more particularly of relative prices, or the 'terms of trade' between primary commodities and manufactured goods.

The consequences of violent shifts in the terms of trade between industrial and agricultural goods, and of a disequilibrium terms of trade, points to the need for mechanisms and institutions that can contribute to equilibrium and stability both within individual countries (and in the world economy) if growth is to be maximised. This issue is addressed in Chapter 11 where some of Kaldor's schemes for primary product price stability are discussed.

CREDIT, FORCING THE PACE OF GROWTH, AND INFLATION

So far in the model capitalists in the industrial sector are assumed to play a passive role, simply investing the surplus steel. There are no mechanisms by which manufacturers may invest in excess of this. In practice, finance and credit mechanisms exist which allow capitalists to force the pace of industrial growth if 'animal spirits' move them. Within the structure of the model we can see the processes by which the industrial growth rate may be raised, and the various constraints. If credit is increased to finance extra capitalist investment, the markup will rise in line with the extra aggregate demand for industrial goods, and the money price of steel will thus be higher. What happens then depends on three major responses. First, is the agricultural sector willing to supply more food at the existing money price? If so, this amounts to 'forced saving' in agriculture to finance the investment; the g_d curve shifts out to validate an upward move along the g_s curve. But the agricultural sector may resist such forced saving by attempting to raise the money price of food. Secondly, are industrial workers content with the same money wage in the face of a rise in the price of food as the demand for food expands? If so, this reduces k and pushes out the g_s curve along the g_d curve. If, however, there is real wage resistance, workers will demand higher money wages restoring k and pushing the g_s curve back to its original position. This is the idea of the 'inflation barrier' familiar from neo-Keynesian growth theory (see Chapter 6) and structuralist theories of inflation. Thirdly, are some individual capitalists unable to increase their money expenditures fully in line with the rise in the price of steel? If so, this will dampen the initial increase in investment. Monetary restraint will work in this direction. If, however, all producers and industrial workers are able to defend themselves against rising prices, there is a real danger of explosive inflation.

There remains the possibility that the government may force savings to match the increased investment by taxing the workers (shifting out the g_s curve) or the corn producers (shifting out the g_d curve). Even here the tax may be resisted with similar inflationary consequences which dampen or abort the development effort.

Kaldor had little sympathy for the monetarist explanation of inflation in developing countries. In the Latin American debate on monetarist versus structuralist explanations of inflation, he sided with the latter (see 1974a; 1979c). According to monetarist doctrine, if only the monetary authorities would control the money supply there would be no inflation. Apart from the obvious question, 'at what price?', on this view, low inflation countries, such as Venezuela and Mexico, avoided inflation because their monetary authorities were clever and/or virtuous, and high inflation countries, such as Chile and Brazil, succumbed to inflation because their monetary authorities were stupid and/or wicked. But why should some countries be luckier with their monetary authorities than others? The truth of the matter is that pressures differ between one set of countries and another, which is another way of saying that the money supply cannot be easily controlled because the supply of money responds in a variety of ways to demand. In Kaldor's view, what has distinguished high inflation countries from low inflation countries is the degree of agricultural supply response to demand and the ability to export enough to pay for imports which determines the degree to which the exchange rate may have to fall. Low supply response and currency depreciation leads to rising food and import prices which then induces high wage demands, raising industrial costs and impeding industrial growth. If monetary and fiscal policy has appeared lax it is because monetary policy cannot easily be tightened in the face of high wage demands and the need to provide industry with sufficient working capital; and government deficits emerge if tax payments lag behind expenditure in periods of inflation.

TECHNICAL PROGRESS, GROWTH, AND THE TERMS OF TRADE

For growth to be maximised demand growth for industrial goods must grow in step with supply growth. A lower price of steel has a positive effect on demand growth for industrial goods and would appear to be necessary in order that the rate of industrial growth be higher. This would seem to imply that higher rates of industrial growth must be associated with a worsening of the industrial terms of trade, and would appear to conflict with historical experience which suggests that economies grow faster when the terms of trade move in industry's favour. The explanation of this apparent contradiction lies in the fact that technical progress in both sectors causes *both* curves to shift about, and more so in agriculture where productivity improvements are not so quickly or automatically matched by increases in agricultural consumption. In industry, where labour productivity improvements tend to be matched by increases in real wages (and often more than matched) the share of wages in industrial output remains fairly stable (or increases), and the g_s curve is therefore relatively stable. Variations in the rate of land-saving innovations, however, both embodied and disembodied, will shift the g_d curve outwards by varying degrees, and the growth of industrial output can then increase without any deterioration in the industrial terms of trade. An outward movement of the g_d curve due to an increasing rate of technical progress, and the relative stability (and perhaps leftward shift) of the g_s curve for the reasons mentioned, would account for a secular tendency of the industrial terms of trade to improve relative to agriculture – the so-called Prebisch effect – despite the fact that industrial activities tend to be subject to increasing returns while agriculture is a diminishing returns activity, and despite the fact that technical progress tends to be faster in industry than in agriculture. Spraos[19] has confirmed the Prebisch thesis for the period 1870 to 1940, and the downward trend (excluding minerals) has continued in the post-war period since 1954.[20] In the short-run equilibrium of the model, the importance of technical progress in agriculture is clear. If there are diminishing returns to land as a fixed factor of production, successive applications of capital will lower the productivity of investment in agriculture, shifting inwards the g_d curve and lowering the industrial growth rate. In the long-run equilibrium of the model it can be shown formally how variations in the pace of industrial growth depend fundamentally on the rate of land saving innovations, and that technical progress in industry affects only the equilibrium terms of trade (by changing k), but not the long-run equilibrium growth rate.[21]

As far as the long-run terms of trade are concerned, nothing concrete can be said. It has been shown that diminishing returns in agriculture cause the terms of trade to turn progressively against industry but that this tendency can be offset by the increased availability of land and land saving technical progress. And we know that a rising real wage (by raising k) turns the terms of trade in favour of industry, which may be offset by labour saving technical progress. Long-term secular movements in the terms of trade are thus the outcome of geographical discoveries, invention, and institutional pressures. There can be no 'iron law' of the industrial terms of trade, either deteriorating (as in Ricardo) or improving (as in Prebisch). What happens depends on the balance of these economic and social forces.

LABOUR SUPPLY AS A CONSTRAINT ON INDUSTRIAL GROWTH

It is possible that in certain countries, at certain times, the rate of growth of industry may be constrained by a shortage of labour. Only if labour supply is strictly exogenous and unresponsive to demand can labour supply growth be regarded as a constraint on industrial growth in a direct sense. But this is not the case in the real world (see Kaldor 1968a; 1975c). In the process of development – at least up until the stage of maturity where the marginal product of labour in different sectors of the economy is roughly equal – there is not likely to be a shortage of labour to the industrial sector, and given the demand it may even be forthcoming at a constant real wage. Employment is then endogenous in the industrial sector at an exogenous wage. In the world economy at large there are ample supplies of labour for use in industry. Even in highly industrialised countries, when they have required labour, they have obtained it – often from other countries with surplus labour. Many countries, such as Germany, Canada, the USA, Australia and France, operated generous immigration policies in the 1950s and 1960s specifically for this purpose. There has also been a big increase in female participation in the labour force in recent years which has partly been a response to the pressure of demand. The informal service sector, too, provides a source of labour for the industrial sector not unlike that provided by agriculture. There are a variety of ways in which the stock of labour can adapt its services to the need for labour if the demand is there, including variations in the number of hours worked. With 70 per cent of the labour force still on the land in the developing countries, and with the new electronic revolution in developed countries, a global shortage of labour to produce industrial output seems a remote possibility for many years to come.

To obtain more labour, however, a higher real wage may have to be paid. This means that k and the g_s curve will be higher than otherwise would be the case, thus raising the industrial terms of trade and lowering the rate of growth of industrial output in the short-run equilibrium of the basic model.[22] In this sense labour supply can exert a constraint on industrial growth.

THE OPEN ECONOMY

Let us now move from the closed economy and think explicitly of the model applying to a particular country which may trade. The importance of trade in this model is not that it may affect growth favourably through raising the overall rate of capital accumulation or improving the productivity of investment, but that export demand becomes another source of autonomous demand for industrial output which, in practice, will come to dominate the growth of demand from agriculture. Trade by itself will not affect the rate of capital accumulation unless a country is allowed to import more than it exports or *both* industry and agriculture are able to buy their inputs cheaper abroad than domestically.[23] If goods are homogeneous, however, a more favourable international than domestic terms of trade for agriculture would mean a less favourable international than domestic terms of trade for industry. Only if goods are sufficiently heterogeneous, and the mix of inputs into each sector could be altered without affecting productivity, might both the agricultural and industrial sector of a country benefit simultaneously from being able to trade internationally as well as internally.

But, as mentioned above, the real significance of trade is that the rate of growth of export demand for industrial output (g_d^w) will, as development proceeds, become an important source of autonomous demand for industrial goods in addition to the rate of growth of demand emanating from the agricultural sector (g_d). In a steady state the rate of growth of demand for industrial output $(g_d{}^I)$ will be a weighted average of the two rates of growth, where the weights represent the proportion of autonomous demand accounted for by agriculture and exports respectively: i.e.

$$g_d{}^I = \theta(g_d) + (1 - \theta)g_d{}^w \qquad (8.13)$$

The growth of demand for a country's industrial exports is a function of the growth of world income and a country's relative competitiveness so that:

$$g_d{}^w = \epsilon(g_w) + \psi p_d \qquad (8.14)$$

where g_w is the growth of 'world' income, p_d is the rate of change of relative prices measured in a common currency; ϵ is the income elasticity of demand for exports ($\epsilon > 0$) and ψ is the price elasticity of demand for exports ($\psi < 0$).

It would be unrealistic, however, to assume a steady state, with the two sources of autonomous demand growing at the same rate through time. In every country's economic history there is a date when export demand for industrial goods grows more rapidly than agricultural demand, and so the ratio of export demand to agricultural demand inevitably grows. This results from a combination of a number of factors. First, the growth in agricultural income and purchasing power will come to lag behind the growth of world income owing to the lower income elasticity of demand for agricultural goods. Second, the income elasticity of demand for industrial goods in the agricultural sector is likely to become less than the income elasticity of demand for the country's goods in world markets as the country begins to acquire the technology to make goods for which the income elasticity of demand in world markets is high.

There is a third reason why export demand may come to dominate. If the income elasticity of demand for imports of the industrial sector is greater than unity then industrial imports will grow more rapidly than industrial output. The rate of growth of industrial exports must be faster than the rate of growth of industrial output as a whole if overall balance of payments equilibrium is a requirement and the deficit in industry cannot be matched by a payments surplus in agriculture. Now if the growth of industrial exports is limited by the growth of demand in world markets[24] then this limit will impose an upper ceiling on the growth of the industrial sector consistent with balance of payments equilibrium. Growth becomes balance of payments constrained, at a rate independent of the rate of growth of demand emanating from the agricultural sector. This is also a significant turning-point in a country's economic history, which might occur before the point when the growth of agricultural demand falls below the growth of world demand for industrial exports.

If in the long run, $g_{dw} > g_d$, then $\theta \to 0$ and equilibrium industrial growth becomes determined by the growth of demand for exports. Export growth becomes the driving force in the system to which other components of demand adapt.[25] If relative prices in international trade are sticky so that $p_d \to 0$; then equilibrium industrial growth approximates to ϵg_w, which is the dynamic Harrod trade multiplier result assuming balanced trade, a constant terms of trade, and an income elasticity of demand for imports equal to unity.[26]

If industrial output growth and productivity growth are positively related (through Verdoorn's Law) a process of circular and cumulative causation may set in which benefits industry relative to agriculture, widening disparities in living standards and income per head. This is the essence of centre–periphery models of growth and development articulated by Prebisch and Seers in the international context, and Kaldor in a regional context.[27]

CONCLUSION

The basic conclusion of the Kaldor two-sector development model is that agriculture must be seen as the driving force behind industrial growth in the early stages of development, superseded by export growth in the later stages. In this sense the model reinforces the belated recognition of agriculture's importance in the early stages of development, and lends support to export-led growth theory in the later stages. The extension of the basic model provides several interesting and important insights: (i) the joint determination of industry's growth rate and its terms of trade with agriculture, and the consequences of disequilibria in the terms of trade for the growth process in individual countries and in the world economy); (ii) the conditions under which the pace of industrialisation can be forced; (iii) a rationale for the 'Prebisch effect', but a demonstration that there is no 'iron law' of the terms of trade; (iv) the importance of land saving innovations in agriculture as an offset to diminishing returns; (v) the consequence of labour shortages and rising real wages for industrial growth, and (vi) the ultimate role of foreign trade and export demand as the fundamental source of autonomous demand for a country's industrial goods.

EXCHANGE RATE POLICY, TARIFFS AND SUBSIDIES

Given the importance of export growth in the intermediate stage of development, the policy question becomes how best can export growth be accelerated. Kaldor's first major discussion of this issue followed his visit to ECLA in 1963. At that time he was still inclined to the view that relative prices are an important determinant of differences in the strength of demand for countries' goods. Even though he lost faith subsequently, the question of exchange rate policy and the role of tariffs and subsidies is still a key policy issue in developing countries attempting to promote the growth of manufactured good exports. In the paper referred to earlier on 'Dual Exchange Rates and Economic Development' he argued that the important obstacles to a high and sustained growth of manufactured exports lie on the side of marketing rather than in production. Apart from trade restrictions imposed by developed countries, the major obstacle lies in the internal cost and price structure of developing countries as between primary and manufactured goods. In the initial stages of industrialisation, because production runs are limited and 'learning by doing' is rudimentary, unit costs of production are high. But the social cost of production is much less than the private cost because of surplus labour and pecuniary external economies of scale. This is the justification for protection, to equalise the difference between private and social costs. The way to equalise the difference, however, is not to impose tariffs, which was the policy adopted in Latin America, but to subsidise industrial products. That subsidies are first-best and tariffs are second best is now a well-established welfare theorem in development economics if the purpose is to increase domestic output and the distortions preventing a welfare optimum are domestic.[28] There is no loss of consumer surplus with subsidies, although how the subsidies are financed is a question that tends to be left unanswered. Kaldor's advocacy of subsidies was on rather different grounds, however. If the object is to encourage exports it is important to adapt the internal cost structure to the external price structure rather than accommodate the internal price structure to the internal cost structure. Tariffs can only promote industrialisation so long as there is scope for creating an internal demand for home manufactured goods in substitution for imports. But what happens when the limits of import substitution have been reached? Industries that grow up behind tariff barriers are not competitive in world markets because they are dependent on the maintenance of an internal price ratio between industrial and agricultural products which is higher than the prevailing world price ratio. Thus exports are not able to grow in line with domestic income and import requirements unless the home market is large enough to allow production at minimum average costs (as, for example, in the case of cotton textiles and steel in some countries with a large population). This basic fact is enough to explain why import substitution policies generally fail with total imports continuing to rise faster than export earnings even though the ratio of imports to GNP might fall.

To rectify an imbalance between imports and exports, exchange rate depreciation is a possibility, but there are few economic policies more fraught with danger and less certain of success than a *uniform* currency devaluation to balance the trading account of a developing country. Foreign exchange receipts cannot be guaranteed to rise, and many imported goods are price inelastic. Even as a means of deflating real expenditure devaluation cannot be relied on, but in any case there are easier ways to deflate if excessive expenditure is the problem. It also has to be taken into account that a devalued currency to promote manufactured good exports would represent an undervalued currency as far as primary products are concerned if their price is determined in world markets or demand in price inelastic. In other words, it is unlikely that a *single* rate of exchange can ensure internal and external equilibrium in a developing (dual) economy. Either a dual exchange rate is required, or some system of combined taxes and subsidies to achieve the same effect.[29] Under a dual exchange rate system a fixed (official) rate could apply to primary commodity exports and all essential imports, and a free rate could apply to non-essential imports and exports of manufactured goods. With a foreign exchange shortage, the free rate would produce a domestic price of foreign exchange considerably above the official rate. The higher the free rate the greater the discouragement to inessential imports and the greater the encouragement to manufactured exports. The major administrative problem is to ensure that export proceeds from primary commodity exports are surrendered at the official rate. This can be achieved through state-owned marketing boards. To ensure that foreign exchange bought at the official rate is used for essential imports a system of advance deposits of local currency could be instituted. If a free rate of exchange were to replace all the alternative forms of import restriction, it would possess two advantages. First it would mean that the differential tax on imports was matched by an equivalent differential subsidy on exports. Secondly, it would combine the advantages of free trade with the promotion of exports and industrialisation. The more backward the country the higher the free market rate is likely to be relative to the official rate so that backwardness would not necessarily put countries at a relative disadvantage in export markets. In the 1960s, dual exchange rates were generally discouraged and frowned on by the International Monetary Fund, but in more recent years greater tolerance has been shown.

CHOICE OF TECHNOLOGY

Apart from the balance of payments, the issue which has come to the forefront in recent years in the discussion of development strategy is the question of the choice of technology and the location of industrial activities with the rapid increase in urban unemployment. The increase in agricultural productivity and the growth of towns have caused between them a rural–urban migration process of unprecedented scale. The incapacity of the urban sector to absorb the migrants as well as its own indigenous increase in the workforce has raised the question of whether the use of more labour-intensive techniques of production located in the rural areas themselves would not help to alleviate the problem and represent a welfare gain to society. The question is closely bound up with the more fundamental question of what developing countries are trying to maximise, for there may be a conflict between increasing employment and reducing unemployment on the one hand and maximising the long run growth rate, because the choice of techniques and location of activities which minimise unemployment may reduce the investible surplus and not create the conditions for a sustained growth of industrial output and exports on which long-run growth depends.

Kaldor's view was that small-scale industry cannot be taken to the villages if successful industrialisation is to take place. 'The fact that in all known historical cases the development of manufacturing industries was closely associated with urbanisation must have deep-seated causes which are unlikely to be rendered inoperative by the invention of some new technology' (1972a). The explanation lies in external economies arising from the spatial concentration of industry. On the matter of the choice of technology he doubted whether more labour-intensive technology would mean a lower capital:output ratio and therefore doubted whether countries can gain from choosing a lower capital:labour ratio. Rather than focus directly on employment, Kaldor would apply the rule of choosing techniques which yield the highest rate of profit per unit of investment because this will tend to maximise the ratio of output to additional consumption and thus maximise the rate of reinvestment. This does not necessarily imply the latest techniques because they may be more costly to maintain, and the output required from advanced technology may be too large for its optimal utilisation. It may be more profitable to instal second-hand machinery if this can be purchased at lower costs. Kaldor's arguments in this field have largely been refuted by empirical research. There is now plenty of evidence that labour-intensive technologies do not necessarily have higher capital:output ratios than capital-intensive tech-nologies and that labour-intensive technologies need not im-pair the overall investible surplus of a country when all factors are taken into account.[30] Thus focusing on employment and present welfare need not involve a sacrifice of growth and future welfare in the way implied by Kaldor and many of his generation who used to argue this way in the 1950s.

NOTES

1. W. A. Lewis, 'Economic Development with Unlimited Supplies of Labour', *Manchester School,* May 1954.
2. Hints of the model are contained in Kaldor (1975a; 1976b; 1979a), and in his 1984 Mattioli Lectures.
3. The lectures predate the publication of Myrdal's book *Economic Theory and Underdeveloped Regions* (Duckworth) in 1957, but not Myrdal's lectures at the National Bank of Egypt in October 1955 on which the book is based.
4. *Strategic Factors in Economic Development* (Ithaca: Cornell University, 1967).
5. J. A. Schumpeter, *The Theory of Economic Development* (Havard University Press, 1934).
6. A. O. Hirschman, *The Strategy of Economic Development* (Yale University Press, 1958).
7. The bulk of the remainder of this chapter is taken from the author's paper 'A General Model of Growth and Development on Kaldorian Lines', *Oxford Economic Papers,* July 1986. I am grateful to the Editors and Oxford University Press for allowing me to use substantial sections of the article.
8. e.g. D. Jorgensen, 'The Role of Agriculture in Economic Development: Classical versus Neo-Classical Models of Growth', in C. R. Wharton (ed.), *Subsistence Agriculture and Economic Development* (Chicago: Aldine, 1969).
9. *Op. cit.*
10. B. F. Johnston and J. W. Mellor, 'The Role of Agriculture in Economic Development', *American Economic Review,* September 1961.
11. W. A. Lewis, 'Reflections on Unlimited Labour', in L. di Marco (ed.), *Inter-*

national Economics and Development: Essays in Honour of Raul Prebisch (Academic Press, 1972).

12. The capitalist non-capitalist distinction is not wholly synonymous with the division between industry and agriculture, but it is clearly the growth of industry that Lewis is concerned with.

13. R. Prebisch, *The Economic Development of Latin America and its Principal Problems* (ECLA, UN Dept of Economic Affairs, New York, 1950).

14. See, for example, R. Findlay, 'The Terms of Trade and Equilibrium Growth in the World Economy', *American Economic Review*, June 1980.

15. Allowing the industrial sector to produce a composite good, which can be either invested or consumed, would be more realistic, but it makes the model more complicated without changing the insights. See A. P. Thirlwall, 'A General Model of Growth and Development on Kaldorian Lines', *op. cit.*

16. In other words, the natural growth rate is assumed to exceed the warranted rate, typical in developing countries. There is no independent investment function of the Keynesian type, but there is a discussion later of what is likely to happen in the model if the industrial sector attempts to 'force' the pace of industrial growth.

17. It would have been attractive to incorporate in the model an above-unitary income elasticity of demand for industrial goods; and likewise a below-unitary income elasticity of demand for agricultural goods. This has not been done for several reaons. First, it makes no difference to the structure, or basic insights, of the model. Secondly, it would be difficult to have income elasticities of demand different from unity with at the same time holding constant the ratio of food consumption to output in both sectors, as is assumed in the present analysis. Undoubtedly, if the income elasticity of demand for industrial goods in the agricultural sector is greater than unity, the sector would partly meet this growing (proportionate) demand by consuming proportionately less food. Thirdly, in the two-sector model the income elasticities of demand for industrial and agricultural goods would have to be the reciprocal of each other for there to be a constant terms of trade which balances the growth of demand and supply in the exchange of food for steel. This would be a restriction on the model which would be difficult to swallow empirically. By ignoring the different elasticities of demand for agricultural and industrial goods, the equilibrium growth rates of the two sectors at the equilibrium terms of trade are constrained to equal each other.

18. See A. P. Thirlwall, 'A General Model of Growth and Development on Kaldorian Lines', *op. cit.*

19. J. Spraos, 'The Statistical Debate on the Net Barter Terms of Trade Between Primary Products and Manufactures', *Economic Journal*, March 1980.

20. A. P. Thirlwall and J. Bergevin, 'Trends, Cycles and Asymmetries in the Terms of Trade of Primary Commodities from Developed and Less Developed Countries', *World Development*, July 1985.

21. The reason for this is that when the capital:output ratio in agricultura is constant, the g_d curve in Figure 8.1 becomes a vertical line emanating from the horizontal axis.

22. However, it does not lower the long-run equilibrium rate of growth since this is independent of k.

23. Trade may raise the productivity of investment in industry if the availability of foreign exchange allows a fuller or more efficient use of domestic resources. We are not concerned with this issue here.

24. Because ψ is low so that it is not possible to greatly increase industrial

exports by continuously cheapening them, or because the price of industrial exports is sticky ($p_d \cong 0$) due to oligopolistic market structures.

25. This is the idea of the Hicks super multiplier which Kaldor had in mind in developing his export-led growth model in a regional context (see Chapter 7).

26. If, empirically, the ratio of imports to output in the industrial sector was increasing, the income elasticity of demand for imports would exceed unity, and growth would approximate to $(\epsilon/\pi)g_w$, where π is the income elasticity of demand for imports. For a summary of the Harrod trade multiplier result and its implications, see A. P. Thirlwall, 'Foreign Trade Elasticities in Centre–Periphery Models of Growth and Development', *Banca Nazionale del Lavoro Quarterly Review*, September 1983.

27. Ibid.; and see Chapter 7.

28. See H. G. Johnson, 'Tariffs and Economic Development: Some Theoretical Issues', *Journal of Development Studies*, October 1964.

29. For example, a tax on primary commodity exports combined with export subsidies on manufactured goods. For a country obtaining X per cent of its export earnings from primary commodities, a d per cent duty would finance an Xd subsidy on manufactured exports. The subsidy would decline the the higher the proportion of export earnings from manufactures.

30. For a useful survey, see H. Pack, 'Aggregate Implications of Factor Substitution in Industrial Processes', *Journal of Development Economics*, August 1982.

9 ECONOMIC ADVISER TO LABOUR GOVERNMENTS

Kaldor was a Special Adviser to three Labour Chancellors of the Exchequer: to James Callaghan 1964 to 1967; Roy Jenkins 1967 to 1968 and Denis Healey, 1974 to 1976; and a Special Consultant to the Treasury and Adviser to the Department of Health and Social Security between 1968 and 1970. He was a natural choice. For many years he had been prominent in Labour Party circles, as a member of the Economic and Finance Committee of the Labour Party's National Executive Committee, and was the Party's foremost all-round academic economist with a particular expertise in tax matters. He also had a long-standing friendship with Hugh Gaitskell, who had been Chancellor of the Exchequer in 1950–51 (and Shadow Chancellor in Opposition) and had promised Kaldor an advisory position in the event of a Labour victory. Both Callaghan and Healey knew and liked him well, and Callaghan kept Gaitskell's pledge.[1] Healey regarded Kaldor as the most interesting and innovative economist in Britain. Kaldor left his mark on economic policy, particularly in the period 1964–67, probably to a greater extent than any other economist in the post-war years, and second only to Keynes this century. Before considering his influence, however, the years need to be put into context.

When the Labour Party assumed office under Harold Wilson in October 1964, it was their first taste of power for thirteen years. During the intervening period, the economy had performed tolerably well by historical standards, but there was growing frustration in the country that living standards were falling relative to other countries. Since the Second World War, Britain had experienced the slowest growth rate of any industrialised country, averaging only 2.7 per cent per annum compared with a

European average of 4.3 per cent. In an attempt to rectify this, the Conservative Chancellor, Reginald Maudling, embarked in the early 1960s on a 'dash for growth' through demand expansion which precipitated, in 1964, the worst balance of payments deficit in the nation's peace-time history: a deficit of £749 mlllion on current and long-term capital account, and a balance for official financing of roughly equal magnitude. Maudling claimed that the difficulties were only temporary due to a restocking boom; that export growth would rise substantially and import growth slow down. In the letter columns of *The Times* (e.g. 28 June 1964), Kaldor took issue, pointing out that imports had been growing persistently faster than exports for some time and that the upsurge in imports was in manufactured goods as well as in raw materials. There had been a 36 per cent increase in imports of machinery and transport equipment alone. As a measure of overheating in the economy, the unemployment rate was only 1.5 per cent, and there were three times as many unfilled vacancies as unemployed in the fourth quarter of 1964. Kaldor warned of the action that would be necessary to deal with the economic consequences of Mr Maudling.

This was the legacy that Labour inherited that was to continue to constrain and undermine economic policy-making throughout its period of office. A weak foreign trade sector and balance of payments at full employment has dogged the British economy throughout the post-war years, to which no administration has found a satisfactory solution. Kaldor initially pinned his faith in devaluation. In a letter to *The Times* (3 March 1963) he wrote:

The British economy is incapable of maintaining high rates of economic growth, or continued full employment, without either severe import restrictions or devaluation. The introduction of severe import restrictions would run counter to the spirit of our age; to our long run interest as a trade nation and to our proclaimed international aim to make trade freer and less discriminatory all over the world. Sooner or later, therefore, the choice has to be faced between the maintenance for prestige reasons of a fixed value of the pound and the avoidance of economic stagnation and mass unemployment.

The Labour Party believed it could break the syndrome of slow growth and balance of payments difficulties through a combination of planning on the one hand and industrial regeneration and export promotion on the other based on rationalisation and the adoption of modern technology. It was less united on currency devaluation, and Harold Wilson was positively hostile. A concise statement of Labour aims was contained in the 1964 Party Manifesto: 'We want full employment; a faster rate of industrial expansion; a sensible distribution of industry throughout the country; an end to the present chaos in traffic and transport; a break on rising prices, and a solution to our balance of payments problems.' The Manifesto continued: 'none of these aims will be achieved by leaving the economy to look after itself ... they will only be achieved by Socialist Planning'. New and revitalised ministries were to play a key role, in particular the Ministry of Technology, to sponsor industrial research schemes through the National Research Development Corporation, and the Department of Economic Affairs charged with the task of formulating a National Plan. Great euphoria surrounded the eventual publication of the Plan in September 1965, setting a growth target for the economy as a whole of 3.8 per cent per annum, some 40 per cent higher than the historical average of the preceding fifteen years. In addition, there were major innovations in the field of tax policy, investment incentives, regional policy, manpower policy, industrial policy, and in attempts to control the insidious process of inflation. The early years saw the introduction of corporation tax, capital gains tax, a selective employment tax to favour the growth of manufacturing industry, a regional employment premium to promote growth in Development Areas, investment grants, the establishment of an Industrial Reorganisation Corporation to promote industrial rationalisation, and a National Board for Prices and Incomes to control inflation, headed by Aubrey Jones, one of Kaldor's former pupils at the LSE. The number of Economic Development Committees of the National Economic Development Council was also increased to cover all major industries, and regional planning machinery was established. Professional economists were recruited to all the ministries and new agencies in unprecedented numbers in the conviction that they could, by wise decision-making reminiscent of Plato's philosopher-kings, produce economic results superior to the invisible hand of *laissez-faire*. An epidemic sense of excitement and optimism pervaded the air in Westminster and Whitehall, as those involved will testify, in the belief that a mixture of planning and the application of economic expertise could and would lift Britain out of the economic doldrums.

Kaldor's title in the Treasury was Special Adviser to the Chancellor of the Exchequer on the Social and Economic Aspects of Taxation Policy. His Hungarian compatriot, Thomas Balogh, was appointed at the same time as Adviser on Economic Affairs to the Cabinet, and they were depicted together in press cartoons and photos as if a sinister Eastern European economic experiment was about to be launched on the British people. The 'Hungarian

Mafia', 'Terrible Twins' and 'B and K' (after Bulgarin and Kruschev) were typical descriptions. Kaldor's appointment was not well received in the City and financial press, which portrayed him as some form of tax ogre employed to squeeze the capitalist class.

On his appointment, Kaldor himself had to resign from his various City posts on the Boards of Investing in Success Equities, Investing in Foreign Growth Stocks, the Anglo-Nippon Trust and Acorn Securities. He chose at the beginning to be part-time in the Treasury, realising that this might undermine his influence, but wanting to keep a foot in Cambridge knowing that a Chair in Economics was in the offing. At the age of 56, with a lifetime of scholarship behind him, he might have expected to have been elevated sooner. There was some comfort, perhaps, in the fact that Joan Robinson was also still a Reader. Both were eventually promoted together in January 1966. In the Treasury, in his first year of office, he was housed in the Inland Revenue at Somerset House, headed by (Sir) Alexander Johnston, and worked primarily on proposals for tax reform. In the autumn of 1965 he became full time and moved to the Treasury building closer to the centre of power. His salary rose commensurately from £4000 to £6500 per annum. His friend from Geneva days, Robert Neild, was installed as Chief Economic Adviser to the Treasury, having replaced (Sir) Alec Cairncross in 1964. Kaldor (1982b) denied that Neild's appointment was 'political' but it is difficult to interpret it in any other way, and certainly this is the way that it was perceived by the Civil Service. Alec Cairncross stayed on as Head of the Economic Section of the Treasury, which was shortly absorbed into a newly created Government Economic Service, but now for the first time politically-committed economic advisers overlapped with the Economic Section of the Treasury.

Neild and Kaldor worked well together and, in the words of *The Observer* newspaper (4 April 1965), they made a formidable pair, with Kaldor sparking off ideas and Neild filtering and steering them through the Treasury machine. Callaghan used Neild as a moderating influence on Kaldor, as well as an independent source of advice. The normal practice in government is for the Permanent Secretary to act as a Minister's principal channel of day to day advice, with the appointed economic adviser keeping in close contact with the Permanent Secretary. In other words, the economic adviser advises the administrators far more than he advises the Minister. This was largely true in Kaldor's case. He had free access to William Armstrong, the Permanent Secretary, and saw him on a regular basis, but there was no regular meeting with

Callaghan. In any case, as Cairncross has observed,[2] it is difficult for an adviser who attempts to work through the Minister and to by-pass the administrative machine to have any great impact unless the Department is very mediocre: not a description one would use of the Treasury.

Kaldor found both the Inland Revenue and Treasury very congenial places to work. During his membership of the Radcliffe Commission (1951–54), Kaldor had come into close contact with the Inland Revenue civil servants and formed a high opinion of them. The respect was mutual, not least because he, unlike some other 'outside' advisers, was always concerned to offer advice on policies and options with due regard to the administrative complexities involved. For instance, he used to show great interest in the administrative procedures involved in PAYE and this enhanced his effectiveness in those areas where he was able to make an impact. At the same time, this attention to administrative detail enabled him to expose any Revenue obstructiveness based on general assertions that such and such a new scheme would involve thousands of extra staff. He enjoyed being at the centre of things, and collaborated well with his Civil Service colleagues, particularly the younger generation whom he treated rather like his Cambridge students as a sounding board for ideas. For much of the time, he was concerned with the general economic situation and in this respect worked as a straightforward Treasury official, sitting on the appropriate committees. It is, of course, one thing to describe the role and activities of an economic adviser; it is quite another to gauge their precise impact on policy, particularly if they are immersed in the routine affairs of a Department. Kaldor's innovative mind, however, and the sheer force of his personality, makes his contribution perhaps easier to evaluate than most. As we shall see, his name is clearly associated with major policy initiatives and innovations, particularly in the tax field.

The first months of the Labour Government, however, were dominated by the deficit on the balance of payments and the question of whether the pound should be devalued. Mr Maudling, the outgoing Chancellor, apparently had in mind the possibility that the pound might float if his own ambitious growth target of 4 per cent led to insuperable balance of payments difficulties, but this option, or a straight devaluation, was ruled out by Wilson and his colleagues virtually the day after taking office. Wilson was strongly opposed because he did not want the Labour Party to be branded as the Party of devaluation, giving the political opposition damaging ammunition in a politically precarious situation; Callaghan was opposed because he felt that Britain had a moral obligation to the holders of sterling; and George Brown, the First Secretary of State and Minister of Economic Affairs, in charge of the newly-created Department of Economic Affairs – a brisk three-minutes walk down the Treasury corridors – was also opposed. The Treasury itself had mixed views, but the Bank of England was strongly opposed. The government's advisers were divided. Kaldor was in favour of floating, and both Neild and (Sir) Donald Macdougall, the Director General of the Department of Economic Affairs, were in favour of some form of exchange rate adjustment. On the other hand, Cairncross was against, or rather sceptical of its feasibility and ultimate 'success'. He knew well Wilson's antipathy, and was worried that the United States might also decide to devalue, jeopardising the whole Bretton Woods system. Balogh, Wilson's influential adviser, was also initially against, preferring other forms of expenditure switching policies. By contrast, Kaldor in this period was never an advocate of unilateral quantitative restrictions on imports in the form of tariffs or quotas. In fact, Balogh frequently castigated Kaldor for being a 'free-trader'. At this time, Kaldor was giving his support to an expanded European Free Trade Association as an alternative to Britain's entry into the Common Market. He was in favour, however, of tighter controls on direct investment overseas and for taxes to be raised in the first budget of November 1964. There were clear signs in Kaldor's thinking of what later came to be called the 'New Cambridge' view, that the balance of payments position and the budget deficit are causally related.

Devaluation having been rejected, a 15 per cent surcharge on imports of manufactures and semi-manufactures (coupled with an export rebate scheme) was immediately introduced as a temporary measure, much to the annoyance of Britain's EFTA partners who were not consulted. The surcharge had been part of a contingency plan to protect the balance of payments and had nothing to do with Kaldor, although in the event he did not object to it. Despite the surcharge, speculation against sterling continued such that not only was bank rate raised from 5 to 7 per cent in late November, but the whole matter of devaluation was reconsidered by the government. The Treasury came down in favour of deflation, while Kaldor, Neild and MacDougall continued to press for an immediate devaluation. The Bank of England meanwhile managed to arrange Central Bank credits of some $3 billion which gave some temporary respite. Orders were given, on Wilson's instructions, to destroy all copies of papers advocating devaluation and to refrain from mentioning the idea. Devaluation became, in effect, a taboo word; the 'great unmentionable' as it was jokingly

referred to in advisory circles. Cairncross says that from October
1965 no paper was ever asked for by a Minister setting out the pros
and cons of devaluation.[3] Kaldor, however, was continuing to
write 'Top Secret' memos to his Permanent Secretary on exchange
rate alternatives, advocating a type of crawling-peg system, or
what he described as 'progressive adaptation' of the exchange rate.
But Wilson firmly believed that *ad hoc* intervention could
eventually improve the balance of payments without any form of
exchange depreciation. Incomes policy would be used to improve
competitiveness; deflation would be used to check excess demand;
exchange controls could be tightened (which they were), and a
variety of alternative measures might be taken to promote exports
and limit imports more directly. Despite action on these various
fronts, sterling's fragility and vulnerability remained, due largely
to pressure on the capital account. Indeed, over the period from
October 1964 to the eventual devaluation of the pound in
November 1967, the deficit on current account was only £90
million. Virtually all of the £1.5 billion of official financing
required was to offset short-term capital and monetary
movements. In July 1965 there was a speculative crisis which
finally converted George Brown to the devaluation case for fear
that his National Plan would be jeopardised. There was a further
crisis in July 1966 which led other senior ministers, including Roy
Jenkins, Tony Crosland and Richard Crossman, to advocate that
the pound should be floated. Instead, tighter exchange controls
were imposed, and a large deflationary package was announced,
killing the National Plan. George Brown duly resigned from the
Department of Economic Affairs and temporarily from the
government, returning on persuasion to the Foreign Office.
Robert Neild, disillusioned with the course of economic policy, also
took the opportunity to resign as the Chancellor's Chief Economic
Adviser to become Director of the Stockholm Institute of
International Peace Research. Callaghan approached Kaldor to
explore the possibility that he might take Neild's position, but
Kaldor was also out of sympathy with the policies being pursued
and said so in no uncertain terms, effectively talking himself out of
the post. Michael Posner assumed the mantle. Earlier, in the
autumn of 1965, Dick Crossman had tried to seduce Kaldor to be
his adviser in the Ministry of Housing, but Dame Evelyn Sharp,
the Permanent Secretary, was against and other Ministers were
suspicious, and the approach came to nothing.

The import surcharge was still in force at a reduced rate, but due
to terminate in November 1966, the prospect of which further
weakened sterling. Problems continued in 1967 with the six-day

Arab-Israeli war, and the closure of the Suez Canal, raising the price of oil. The continual pressure on sterling made devaluation look almost inevitable. The final straw was the London and Liverpool dock strikes in September which highlighted once again the vulnerability of sterling to exogenous influences. According to Wilson's own account of the events leading up to devaluation,[4] the Chancellor called on him on 4 November to express doubts about the parity. Wilson said he preferred, if anything, to let the pound float. A special meeting of the Inner Cabinet on Economic Policy was then called on 8 November to discuss the possibility of devaluation. On the 13th, Wilson and Callaghan decided to submit devaluation plans to the Cabinet and it was agreed on two days later that sterling should be devalued on the 18th from $2.80 to $2.40. Callaghan's reputation was now in tatters and he resigned as Chancellor a week later with his tail between his legs. He actually tendered his resignation from the government but was persuaded to stay on as Home Secretary, with Roy Jenkins becoming the new Chancellor. Kaldor's view was that the 14.3 per cent reduction in the value of the pound was insufficient, particularly as it would be politically suicidal to have a second devaluation. Indeed, the whole of economic policy thereafter was designed to prevent such an outcome. None the less, Kaldor appears to have been optimistic, writing to *The Times* at the end of 1968 (13 December) that Britain's economic prospects look better than for many years as a result of correcting the overvalued pound caused by too much deficit finance, and going so far as to predict a balance of payments surplus on a lasting basis.

Devaluation is always slow to work (if it works at all) and the hopes pinned on devaluation appear in retrospect to have been exaggerated. In fact, because of adjustment lags and other factors, the balance of trade continued to deteriorate in 1968, so much so that not only was further deflation imposed, but an entirely new import deposit scheme was also introduced in November requiring one-half of the value of imported manufactured goods to be deposited before goods could be imported, designed to squeeze liquidity and raise the cost of importing. This was Jenkins' own creation, and had nothing to do with Kaldor. By this time he had been banished from the second floor of the Treasury to Palace Chambers in Bridge Street across the road. Jenkins wanted to distance himself from Kaldor, although was reluctant to dismiss him entirely. Kaldor continued to act as his Special Adviser (at first full-time and then part-time), and was fully involved in the budget preparations of 1968, but they saw very little of each other, and in September 1968 Kaldor decided to return to Cambridge full time, remaining in the Treasury only as an unpaid consultant. He retained a small research staff, however, of Roger Tarling, Francis Cripps and Christopher Allsopp, and worked on various projects including the relationship between budgetary and balance of payments deficits (the 'New Cambridge' theory); the relationship between employment, output and productivity growth following his 1966 Inaugural Lecture (Chapter 7), and the employment effects of the Selective Employment Tax (see later). During this period, Dick Crossman at the Department of Health and Social Security was also seeking his advice on an unofficial basis, and in November 1969 it was agreed with Jenkins that Kaldor should be released from the Treasury to become special adviser to Crossman at a salary of 1000 guineas a year with an office in Alexander Fleming House. In this capacity, he became involved in discussions relating to deferred retirement, a negative income tax, new pension proposals and contracting out of the state scheme, earnings-related National Insurance contributions and benefits, and a scheme for minimum earned income relief in order to reduce the burden of tax in the lower income ranges. At this time, he was also responsible for persuading the government to increase family allowances and at the same time to 'claw back' some of the increase through the tax system: a measure to benefit poor families relative to the rich.

Not until 1969 did the balance of payments improve substantially and move into healthy surplus, and not until 1972 were all official debts incurred to support sterling in the 1960s discharged. Throughout his period as Special Adviser, Kaldor never flinched in his faith in exchange rate depreciation, although he subsequently changed his mind on its efficacy particularly as a result of the perverse experience in the years after exchange rates began to float in 1972 when countries appreciating experienced growing surpluses and countries depreciating experienced growing deficits (1977a).[5] As far as the 1967 devaluation is concerned, most of the subsequent improvement in the balance of payments can be attributed to domestic deflation and the revival of world trade. More importantly, there is no evidence that the country was lifted to a higher *growth* path consistent with balance of payments equilibrium. Whether a once-for-all exchange rate adjustment can do that is a controversial theoretical and empirical question.

Despite his heavy schedule as an Economic Adviser, Kaldor continued to travel extensively in an unofficial capacity giving academic lectures all over the world. He was also still much in demand as an adviser to foreign governments. 1967 was a particularly hectic year. In June–July he toured four countries. He paid his first visit to the Soviet Union where he lectured to the Institute of World Economy and International Relations in Moscow on the theme of the 'Rate of Profit in Advanced Capitalist Economies', reminiscent of his 1956 Peking lecture. From the Soviet Union he went on to Tokyo at the invitation of the Econometric Society where he presented a paper on 'Factors Determining the Rate of Growth of Advanced Countries'. Additional lectures were arranged at Osaka and Keio Universities, and a more popular lecture for one of Japan's national newspapers on 'The Economic Problems of the British Labour Government'. From Japan he flew to India to advise the Planning Commission on the budgetary implications of the fourth Five Year Plan and to talk with various officials including the Prime Minister, Indira Gandhi. He returned via Israel where he attended a seminar on economic development and held talks with officials of the Central Bank.

Kaldor's major influence during this period of the Labour government was not on international economic affairs, but in the field of tax policy, where he was recognised as a tax expert and where his views and advice were extremely influential. There are not many economists who have believed as strongly as Kaldor in the importance of the tax structure for economic performance; and he espoused his beliefs with missionary zeal. It is true that the Labour Party was already committed to such reforms as capital gains taxation and the introduction of corporation tax, but this itself was largely the result of his influence in Labour Party circles and his advocacy of such reforms ever since his Minority Report for the Royal Commission on the Taxation of Profits and Income in 1955 (see Chapter 4). The City's hostility to Kaldor's appointment has already been mentioned. Harold Wincott in the *Financial Times* (15 December 1964) likened Kaldor's Minority Report, and its influence on Labour's tax policy, to Hitler and *Mein Kampf*. Wincott's advice to Callaghan was: 'send him back to Cambridge ... and rely on your own good common sense'. There were unseemly references to his academic respectability, prompting nine of his Cambridge colleagues, and Callaghan separately, to respond, defending Kaldor's academic credentials and protesting against the charge of political extremism. Other newspapers remembered his advice to less developed countries and its alleged repercussions, and warned against the dangers of introducing tax changes too quickly. In addition to his influence behind capital gains and corporation tax, he was responsible for the invention and introduction of the completely new Selective

Employment Tax which proved to be not only an efficient revenue raiser but also a major factor in raising productivity in the service industries after its introduction in 1966. On the investment front, he was instrumental in the overhaul of the investment incentive system in 1966 which introduced for the first time investment grants for manufacturing industry differentiated on a regional basis: 45 per cent in the Development Areas and 25 per cent in the rest of the country. He would have preferred the investment grants also to have been industry-specific, for particular plant and equipment identified by technological working parties, but the new system was at least superior to investment allowances which it replaced. The Inland Revenue had never believed that investment allowances mattered as far as investment is concerned. Kaldor was also very concerned with tackling tax avoidance, and, together with the Revenue, he played a major part in eliminating various anomalous concessions in the tax system; for example, stock options, entertainment allowances, covenants and the deductability of interest payments on personal loans. Very little was done, however, to improve the equality of tax treatment of Schedule D and Schedule E taxpayers.

To set against the successes, many of his tax ideas were not implemented. His desire for a wealth tax, as an integral component of an equitable taxation system, was resisted by the Inland Revenue because of its time-consuming administrative complexities. Nor was the idea of a wealth tax enthusiastically supported by Callaghan (or Healey later in the 1970s), who found the Inland Revenue's resistance as a convenient excuse for prevaricating on the issue, particularly with more pressing economic difficulties on their hands. The more revolutionary idea of an expenditure tax was never seriously suggested. Kaldor learnt early on the political limitations on economic policy-making. He felt ambivalent about a new value added tax. The introduction of such a tax had already received a cold shoulder from the Richardson Committee on Turnover Taxation in 1963, to which he gave evidence (1963c). On the other hand, it could have been used as an instrument for export promotion. He suggested so immediately after the 1964 election, but afterwards did not press the matter further largely because of its regressive effect and its likely impact on inflation. Some of the details of the tax changes that took place were against Kaldor's advice, but many more things united than divided him and the Revenue, and relations in general were extremely amicable. He had access to a very competent staff – including Alan Lord and H.V. Lewis – and he had an easy working relation with (Sir) Alexander Johnston, Head of the Revenue. Kaldor would attend for tea every afternoon that he was in the Revenue, and then see Johnston regularly at 5 p.m. He was generally consulted on matters at the stage when the Revenue had decided what it wanted to do, but this did not prevent his influence being felt, and he revelled and excelled in the role of grit in the oyster. Initially, the Revenue did not want capital gains and corporation tax to be introduced at the same time. While recognising that the taxes were interrelated in various aspects, it feared that the workload would be too great. The government was, however, pledged to introduce a tax on capital gains, while Kaldor believed that the corporation tax should have priority in order to stimulate domestic investment. In the event, the Revenue agreed to take the risk and both taxes were introduced in the April budget of 1965.

A good deal of preparation had already been done for the introduction of an extended capital gains tax. The previous government had introduced a short-term gains tax under Selwyn Lloyd in the Finance Act 1962, and questions such as the definition of a capital gain had already been thrashed out. When the Finance Bill 1965 was introduced, Kaldor would not have discriminated between short- and long-term gains because of the difficulty of distinguishing between the two, but the Revenue persuaded him otherwise, and in the event gains realised within a year were subject to the full marginal rate of tax while gains realised after one year were taxed at the lower rate of 30 per cent. Both Kaldor and the Revenue were united against the Treasury that gains from gilt-edged securities should be taxed and won the argument, only to be defeated in 1969 by Treasury arguments that the gilt-edged market then needed to be strengthened. Kaldor and the Revenue were also in agreement that capital gains tax should be levied on death and this prevailed till 1971 when the Conservative government changed the rules.

The changes in company taxation introduced at the same time were very much in accordance with Kaldor's thinking, and the Revenue had done a good deal of preparatory work in this field too. Up to 1965 profits were taxed at the standard rate of income tax (which the shareholder could recover if he was liable to less than the standard rate) and were then subject to a separate profits tax which up to 1958 discriminated against distributed profits to varying degrees. The new corporation tax in 1965 introduced the so-called classical system under which the tax liability of the company is separated from the tax liability of its shareholders. Companies would pay a flat rate corporation tax of 40 per cent on their profits, and shareholders would pay income tax on their dividends (plus capital gains on any gains arising from the retention of profits). Kaldor hoped that the rate of corporation tax would fall to 30 per cent, but in fact it was raised to 42.5 per cent in November 1967 and to 45 per cent in April 1969. Since dividends are subject in effect to both corporation tax and income tax, the classical system is said to favour retention compared with alternative systems and to encourage loan stock rather than equity capital. Kaldor had campaigned for the classical system for many years and the Revenue were in sympathy with it. The only major disagreement came over the franking of dividends; that is the arrangement under which dividends received from a UK company by another UK company (subject to corporation tax) is not subject to corporation tax a second time. Kaldor wanted franking to apply only to the subsidiaries of companies and not to independent companies. Ministers eventually accepted the Revenue proposals for franking and Kaldor later agreed that there would have been a storm of protest if his view had been accepted.

Because of the discrimination against equity finance, when the Conservatives came to power in 1970 discussions started almost immediately to reform the corporation tax in the belief that discrimination in favour of retained profits distorts market forces and leads to the misallocation of investment resources. A Select Committee of the House of Commons was set up to consider the relative merits of two alternative systems: the imputation system and the two-rate system. The imputation system, which the Conservative government eventually introduced in 1973, avoids the 'double taxation' of dividends. It gives shareholders credit for tax paid by the company (at the standard rate), which is used as an offset against tax liability so that no further tax on the dividends is paid (unless the shareholders are subject to a higher marginal tax rate than the standard rate in which case they pay the difference in tax due). Kaldor gave evidence to the Select Committee and was strongly against the change (1971a). On the assumption of equal tax yields from the classical system and the imputation system, he expressed four major objections. First, it would involve a higher marginal rate of tax to compensate for distribution relief. Secondly, fast-growing companies with a high retention rate would pay more tax and this would reduce investment. He stressed that fast-growing companies need both internal and external finance, and the two are complementary not substitutes. The ability to raise external finance partly depends on own resources; and the ability of companies to sell new issues does not depend on shareholders using their saved-up dividends. It depends on the attractiveness of new issues. Thirdly, Kaldor pointed out that the change would increase consumption since the propensity to consume out of dividends is likely to be considerably higher than the propensity to consume out of capital gains. To compensate there would need to be an increase in public saving (general taxation) to maintain the economy's growth rate. Finally, and indefensible from an equity point of view, the imputation system insulates shareholders against personal tax increases since they always receive credits equal to the amount of the increase in tax (unless company tax is increased at the same time). In Kaldor's view, a second-worst system would have been the two-rate system which would have preserved the separation of company and personal taxation and charged a lower rate of corporation tax on distributed profits than on undistributed profits. The 1971 Green Paper on the Reform of Corporation Tax (Cmnd 4360) had originally recommended this system. The imputation system survived the Labour administration 1974 to 1979, as we shall tell later.

Of all the tax changes between 1964 and 1969, the most radical and innovative of all was undoubtedly the selective employment tax (SET), solely attributable to Kaldor. It was introduced in September 1966 as a tax on all labour, but rebatable in the public sector and transport, and rebatable with a subsidy to labour in manufacturing industry. The statistical basis for the classification of which industries should be taxed and which should be subsidised, was prepared by Wynne Godley in the Economics Section of the Treasury. This was the start of Kaldor's close friendship with Godley, which further blossomed in Cambridge after Godley was appointed, on Kaldor's initiative, as Director of the Department of Applied Economics in succession to Brian Reddaway. SET thus represented a tax on the service sector affecting over 7 million employees, and a subsidy to manufacturing. The weekly rates of tax were initially £1.25 per man, 62.5p per woman and boys under 18, and 40p for girls under 18, representing a tax on services of about 7 per cent of total costs. The subsidy to manufacturing was 37.5p per man, with smaller amounts for women, boys and girls, giving a refund to manufacturing of some 130 per cent of the tax paid. The rates of tax and subsidy were periodically raised. The Inland Revenue was generally hostile to the tax. It foresaw several practical difficulties, and convinced Ministers that because of the pressure of other work, it could not administer the new tax. Instead, the tax was collected through the National Insurance stamp, and the subsidy to manufacturing was paid by the Ministry of Labour under the

Selective Employment Payments Act. Many in the Treasury, including Cairncross, thought it a 'monstrous scheme' as a way of raising money, but did not fully understand its rationale. Its proximate cause, one might say, was indeed to raise additional revenue by non-conventional means of taxation, in a way unlikely to fall directly on the consumer, but for Kaldor this was secondary. Callaghan had promised during the election campaign of 1966 that there would be no increase in conventional taxation. As the international economic situation deteriorated and the need for further deflation of the economy became apparent, Callaghan would either have to eat his words and break his promise or find something new. Kaldor, virtually out of the blue, provided him with a Godsend – or so it seemed – which would take money out of the economy as required without the Chancellor breaking his word. Callaghan did not pretend to understand Kaldor's main motives behind the tax, which he expounded publicly later, but embraced the tax with alacrity. In fiscal year 1969/70, the tax was yielding £600 million at very little administrative cost.

What were Kaldor's main motives? First of all, in a Machiavellian way, he clearly saw the tax as a substitute for devaluation. He had argued on these lines in his Memorandum on Value Added Tax submitted to the Richardson Committee on Turnover Taxation in 1963, in which he expressed a preference for VAT, not as a substitute for the existing profits tax and purchase tax, but as an additional tax which could be used as a general subsidy to labour in manufacturing industry to achieve effective devaluation. The liability of each firm would have been equal to the tax on *domestic* sales minus the purchases of goods and services from other firms less the subsidy on total wage and salary payments. This would not have contravened GATT or other trade agreements since it would not represent a direct subsidy to exports. Later in one of his first memos to the Chancellor of the Exchequer after the decision had been taken not to devalue, Kaldor recommended a 10 per cent VAT on all consumption combined with a 12.5 per cent subsidy on all payrolls, arguing that anything devaluation can do, VAT-cum-payroll subsidies could do better. Devaluation through payroll subsidies is less inflationary; it combines in one package the beneficial effects of devaluation and investment grants; it could be regionally differentiated, and it could be used as a much more useful economic regulator than the existing tax system, affecting exports and investment and not just consumption. Indeed, Kaldor claimed in retrospect at a conference on VAT held in 1972 (before its eventual introduction in January 1973 to meet the requirements of the EEC) that: 'had we had VAT in 1964 the whole history of the years 1964–1970 would have been very different; there would have been no currency crisis or devaluation and we could have dealt with the problem of regional unemployment far more effectively.'

As well as SET being an effective substitute for devaluation (albeit a small one), it was also apparent to Kaldor that because of differences in cost conditions between manufacturing and services, and in the way goods are priced, a discriminatory tax against services and in favour of manufacturing would raise productivity in both sectors. The existing purchase tax discriminated against manufacturing and SET reversed this bias. Manufacturing industry is subject to increasing returns, while most service activities are subject to diminishing returns. A redistribution of resources between services and manufacturing alone would increase productivity, and this was the gist of the argument used by Kaldor in his Cambridge Inaugural Lecture in 1966 on the *Causes of the Slow Rate of Economic Growth of the United Kingdom* (see Chapter 7). Much later in his *Collected Essays*, Volume 7 (1979b) he gave a more sophisticated theoretical exposition of how he expected the tax to work in raising productivity in the service sector, related to the nature of pricing and the characteristic of free entry into most service trades. The theory goes back, at least in part, to his 1935 paper on 'Market Imperfection and Excess Capacity' (1935a).

The first question to ask is, are all selective taxes passed on in prices, or are they absorbed by the producer? The answer depends first, on whether the tax enters into the prime cost of production or whether it comes out of 'overheads', and secondly, on the state of competition. The selling prices of virtually all traders in the tertiary and secondary sectors of the economy are arrived at by calculating the direct (or prime) costs of the article sold plus a percentage markup for overheads. In a competitive industry the maximum permissible mark-up for overheads is the outcome of competitive forces. An inefficient business with high overhead costs per unit of sale cannot compensate by charging a higher mark-up because it would lose business by doing so. It follows from this that a tax on elements of overhead costs will *initially* come out of profits. At the same time it will increase the minimum turnover (or break-even point) at which the firm will earn a normal return on capital. The consequence of the tax will then be to accelerate the exit of marginal firms (or decelerate the entry of new firms) until the increase in the turnover of existing firms is just sufficient to offset the increase in the cost of overhead inputs. Kaldor believed that it is a feature of many service trades –

particularly wholesale and retail distribution, restaurants, etc. – that the trader's mark-up relates exclusively to the wholesale price of the article and does not include the cost of the selling staff. In other words, the whole of the wage and salary bill becomes a charge on gross margins because labour costs are only a small fraction of the wholesale price. In effect, labour is treated as an overhead cost and, as such, a tax on labour in these service trades will not be passed on but absorbed either by a reduction in profits or by a reduction in overhead costs per unit of sale from the increase in the volume of turnover of the average business, i.e. by an increase in productivity. The inability to pass on the tax in the form of higher prices was the major reason why it was so unpopular with most of the service trades. In addition, the rise in the cost of labour in services makes labour more expensive relative to labour saving equipment of all kinds which one might expect to lead to more efficient means of retail distribution, further increasing productivity.

It also follows that given the percentage mark-up, the amount of labour employed in distributing goods, as opposed to manufacturing them, will be higher the lower the relative cost of labour in the service trades compared to manufacturing, and vice versa. This is the main reason, Kaldor argued, why productivity growth is pro-cyclical: when the demand for labour falls, wages in services fall relative to wages in manufacturing, and more workers are employed in services relative to manufacturing, depressing overall productivity.

Anxious to know the effects of the tax, it was Kaldor who suggested to the Treasury in 1967 that an Inquiry should be set up under Brian Reddaway, the Director of the Department of Applied Economics at Cambridge. This was duly done with the following terms of reference: 'To examine and report on the effects of the Selective Employment Tax on prices, margins and productivity on which the tax falls as a net burden and the consequent effects on the economy generally'. Work started almost immediately, although announcement of the Inquiry was delayed until after the 1968 budget to avoid embarrassment to Roy Jenkins, the new Chancellor, who had not had time to consider its merits. The Inquiry concentrated on retailing, as did other independent investigators including the Department of Economic Affairs, the Department of Employment and Productivity, and Kaldor himself with his research assistants, Christopher Allsopp, Francis Cripps and Roger Tarling. Kaldor was also sent preliminary results and drafts of the Reddaway Report and he spent most of Christmas 1969 commenting in the minutest detail on various aspects.

From the tenor of the draft, Reddaway seemed to assume from the start that the tax would be passed on like VAT, and seemed surprised by the statistical results which showed the opposite. Kaldor criticised the draft for not discussing in greater detail the theory of the incidence of the tax to derive *a priori* predictions, and accused him of giving the wrong reasons for expecting a productivity effect namely firms moving along a labour demand schedule as labour becomes more expensive. Reddaway failed to appreciate most of the points Kaldor made, regarding most of the criticisms as 'misconceived'. The fact remains, however, that the Reddaway Report, published in March 1970, vindicated Kaldor's theory of the effects of SET.[6] None of the tax seems to have been recovered from the consumer (although it is difficult to disentangle the effects of SET from the abolition of resale price maintenance at the same time). About one-half of the tax was paid by increased productivity; the other half by reduced profits. Productivity in retailing in 1970 was nearly 9 per cent higher than would have been expected on the basis of past trends; equivalent to the saving of 130,000 full time jobs. Indeed, interestingly, one year after SET was abolished in January 1973, employment in retailing rose by 134,000 and remained roughly constant thereafter.

According to the Treasury model of the economy, the *total* effect of SET at its peak was to reduce employment in services by 400,000 below what it would otherwise have been. In every way, SET appears to have been a desirable tax. The press called it 'the miracle tax'. It was not inflationary, it raised substantial revenue, and it improved productivity in major sectors of the economy. In terms of altering the allocation of resources, however, Kaldor judged the tax to have failed because it operated against a background where major improvements in performance did not depend on increased efficiency in the allocation of labour resources but on general (macro) economic conditions. In particular, manufacturing growth was not constrained by a shortage of labour as it probably was in the 1950s and early 1960s. His faith remained undimmed, however. In a Labour Party research document in 1970 he wrote: 'it is possible through the periodic increase of SET in successive budgets to enhance the rate of growth of our productive potential for a fairly long time to come, and to provide substantial additional revenue which could offset the cost of badly needed tax concessions in the income tax field.' He continued to argue for the reimposition of the tax during the 1970s.

One year after SET was introduced, it was further

differentiated regionally, as Kaldor had suggested it might, through the introduction of the Regional Employment Premium (REP). This innovation again was entirely his creation. The new Department of Economic Affairs was concerned with revitalisation of the regions, and the REP was discussed by an Inter-Departmental Committee chaired by (Sir) Eric Roll, the Permanent Secretary. A Green Paper was published on the subject in 1967 (Cmnd 3310) laying out the case for the Premium. When it was introduced, labour employed in manufacturing in the Development Areas received an extra subsidy to that already given of £1.50 per man week (with lower rates for other employees). Kaldor wanted at least £2 per week. Payment was guaranteed for seven years. The scheme itself lasted nine years, being withdrawn during the financial crisis of 1976. The rationale for REP, as Kaldor was to make clear in his 1970 address to the Scottish Economic Society (1970d) was to revive regional activity in a labour-intensive way, and at the same time to allow the economy to be operated at a higher level of demand without bottleneck inflation arising. In this way, the REP was supposed to be 'self-financing' (out of higher tax revenue). The average annual cost up to 1971/72 was £57 million, and £143 million from 1972 to 1975/76. The premium was effectively a form of regional devaluation which could either be taken in the form of lower prices or higher profits, or a combination of both. The original subsidy equal to 7.5 per cent of labour costs was estimated to raise manufacturing output in the Development Areas by some 8 per cent and to raise employment by 50,000. The employment forecast turned out to be reasonably accurate. According to the extensive research of Moore, Rhodes and Tyler the net addition to employment in 1971 was 44,000.[7]

1970–1974

In his official Treasury positions, Kaldor was unable to pronounce publicly, in the press or otherwise, on matters of economic policy. Out of office, he relished his freedom. Through a flood of letters to *The Times* and in newspaper articles, he became a vociferous critic of the economic policies pursued by the Conservative administration under Mr Heath from 1970 to 1974. The Conservatives inherited an economic climate much healthier than Labour in 1964. The heavy doses of taxation and the 1967 devaluation had lowered consumption and shifted resources to exports. Both the government budget and the balance of payments were in surplus in 1970. The new government started life strongly committed to the pursuit of economic *laissez-faire*. The frontiers of the state were to be rolled back; taxes and government expenditure slashed; parastatal organisations banished, and sound finance maintained. By 1972 the government had done a complete *volte face*, and the experiment ended in a frightful economic mess, impaled on a miners' strike. Kaldor described Heath's disastrous period of office as on a par with Ethelred the Unready, Lord North, Lord Liverpool and Neville Chamberlain (*New Statesman*, 22 February, 1974). Several factors conspired together, but two stand out. One was the excessive expansion of demand, particularly of consumption, generated by an extremely lax fiscal and monetary policy. The other was the difficult and bitter struggle to control inflation, fuelled by rising world commodity prices, currency depreciation from 1972, entry to the Common Market at the beginning of 1973, and the four-fold increase in the price of oil at the end of 1973.

Policy started to go astray in 1971. In that year, the policy of Competition and Credit Control, designed to make the banking system more competitive, considerably increased the liquidity of the banking system. In Douglas Jay's graphic words, 'more pounds sterling were created in these years than in the whole twelve hundred years' history of the pound since King Offa'.[8] The total assets of British banks rose from £37 billion in 1971 to nearly £200 billion in 1974, created largely for consumption spending and property speculation. Consumption was further encouraged in the budget of 1972 with nearly £2 billion of tax reductions. In June, sterling was allowed to float and depreciated by 15 per cent in a year, but no leeway was made for an improvement in the balance of payments to take advantage of improved competitiveness and the revival of world trade. The balance of payments deteriorated from a current account surplus of £1.1 billion in 1971 to a £3.2 billion deficit in 1974. Throughout the period Kaldor repeatedly argued that there was no prospect of improving the balance of payments while the public sector remained in deficit. In a letter to *The Times* (21 August, 1973), he wrote that the £1.3 billion balance of payments gap and the £4 billion PSBR are 'causally related to each other as clearly and definitely as daylight is to sun'. Taxation must be increased or government spending reduced. By the budget of 1973, £4 billion had been given away in tax cuts which he strongly condemned (*New Statesman*, 1 March, 1974), criticising Tory governments for always diverting resources to consumption and neglecting the foreign trade sector. By the 1960s Kaldor had become convinced that Britain's slow growth and rising unemployment had little, if anything, to do with Keynesian oversaving, but rather with an insufficiency of exports to match the propensity to import at full employment. The price of using budget deficits to maintain employment was inevitably an excess of imports over exports. In other words, a large part of Britain's economic failure must be traced to inappropriate techniques of economic management: the pursuit of consumption-led growth rather than export-led growth. This was the theme of his influential Presidential Address to the British Association for the Advancement of Science in Durham in 1970 (1971c). In 1974 Kaldor wanted to see the Selective Employment Tax reintroduced both to raise revenue and to stimulate the tradeable goods sector.

On the inflation front, wages and prices had risen on average during the period of the Labour government (1964 to 1970) by 7 per cent and 5 per cent per annum, respectively, partially controlled by the Prices and Incomes Board. One of the first acts of the Heath government was to abolish the Board, but it soon became clear that without some form of incomes policy the control of inflation would be impossible. In 1971 and 1972 wage settlements were running at close to 15 per cent on average, while prices rose by 8 per cent. The government first tried to concoct a voluntary incomes policy, but this failed, and in the autumn of 1972 the first phase of a compulsory three phase prices and incomes policy was introduced: phase 1 lasting from November 1972 to March 1973: phase 2, from April to September 1973, and phase 3 from November 1973. Kaldor thought Heath's conversion to incomes policy was as dramatic and significant as Peel's conversion to free trade, and Gladstone's conversion to Home Rule for Ireland (*The Times*, 30 October, 1972). At the time of its introduction, he praised the government for its realism, and in optimistic mood argued that if the policy could be made to work, it could, combined with the floating pound, 'usher in a period of social and economic progress exceeding in scale and duration that of any previous era of British history' (*Sunday Times*, 8 October, 1972).

The first phase involved a virtual freeze of pay, dividends, rents and most prices, and was largely successful, with average earnings rising by less than 1 per cent. Kaldor doubted, however, whether the trade union movement would cooperate with the policy. He was sceptical whether the government could deliver its promise of keeping price increases down to 5 per cent, particularly in view of the effect of the Common Agricultural Policy (CAP) and sterling depreciation on the price of food. Heath had made it clear in his

Downing Street statement of 2 November 1972 that 'no government... could possibly undertake to hold the retail price index irrespective of what happens to wages or to world prices, to a predetermined figure'. Kaldor's response was that the trade unions could hardly agree to proposals where prices are allowed to rise by much more than 5 per cent for unspecified reasons such as world price increases, depreciation, CAP, etc. (*The Times*, 6 November, 1972). He was equally clear that there was no chance of an incomes policy working with a large (inflationary) budget gap. Either excess demand from the public sector must raise prices and swell profits making wage control difficult, or it spills over into the balance of payments. Either way there is trouble.

Under phase 2 of the incomes policy, pay increases were limited to £1 per week plus 4 per cent with a maximum increase of £250 a year. The trade unions did not support it. Phase 3 was intended to run for six months from November 1973, but the policy was challenged by the miners from the very start. They rejected a 16 per cent pay offer and resorted to an overtime ban. A state of emergency was declared, and a three-day working week was introduced from 1 January, 1974. The miners then decided to use their muscle and called for an all-out strike in early February. Heath's response was to call an election for the end of February to be fought effectively on the issue of 'who runs Britain'. Kaldor believed that the government's showdown with the miners was pointless, it being less costly to concede the miners' claim. The Pay Board was instructed to adjudicate the miners' case, and in the meantime, as a compromise, Kaldor suggested that industrialists should buy off the miners by raising a voluntary contribution from their members to give each miner a weekly *ex gratia* payment – another of his ingenious, potentially Pareto-optimal schemes! A voluntary levy of £1 million would have given each miner £4 per week. In the end, the election was held and the government was narrowly defeated. Labour assumed power once again under Harold Wilson. The miners' strike ended, and so too did the statutory incomes policy, although the phase 3 threshold policy was mistakenly retained giving wage increases for every 1 per cent price increase over 6 per cent. This proved to be a disaster at a time when commodity prices were rising rapidly, and was the start of a wage–price explosion. Earnings and prices both began to rise at over 25 per cent per annum, while the balance of payments deficit was running at an annual rate of over £3 billion. This was the economic legacy that Labour inherited.

1974–1976

In 1974, a general system of 'special' or 'political' advisers was introduced of appointments from outside the Civil Service on a temporary basis paid for out of public funds.[9] By the end of 1974 there were nearly thirty Special Advisers in posts attached to various ministries, including six at Number 10 Downing Street. These were all political appointments; indeed several had already been working for the politicians concerned, financed from outside sources. Kaldor, recently elevated to the Peerage as Baron Kaldor of Newnham, became Special Adviser to Denis Healey, the Chancellor of the Exchequer, with wider responsibilities than just taxation, and based in the Treasury building from the start. Indeed, he insisted on this as a condition of appointment. His salary was £11,000, nearly double the minimum professorial salary at the time. Healey had only recently become the Labour Party's economic spokesman in succession to Roy Jenkins, who resigned in 1972 over Labour's hostile attitude towards the Common Market. He first thought of appointing Robert Neild as adviser but then plumped for Kaldor despite reservations by some of his political colleagues and civil servants in the Treasury. Harold Wilson was concerned with Kaldor's image in the City. The Chief Economic Adviser to the Treasury at the time was (Sir) Kenneth Berrill. There was no love lost between him and Kaldor, and Berrill was conveniently and diplomatically transferred to Number 10 as Director General of the Central Policy Review Staff on the resignation of Victor Rothschild. (Sir) Bryan Hopkin, on leave from Cardiff University and previously Deputy Chief Economic Adviser, succeeded him, but relations between him and Kaldor were also somewhat strained. They certainly did not see eye to eye on economic policy.

On the whole, however, Kaldor was well liked by the Treasury during this period. He was generous with his time, and had a particularly good working relationship with (Sir) Douglas Wass, the Permanent Secretary. Wass and Kaldor knew each other from the previous Labour administration and had remained personal friends, and they saw each other frequently outside the formal structure of Treasury Committees and meetings. Kaldor sat on all the Treasury Committees that he wanted, including the Fiscal Policy Committee and the Short Term Economic Policy Committee consisting of all Heads of Departments, and he attended all the important meetings with Healey present. But his influence on the Chancellor was minimal. For a Labour Chancellor, Healey was disappointingly orthodox like Jenkins before him, and was inclined to accept the advice of the Bank of England and the more conventional economists in the Treasury, such as Hopkin, Michael Posner, Andrew Britton and Hans Leisner, despite the appalling economic difficulties facing the country relating to inflation, the balance of payments, and the Public Sector Borrowing Requirement (PSBR). Kaldor stuck to the New Cambridge view that the deficit on the balance of payments was the mirror image of the government's budget deficit, but if the latter was cut unemployment could not be prevented from rising by allowing the exchange rate to depreciate. Hence import controls of one form or another were required.

The New Cambridge doctrine had a curious history. It was originally espoused by Kaldor in the 1960s, and he must be considered the intellectual father of the doctrine. Some of his close academic colleagues were at first sceptical, but after 1970 appear to have been converted, particularly Wynne Godley and Francis Cripps who became its chief protagonists. Other Cambridge colleagues, such as Richard Kahn and Michael Posner, were highly dubious. It was a doctrine arising out of an identity and as such, as a theory of behaviour, suffered all the familiar problems of any theory arising from an identity, relating to the stability of other behavioural relationships within the identity and to what is exogenous and what is endogenous (or to what is cause and what is effect). The assumed direction of causation was never entirely clear, whether it was from the budget deficit to the balance of payments deficit or from an (autonomous) payments deficit (caused by import penetration) to the budget deficit. Kaldor never expounded at length in print on the doctrine, and later admitted scepticism over the stability of the assumed relationship, but continued to urge for a reduction in the budget deficit and measures to control imports. He was unable to convince, however, on the desirability of import controls. The Chancellor was worried about the international repercussions of any import control scheme, and the Treasury were worried by the administrative difficulties. The other top Treasury economists all seemed to be sanguine about exchange rate depreciation despite the Treasury's own model showing that a 10 per cent depreciation would have a net effect on the balance of payments of only £250 million over two years.

Kaldor's warnings in the Treasury turned out to be prophetic. In memo after memo from 1974 on, and in personal letters to the Chancellor, he warned continually that if immediate action were not taken to control the PSBR and to rectify the balance of payments, even more draconian measures would have to be taken in the future under the auspices of the International Monetary Fund, which is exactly what happened at the end of 1976. Kaldor floated several ideas for the control of imports under the code name, 'Delve Exercise'. His first suggestion was the use of quotas to curtail inessential imports to the tune of some £3 billion, as if the country was in a state of national emergency, which in his view it was. This was followed by the advocacy of a dual exchange rate system, which would consist of a 'devalued' 'industrial' pound applying to manufactured exports and imports. Exporters would receive a sterling credit, and importers would be debited an amount equal to the difference between the two rates of exchange, making the scheme equivalent to an *ad valorem* duty on manufactured imports and a subsidy to manufactured exports. A third possibility actively discussed was a voucher scheme for balancing the imports and exports of manufactures, whereby vouchers for imports would be issued equal to the value of exports, allocated partly by direction and partly through the free market. No action was taken. The Chancellor and the Treasury continued to pin their faith in exchange rate depreciation.

In 1976 there were sharp exchanges of view between Kaldor on the one hand, and Posner and Britton on the other on the size of export and import price elasticities which the Treasury claimed were approximately 2.2 and 1, respectively. Kaldor thought these far too high on the basis of the balance of payments experience since 1972 when the exchange rate had been floated. By mid-1976, almost in desperation, Kaldor was arguing for an import deposit scheme applied to manufactures of 200 per cent, lasting for 12 months, plus a special car tax surcharge to discourage the purchase of foreign cars. The Chancellor continued to remain unconvinced by the necessity of such measures, but none the less Kaldor urged him in his speech of 23 July 1976 to announce in advance that he was seeking approval from the EEC and IMF for such a scheme in view of the serious balance of payments position. A deflationary package would not be enough, he argued, and, in any case, with 1.3 million already unemployed such a policy would be a complete break with the most basic tenets of the Labour Party. He drew the comparison with Philip Snowden's measures of 1931 which destroyed the first Labour government. In a memo to the Principal Private Secretary he expressed the fear 'that the Chancellor does not see clearly enough that he is being driven into a course of action that will destroy him and the Labour Party with the inevitableness of a Greek tragedy'.

Linked to the concern over the balance of payments, and the need for direct action to control imports, was his worry over the size of the PSBR. The PSBR swelled alarmingly from 1974 as a result of a combination of recession and inflation, particularly from public sector pay increases. The forecast in the March budget of 1974 was for a deficit of £2.75 billion. By November the actual deficit was £5.5 billion. The forecast in the April 1975 budget for the following fiscal year was £9 billion, and £12 billion for the year after. The government's main response was to axe public expenditure, not a palatable socialist measure to take. There were cuts of over £1 billion in 1975 followed by further cuts of the same order in 1976, plus the imposition of a National Insurance surcharge to raise a further £1 billion in revenue. In addition, for the first time, an official money supply target was announced. Kaldor continually argued for increases in indirect taxes to reduce the size of the PSBR further and for the reintroduction of the selective employment tax. At the same time he would have excluded the effect of indirect tax increases from the calculation of the retail price index (RPI) so that wages would not respond *pari passu* and real consumption could be reduced. The *quid pro quo* would have been a guarantee to workers that they could have wage increases equal to the adjusted RPI, to be sure therefore that they would not have to shoulder a disproportionate burden of the adjustment necessary. In June 1976 he also urged a 5 per cent payroll tax to yield £3 billion, with any adverse effects on employment compensated by a marginal employment subsidy (the so-called Layard Scheme.)[10] The planned increases in taxes in the budget for 1975/76 and 1976/77 amounted to only £1.9 billion and £2.2 billion, respectively. Kaldor urged tax increases of £3–4 billion. He estimated consumption to be some 10 per cent higher than if the balance of payments were in equilibrium. He accused Bryan Hopkin of complacency over both the size of the PSBR and the balance of payments deficit, and criticised economic strategy as a whole for neglecting exports and investment. Kaldor wanted planning agreements with the 50 largest firms, to increase production and export capacity.

Through successive doses of deflation the current balance of payments improved in 1975 and 1976, but owing to speculation against the currency and short-term capital outflows, the balance for official financing increased in 1976 to £3.6 billion. The government continued to rely on exchange depreciation as an equilibriating mechanism, and by the autumn of 1976 the pound had depreciated by nearly 50 per cent against its Smithsonian parity of 1972. Kaldor warned of a spiral of depreciation and inflation – a German-style hyper-inflation – and recommended controls over capital flight. In July he wrote at least two strong memos to the Principal Private Secretary urging the need for a severe package of measures to re-establish international confidence, to stop currency speculation, and to avoid going cap in hand to the IMF which would only lead to further deflation and preclude any quantitative restriction over imports. His package would have included £1 billion of expenditure cuts, a 5 per cent payroll tax, a 200 per cent import deposit on manufactures, a car tax surcharge, a marginal employment subsidy, and further controls on capital exports. His advice went unheeded, although further monetary measures were taken, including the imposition of special deposits and a rise in the minimum lending rate to a record level of 11.5 per cent, but the tide of speculation could not be stopped. Finally, in desperation, the government was forced to turn to the International Monetary Fund to seek credits of $3.9 billion over two years. In return, in the Letter of Intent to the IMF, the Chancellor announced further cuts in public spending over two years of nearly £3 billion (including abolition of REP); a 10 per cent surcharge on tobacco and alcohol, and new monetary targets expressed in terms of figures for domestic credit expansion (DCE).[11] The target for 1976–77 was £9 billion, and £7.7 billion for the following year. This was deemed consistent with the forecast size of the PSBR of £8–9 billion and the forecast balance of payments. What Kaldor had foretold, had come true: 'an IMF Budget'. By this time, however, Kaldor had resigned from the Treasury dispirited and disillusioned. Healey was not sorry to see him go, and he went in early August. Kaldor continued his campaign against currency depreciation, and in favour of import controls, in the columns of the press.

While Kaldor had failed to convince with respect to the broad thrust of macroeconomic policy, he did have a little more success in the field of tax policy although by no means to the same extent, or with the same impact, as in the period 1964 to 1967. One major success, which inside the Treasury was entirely Kaldor's invention, was the introduction of stock appreciation tax relief for companies which took effect in 1975 and saved several companies from bankruptcy.[12] When the Labour government took office in 1974, the Treasury advisers not only underestimated the future size of the PSBR, but also grossly underestimated the financial squeeze on industry. The ratio of stock appreciation to gross trading profits had risen from £881m/£4429m in 1971 to £3330m/£2930m in the first half of 1974, causing a severe liquidity crisis since companies had to pay tax on profits inflated by stock appreciation and stocks themselves needed to be replaced. It was assumed that industry would borrow its way through but instead the banks reined in. Out of the blue, rather like SET, Kaldor suggested that companies should be given relief on increases in the value of stocks in excess of a certain percentage of trading profits. Above 10 per cent the relief would have amounted to £1.2 billion in 1975/76, and this was the percentage chosen.

Another new fiscal reform, which he strongly supported, was the introduction of a capital transfer tax to replace death duties, although it was not levied on the recipient as he wanted. Unrealised capital gains on death were also to be taxed. The general attack on tax avoidance was strengthened and income tax was made more smoothly progressive, helping the lower paid.

In the field of social security, the Conservative government's proposals to replace tax allowances and various discretionary social security payments with tax credits, as proposed in a Green Paper on the subject, were rejected. Kaldor had written a long critique in evidence to the Select Committee of the House of Commons on Tax Credits in March 1973 (1973b), and with the Labour Party in office his arguments proved decisive. He also gave oral evidence to the Committee. So powerful was Kaldor's attack that the Chairman of the Committee, William Clark, described the Professor as having left the Committee speechless! What Kaldor showed was that for the low-income groups the benefits of the credits would have been more than offset by the saving in supplementary benefits and other social security payments and that of the net cost of the scheme of £1300 million, only £150 million would go to those on less than £1000 per annum. The cost of the scheme could be attributed entirely to raising tax allowances and had nothing at all to do with the tax credit proposal since net tax credits of £850 million would be offset by savings of £1,040 million on social security payments. Thus the whole scheme would have been highly regressive. Kaldor proposed instead a unified system of family endowment, which would replace existing family allowances and tax allowances for children with a system of tax-free age-graduated allowances paid to the mother. Child benefits were duly instituted by the Child Benefit Act of 1975. Such a scheme had, in fact, been suggested by Kaldor and Douglas Wass in 1967 and 1968, but the government had backtracked because it would represent an income transfer from wallet to purse which might have had adverse effects on wage bargaining.

Kaldor also wanted a reform of the corporation tax structure, or imputation system, introduced by the Conservatives, and a return to the classical system, but he was thwarted. In this he was supported by the Treasury officials, but the Inland Revenue insisted on consulting the Confederation of British Industry (CBI) who felt another change in company taxation would be too disruptive. The Revenue accepted the CBI's advice, and the Treasury felt obliged to advise the government against the change. Likewise no action was taken on a wealth tax, despite the intention to introduce one announced in the March 1974 budget. A Green Paper appeared on the matter which was referred to a House of Commons Select Committee and the Liberals conspired with the Tories against the idea. The government decided to shelve the issue, having more pressing problems on its hands and being reluctant in any case to antagonise the wealth-owning class.

After his resignation as Adviser in 1976, Kaldor was able to carry on his political life, and to campaign for economic reform and economic sanity, in the public domain in the House of Lords. He chose to stick to the back benches, but spoke frequently none the less. His maiden speech (25 November) addressed the problem of the trade imbalances arising from the high price of oil. Through the remaining years of the Labour government to 1979, and throughout the Thatcher years, he made a series of pungent speeches on topical issues of the day. The bankruptcy of the doctrine of monetarism, the waste of oil revenue, unemployment, and the devastation of British manufacturing industry particularly preoccupied him. Some of his best speeches, which remain still fresh, were collected together in a Fabian booklet under the title *The Economic Consequences of Mrs Thatcher* (1983).

NOTES

1. Hugh Gaitskell died when Leader of the Labour Party in 1963.
2. 'Economists in Government', *Lloyds Bank Review*, January 1970.
3. A Cairncross and B. Eichengreen, *Sterling in Decline* (Oxford: Basil Blackwell 1983), p. 24.
4. H. Wilson, *The Labour Government 1964-1970: A Personal Record* (London: Weidenfeld and Nicolson, 1971), pp. 447-8.
5. See also R. Triffin, *Gold and Dollar Crisis: Yesterday and Tomorrow* Essays in International Finance, No. 132 (Princeton University, 1978).
6. W.B. Reddaway, *Effects of the Selective Employment Tax: First Report on the Distributive Trades* (London: HMSO, 1970).
7. B. Moore, J. Rhodes and P. Tyler, *The Effects of Government Regional Economic Policy* (London: HMSO, Department of Trade and Industry, 1986).
8. D. Jay, *Sterling, Its Use and Misuse: A Plea for Moderation* (London: Sidgwick and Jackson, 1985).
9. See N. Chester, 'The Role of Economic Advisers in Government', in A.P. Thirlwall (ed.), *Keynes as a Policy Adviser* (London: Macmillan, 1983).
10. After Professor Richard Layard of the London School of Economics.
11. Domestic Credit Expansion is equal to the supply of money minus the balance of payments surplus. A target for DCE means that the money supply

then varies inversely with the balance of payments, rather like under the gold standard.

12. The subject of inflation accounting was at the time being widely discussed in academic circles and in the press.

10 THE COMMON MARKET DEBATE

The Treaty of Rome was signed on the 25 March 1957, and the European Economic Community (EEC) came into being on the 1 January of the following year, binding together the 'Six' – France, Germany, Italy and the Benelux countries of the Netherlands, Belgium and Luxembourg – in a formal Customs Union. There was also a commitment to the free mobility of the factors of production and to what was described, imprecisely, as 'ever closer union'. The Customs Union has materialised (with transitional arrangements for new members), and progress has been made in breaking down barriers to factor mobility, but full economic and political union (if that is what 'closer union' meant) is still a long way off.

From its inception, and Britain's first application to join in 1961, Kaldor was sceptical of the alleged political and economic benefits that the country would derive from membership, particularly if its initial economic starting position was weak. The scepticism was to turn to outright hostility at the time of eventual entry in 1973, on the terms negotiated, and the antipathy remained as Britain's economic situation deteriorated relative to its European partners. Between 1970 and 1973, he wrote over twenty letters to *The Times* alone, in addition to several articles in newspapers and magazines, warning of the costs of entry and the dangers to Britain's competitive position if the country accepted the Community's Common Agricultural Policy (CAP) and the arrangements governing each country's contribution to the Community's budget (consisting mainly of agricultural levies on food imports, customs duties and up to 1 per cent [now 1.4 per cent] of VAT proceeds).

Many of Kaldor's worries proved to be well-founded, and many of his prognostications on the costs of entry, and the difficulties for Britain's manufacturing industry, have materialised. He was never, however, an isolationist or 'little Englander'. He was not opposed to European economic integration, and argued the case on several occasions for a European free trade area and for the dismantling of tariffs on industrial goods between the countries of Europe including Britain. Paradoxically, in a way, he seemed willing to accept the consequences for British industry of membership of a free trade area, while using the same predicted damage as one of the arguments against entry into the EEC. A European free trade area was the original British stance in the mid-1950s following the initial impetus from the Benelux states in 1955 to establish a wider Customs Union of the Six. Under British initiative in 1956, the Organisation for European Economic Cooperation (OEEC) began to consider the question of whether the OEEC States might form a free trade area, but negotiations broke down partly because of Britain's insistence that each country should be free to set its own external tariff; and a policy for European agriculture was also excluded. It was out of these discussions that eventually the European Free Trade Association (EFTA) was born, on 1 January 1960, creating a second major trading bloc in Europe with Britain as the dominant partner. Kaldor welcomed the Association. There was no commitment to an expensive agricultural policy, and Britain was free to discriminate with its external tariff in favour of any countries it chose, subject to GATT rules.

The ink was hardly dry on the EFTA Treaty, however, when Britain began to reappraise its position. In July 1961, Harold Macmillan, the Conservative Prime Minister, announced that the government had decided to apply for full membership of the EEC. The application was accepted but negotiations made slow progress and in 1963 General de Gaulle, President of France, effectively vetoed the application declaring that the British were not fit Europeans. At the time of the negotiations, Kaldor and other eminent economists expressed doubts over the benefits of Britain joining. In a letter to *The Times* (15 October 1962), Kaldor with (Sir) Roy Harrod, Richard (Lord) Kahn and H. D. Dickinson wrote curtly:

While not wishing to express any opinion on the political argument for or against the U.K. joining the Common Market, we should like to question the view that there is some plain economic advantage in the U.K. joining on the terms now proposed by the government. In our view there is no such clear gain. The free and unrestricted import of food and materials into this country from the Commonwealth is as valuable to us as to the Commonwealth exporters, and any interruption of it would be as harmful to us as to them. The total effects of the diversion of trade which would result from joining on the proposed terms are not easy to estimate, but in our view they are as likely, on balance, to mean a loss to the U.K. as a gain. Whatever the political arguments, therefore, the final choice should not be made on the assumption that there will be any favourable balance of economic advantage for the United Kingdom.

It is also true to say that Kaldor was never enamoured of the political arguments for joining, and some of his disdain for the Common Market may have arisen from an historical dislike of Germany. He was not convinced that western democracy or defence was threatened if Britain remained outside the Community, or that Britain's influence in the world would necessarily diminish unless it joined a wider grouping of States. Indeed, to be economically weak in Europe could weaken Britain's voice politically. In a letter to *The Times* (19 October 1962), and later in *Encounter* (March 1963), he first advanced the thesis that the Common Market might not make Britain more enterprising and efficient, since free trade benefits the strong at the expense of the weak, and growing uncompetitiveness *vis-à-vis* Europe could make Britain a depressed area unable to protect or defend itself. This was to be a consistent and perennial theme in his writings in the years to come.

In the meantime the newly-elected Labour government (1964) took a renewed interest in the possibility of joining the Community, and in May 1967 a second application was submitted which was again vetoed by de Gaulle, although he was not averse to Britain taking associate membership. Britain did not withdraw its application, and when de Gaulle resigned in 1969, the Six agreed to open discussions again. By the time the negotiations started, the Conservatives had come to power under Edward Heath, fully committed to Britain's membership. In February 1970, the Government published its White Paper, *Britain and the European Communities: An Economic Assessment* (Cmnd 4289), laying out the potential costs and benefits of entry. It recognised that the impact effects would be negative – at the worst, a cost of some £1.1 billion per annum was estimated – but offsetting these there would be, it was argued:

dynamic effects resulting from membership of a much larger and faster growing market. This would open up to our industrial producers substantial opportunities for increasing export sales, while at the same time exposing them more fully to the competition of European industries. No way has been found of quantifying these dynamic effects, but if British industry responded vigorously to the stimuli, they would be considerable and highly advantageous. The acceleration of the rate of growth of industrial exports could then outpace any increase in the rate of growth of imports, with corresponding benefits to the balance of payments. Moreover, with such a response, the growth of industrial productivity would be accelerated as a result of increased competition and the advantages derived from specialisation and larger scale production. This faster rate of growth would, in turn, accelerate the rate of growth of national production and real income.

An addition to the growth rate of 0.5 per cent for five years was reckoned to be enough to offset the transitional cost of entry on the most unfavourable assumptions. Interestingly, the White Paper also recognised, however, that 'if the total burden on our balance of payments as a result of membership becomes excessive we might find that we were unable to pursue economic policies which enabled the full benefits of membership to be realised'. Having said that, it expressed the view that 'since such an outcome would be as contrary to the interests of the Community as of the U.K., the government would expect to find its avoidance a common aim of all concerned with the negotiations'. The hope, as it turned out, was a forlorn one; a case of economic wishful thinking driving out political common sense.

There were three main potential costs of Common Market entry, conceptually distinct, but overlapping in their impact. First, the costs of higher food prices and the contribution to the Community budget to support agriculture (approximately 70 per cent of the budget has been regularly spent on agriculture). Secondly, the costs to the balance of payments consisting partly of the trade effects from tariff dismantling and the common external tariff, and partly of the effects of higher food prices and contributions to the budget. Thirdly, the real income and resource costs involved in adjusting the internal economy to meet the needs of the balance of payments. Kaldor's position throughout the negotiations until final entry into the Community on 1 January 1973 was that the government had grossly underestimated the various costs of entry and grossly exaggerated the dynamic benefits of entry if the country was forced to enter in a weak position as a result of unfavourable terms. Of particular concern to all 'anti-marketeers' was that joining the Community would deny Britain access to cheap food imports from outside the EEC with all its repercussions on the balance of payments, wage inflation and the standard of living. Kaldor was a bitter opponent of CAP and in January 1970 delivered a fierce attack on Community farm policy to the International Press Institute in Paris, which was subsequently published in the New Statesman.[1] The socialist weekly, under the editorship of Dick Crossman, became one of Kaldor's major outlets of protest outside the columns of The Times. The attack on farm policy was followed a year later by his powerful and prophetic essay on 'The Truth about the "Dynamic

Effects" '.[2] The objectives of the CAP, as set out in Article 39 of the Rome Treaty, were: to increase agricultural productivity, to secure a fair standard of living for the agricultural community, to stabilise markets, to assure availability of supplies, to ensure that supplies reach consumers at reasonable prices, and to ensure uniform prices for food in the interests of free and fair competition between industrialists so that some producers are not confronted by a worse terms of trade than others. It is not easy to explain, however, why the CAP should have been regarded as one of the major cornerstones of the Community, as if the political and economic objectives could not be realised without it, except for the historical-political power of the agricultural lobby, particularly in France. Indeed CAP has been described as the French *quid pro quo* for free trade in manufactures which everyone recognised would benefit the Germans most. In the words of one French official, 'without a CAP the Common Market is nothing'.

By supporting artificially high uniform prices to producers, Kaldor believed the CAP to be fundamentally misconceived in terms of the objectives which European integration was intended to serve. It hampers the growth of welfare of the peoples of Europe, and also of the rest of the world by depriving countries, particularly in the developing world, of markets for their cheaper produce. It impedes the rationalisation of agriculture, impairs the efficiency of resource allocation between agriculture and industry, and slows the growth of industry and exports by artificially worsening the industrial terms of trade. If the CAP continued, Kaldor predicted 'a growing burden on both consumers and taxpayers which threatens to become intolerable sooner or later' and 'makes it very difficult ... for countries like Britain to join the Common Market'. In 1970 the budgetary cost to the Community of the CAP to buy up surpluses and subsidise exports was over £2 billion, having risen from under £1 billion in 1960 (roughly one-half of the cost in 1970 being met from the Community Guarantee Fund and the other half by national governments). The cost of higher EEC food prices compared to prevailing world prices (the 'hidden cost' of CAP), paid for by the consumer, was another £2.5 billion giving a total direct cost of nearly £5 billion or some 3 per cent of the Community's GNP. By 1984, the cost of supporting agriculture had risen to £12 billion, and the Community reached the limit of its own resources. The 1970 White Paper estimated that if Britain joined food prices would rise by between 18 and 25 per cent, representing a 4–5 per cent permanent increase in the cost of living, and that the contribution to the Agricultural Fund might initially be between

£190 million and £250 million, rising to between £270 million and £350 million in 1977 depending on the relation between EEC and world food prices. Kaldor put the cost of CAP to Britain at between £400 million and £800 million, composed of higher food prices on the one hand, and the levies on cheaper imported food paid into the Community budget on the other; a cost far too high in his view. If any scheme had to be adopted he would have preferred the substitution of CAP by the existing British system of deficiency payments to farmers financed by an appropriate increase in VAT on goods other than food. He would also have adopted the Mansholt Plan for the rationalisation of European agriculture based on the use of Community expenditure not to buy up agricultural surpluses at disequilibrium prices but to encourage modernisation and consolidation of the farming sector and to compensate small and inefficient farmers who leave the land.[3]

The later diagnosis of the alleged dynamic benefits of joining the Common Market brought into play consideration of his complete model of the growth and development process as a cumulative disequilibrium phenomenon in which growth and competitiveness become self reinforcing so that in the process of trade some countries inevitably gain at the expense of others. Immediately after the 1970 White Paper was published he warned in a letter to *The Times* (16 February) of the possibility of dynamic *disadvantages* unless efficiency wages were free to adjust, and he repeated the warning in his much publicised Presidential Address to Section F of the British Association for the Advancement of Science held at Durham University in September. By this time Kaldor was beginning to receive a good deal of press coverage for his Jeremiah forecasts that Britain might become 'the Nothern Ireland of Europe' if she entered the Common Market on the wrong terms. He was, and remained, in the forefront of academic economists opposed to entry without prior institutional reform and on the terms envisaged by successive governments, and lent his name to the Common Market Safeguards Campaign established to fight for a national referendum on the issue of Common Market entry. With his recent conversion to the importance of export-led growth for Britain, he was also at this time concerned with the question of exchange rates. He frequently repeated that he was not against Common Market entry on the right terms, but he became increasingly concerned about the prospect of full economic and monetary union that the Community endorsed in 1969 which would preclude the use of the exchange rate as an adjustment weapon to reconcile internal and external equilibrium.

He was still sanguine then that the exchange rate was an efficient instrument of adjustment.

The attack on the promised benefits of entry in his *New Statesman* article of March 1971 was devastating. He ridiculed the vagueness and impreciseness of the measure of dynamic effects and argued that whether they accrue or not depends on whether there are constraints on output growth in the first place. A common market does not confer equal benefits on all members and the initial starting-point is crucial. If the impact effects are negative and growth is constrained as a result, the dynamic effects will be adverse not beneficial because growth will be slower, and competitiveness will therefore deteriorate rather than improve. This raised the question of the balance of payments costs of entry in addition to the budgetary costs. The net effect on the balance of payments of entry comprised three parts (i) the change in the balance of trade in manufactures as a result of tariff reductions; (ii) the higher cost of food from the EEC and the levies on imported food, and (iii) the net contribution to the Agricultural Fund in addition to the levies. The 1970 White Paper did not venture a precise up-to-date cost to the balance of payments except to say that it would have been between £175 million and £250 million in 1967 and higher in 1970. Kaldor put the estimate at close to £1000 million. The balance of trade in manufactures could be expected to deteriorate initially by some £300 million to £400 million. British exports to the EEC, already growing fast, were faced with only a 7 per cent tariff, while British producers were protected by an 11 per cent tariff. In addition, Britain would lose Commonwealth and EFTA preferences. The higher cost of imported food would be approximately £400 million. At the time EEC farm prices were some 45 per cent higher than world prices. The net contribution to the Agricultural Fund would be between £190 million and £370 million. Clearly the balance of payments cost of £1000 million would have to be met either by an increase in exports or a decrease in imports. In Kaldor's view there would be no way of achieving the required increase in exports without a large devaluation. If there was no devaluation, or a devaluation was not successful, the only alternative would be the contraction of demand to reduce imports, in which case the dynamic effects would be adverse, aggravating the initial adverse impact effects making entry into the Community 'a national disaster'. The commitment to an economic union, on Kaldor's reasoning, would make the situation even worse.

At The Hague in December 1969 the Six agreed in principle to work towards full economic and monetary union. The Werner

Committee was appointed to work out a programme of action and recommended a time-table for monetary union, fiscal (tax) harmonisation, and central Community control over national budgets, to be achieved in three stages, each of three years, with full union by 1979/80. Naturally Kaldor was apprehensive. Monetary union would preclude exchange rate adjustments, and fiscal harmonisation without fiscal integration would damage the poorer members whose tax base is lower and whose expenditure needs are greater, thus reinforcing the circular and cumulative tendencies making the rich richer and the poor poorer. For this reason he believed that any economic union must be preceded by political union and fiscal integration. Adopting economic union before political union could jeopardise the eventual establishment of political union by causing the Community to disintegrate.

The reaction of the pro-Marketeers and the pro-Market press was predictable: that Kaldor had exaggerated the costs, particularly the budgetary contributions and the rise in food prices. *The Economist* (13 March, 1971) carried a photo of Kaldor captioned 'Soberly wrong'. The paper dismissed the claim that the budgetary arrangements would be a burden to the balance of payments, that spending on farm subsidies would rise and that agricultural surpluses would grow. Indeed, it predicted that surpluses are likely to diminish as the exodus from the land exceeds the effect of increased efficiency! Dick Taverne in the *Guardian* (12 March, 1971) argued that once in, Britain would be able to control EEC food prices to prevent surpluses arising. Andrew Shonfield argued in *The Times* (1 April, 1971) that the EEC would not allow Britain to be weakened economically. Kaldor carried on the argument in *The Times*,[4] repeating his *New Statesman* points and pointing out that if all Britain wanted was a whiff of competition it would be more sensible to allow free trade than to join the Community. The low external (EEC) tariff could be easily offset by devaluation and all the ramifications and costs of EEC entry would be avoided. In May 1971, Kaldor thought he detected signs of monetary disintegration of the Community when Germany and the Netherlands announced that the Deutschmark and Guilder would float against other currencies, which might then force changes in the CAP and reduce the costs of British entry, particularly if the pound itself was also allowed to float.[5] In the event the Community structure survived these temporary hiccups. The Paris Communiqué, 19–20 October, 1972, reaffirmed the Community's determination to achieve economic and monetary union by the end of 1980. The pledge was made to restore fixed parities and to develop a European Unit of Account. At the same time, the British government also committed itself to the ideal of economic and monetary union, which again Kaldor attacked unless there was a parallel commitment to greater political union and fiscal federation. The monetary union was solidified by the formation of the European Monetary System in 1979.

While the pros and cons of Britain joining the Community were being debated in the press, the negotiations for entry were proceeding in Brussels, conducted first by Anthony Barber and then by Geoffrey Rippon. The entry talks were finally completed in June 1971, after meetings of Mr Heath and President Pompidou to clear the ground of remaining obstacles, and the proposals for entry were set out in the White Paper, *The United Kingdom and the European Communities* (Cmnd 4715), July 1971. The White Paper first emphasised the political case for joining Europe, before turning to the economic benefits. The miserable economic performance of the British economy was compared with the vastly superior perforformance of the EEC, with the optimism expressed that 'Her Majesty's Government is convinced that our economy [will be] stronger and our industries and peoples more prosperous if we join the European Communities than if we remain outside them.' If Britain joined the EEC 'improvements in efficiency and competitive power should enable the U.K. to meet the balance of payments costs of entry over the next decade as they gradually build up... [the] advantages will far outweigh the costs, provided we seize the opportunities of the far wider home market now open to us'.[9] On the other hand, the White Paper admitted 'the government does not believe that the overall response of British industry to membership can be quantified in terms of its effect on the balance of trade' but 'they are confident that the effect will be positive and substantial, as it has been for the Community'. The estimated extra cost of food imports after the transitional period of five years was put at only £50 million, while the estimated cost to the balance of payments of the budgetary contribution was put at no more than £200 million in the fifth year (1977). From 1975 the system of Community financing was due to change from food import levies and national exchequer contributions to a system of 'own resources', composed of 90 per cent of the total of agricultural levies and customs duty receipts from the common external tariff plus up to 1 per cent of VAT receipts (subject to various correctives up to 1978). The White Paper said, 'it is not possible to make any valid estimate of the size of our levy and duty receipts in the 1980s'. As a form of sweetener, however, there was the clear promise from the Community that if unacceptable situations should arise 'the very survival of the Community would demand that the institutions find equitable solutions'.

Kaldor reacted angrily to the White Paper, again in the columns of the *New Statesman*.[6] If nothing can be estimated, he claimed, where does the government's confidence come from that 'membership of the enlarged Community will lead to much improved efficiency and productivity in British industry, with a higher rate of investment and a faster growth of real wages'? He likened the vagueness of the prospectus for entry to the basic tenets of religion, arguing that they were no more amenable to logical scrutiny or empirical verification than the doctrine of the Holy Trinity. He referred to the White Paper's 'crudities, disastrous logical contradictions, vagueness and deliberate omissions', and attacked the government's cost estimates as fraudulent in the sense of misleading and disingenuous. He called for a Select Committee enquiry so that officials who drafted the White Paper could be questioned. The treatment of food prices was particularly disingenuous based on an abnormally small difference between EEC and world prices in 1971, whereas the historical difference averaged 50 per cent. The likely increase in food prices up to 1977 could be 20–22 per cent, not 15 per cent as estimated in the White Paper, implying that the extra cost of food imports would also be in excess of the estimated £50 million, a figure which seemed to have been plucked from the air. Devaluation of the pound on entry, which might be necessary, would raise the cost even more. Likewise Kaldor regarded as far too low the estimated net budgetary cost of £200 million in 1977. The forecast EEC budget for 1977 was £1600 million, way below an estimate based on the extrapolation of past trends. Britain's gross contribution to the Budget was estimated at 19 per cent, broadly comparable with its share of total GNP. This forecast of the proportionate contribution proved to be broadly correct, although it was to soar to 24 per cent in 1982, while Britain's percentage contribution of total GNP shrunk. Finally, Kaldor found it incredible that the White Paper made no attempt to estimate the total balance of payments costs or resource costs of entry; a major omission from the prospectus which could radically alter the scenario of entry.

None the less, broad terms of entry or 'heads of agreement' were put to the House of Commons on 28 October, 1971, with 356 votes cast in favour of entry and 244 against. Negotiations were taking place at the same time for the entry of Eire, Denmark and Norway. Negotiations were concluded successfully, but Norway eventually voted 'no' in a referendum, so that only Britain, Eire and Denmark formally joined the Six on 1 January, 1973.

The Labour Party, and indeed the nation itself, was deeply divided on both the issue of entry and the proposed terms. In response to Kaldor's tirade against the White Paper, the Labour Committee for Europe placed a full page advertisement in the *New Statesman* chiding him for being so pessimistic and blinded by statistics, and for not appreciating the opportunities to be seized. *The Times* thought it significant that Kaldor and Peter Shore, both opponents of entry, should have been voted off the Executive Committee of the Fabian Society. The overwhelming mood in the Labour movement, however, was against entry. Academic economists were more evenly divided. Kaldor with Professor Harry Johnson of the LSE (himself against entry) organised a poll among university economists to gauge opinion whether they thought Britain would experience a net gain: 142 respondents replied that they thought the net effects would be favourable, while 154 thought the net effects would be unfavourable. In a series of letters to *The Times* in 1972, Kaldor appealed for a referendum to decide the issue of entry, reminding Edward Heath that he had promised in 1970 that he would not take Britain into the Community without the full-hearted consent of Parliament and the British people. In the 1950s and 1960s, British public opinion seemed to be broadly in favour of joining, but around 1968 there seems to have been a shift of sentiment, and by the early 1970s, according to the public opinion polls, the majority were hostile. The official position of the Labour Party was that it would take Britain out of Europe if better terms could not be negotiated. Harold Wilson declared in Parliament that the terms involved 'an intolerable and disproportionate burden on every family in the land and, equally, on Britain's balance of payments'. When Heath's government fell in March 1974, and the Labour Party assumed office, it issued a White Paper[7] outlining its objectives in renegotiating the terms of entry, including: (i) major changes in CAP; (ii) new and fairer methods of financing the Community budget; (iii) no requirement to maintain a fixed parity for sterling within an economic and monetary union; (iv) the retention by Parliament of powers over regional, industrial and fiscal policy, and the ability to control capital movements; (v) safeguards for the Commonwealth and those developing countries not eligible for association; and (vi) no harmonisation of VAT which would require the taxation of necessities. These were similar in substance, although much less specific, to the conditions that Kaldor argued Britain ought to insist on if the Six were really anxious to strengthen the Community by accession of the UK, namely that (i) CAP should be liquidated in a series of steps over eight years, and from 1980 there should be no agricultural protection other than a fixed import duty of not more than 10 per cent; (ii) new members should not be compelled to adopt the variable import levy system or contribute to the Agricultural Fund; (iii) no country should be compelled to adopt VAT; and (iv) no country should be denied associate membership provided it is willing to grant free access to EEC products on a reciprocal basis. Realistically, there was no chance of these conditions being met. If they were regarded by Kaldor as the 'right terms', laying out such conditions might well be regarded as simply a coded way of expressing continued outright opposition to entry.

The government entered negotiations and concluded new terms which were deemed mutually satisfactory to both sides, and these were put to a national referendum in June 1975. Seventeen million voted 'yes' and eight million voted 'no'. |Kaldor thought the new terms feeble and voted 'no'. Owing to his official position as Special Adviser to the Chancellor of the Exchequer, however, he could make no public comment and, in fact, he had already been silenced for nearly a year. By the time he left government service in August 1976, the years had mellowed his attitude to the Community and he accepted membership as more or less a *fait accompli*. He consistently argued for institutional reforms, but never actively campaigned for Britain's withdrawal which he regarded as futile without a broad political consensus in favour. He continued to oppose, however, Britain joining a European monetary union and made a strong speech in the House of Lords to this effect in June 1978 warning against a further loss of sovereignty; a loss of power, and a strengthening of the centrifugal economic forces which would make political union more difficult.

In retrospect, there can be little doubt that much of Kaldor's pessimism concerning the economic implications of Britain joining the Community seems to have been justified. In a letter to *The Times* (16 June) in 1977 with Robert Neild he compared what had happened up till then with the predictions of the 1970 and 1971 White Papers. British manufactured imports from the EEC exceeded exports by £1.2 billion. The outflow of investment to the EEC had increased from £80 million in 1970 to over £500 million, while EEC investment in the UK had hardly changed. The trade deficit with Germany deteriorated from £95 million in 1970 to £1.4 billion in 1977. Industrial production had grown in the UK since entry by 7 per cent, compared with 20 per cent in the EEC. After 1977, Britain's comparative position worsened further, particularly in the trade field. When Britain joined in 1973 the UK deficit in manufactured trade with the EEC was only £275 million. By 1984, the deficit was a colossal £8 billion, largely with Germany. While export volume to the EEC grew by 66 per cent from 1973–84; import volume from the EEC grew by 300 per cent. Latest evidence suggests that as a result of Britain's accession to the Community, UK imports of manufactures from her new partners increased up to 1979 by £8 billion, home sales fell by £8 billion, exports to partners increased by £4.5 billion and exports to non-partners fell by £1.5 billion.[8] In other words, as a result of the reduction in tariff barriers, EEC manufacturers have succeeded in increasing their penetration of the UK market much more successfully than the British in EEC markets, causing a welfare loss of jobs and real income. The car industry provides a classic case study where UK car production peaked in 1972 and declined thereafter – by over one million vehicles from 1972 to 1984 – as tariff reductions took effect. The alleged dynamic benefits of Common Market entry have proved illusory, as Kaldor predicted.

The budgetary cost has also been enormous. By 1979 Britain's net contribution to the Community budget had risen to over £1 billion. Following negotiations started by Mrs Thatcher in that year to reduce the size of Britain's contribution, rebates have since been secured in most years, but the country still remains a large net contributor, while richer countries are net beneficiaries or pay proportionately less relative to GNP and per capita income.[9] Most of the problem lies with the Common Agricultural Policy and the fact that Britain imports a larger quantity of food than other European countries. EEC food prices have sometimes been more than double world prices. On average the EEC price of wheat, maize, barley and meat have exceeded world prices by about 100 per cent, while the prices of dairy products and sugar have exceeded world prices by 200–300 per cent. In 1978/79, the price of EEC milk and butter was 400 per cent higher. All this has caused food prices to be about 20 per cent higher than otherwise would have been the case, which in turn has raised labour costs and reduced industrial competitiveness. It was estimated that in 1978 consumers lost £1.8 billion by having to pay higher than world prices, at a balance of payments cost of £900 million. Without reform of the financing of the Community's budget, Britain will continue to lose; and the trade prospects look particularly bleak. This remained Kaldor's considered view: 'if we stay in Europe, we must ensure, by fresh institutional arrangements, that we derive some genuine benefits from membership and not just costs; and these could come only through fresh "ground rules" governing trade in manufactured goods, as well as trade in agricultural products.'[10] Free trade, as Prince Bismarck once remarked, is a policy for the strong.

NOTES

1. 'EEC Farm Policy is Fundamentally Misconceived', 3 April, 1970.
2. *New Statesman*, 12 March, 1971.
3. Mansholt Report, *Memorandum on the Reform of Agriculture in the European Community*, submitted to the EEC Council of Ministers 1968.
4. 'Would Britain Really Benefit from the EEC?', 14 April, 1971.
5. N. Kaldor, 'The Money Crisis: Britain's Chance', *New Statesman*, 14 May, 1971.
6. 'Distortions of the White Paper', 16 July 1971.
7. 'Renegotiation of the Terms of Entry into the European Economic Community', Cmnd 5593, (London: HMSO, 1974).
8. L. A. Winters, 'Britain in Europe: A Survey of Quantitative Trade Studies', CEPR Discussion Paper No. 10, 1986.
9. The Fontainebleau agreement of June 1984 improved Britain's position but still left her a net contributor. It provided for a rebate of two-thirds of the difference between adjusted payments ('basis for correction') and receipts.
10. House of Lords, 15 March 1984.

11 The International Monetary System and Balance of Payments Adjustment

REFORM OF THE INTERNATIONAL MONETARY SYSTEM

In 1944 some semblance of order was restored to international monetary relations by the Bretton Woods agreement and the establishment of the International Monetary Fund (IMF). The pre-war chaos of competitive devaluations, protectionism and beggar-thy-neighbour policies was replaced by agreement that fixed, but adjustable, exchange rates should be established between countries, and that balance of payments finance should be made available to avoid protection and enable the world to move towards a more liberal economic order. The dollar would have a fixed price in terms of gold, and be convertible into gold, while other national currencies would have a fixed price in terms of dollars. Hence there emerged from Bretton Woods a gold exchange standard, with the American dollar as the 'key' reserve currency. The maintenance of a system of this nature depended, on the supply side, on the willingness of the 'key' currency country to continue to supply its currency as a reserve asset and, on the demand side, on confidence in the key currency and faith in its convertibility into gold. But there was an inherent contradiction in such a system. For confidence, the currency must be strong, but for there to be an adequate supply of reserves, the key currency country must run a balance of payments deficit (or export capital), and issue liabilities (IOUs) which weakens the currency. Ultimately the costs to the country of running persistent balance of payments deficits may become too high, and liabilities may come to exceed assets, making the promise of convertibility of the currency into gold impossible. This is precisely what happened in 1971 when on 15 August, the United States was forced to suspend convertibility of the dollar and the Bretton Woods system came to a sudden end.

The collapse had been foreseen by several economists, most notably by Robert Triffin in his book *Gold and Dollar Crisis* (1959), and also by Kaldor. Throughout the 1950s, Kaldor warned, mainly in correspondence, of the fragility of the system; of the excessive increase in dollar liabilities, and of the consequences of what he considered to be the overvaluation of the US dollar. In 1960 he wrote to Walter Heller, the newly appointed Chairman of the Council of Economic Advisers under President Kennedy, urging a devaluation of the dollar of some 17.5 per cent. Later, in 1968, he repeated the advice to his friend Arthur Okun, holding the same position, suggesting a devaluation of between 10 and 12 per cent. It was his worry over the inherent fragility of the system that inspired his various plans to replace the gold exchange standard with a commodity-backed international money independent of the US dollar.

While the Bretton Woods system lasted, there can be little doubt that it conferred substantial benefits on the world economy by providing an economic environment in which the major industrialised countries could expand their economies without running into balance of payments difficulties. Without the dollar deficit, countries such as Germany, Italy and Japan could not have grown at the rate they did; nor could countries have liberalised trade with such ease. The dollar standard permitted a steady increase in world effective demand and benefited particularly those countries that were able to remain competitive. For countries not so competitive, however, such as the UK, the fixed exchange rate system posed problems and this became an additional strain on the system. Not surprisingly, after many years without any adjustment, some exchange rates deviated substantially from their fundamental equilibrium rates. The growth of capital flows and capital movements likewise made the maintenance of the system difficult when fixed rates provided a one-way option for speculators. All these factors, together with the reluctance of the Americans to supply more dollars, made the breakdown of the existing Bretton Woods system inevitable. When it finally cracked, Kaldor predicted, in a series of three articles in *The Times* ('Bretton Woods and After', 6, 7 and 8 September 1971): 'a new era of floating exchange rates which will be of fairly long duration'.

Up to that time, Kaldor had always favoured a floating rate system, at least for structurally weak countries, in order to maintain full employment and to minimise currency speculation. He shed no tears, therefore, over the collapse of the Bretton Woods system, but he wanted to see instituted a true system of floating which would require the dollar to be demonetised internationally with existing dollar balances transformed into some new international unit (call it bancor) divorced from the domestic currency of the United States, so that the US could vary the dollar in terms of the new unit in the same way as other countries. To be acceptable, and to be independent of individual currencies, a new international medium of exchange should be backed, he argued, by *real* assets and convertible at the discretion of the holder. It would be possible for gold to perform the role with a high enough price to ensure the growth of new production equal to the liquidity needs of the world to finance the growth of trade and the demand for output. To play the same role as the US balance of payments deficit, however, Kaldor calculated that an annual value of gold output of $10 billion would be required, rising at the rate of 10–15 per cent per annum. He thought a gold price of $100–150 an ounce might achieve this, but shuddered at the prospect of conferring so much power and riches on the world's two major gold producing nations, Russia and South Africa. How much better to have a whole bundle of commodities, of which gold might be one, with the supply of international money linked to the supply of the commodity bundle, which would ensure at the same time enough purchasing power over the commodities to keep their price stable and to maintain a stable growth of demand for industrial output.

This was the essence of the scheme for an international commodity reserve currency that Kaldor first proposed in a Report for UNCTAD in 1964, co-authored with Albert Hart and Jan Tinbergen[1] and presented in a simplified version to the World Trade Conference in Geneva in April. The plan was Kaldor's brainchild, which he had been working on since April 1963, and he wrote the document. Hart, from Columbia University, and a friend from Kaldor's LSE days, advised on the commodities that might be suitable for inclusion in the bundle, and Tinbergen did little more than sign the Report to give it prestige. But the idea of a commodity reserve currency was not new. Alfred Marshall once proposed what he called a 'symettalic' currency system according to which a currency would be expressed not in terms of a particular quantity of a particular metal (e.g. gold) but in terms of several metals in fixed proportions to each other.[2] The Kaldor scheme was also reminiscent of the commodity-backed currency scheme advocated independently by Benjamin Graham and Frank Graham designed to avoid a repetititon of the catastrophic depression of commodity prices that occurred in the 1930s.[3] Friedrick von Hayek once endorsed such a plan for the monetary authorities to buy and sell the specified commodities so that their aggregate price remained stable[4].

Kaldor's precise proposal was as follows. First, the IMF should establish its own currency (bancor) convertible into both gold and a bundle of, say, 30 principal commodities in world trade. Secondly, bancor should be fully covered by gold and commodities except for a fixed fiduciary issue. Thirdly, only central banks of member countries should be entitled to hold bancor balances with the IMF, and countries should accept bancor in settlement of claims in the same way as gold. Fourthly, $30 billion of bancor might be issued in the first instance – $5 billion in exchange for gold, $20 billion in exchange for commodities, and $5 billion as the fiduciary issue.

The commodities included in the bundle should satisfy four criteria: low storage costs, durability, possess a well-defined world price, and be free from price manipulation. The weight of each commodity in the bundle should approximate to the proportional importance of that commodity in international trade. The IMF should build up its purchase of stocks gradually from member countries and be responsible for storage and maintenance. Once the initially agreed reserves had been built up, the IMF would then announce the final composition of the commodity bundle and the bancor value of the commodity unit. For example, if there were 30 commodities and the relative number of tons held of the various commodities varied at an even rate from 1 to 30 (i.e. 1, 2, 3, 4, etc.), then a commodity unit would contain 465 composite tons. Suppose that the par value of a commodity ton was equal to 1.15 units of bancor, the par value of a commodity unit would then be 534.75 bancor. Parity between bancor and the current market price level of commodities would be assured by the arbitrage of private traders who would buy commodities in the open market for tendering to the IMF when the price was below par, and buy commodities from the IMF whenever there was a profit in doing so. The IMF, in turn, should undertake to maintain parity between bancor and the world free market price of gold so as to maintain parity between gold and the bundle of commodities. Countries would be free to maintain a fixed rate of exchange in terms of bancor, or a variable rate, provided it is not continually undervalued leading to large accumulations of gold and bancor.

The Kaldor plan received short shrift at the World Trade Conference and was referred instead to a study group. Such a scheme is no nearer the drawing board than it was in 1964. It continues to possess, however, a number of attractive features. At the time it would have eliminated (and was designed to do so) the inherent weaknesses of the gold exchange standard already referred to. Above all, in any environment, it would lend greater stability to the functioning of the world economy. The scheme guarantees that any increase in primary production will generate an equivalent increase in the demand for industrial products since any excess supply of commodities at existing prices would be absorbed into IMF stocks. This would prevent the contraction of the world economy when there was a tendency for the prices of primary commodities to fall. Then if IMF reserves rise faster than the production of primary commodities, manufacturing countries will find their sales rising faster than their purchases, i.e. they will experience growing export surpluses which will accelerate their expansion, thus adding to the demand for primary commodities so that the whole process will tend to be self-balancing. The growth of the consumption and production of primary commodities will converge towards balance, and the growth of reserves will match the growth of production and the use of primary commodities. Thus the scheme would provide the world with an international reserve asset more responsive to the needs of an expanding world economy, and the greater stability of the world economy would be an encouragement to investment and growth in both developed and less developed countries.

The IMF did produce a new international monetary unit in 1969 in the form of Special Drawing Rights (SDRs), the first issue of which was in 1970. But the SDR is valued in terms of a basket of currencies (not backed by commodities) and, as yet, it has not replaced the dollar as the reserve asset of the international monetary system. Moreover, there is no provision for the automatic increase in SDRs as the need arises and no specific role for SDRs to serve internationally agreed purposes of a social nature such as aid to less developed countries or for the purchase of primary commodities to support their price. If ever there was an instrument in search of a policy it is SDRs! There has been frequent discussion of the world moving towards an SDR standard. When the British Chancellor of the Exchequer, Anthony Barber, made such a proposal in 1971, Kaldor wrote to *The Times* (1 October 1971) reiterating the importance and superiority of a commodity-backed standard. He never budged from this position. The only modification he later made to his 1964 proposal was to allow bancor to be separately convertible into a series of individual commodities instead of only into a basket of commodities. This would require the periodic revision of relative bancor prices of individual commodities, which could be done through a worldwide buffer stock scheme financed through bancor.

PRIMARY PRODUCT PRICE INSTABILITY

The case for a commodity-backed currency is conceptually distinct, of course, from the stabilisation of primary product prices. The instability of primary product prices presents problems of its own and can be tackled independently of devising new currency arrangements. Kaldor was equally interested in this separate issue, as Keynes had also been towards the end of his life. The volatility of primary product prices has a number of detrimental consequences. First, it leads to a great deal of instability in the foreign exchange earnings and balance of payments position of producing countries (particularly developing countries) which makes investment planning and economic management much more difficult than otherwise would be the case. Secondly, because of asymmetries in the economic system, volatility imparts inflationary bias combined with tendencies to depression in the world economy at large. This was the major theme of Kaldor's Presidential Address to the Royal Economic Society in 1976 (1976b) which he repeated in a paper to a conference in Dubrovnik in October 1977 under the title of 'World-Wide Inflation and the Effects on Developing Countries'.

The theory is straightforward. First, it is important to recognise the different pricing behaviour in primary product markets and the markets for manufactured goods. Prices in the primary sector are generally market-determined (flexiprice) whereas in the secondary sector they are cost determined and prices are relatively sticky (fixprice). Because industrial prices are sticky, the burden of disequilibrium between the growth of primary production and industrial output is thrown entirely on the commodity market, the behaviour of which is erratic because of lags and speculation. Falling prices for primary commodities can precipitate depression in industry because the buying power of agriculture falls more than the stimulus to demand from rising real income in the industrial sector. In terms of Allyn Young's model, the demand for primary products is not elastic and there is not a self-generating interactive process between supply and demand.[5] Rising commodity prices do not have the opposite effect because industrial prices are quick to follow suit and governments depress demand to control inflation. Inflation itself has a deflationary effect on effective demand for industrial goods in real terms partly because a rise in the profits of primary producers is not matched by an increase in their expenditure, and partly through real balance effects. Thus, whether primary product prices rise or fall, their instability tends to dampen industrial activity: the end result is stagflation. This asymmetrical behaviour is sometimes referred to as the 'Kaldor kink'. Thirdly, the volatility of primary product prices leads to volatility in the terms of trade which may not reflect movements in the equilibrium terms of trade between primary products and industrial goods in the sense that supply and demand are equated in both markets. In these circumstances, world economic growth becomes either supply constrained if primary product prices are 'too high' or demand constrained if primary product prices are 'too low' (see Chapter 8).

There are three broad ways to control fluctuations in primary product prices. First, to have multilateral purchasing agreements for all commodities; second, to establish buffer stocks, and thirdly, to institute restriction schemes. The 1948 Havana Charter had in mind the first two methods, but to date they have not been successful. There has been only one major multilateral purchasing agreement, and that was under the 1949 International Wheat Agreement when the actual agreed selling price turned out to be less than the market price thereby benefiting importers! Buffer-stocks have never been given the finance and international encouragement that they need to be effective. Keynes devoted considerable attention to the instability of primary product prices both during the Second World War and in the years immediately preceding the war. He favoured buffer stock schemes, and was against restriction schemes, although he recognised that if stocks accumulated excessively the agreed 'normal' price could not be held above the market price for ever. There would either have to be a downward revision of the normal price, or output restriction to raise market prices. In a paper in 1938 read to Section F of the British Association,[6] Keynes advocated that the British government should offer storage facilities to all Empire producers of specific raw materials, either free of warehouse charges and interest or for a nominal charge, provided they ship the surpluses to approved warehouses. This, he believed, would not only provide security, but also the moderation of price fluctuations would ensure a more continuous scale of output in the producing countries with corresponding benefits to the industrialised countries. In 1942 Keynes then produced a more detailed plan for what he called Commod Control[7], an international body representing leading producers and consumers that would stand ready to buy Commods (Keynes' name for typical commodities), and store them, at a price (say) 10 per cent below the fixed basic price and sell them at 10 per cent above. Finance for the storage and holding of Commods would have been provided through his proposal for an

International Clearing Union, acting like a World Central Bank, with which Commod Controls would keep accounts. Keynes believed, with some justification, that such a Commod Control scheme would make a major contribution to curing the international trade cycle.

Kaldor's interest in commodity policy dates from 1952 when he was employed as a consultant to the Food and Agricultural Organisation (FAO) in Rome. The International Wheat Agreement was due for renewal and a former research student from the LSE working in Rome, Gerda Blau, invited him to participate in the discussions. The result was a paper on a reconsideration of the economics of the Agreement published in the FAO's Commodity Policy Studies Series.[8] The Wheat Agreement was an interesting scheme whereby a certain bloc of output was traded at a fixed price, and above which there was a free market price. This was also the essence of the Grondona scheme for primary product price stabilisation which would support the price in blocs of commodities, with successive blocs being supported at lower and lower prices. Prices are thereby stabilised but not fixed, thus avoiding the problem of continuous excess supply/demand. Kaldor lent support to the Grondona scheme by writing a preface to one of his books (1975b). Later, in 1963, on a visit to the Economic Commission for Latin America (ECLA) in Santiago, he expressed concern, not only over the instability of primary product prices, but also over the deterioration in the terms of trade for developing countries producing and exporting primary commodities (1964a). The secular trend deterioration in the terms of trade of primary commodities was first articulated independently by Raul Prebisch[9] and Hans Singer.[10] Prebisch was Executive Secretary (and later Director) of ECLA and put the historical trend deterioration at 0.9 per cent per annum. Subsequent, more refined, research has estimated the decline to be about one-half this figure, and the decline has continued post-war.[11]

Like Prebisch and others, Kaldor believed that the only solution lies in enhancing the importance of manufacturing industry within a broader-based industrial structure. As a precondition, however, there must first be the stabilisation of commodity prices with the control of production and export of particular commodities to bring supply and demand into line at an agreed price. This led him to recommend restriction schemes, although recognising their monopolistic nature and the difficulties of maintaining them. To secure full participation and to minimise the risk of breakdown through overproduction, several measures were suggested, including importers agreeing not to buy from non-participants and the imposition of variable export duties or levies depending on the level of stocks. To maintain efficiency, quotas could be redistributed to the most efficient producers in small gradual steps. In the 1970s the problem became not one of depressed prices of primary commodities, but of rising prices contributing to world wide inflation. The experience convinced Kaldor that only by stabilising the price of basic commodities could world inflation be beaten. In 1977 he wrote to Charles Schultze, the new Chairman of the Council of Economic Advisers in America, proposing an initiative to stabilise the world price of wheat. It received a sympathetic reply but to no avail.

Despite the schemes proposed by Kaldor and others, very little action has been taken at a world level to control primary product price instability. If anything, commodity price fluctuations have been greater since the Second World War than pre-war, and certainly much more sensitive to world industrial production since the breakdown of Bretton Woods. In the face of growing instability Kaldor eventually endorsed the original Keynes Plan for Commod Control, advocating a new International Agency for Commodity Control financed by the issue of SDRs (1983c). The purpose of the scheme would be 'to secure the highest sustainable rate of economic growth, to the world as a whole, i.e. the highest rate of growth of world industrialisation which the growth of availabilities of primary products permits'. In other words, keeping the rate of output growth of the two sectors of primary product production and manufacturing in line would be done not through primary product price variations, but through variations in the rate of investment in stocks by the International Commodity Control Authority. The Control Authority would buy and sell commodities in exchange for SDRs to keep the price of basic commodities within, say, 5 per cent of their value in terms of SDRs. Net purchases by the Authority would cause an equivalent increase in SDRs thus increasing world liquidity when most needed. The price stability would also give the incentive to invest in, and expand the production of, primary commodities, the supply of which in the Kaldor model is the only true long run constraint on industrial growth (see Chapter 8). We have now, of course, turned full circle, because a buffer-stock scheme linked to the issue of SDRs could provide the world with a basic money unit which would be guaranteed to be stable in terms of basic commodities with the commodities included in the scheme convertible into SDRs at a fixed rate. We are led back to the 1964 Kaldor scheme for a commoditity backed currency which could kill at least two birds with one stone, if not more.

BALANCE OF PAYMENTS ADJUSTMENT

The cyclical instability of the world economy is not only related to the behaviour of primary product prices but also to the demand management and employment policies pursued by industrial countries and to methods of balance of payments adjustment. Kaldor presented a paper on this theme to the meeting of the International Economic Association in Monte Carlo in September 1950 (1950a). Many of his early ideas he maintained, and they stood the test of time; others he changed. In the analysis of the international repercussions of domestic demand management policy he distinguished two aspects – structural and cyclical – the former relating to one country maintaining permanently higher employment than others; the latter relating to one country attempting to maintain its domestic income and employment in the face of contraction by other countries. The higher the level of employment relative to other countries, the higher the level of imports relative to exports and the lower the equilibrium rate of exchange and terms of trade. If the exchange rate adjustment must be large, there may be a case for import restrictions. Kaldor makes the important distinction here between import restrictions preventing an *expansion* of imports beyond a level that cannot be financed by exports, and restrictions which reduce imports below the level of exports which is a policy of exporting unemployment. The former policy is designed to allow expansion towards full employment, implying a fall in the import *ratio* but not necessarily a fall in the absolute level of imports. It is not, therefore, a beggar-thy-neighbour policy. The Cambridge Economic Policy Group's case for import controls in the United Kingdom in the 1970s was based on a reduction in the import ratio which need not then provoke retaliation.

The cyclical problem arises because countries are linked through trade. Depression in one country causes the balance of payments of other countries to move into deficit as export demand falls, and if the deficits cannot be financed, income and employment falls elsewhere. If saving falls relative to investment, the multiplier effect of falling exports will not reduce imports commensurately, so that a residual deficit might still remain at a lower level of employment. There are four possible remedies: first, further deflation; second, import restrictions; third, exchange rate adjustment; and fourth, discriminatory exchange or trade restrictions. Deflation simply further reduces income and employment. Import restrictions reduce the volume of world trade. The least damaging policy probably lies in devaluation and discriminatory exchange controls. But the important point is that whatever policy is pursued, countries can rarely isolate themselves from the adverse effects resulting from a cyclical depression emanating from a major industrial country. The world is no nearer solving this particular problem which becomes more acute the larger the number of countries that participate in autonomous deflation, as became apparent in the world economy between 1979 and 1982. Ideally, depressed surplus countries should lend their currencies to enable other countries to continue to import to prevent cumulative contraction. While this happens to a certain extent, there are not the institutional mechanisms which can guarantee this process to the required extent. To remedy this defect was one of the major recommendations of the UN Report on *National and International Measures for Full Employment* 1949 for which Kaldor was largely responsible.

Kaldor took up again the theme of international cyclical instability in a paper presented to the Oxford Conference of the International Economic Association in September 1952 (1955a). He pointed out that even if there was complete synchronisation of the investment cycle across countries, some countries would move into surplus and others into deficit, firstly because one country's demand for imports varies more or less than the world demand for its exports (i.e. the income elasticities of demand for imports and exports differ), and secondly because the terms of trade will change with export prices falling more or less than import prices as a result of differences in supply elasticities. If cyclical movements (investment cycles) are not synchronised there is even more reason to suppose international payments disequilibrium. What is needed is international finance to sustain cyclical deficits. The preoccupation at the time was with disequilibrium between the United States and the rest of the world, and Kaldor's prescription was for discriminatory restrictions on imports from the dollar area, in the spirit of the IMF's scarce currency clause, rather than devaluation by the rest of the world or deflation. Making other countries' goods cheaper and choking the demand for US goods in this way would not be sensible because it would make the rest of the world poorer, reducing the world's ability to buy American goods. Deflation by the rest of the world would not be sensible either because it would not only make countries poorer but also be largely ineffective. The US demand for imports would not increase and America's exports would not decrease very much because a large part of the export surplus comprised essential commodities. The demand contraction would have to be very severe. In the interests of world welfare, it would be much better to restrict dollar imports. As it turned out, the dollar soon ceased to be scarce as the world embraced a dollar standard, but the same argument applies against any country in perpetual balance of payments surplus which for some reason is either unwilling or unable to adjust to eliminate its surplus. It is these countries that exert deflationary bias on the global economic system. Japan, with huge trade surpluses, would be an example in the modern era.

Kaldor was to reiterate these arguments in an essay written for the Fabian Society (1952a), where he also turns to the specific balance of payments problems of the United Kingdom. He warned of the necessity and problems of adapting the internal economic structure to the need for sufficient exports to pay for necessary imports to maintain full employment. Britain's immediate post-war export performance had been very creditable but was still inadequate, in Kaldor's view, particularly if the country was to build up its foreign exchange reserves and to lend abroad to developing countries. He urged the government to invest more to increase the supply capacity of exportables, particularly in the steel and engineering sectors using indigenous materials.

The Fabian essay is noteworthy for Kaldor's first assault on the doctrine of the mutual profitability of free trade for all participating nations. The numerous qualifications to the doctrine are emphasised, particularly that welfare may not increase if free trade leads to unemployed resources and terms of trade deterioration. Free trade for a less developed country may put obstacles in the way of its development without compensating advantages to the world as a whole, and may produce an undesirable distribution of 'regional' income bearing no relation to the amount or productivity of the resources involved in production. Furthermore, terms of trade changes may not rectify balance of payments deficits, in which case it would be preferable for a country to restrict imports directly to avoid the necessity of internal deflation.

EXCHANGE RATE ADJUSTMENT VERSUS PROTECTION

In the British context, as early as 1952 in his Fabian essay, Kaldor supported a floating exchange rate for the United Kingdom, as dollar earnings fluctuated, although he was aware of the institutional constraints and difficulties. For one thing, floating would have been contrary to the IMF Articles of Agreement. Secondly, it would have been difficult to combine floating with discrimination against dollar goods, but the abandonment of discrimination would aggravate the long-run problem of attaining dollar balance and could involve a serious deterioration in the terms of trade. Throughout the 1950s and 1960s he retained his faith in exchange rate adjustment as an efficient instrument for rectifying balance of payments disequilibrium, although in the 1950s, at least, he did not believe that the pound was overvalued.[12] His 1970 Presidential Address to the British Association for the Advancement of Science (1971c) was devoted to exchange rate policy in which he criticised successive British governments for wrongly perceiving the task of securing full employment as one of internal demand management through fiscal policy as opposed to one of balancing exports and imports. Export-led growth through exchange rate adjustment, as opposed to consumption-led growth, would have led to a higher ratio of investment to output, a faster rate of growth of productivity and a virtuous circle of growth. In this spirit he welcomed Britain's decision to float the pound in June 1972, and in 1973 he was still expressing optimism that a floating rate system could reconcile internal and external balance across the major industrialised countries of the world. In both *The Times* (9 July 1973) and in *The Banker* (1973a) he argued against any return to rigid rates of exchange or pegs (even with greater flexibility) because of what he described as the built-in tendencies towards disequilibrium in trade and payments resulting from self-reinforcing trends of industrial productivity and competitiveness: 'it is only by adjustments of the exchange rate ... that the trade losing countries can counter the cumulative disadvantages resulting from increased inroads by the trade earning countries both in their own markets and in third markets.'

From the time he became Special Adviser to the Chancellor of the Exchequer in 1974, however, his optimism over the efficacy of exchange rates as an adjustment weapon changed perceptibly. With the mounting evidence of growing imbalances in the world economy, despite the floating system, he became more and more sceptical that nominal exchange rate changes could bring about sufficiently large real exchange rate changes, or that the price elasticities were high enough in the short term to guarantee movement towards equilibrium. He became convinced that in practice price elasticities of demand are dominated by income elasticities of demand determined by the characteristics of goods, and in the final analysis it is movements in income and output that preserve long run balance of payments equilibrium not relative price movements. This realisation converted him to the doctrine of the Harrod trade multiplier and its importance for understanding growth performance between open economies.

Roy Harrod had suggested as long ago as 1933[13] that the pace and rhythm of growth in industrial countries was to be explained by the workings of the foreign trade multiplier – or $Y = X/m$, where Y is output, X is exports, m is the marginal propensity to import and $1/m$ is the trade multiplier.[14] This result is derived on the assumption that trade is always balanced and the terms of trade remain unchanged. The dynamic analogue of this static multiplier on the same assumptions is $y = x/\pi$, where y is the growth of output, x is the growth of exports and π is the income elasticity of demand for imports.[15] Given that, as an approximation, $x = \epsilon(z)$, where z is the growth of world ouput and ϵ is the income elasticity of demand for exports, this means that $y = \epsilon(z)/\pi$ or $y/z = \epsilon/\pi$; in other words, one country's growth relative to all others is equal to the ratio of the income elasticity of demand for its exports and the income elasticity of demand for imports.

It was not until 1977, however, that he was able to prove conclusively to himself what was becoming increasingly apparent that flexible exchange rates were not working as expected. In a paper prepared with the assistance of Mr I.F. Edwards entitled 'The Effect of Devaluations on Trade in Manufactures' (1977a), he showed exactly the opposite of what he previously argued and believed. Using data over the period 1956–76 it appeared that in countries such as the United Kingdom and the United States where relative unit labour costs and the exchange rate had fallen relative to other countries, their export share of manufactured goods also fell – in the UK from 18.7 to 8.7 per cent and in the US from 25.5 to 17.3 per cent. By contrast, in countries such as Germany and Japan, where relative costs and the exchange rate had risen, their export shares also rose. In other words, there was a generally perverse relationship between changes in competitiveness and changes in export performance despite movements of exchange rates in an equilibrating direction – what might be called the 'Kaldor paradox'. The explanation probably lies in a combination of reasons. A low price elasticity of demand for goods would be one obvious explanation, but that would have to be separately verified. A more likely explanation would be that income effects simply dominated price effects; in other words, the apparent perversity would have been even greater had exchange rates not changed. Another possibility is that there was an exaggerated rise in unit labour costs in successful countries with productivity growth in the successful export industries far higher than for the manufacturing sector as a whole. The apparent failure of exchange rate changes can also be seen by observing the trade balances of the devaluing countries such as the UK and the US. The deficit grew between the UK and Germany, Japan, France and Italy, with the largest deficits emerging with Germany and Japan where competitiveness had improved the most. The US deficit also grew with Japan despite a reduction of nearly 50 per cent in relative unit labour costs. Robert Triffin showed the same paradox.[16] Kaldor admitted in the General Introduction to his eight-volume *Collected Essays* that the subject of exchange rate adjustment, and its efficacy, was one of the few important matters on which he changed his mind during his academic life. Non-price factors in international trade appear from the evidence to be far more important than price competitiveness in determining trade patterns and trade balances between countries. If exchange rate adjustment goes far enough or lasts long enough it may work, but there may be a great deal of chaos and loss of real income in the meantime which call for alternative methods of adjustment.

If exchange rate changes are ruled out as an efficient adjustment mechanism, and instead income and employment suffer, trade imbalances will incur welfare losses. Some form of managed trade or protection may be superior if trade imbalances and demand constraints in deficit countries lead to deflationary bias in the whole world economic system. The assumption of full employment is quite crucial to the welfare predictions of (neo) classical free trade theory, but cannot be guaranteed even where trade is balanced. It partly depends on the conditions of production. Take, for example, Ricardo's classic demonstration of the gains from trade with Portugal and England specialising in wine and cloth, respectively. The fact that some activities are subject to diminishing returns, for example, means that there will be a limit to employment in those activities so that if resource reallocation occurs some previously employed labour may find it difficult to be reabsorbed. Viniculture, since it is land-based, may be characterised as a diminishing returns activity, while cloth manufacturing is subject to constant or increasing returns. Portugal may have a comparative advantage in wine, but not all those thrown out of work in the cloth industry may be able to find work in the vineyards, and the welfare gains from trading wine for cloth from England may be offset by the unemployment of resources. In theory, factors of production should stop moving when they are no more productive growing wine than producing cloth in exchange for wine with England, so that specialisation is only partial. In practice, protective barriers may be reduced beyond the optimum point. Ricardo conveniently assumed trade balance and constant returns in all activities, but as soon as these assumptions are relaxed it is easy to appreciate that free trade may not guarantee full employment or a net increase in welfare for each trading partner.

In the case of two countries that both specialise in manufacturing, whether both gain from specialisation depends on whether trade remains balanced. If it does not, because one country is technologically superior, for example, the deficit country will be constrained in its activity, and unless the entire (*ex ante*) deficit can be financed, the output of both countries will be reduced below potential.

There are several ways of attempting to achieve a greater degree of trade balance between countries to avoid deflationary bias in the economic system. Systems of tariffs and quotas on goods are one possibility, although they only make welfare sense on a selective basis against countries in surplus, otherwise activity will be further constrained in other deficit countries, not to mention the threat of retaliation. Kaldor was never a strong advocate of these forms of expenditure switching, preferring less 'inward-looking' forms of 'protection'. Tariffs adjust the internal price structure to the internal cost structure, whereas what is required for a dynamic growth strategy is to adjust the internal cost structure to the external price structure. The subsidisation of production and exports is much superior to the restriction of imports. It would be difficult, though, to subsidise exports only to selective destinations where imbalances are greatest. Voluntary export restraints from surplus countries might be another possibility, or a system of bilateral agreements between countries that a certain level of imbalance would be tolerable, but above that level voluntary or other action would have to be taken. Kaldor's preferred method of control, however, to ensure balance, was to use import licences or vouchers to limit the import of particular categories of goods in a certain proportion to the value of the exports of those goods. He aired this scheme in the British Treasury in the 1970s with the idea of applying it to British imports of manufactures in the face of growing trade imbalances with Japan and the EEC. After leaving the Treasury in 1976, he carried on the campaign for managed trade in the columns of the press.[17] He prepared a more detailed plan at the request of the French government in 1982 that would allow equilibrium on the balance of payments with the simultaneous expansion of demand. First, a distinction would be made between substitutable and non-substitutable goods. In the context of Europe the major non-substitutable goods consist of fuels and raw materials and some semi-manufactures, while substitute goods consist largely of manufactures. The estimated imbalance of trade in non-substitutables (or complementary) goods then determines the surplus that must exist in manufactures for there to be overall balance of payments equilibrium. To ensure the required trade surplus in manufactures, exporters would receive certificates of exportation, which could then be sold to importers in the same broad field, but the entitlement to import would be only some fraction to the value of the certificate. For example, if the required excess of exports over imports was 33 per cent, importers would be able to import up to 75 per cent of the value of the exports (a ratio of 0.75). The certificates could be sold in a free market and if there was excess demand, the premium over the official exchange rate would represent a form of devaluation – with the big difference, however, that the devaluation would be the uncertain outcome of the desired (fixed) ratio of imports to exports allowed rather than the balance between exports and imports being the uncertain outcome of a given devaluation. If required, the scheme could favour intra-EEC trade by allowing the permitted ratio of imports to exports to be higher for EEC countries than for others. Kaldor gave an illustrative figure for France of how the scheme might work. Given France's trade flows then prevailing, the ratio of imports to exports might be (say) 1 for imports from other EEC countries and 0.6 for imports from the rest of the world to achieve a required surplus on manufactured trade of 106 million francs equivalent to an overall import:export ratio of 0.75.

There are obvious problems with such a scheme and disadvantages compared with more conventional methods of achieving trade balance, but none would be insurmountable. There might be speculative hoarding and dis-hoarding of certificates, but to prevent this the certificates could be given a fixed life of, say, no more than six months. The right to import would go to the highest bidders for the certificates of exportation; in other words, to where the private return is highest. These uses for imports may not be where the social return is highest. It would be possible, however, to distinguish between essential and less essential manufactures and semi-manufactures and to allocate only the latter via the market mechanism. In any case, there would be a general problem of the classification of goods as to whether they would be covered by the scheme, but no greater than with other forms of discrimination and control. As opposed to tariffs, the government would get no revenue from the scheme, unless profits to exporters from the sale of certificates were taxed. This would be possible if they were sold at a premium. To the extent that the scheme reduced trade and specialisation, welfare would be reduced, but the overriding advantage of the scheme of permitting expansion and the fuller utilisation of resources while preserving trade balance could more than outweigh such static losses.

As well as control over imports, the promotion of exports must not be ruled out. Having once seen payroll subsidies as only a substitute for devaluation, Kaldor later came to prefer them. Apart from avoiding the inflationary consequences of a conventional devaluation, payroll subsidies can be shown to be superior in shifting resources from consumption to exports in the sense that a lesser reduction in the real wage is necessary with a payroll subsidy than with devaluation. The reason is that devaluation raises the share of profits in GNP, while a wage subsidy does the opposite. Thus devaluation increases consumption out of profits and the required cut in consumption out of wages is that much greater. A payroll subsidy also has the advantage that it can be regionally differentiated as an instrument for encouraging regional development and rejuvenation at the same time, as it was in the UK from 1967 to 1976.

Kaldor's experience in trying to persuade the Treasury to adopt non-orthodox measures to rectify Britain's growing trade imbalance, particularly in manufactures, has been related in Chapter 9. He remained a strong critic of the country's doctrine of 'laissez-faire, laissez-passer': 'The nemesis of the belief in free trade and in free markets, after a century of failure, haunts us still' (Spectator, 27 August, 1977). Such an attitude was perhaps excusable and tolerable up to the great depression of the 1870s when Britain dominated the industrial world. Since that time, however, there has been virtually persistent relative decline in the face of superior foreign competition. No other European economy based its growth and development strategy on free trade, before its domestic market was ready.[17] The only respite in Britain's fortunes was between 1932 and 1937 behind a protective wall which helped to accelerate industrial growth to a rate of 8 per cent per annum. Nothing changed Kaldor's view that 'with a protected home market [the British] could have enjoyed much higher growth rates and as a result we could now have much higher living standards and more secure employment' (Spectator, op. cit.). His last major research project, financed by the Economic and Social Research Council, was on the effect of tariffs relative to other factors on industrial recovery in Britain in the 1930s (see 1986e).

1. *The Case for an International Commodity Reserve Currency*, (Geneva: UNCTAD, 1964).
2. For a systematic treatment see his *Money Credit and Commerce* (London: Macmillan 1923). He had first expounded his views, however, in 1886 to the Royal Commission on the Depression of Trade and Industry and in evidence to the Gold and Silver Commission in 1887 and 1888.
3. B. Graham, *Storage and Stability* (New York: McGraw Hill, 1937); and F.D. Graham, *Social Goals and Economic Institutions* (Princeton University Press, 1942).
4. F. von Hayek, 'A Commodity Reserve Currency', *Economic Journal*, June–September 1943.
5. A. Young, 'Increasing Returns and Economic Progress', *Economic Journal*, December 1928.
6. J.M. Keynes, 'The Policy of Government Storage of Foodstuffs and Raw Materials', *Economic Journal*, September 1938.
7. See D. Moggridge (ed.), *The Collected Writings of J.M. Keynes, Vol. XXVII: Activities 1940–1946 Shaping the Post-War World: Employment and Commodities* (London: Macmillan, 1980).
8. *A Reconsideration of the Economics of the International Wheat Agreement*, Commodity Policy Studies No. 1 (FAO, Rome, September 1952).
9. R. Prebisch, *The Economic Development of Latin America and Its Principal Problems*, (UN Dept. of Economic Affairs, New York: 1950).
10. H. Singer, 'The Distribution of Gains Between Investing and Borrowing Countries', *American Economic Review*, Papers and Proceedings, May 1950.
11. A.P. Thirlwall and J. Bergevin, 'Trends, Cycles and Asymmetries in the Terms of Trade of Primary Commodities from Developed and Less Developed Countries', *World Development*, July 1985.
12. See Kaldor's article 'Three-Way Dilemma', *The Spectator*, 24 January 1958.
13. R. Harrod, *International Economics*, (London: Nisbet, 1933).
14. Kaldor drew public attention to this important contribution of Harrod in a supplementary obituary of Harrod written with Wynne Godley for *The Times* (15 March 1977).
15. See my book, *Balance of Payments Theory and the United Kingdom Experience* (London: Macmillan, 3rd edition 1986), Chapter 10.
16. R. Triffin, *Gold and Dollar Crisis: Yesterday and Tomorrow*, Eassy in International Finance No. 132 (Princeton University, December 1978).
17. See, for example, his article 'Group therapy for world growth', *Guardian*, 8 March 1978.
18. D. Senghass, *The European Experience: A Historical Critique of Development Theory* (Berg Publishers, 1985).

12 MONETARISM

Prior to his submission of evidence to the Radcliffe Committee on the Working of the Monetary System in 1958 (1958f), Kaldor devoted relatively little attention to monetary theory and policy. He was not a monetary economist in the sense of Keynes or Dennis Robertson. From the time of the Radcliffe Report,[1] however, he became increasingly concerned with monetary issues, and in the 1970s and 1980s it was Kaldor who led the intellectual assault on the doctrine of monetarism that spread from the University of Chicago with the virulence of a plague, first affecting susceptible academic communities and then the governments of several advanced industrialised countries.

The doctrine comes in several versions, varying in character and strength according to source and assumptions. The father of modern monetarism was Professor Milton Friedman, and his monetarism is sometimes labelled Mark I monetarism to distinguish it from stronger versions of monetarism identified with the 'new classical macroeconomics' which embraces Friedman monetarism but goes further in denying the effectiveness of government stabilisation policy not only in the long run but also in the short run, on the assumption that agents behave on the basis of rational expectations.[2] Kaldor was not primarily concerned with the finer nuances and distinctions between the different versions of monetarism, but with the core propositions which distinguish monetarist thinking from the outlook of Keynesians. He also became deeply concerned with the practical application of monetarism in the United Kingdom after 1979 which differed in some respects from the theoretical doctrine.

Modern monetarism, as developed by Friedmen, is really nothing more than a refinement and extension of the old classical quantity theory of money first propounded by the English philosopher David Hume in his essay 'Of Money' (1752):[3] the

291

proposition that in the long run money affects only money things and not the real economy; the stock of money determines money income. The doctrine is profoundly anti-Keynesian, and that was the inspiration for its revival. Keynes thought he had undermined the quantity theory of money by | destroying the theoretical presumption of a stable velocity of circulation of money. It was on these Keynesian grounds, combined with a belief that expenditure is relatively insensitive to changes in the rate of interest, that Kaldor expressed doubts to the Radcliffe Committee concerning the efficacy of monetary policy.

The 'Keynesian' attack on monetarism led by Kaldor, however, took a somewhat different approach. Friedman and other monetarists claimed from their empirical investigations to have discovered a long run stable (not necessarily constant) velocity of circulation of money which for them was enough to support the proposition that variations in the money supply will have predictable effects on the price level and money income. The stock of money *determines* money income, and more strongly, 'inflation is always and everywhere a monetary phenomenon' in a *causal* sense. The basic issue dividing monetarists and Keynesians concerns this presumed direction of causation, and whether the money supply can be treated as exogenous and controllable. A stable velocity of circulation of money (if indeed velocity *is* stable) could be evidence that as costs and prices rise autonomously, or as plans to spend increase, the supply of money responds passively to increases in the demand for it. The debate on this matter is reminiscent of the Currency versus Banking School controversy of the nineteenth century, the Currency School being the quantity theorists arguing that output is determined from the supply side, and the Banking School believing in the importance of credit as a stimulus to trade.

Keynes in the *General Theory* was critical of the classical quantity theory of money on several counts, including the assumptions of full employment; a constant velocity of circulation of money; and constant prices before the full employment level of output is reached. Although in his own analysis he proceeded *as if* the money supply was exogenously determined by the Central Bank (since he wanted to analyse the predictions of the quantity theory on its own ground) he saw money as only one of many sources of inflation in a modern capitalist economy. Equally important are structural factors (e.g. bottlenecks) and strong institutional pressures which raise the cost unit and cause prices to rise independently of prior increases in the money supply and the level of employment. Then money responds to the needs of trade. There is recognition that when money is 'relatively scarce' some means is found to increase the effective quantity of money.[4] Indeed, this is given as the reason why in the long run a stable ratio between the national income and the quantity of money may be observed. Keynes had already observed in the *Treatise on Money*, Volume 2 (1930) that 'if there are strong social or political forces causing spontaneous changes in the money rates of efficiency wages, the control of the price level may pass beyond the control of the banking system'.[5] Kaldor accepted this position, although emphasising even more strongly the cost basis of price determination, at least in industrial activities, and sometimes castigating Keynes for placing too much emphasis on the determination of the money supply by the Central Bank, as if the money supply is exogenously determined and controllable (1983d).

It is easily forgotten that the sustained inflation witnessed in industrial countries over the last forty years since the Second World War is unprecedented historically. The index of retail prices at the end of the great depression of the 1930s was no higher than at the time of Cromwell. Since 1945 industrial prices have risen twenty-fold. What has changed is not primarily attitudes to monetary restraint but the economic and institutional environment in which workers and business operate, namely the growing strength of trade unions in the labour market, in an environment up till recently of relatively full employment, and the adoption of 'mark-up' pricing by large corporations which dominate the product market. Inflation is a wage or cost phenomenon propagated, but not originated, by an elastic supply of money through the commercial banking system and other credit mechanisms. In Kaldor's words: 'all inflationary processes that proceed in time, that is to say, which do not peter out of their own accord, are cost induced inflations: they reflect the failure of society to distribute its real income in a manner that is acceptable to the great majority of its inhabitants.'[6] He had reached this conclusion at least thirty years earlier. In 1950, he submitted a memorandum to the Chancellor of the Exchequer, Stafford Cripps, outlining a strategy for wages and dividends, fearing that full employment would lead to excessive money wage demands jeopardising price stability (1950b). A Wages Board was proposed consisting of the Trade Union Congress and government to review wage agreements within a stated annual wage and salary target with powers to postpone particular wage increases. Prophetically he wrote: 'whether the trade union movement can be brought to accept a policy on these lines at the present time, or whether they will only be brought to agreement after further (and perhaps bitter) experience, is open to doubt'.

It was within a framework that treats money as exogenous that Kaldor submitted his evidence to the Radcliffe Committee and answered questions in oral examination. Originally, he was lukewarm about the enquiry. In a letter to David Worswick he wrote, 'I am a little doubtful about the whole thing.... I am not very anxious to give evidence to the Committee and I don't think I would do so unless specially requested' (16 July). He was requested, and his evidence bears close examination since it is clear from the final Report[7] that Radcliffe seems to have been strongly influenced by it, with respect to the ineffectiveness of monetary policy both on account of changes in the velocity of circulation of money and the insensitivity of expenditure to changes in the rate of interest. Sir Roy Harrod was led to remark in a review of Kaldor's Essays: 'there appears to be a certain family resemblance between Mr. Kaldor's point of view on certain central questions and that of the Radcliffe Report, and it is possible that the Kaldor memorandum had an important influence on the Radcliffe Report'.[8] Despite political and philosophical differences, Radcliffe and Kaldor had a strong mutual respect for each other dating from the time when Kaldor served on the Royal Commission on the Taxation of Profits and Income 1951–54 of which Radcliffe was also Chairman.

Monetary policy in the United Kingdom had been revived in 1951, having been in abeyance since the beginning of the war. With the threat of accelerating inflation and a balance of payments crisis in early 1955, increasingly restrictionist monetary measures were taken, but apparently to little effect. Despite the pressure on liquidity, bank advances continued to rise such that both quantitative and qualitative controls were introduced. It became clear to the government and outside observers that a review was necessary of the methods and scope of monetary controls. The Radcliffe Committee of Inquiry was constituted in May 1957 with the following brief terms of reference: 'to inquire into the working of the monetary and credit system and to make recommendations'. Alec Cairncross and Richard Sayers were the two academic economists on the Committee. Over 150 individuals and institutions submitted evidence and were subsequently questioned by the Committee as witnesses. The Final Report was unanimous, but at the price, as Kaldor later put it, of 'vagueness at critical points and omission of important links in the chain of argument' (1960c).

The Committee's overriding conclusion was that there is no direct link between the supply of money and the level of demand in the economy, first because the velocity of circulation of money is variable and secondly, because, as far as spending is concerned, it is not the quantity of money that is important but the wider structure of liquidity in the economy: 'The decision to spend... depends on liquidity in the broad sense, not upon immediate access to the money... spending is not limited by the amount of money in existence but it is related to the amount of money people think they can get hold of, whether by receipts of income (for instance from sales), by disposal of capital assets or by borrowing'.[9] On the velocity of circulation of money, the Committee concluded (in what has become a classic paragraph): 'we have not made more use of this concept because we cannot find any reason for supposing, or any experience in monetary history indicating, that there is any limit to the velocity of circulation; it is a statistical concept that tells us nothing directly of the motivation that influences the level of total demand'. It is, of course, the existence of a wide range of liquid assets that can be converted into spending power when 'money' is short that makes velocity highly variable, but the Committee rejected the view that there should be control over financial institutions other than the commercial banks. Another major conclusion was that control over liquidity should be through control over the *entire structure* of interest rates (not just short term rates). It was by this reasoning that the Committee made its controversial recommendation that interest rate policy, rather than control of the money supply as such, should be the centrepiece of monetary policy. The Committee referred to a 'diffused difficulty of borrowing' by manipulation of the interest rate structure through its effect on the liquidity position of financial institutions of all kinds. Kaldor warmly approved the Committee's attack on the mechanistic quantity theory of money, although in his review of the Report (1960c) he regretted that it failed to probe deeper into the question of the variability of the velocity of circulation of money.

Kaldor began his evidence to Radcliffe by stressing that the rate at which money circulates is not constant. He supported his case by pointing to the increase in velocity between 1955 and 1958 resulting from the failure of the money supply to expand *pari passu* with prices and money incomes. This behaviour of velocity was not an independent event which just happened to coincide with the restrictive monetary policy; it was the direct consequence. The effect of money on activity comes indirectly through the effect of interest rate changes on expenditure. Kaldor listed many reasons, however, why the effect of interest rate changes on expenditure may be limited in practice: for example; to reduce stocks of goods may involve heavy costs if transport costs are raised or there are delays in production; the effect on short term investment can only be temporary while the adjustment of stocks to turnover takes place; the long rate of interest moves only sluggishly with the short rate and may not be expected to last; there may be a large gap between the market rate of interest and the prospective rate of profit so that marginal interest rate changes do not affect the investment decision; at full employment, the capacity of the investment goods industries may act as a stronger constraint on investment than the cost of borrowing, and so on. He conceded that large interest rate movements could no doubt curtail and stimulate demand, but he warned against pronounced interest rate variability which would increase the instability of bond prices in the capital market. This would be undesirable since, owing to the increased risk involved, it would tend to raise the average yield which investors would demand for parting with liquidity, which would mean that the average profit rate would also have to rise to make real investment attractive. Thus fluctuating interest rates would alter the balance of expenditure in the economy in favour of consumption, with adverse consequences for economic growth. Only if a higher rate of inflation matched the higher rate of interest would growth be sustainable.

At this juncture in his evidence Kaldor elaborated on the role of inflation in the growth process; a theme on which he subsequently expanded in two lectures at the London School of Economics in 1959 (1959c). He criticised the first Cohen Council Report on *Prices, Productivity and Incomes* (1958)[10] for neglecting to consider the effect of prices on the rate of profit; a neglect all the more surprising since Dennis Robertson was a member of the Council. After all, it was Robertson, in his book *Money* (1922), who argued the case for a gently rising price level in the spirit of David Hume and others before him:

so long as the control of production is in the hands of a minority, rewarded by means of a fluctuating profit, it is not impossible that a gently rising price level will in fact produce the best attainable results not only for them (the controllers of industry) but the community as a whole. And it is tolerably certain that a price level continually falling, even for the best of reasons, would prove deficient in those stimuli upon which modern society, whether wisely or not, has hitherto chiefly relied for keeping its members in full employment and getting its work done.

Kaldor reckoned (at the time at least) that the inducement to invest required a margin between the gross profit rate and the rate of interest of between 6 and 10 per cent (or 3–5 per cent net of tax), so that a 15 per cent profit rate, for example, would be consistent with a long-term interest rate of something between 5 and 9 per cent. The rate of profit (P/K) is equal to the growth of money GNP (g) divided by the proportion of profits saved (s_p).[11] A 15 per cent profit rate might be made up of a 6 per cent GNP growth rate and a savings ratio out of profits of 40 per cent. Suppose half the GNP growth consists of rising prices which is then eliminated. This would reduce the profit rate to 7½ per cent, and interest rates would have to fall to 1½–2½ per cent to keep real growth moving. The implication of this analysis is that if *real* growth is slow, stable prices will produce a low rate of profit which may not be sufficient to induce enough investment for full employment and future growth. Thus, according to Kaldor, 'stable or falling prices may well be regarded as a luxury which only fast-growing economies can afford'.

The Radcliffe Committee concurred with Kaldor's fears concerning interest rate instability. They strongly favoured stability of the long-term rate of interest in order to preserve stability in the bond market to facilitate finance of the national debt. But, as Kaldor himself noted, there was some inconsistency here between this recommendation and the general view that interest rate policy, through management of the national debt, should become the centrepiece of monetary policy: 'If the . . . policy of the Central Bank in the bond market is not to be understood as deliberately inducing variations in bond prices, but as stabilising them, this is the equivalent of saying that monetary action should play a purely passive role in the regulation of the economy, at any rate in relation to short-term variations in the pressure of demand' (1960c). The Committee themselves concluded: 'we envisage the use of monetary measures as not in ordinary times playing other than a subordinate part in guiding the development of the economy . . . our conclusion is that monetary measures cannot alone be relied upon to keep in nice balance an economy subject to major strains from both without and within. Monetary measures can help, but that is all.'

The Committee refrained from discussion of contemporary economic problems relating to wage inflation and balance of payments difficulties. In his evidence, however, Kaldor questioned the relevance of monetary policy in coping with cost inflation and sectoral difficulties such as the current account of the balance of payments. In these respects monetary policy is crude and blunt. In the light of the monetarist experiment pursued in the United Kingdom from 1979, his strictures on the appropriateness of monetary policy to cope with wage inflation have a prescience about them: 'not unless restriction is carried to the point of such heavy unemployment that the wage-earners in any particular industry are unable to hold out for higher wages on account of the competition of unemployed workers' can any success be expected. He was sceptical of the argument that with a tight credit policy employers will be unable to grant wage increases or to pass on higher wage costs in higher prices and will therefore offer far greater resistance to demands for higher wages. Instead,

tight credit policy, if sufficiently severe, will force employers to reduce their rate of investment, and possibly even to disinvest. But neither their willingness to grant wage increases, nor their ability to pass on higher costs in the form of higher prices will be *directly* affected by it – any such effect will be indirect, and dependent on a prior reduction in the scale of operations.'[12]

This prognostication proved absolutely right in the 1980s.

He also doubted whether it is possible to prevent wage increases from exceeding productivity increases by a moderate reduction in the level of activity, and indeed whether it is possible to sustain an 'under-employment' equilibrium with steady growth. His views here draw on his early models of growth and distribution (see Chapter 6). The international evidence he presented to the Committee showed little connection between wage increases, price increases and productivity increases, nor any close relation between the rate of wage inflation and the level of unemployment (the so-called Phillips curve).[13] Kaldor was an early doubter of the Phillips curve mechanism and the theory underlying it. He addressed himself more fully to the relation in his 1959 LSE lectures on growth and inflation where he put forward an alternative profits-push theory of wage increases (1959c). He disputed the policy conclusion that some economists had derived from the Phillips curve that if the economy was managed at a particular level of unemployment there would necessarily be wage and price stability. If the economy is growing, profits will also be growing and wage demands will also increase. Thus only if unemployment is used to deliberately restrain growth will it constrain wages and prices. Later he subscribed to a productivity-based theory of money wage increases emanating from leading sectors in the economy which then spread to other sectors (see 1982a). In the leading sectors efficiency wages (i.e. wages relative to productivity) may fall, but overall, money wage increases are likely to be greater than average productivity growth in the economy as a whole, thereby causing prices to rise. In the 1970s he naturally recognised commodity price rises as a powerful source of domestic inflation and with a much more pronounced effect on overall prices than the weight of imported commodities in the final value of output would have suggested.

In 1981, Kaldor revisited the Radcliffe Report in his Radcliffe Lectures (1981e) delivered at the University of Warwick where Radcliffe was the first Chancellor. He reviewed the Radcliffe recommendations in historical perspective before launching a scathing attack on modern monetarism. He used as his cue (with some nostalgia) the Committee's reference to 'no limit to the velocity of circulation of money', pointing out that in one sentence: 'they repudiated in one fell swoop the quantity theory of money in all its versions from Cantillon and Hume through Ricardo, Marshall and Walras, Irving Fisher and Milton Friedman (to mention only the most prominent) with their army of camp followers, right down to Mrs Thatcher'! Kaldor's view of the doctrine of monetarism was reminiscent of what Keynes felt about economic policy in the 1920s when in his polemic against the return to the gold standard at the pre-war parity[14] he described monetary policy as 'simply a campaign against the standard of life of the working classes', operating through the 'deliberate intensification of unemployment... by using the weapon of economic necessity against individuals and against particular industries – a policy which the country would never permit if it knew what was being done'. For Kaldor, monetarism and its application was a synonym for deflation masquerading as a scientific doctrine; a reactionary movement to be resisted in every way possible. Most of his energy was devoted to this task in the 1980s through letters to the press, speeches in the House of Lords, lectures throughout the world, books and articles in learned journals.

THE ATTACK ON MONETARISM

Monetarism, and its application, did not become a live issue in the United Kingdom until the late 1960s. It permeated the country from America through official channels, the universities and the press. After Britain devalued the pound in November 1967, targets for domestic credit expansion were imposed under the influence of the International Monetary Fund (IMF). This was the first official taint of the doctrine. Monetary targets were also introduced by Denis Healey in 1977, also under pressure from the IMF. The IMF subscribed to the monetarist creed long before it became fashionable, particularly in its approach to balance of payments problems. Jacques Polak, Director of the IMF's Research Department, was an early architect of the monetary approach to the balance of payments, and he was in attendance at an influential Treasury, Bank of England, IMF Seminar held in London in October 1968 examining the role of Central Bank control of the money supply in economic management. Kaldor also attended and not unexpectedly dissented from the mood of the meeting that monetary policy must be given more prominence in the control of inflation. *The Times* became influential in spreading the doctrine of monetarism through the City and business community. Peter Jay, the paper's Economics Editor, was a clever and persuasive convert. William Rees-Mogg, the paper's editor from 1967, became an arch-monetarist (converted by Jay) who would have returned Britain to the full gold standard. Samuel Brittan of the *Financial Times* was also an early believer and played a similar missionary role. Together they preached the gospel according to Milton Friedman and mesmorised a large section of the political Right. The long-run solution to rising prices (without unemployment?) was simply to pursue a monetary growth rule which kept the growth of the money supply in line with the underlying rate of growth of the economy's productive potential. It was a convenient doctrine for the Right to embrace providing intellectual justification for the withdrawal of government from economic affairs, and for the control of public expenditure on the assumption of a close link between budget deficits and the growth of the money supply.

Kaldor's first major public attack on the theory of monetarism was launched at a lecture given at University College, London in March 1970 (1970b). In the years to follow he was to stomp the world campaigning against what he regarded as a pernicious doctrine without theoretical or empirical foundation. His critique was to culminate in a book, *The Scourge of Monetarism* (1982), reminiscent in its style, topicality and righteous indignation of Keynes' *Economic Consequences of the Peace* (1919). The book contained his 1981 Radcliffe Lectures and his masterly 1980 evidence to the Treasury and Civil Service Enquiry into Monetary Policy (1980c). He gave several public lectures on the subject including the Page lecture at Cardiff University in 1980 on the 'Origins of the New Monetarism', in which he described monetarism as 'a terrible curse, a visitation of evil spirits, with particularly unfortunate, one could almost say devastating, effects on our own country'. The results of the monetarist experiment in the United Kingdom, and the fervour with which the doctrine continued to be preached, reminds one of what Keynes wrote to an American friend at the height of the great depression in 1931:

'to read the newspapers just now is to see bedlam let loose. Every person in the country of super-asinine properties, everyone who hates social progress and loves deflation, feels that his hour has come, and frequently announces how, by refraining from every form of economic activity, we can all become very prosperous again'.[15]

Kaldor predicted in a House of Lords speech (20 July 1977): 'In my opinion monetarism is doomed to failure because it could succeed, if it succeeded at all, only by ruining industry, long before it succeeded in making labour more submissive.' How right he proved to be in the British context.

To understand monetarism it is important to understand the personalities involved and its close affinities with the ideas of the English liberal philosophers spanning the eighteenth and nineteenth centuries (which include the doctrine of the quantity theory of money). First of all, as Kaldor noted, the new monetarism was a Friedman revolution, more truly than Keynes was the sole fount of the Keynesian revolution. Friedman's monetarist beliefs, whatever their empirical basis, coincided with his own political ideology of *laissez-faire*. By the same token, it can be argued that the comparative strength of monetarism in America is related to the country's conservative ideals and antipathy to the state as the enemy of freedom. Equally the question might be raised of whether Kaldor's monetary views presuppose or imply a left-wing ideology. Although he stood on the left of the political spectrum, the argument would be difficult to sustain since his anti-monetarist stance was rooted in what he saw as the autonomous nature of the private sector, in the Keynesian tradition. It had nothing to do with wanting to see more government control of the economy. He did not object to a non-discretionary monetary growth rule, but he thought it a gross delusion to believe that this would stabilise the quantity of money or movements in money income and the price level. He felt the same about Professor Meade's proposal to substitute for monetary targets a target rate of growth of money GNP (the sum of the growth of output and the price level).[16] It may be easier in practice to control the growth of real output through monetary and fiscal policy than to control the money supply but the problem of the price level remains unsolved. Such a target is no guarantee against excessive inflation and rising unemployment since there is nothing to stop prices rising faster than the growth of money GNP. Meade pins his faith in decentralised wage bargaining, but there lies the problem. One is thrown back to wages as the villain of the piece; that there is no way of controlling monetary demand or the price level (if output and employment are not to fall) without controls over nominal wage increases. An incomes policy is a necessary condition for the control of inflation, and a sufficient condition at least before the full employment level of output is reached.

It was mentioned earlier that Hume must be regarded as the intellectual father of monetarism, as the original propounder of the quantity theory of money. Just as the growth of modern monetarism was partly a reaction to Keynes and Keynesianism (e.g. the supposition \ that 'money does not matter', and the 'presuppositions of Harvey Road' – as Harrod[17] called them – that in certain spheres the decisions of wise and disinterested men could improve economic performance *vis-à-vis* the market mechanism), so Hume was reacting to the doctrine of mercantilism and the mercantilist belief that the accumulation of trade surpluses and gold could make a kingdom richer in real terms. Hume remarks:

if we consider any one kingdom by itself, it is evident, that the greater or less plenty of money is of no consequence; since the prices of commodities are always proportioned to the plenty of money . . . . It seems a maxim almost self-evident that the prices of everything depend on the proportion between commodities and money, and that any considerable alteration on either of these has the same effect, either of heightening or lowering the prices. . . . All augmentation [of gold and silver] has no other effect than to heighten the price of labour and commodities.[18]

There could hardly be a clearer statement of the quantity theory of money. Equally Hume believed that price flexibility would ensure stability of the private sector and argued against the mercantilist stress on deliberate policies to secure full employment. He was not, however, paranoic about inflation. He saw benefits in a mild inflationary stimulus to monetise the economy to bring underemployed resources into play:

the good policy of the magistrate consists only in keeping . . . [money], if possible, still increasing; because by that means he keeps alive a spirit of industry in the nation and increases the stock of labour in which consists all real power and riches. A nation, whose money decreases, is actually, at that time, much weaker and more miserable than another nation, which possesses no more money, but is on the increasing hand.[19]

Keynes was later, in the *Treatise on Money*, to invoke Hume in support of policies of mild demand inflation, in the same way that Kaldor invoked Robertson in his evidence to Radcliffe.

So much for the historical origins of monetarism. Let us now turn to the key propositions of modern monetarism, and to Friedman's position as epitomising the theoretical and practical stance which Kaldor attacked so vehemently. The first key proposition is that the stock of money determines money income and that changes in the money stock lead to predictable changes in money income. A stable demand function for money is implied so that changes in the supply of money lead, via the rate of interest, to predictable changes in the velocity of circulation of money. To view money as causal in the income determination process also implicitly assumes that the money supply is exogenously determined, as if all money is commodity money or comes into existence by decree. In some of Friedman's papers it is dropped from helicopters! Secondly, the transmission mechanism from money to money income is through the substitution of money for a whole range of household assets (money and real) not just bonds as in Keynes' *General Theory*. Thirdly, monetary policy should be judged by what is happening to the money stock, not by what is happening to interest rates (since many of the important rates of return on assets are not observable), and, to avoid inflation, monetary policy should be conducted so as to ensure a stable growth of the money supply equal to the underlying rate of growth of the productive potential of the economy. Fourthly, the private sector of an economy is inherently stable, always tending to full employment in the long run, so that government stabilisation policy is at best superfluous and at worst destabilising. Indeed, government expenditure will merely 'crowd out' private expenditure either by absorbing resources that otherwise would have been used by the private sector (resource crowding out) or by raising interest rates and cutting private investment (financial crowding out). Fifthly, there is no long-run trade-off between unemployment and inflation. Attempts by government to spend their way out of unemployment will only lead to ever-accelerating inflation because workers come to anticipate inflation and bid for money wage increases to match price increases. The so-called Phillips curve is really a vertical line emanating from the level of the so-called 'natural' rate of unemployment, which is merely the point of classical labour market equilibrium where the demand for, and supply of, labour are equal. In monetarist thinking it is more important to control inflation than to cut unemployment, despite the fact that according to classical monetary theory money does not affect real variables (the classical dichotomy). Lastly, within the doctrine of monetarism there is a strong belief in the ethics and virtues of the market mechanism.

Friedman would subscribe to all of these propositions. One of the clearest statements of the role of money in the determination of money income, coinciding with Kaldor's first critique of monetarism in 1970, is contained in his paper 'A Theoretical Framework for Monetary Analysis'.[20] There the quantity theory of money, as a causal theory of the inflationary process, is an analysis of the factors that determine the real quantity of money that the community wishes to hold. In Friedman's view, changes in desired real balance holdings take place only very slowly, while changes in the nominal money supply can occur independently of demand. The result is that changes in the price level or nominal income are invariably the result of prior changes in the nominal supply of money. Once the money demand function is specified, all that is needed is a supply function, and prices and nominal income are the result of their interaction. The supply of money depends first, on the amount of high-powered money which is dependent on the activities of the monetary authorities and on the balance of payments; secondly, on the ratio of bank deposits to bank holdings of high-powered money; and thirdly on the ratio of the public's deposits to its holdings of currency. The demand for money depends on: total wealth, the division of wealth between human and non-human forms, the expected rates of return on money and other assets, and the utility attached to the services of money relative to other assets. If the supply of money does not affect the real factors on which the demand for money depends, the effect of changes in the money supply must be on prices in 'full equilibrium'. Friedman is critical of Keynesians for clinging to the view that changes in the supply of money produce changes in the demand for money via the interest rate, so that the velocity of circulation is viewed as adjusting passively to changes in the stock of money. In his model, the demand for money is relatively interest inelastic with changes in the money supply affecting nominal income through the substitution of money for a wide range of assets. The portfolio approach to asset demand is now generally accepted. This is *not* the issue that divides monetarists and Keynesians. The issues which divide monetarists and Keynesians are much more fundamental concerned with such factors as whether the money supply is exogenous or endogenous to an economic system; whether the direction of causation is from money to prices or vice versa and whether prices can rise independently of prior increases in the money supply; whether the private sector of an economy is inherently stable, and whether governments can exert a stabilising influence on an economy. Friedman concludes his essay in a conciliatory way by saying:

the basic differences among economists are empirical not theoretical. How important are changes in the supply of money compared with changes in the demand for money? How elastic is the demand for money with respect to interest rates? Are transactions variables or asset variables most important in determining the demand for money? When changes in demand or supply occur that produce discrepancies between the quantity of money that the public holds and the quantity it desires to hold, how rapidly do these discrepancies tend to be eliminated? Does the adjustment impinge mostly on prices or mostly on quantities? . . . Much of the controversy that has swirled about the role of money in economic affairs reflects, in my opinion, different implicit or explicit answers to these empirical questions. The reason such differences have been able to persist is, I believe, that full adjustment to monetary disturbance takes a very long time and affects many economic magnitudes. If the adjustment was swift . . . the role of money would be clearly and sharply etched. . . But if the adjustment is slow then crude evidence may be misleading and a more subtle examination of the records may be needed to disentangle what is systematic from what is random and erratic. *That*, not the elaboration of the theory, has been the primary aim of the studies of myself and my associates,.[12]

From this seemingly innocuous statement it might be wondered what all the fuss is about. It may be true that the basic differences between monetarists and Keynesians are empirical and not theoretical. The fuss concerns the vehemence with which the propositions of monetarism, reputedly based on rigorous empirical analysis, are enunciated, and which formed in the late 1970s and early 1980s the basis of the conduct of economic policy in several industrialised countries, including the United Kingdom.

The tenets of monetarism which guided the conduct of economic policy in the United Kingdom in 1979 may be reduced to four key propositions. First, that inflation is a monetary phenomenon in a direct *casual* sense, and that trade unions do not *cause* inflation. Secondly, that government borrowing is a major source of increases in the supply of money and that a necessary condition for control of the money supply is the control of government expenditure. Thirdly, that government spending crowds out private spending rendering ineffective the stabilisation branch of the budget. Fourthly, that government spending cannot create 'real' (lasting) jobs because there is no long run trade-off between inflation and unemployment; instead there is a 'natural rate of unemployment' determined by real factors and if governments attempt to maintain unemployment below this rate there will be ever-accelerating inflation. These are the strong claims that Kaldor objected to, both the theory underlying them and the empirical evidence adduced by Friedman and other monetarists to support them.

On the first proposition, that fluctuations in the quantity of money are the dominant *cause* of fluctuations in the price level and money income, a number of things have to be demonstrated if it is to be taken seriously as a scientific theory: first, that the money supply is the determinant of the system and not the determinate or, in other words, that the money supply is exogenous and not endogenous responding to the needs of trade; secondly, that the demand to hold money is stable; thirdly, that money supply changes preceding price and income changes (if they do) necessarily imply that the former is the cause of the latter; and fourthly, that the lags between changes in money and changes in prices and income are uniform.

Is the money supply exogenous or endogenous? Friedman and other monetarists fully recognise that their views on inflation hinge crucially on the assumption that the money supply is exogenous. But Kaldor is quite adamant that in modern, capitalist, credit-based economies, the money supply cannot be treated in this way. The failure to see the different genesis of modern money, as credit not commodity money, was, in his view, the essential mistake of modern monetarism. In the case of commodity money (such as cattle or cowrie shells), or commodity-backed money (as under a pure gold standard), it is true that the money supply may be determined quite independently of the public's demand for it. In this case, the money supply may be treated as exogenous. Then if the demand for money in relation to income is constant, and output is fixed, prices must rise to absorb the new money for an equilibrium to be established; the prediction of the quantity theory. But modern capitalist economies do not use commodity money or commodity-backed money. They use credit money, and credit money issued by banks only comes into existence if it is demanded in the first place. In a pure credit-money economy, supply can never be in excess of the amount individuals wish to hold. Thus, it can never be true to say that the level of expenditure rises in consequence of an increase in the amount of bank money held by the public. On the contrary, it is the rise in the desired level of expenditure which leads to an increase in the amount of bank money. In the absence of quantitative controls, the Central Bank has no direct control over the amount of money held by the non-banking public in the form of deposits with the clearing banks. The only way it can attempt to influence the volume of bank deposits, in the absence of controls, is to influence demand by using interest rates. If the interest elasticity of demand for money is low, this does not augur well for monetary control since high interest rates will not curb demand or supply.[22] The conclusion is the exact opposite to that of the monetarists who infer that if the interest elasticity of demand for money is very low (and stable) the velocity of circulation of money will be almost constant (and predictable) and therefore changes in the supply of money will have direct and predictable effects on money income. If the money supply is endogenous, however, a close correlation between the quantity of money and money income is evidence not of the potential *potency* of monetary policy but of precisely the opposite that the money supply responds elastically to the needs of trade. The greater the response of the money supply to changes in the value of transactions, the more stable the velocity of circulation of money will appear to be. The issue, therefore, is not whether the demand for money is stable and elastic or inelastic, but how money comes into existence. The fact that Friedman in some of his papers has money dropping from helicopters is perhaps indicative of the trouble monetarists have in introducing money in any other exogenous way.

Monetarists who wish to deny the endogeneity of the money supply base their case on two kinds of evidence: first that there are well defined lags between money supply changes on the one hand and peaks and troughs of money GNP on the other, and secondly that banks are always fully loaned up, so that bank deposits are assumed to vary closely with high powered money which the monetary authorities can control. On the question of lags, the mere existence of a time lag, with variations in the money supply apparently preceeding changes in money income, is not in itself evidence of the exogeneity of the money supply or evidence for the direction of causality. For instance, suppose that there was an autonomous increase in plans to spend. The initial impact would be to reduce stocks of goods. To replenish stocks requires financing (Keynes' finance motive for holding money) and takes time. Thus changes in the money supply may be observed to preceed income changes, but the change in money is not necessarily causal. The fact that event A preceeds B does not mean that A causes B, and logically the fact that event B occurs after A does not rule out the possibility that B is the cause of A. Volcanoes erupt after they rumble, and the eruption is the cause of the rumble. Before Christmas there is an expansion of the money supply, but it is Christmas that is causal and not vice versa. More importantly, for the time lag argument to be taken seriously, the lag must at least be uniform. The common article of faith of monetarists used to be that changes in the money supply affect prices with a lag of 18 months. This was then extended to two years, and then became long and variable. But what can be said about a theory, and how can it be tested, which makes the relation between two variables 'long and variable'?

Kaldor showed in his 1980 evidence to the Treasury Enquiry into Monetary Policy (1980c) that for the United Kingdom there was no support for the time lag hypothesis except for monetary growth over the period 1971–76 and inflation over the period 1973–78. But this was completely coincidental and spurious, resulting on the one hand from the introduction of the policy of Competition and Credit Control in 1971, which led to a massive increase in bank lending, and on the other from the commodity price explosion (including oil) in 1972/73 which led to a marked rise in import prices. The closest statistical fit between changes in the money supply and the price level showed no lag at all. The same was true for an average of nine other industrialised countries. The questions of causation and time-lags were the subject of heated public debate in the correspondence columns of *The Times* in 1979 involving evidence produced by the editor himself who supported the two-year lag hypothesis. Kaldor rebutted the evidence (6 April), while *The Times* leader the next day reiterated the monetarist view maintaining that the quantity theory of money is no different from the quantity theory of wheat. Friedman also joined the debate (2 May), admitting that the relation between money and prices can be upset by such factors as: expectations, import prices, exchange rate changes, etc. (no mention of wages), but emphasising the point that no inflation can persist without monetary growth exceeding output growth. To make this point, however, is not the same as maintaining that inflation always *originates* in monetary factors.

On the autonomous nature of the money supply, the evidence of Friedman and Schwartz in their massive monetary history of the United States[23] is not entirely convincing and does not always support their case. The correlation between the monetary base and the money supply is often weak and the money multiplier is sometimes negative. Moreover, the monetary base itself cannot be regarded as exogenously determined if it is altered by the authorities to ensure government debt financing and to stabilise interest rates. Friedman attempts to give a monetary explanation of the great depression in the United States between 1929 and 1933, but in fact the monetary base actually increased during this period. The great contraction of the money supply by over 30 per cent occurred *despite* a rise in the monetary base by 10 per cent. In the UK, the money supply is not under the control of the monetary authorities. Neither the cash ratio nor the liquid assets ratio provide effective controls when the Central Bank acts as a lender of last resort to the banking system, and when there are many ways open to the banks to maintain a given liquidity ratio without resort to Central Bank credit.

Friedman's initial retort to Kaldor was 'if the relation between money and income is a supply response, as Professor Kaldor asserts it is for the UK since the second world war, how is it that major differences among countries and periods in monetary institutions and other factors affecting the supply of money do not produce widely different relations between money and income?'[24] The short answer is that they do! In his evidence to the Treasury Committee of 1980, and also in his 1981 Radcliffe Lectures, Kaldor gave evidence of the relation between the money stock and GNP for ten industrial countries, and reached the same conclusion as he did when he presented his evidence to the Radcliffe Committee in 1958: 'in some communities, the velocity of circulation is low, in others it is high, in some it is rising and in others it is falling, without any systematic connection between such differences and movements and the degree of inflationary pressure, the rate of increase in monetary turnover etc.'

The second proposition to examine is whether government borrowing is a major cause of monetary growth. This is essentially an empirical matter but does not seem to have been true for the United Kingdom in the 1970s and 1980s, nor for many other countries. Government deficits can be financed in three major ways: first by literally printing money; secondly, by selling securities to the banks (which is equivalent to printing money if interest rates are kept stable); and thirdly, by selling securities to the public. Most countries do not resort to the first method. They either try to 'fund' the debt by selling securities to the non-bank sector, thus neutralising the effect of increased government spending on the money supply, or they make it possible for the banks to hold the debt in which case the supply of money may rise to some extent. This is known as 'unfunded' debt.

Kaldor showed convincingly in his Treasury evidence that in the UK over the period 1968 to 1979 there was no relation between the size of the Public Sector Borrowing Requirement (PSBR) and the growth of broad (M_3) money. On the contrary, when the amount of the unfunded PSBR was highest, there was the smallest increase in M_3, and in the latter half of the 1970s when there was a colossal growth of M_3 money averaging £5 billion a year, the unfunded PSBR was very small (less than £1 billion a year), and was actually negative in 1977/78 when M_3 increased by £6.2 billion. Changes in the broad money supply were dominated by bank lending to the private sector which is demand determined. Friedman also gave evidence to the Treasury Committee and charged the Bank of England with incompetence for allowing the money supply growth to exceed the target laid down by the government. He always recognised control of the PSBR as an uncertain weapon of monetary control preferring control of the monetary base. Kaldor concluded this part of his evidence to the Treasury Committee by agreeing that 'there is no doubt that "funding" is an efficient instrument for reducing the growth of the money stock'. The question is, so what? Why should a given budget deficit be less inflationary when funded than when it is not? This question brings us back to the heart of the monetarist controversy. The true monetarist believes that through an unknown and undisclosed mechanism, a reduction in the growth of the money supply must bring inflation to an end if sustained long enough. But Kaldor remarked laconically, 'until it is shown how this mechanism operates it is no better than a fairy tale, or a mystique which, among primitive peoples, takes the form of endowing particular objects, like a tree, or a mountain, with magic powers.'

The third proposition is that government spending and borrowing 'crowds out' private expenditure. This was the so-called British Treasury view in the 1920s and 1930s; a view which Keynes, armed with Kahn's multiplier, attempted to undermine. This is also an empirical matter. First, resource crowding out must be distinguished from financial crowding-out. In conditions of spare capacity and underutilised resources, resource crowding out is logically impossible. On the contrary, there should be 'crowding-in' as multiplier theory teaches, if stocks are replenished. Financial crowding-out may occur if interest rates rise as the government sells its debt. But this is not inevitable. It depends on monetary policy, on expectations held by the public about future rates of interest, and on the degree to which saving rises as output and incomes expand. Kaldor found no evidence for the UK that a higher PSBR required ever-rising interest rates. The government was able to sell gilts at the end of the 1970s at a lower rate than in 1975/6 when the unfunded PSBR was at its highest. Indeed yields on long term securities fell at the same time as the public was buying. There was a reverse yield-gap with the government's minimum lending rate above the yield on gilts. It was this that was responsible for the squeeze on the private sector not the size of the PSBR itself. Very high short term rates were no doubt also responsible for the expectation that interest rates would eventually fall, thus enabling gilts to be sold at a lower yield.

It must also be remembered that if the crowding-out argument has force, one form of private expenditure should crowd out another. There is nothing pernicious about government expenditure as such. The debate then becomes one of the relative merits of public and private spending. Indeed, we see here the ideological, as well as the economic, nature of monetarism. From a strictly economic point of view, monetarism has really nothing to say about whether public borrowing is too high or too low or about the absolute size of the public sector.

Despite the statistics on the money supply and interest rates, Nigel Lawson, the Financial Secretary to the Treasury at the time, told the House of Commons in January 1980:

Let me start with two simple facts – the PSBR and the growth of the money supply and interest rates are very closely related. Too high a PSBR requires either that the government borrows heavily from the banks which adds directly to the money supply; or failing this, that it borrows from individuals and institutions, but at ever-increasing rates of interest, which place an unacceptable squeeze on the private sector.

Kaldor was led to remark that it could be seen from the government's own statistics that the 'simple facts' were not facts at all but fairy tales (1980c).

The last question is whether policies of demand expansion initiated by governments can increase employment and decrease unemployment permanently. The answer to this depends largely on whether unemployment is involuntary or voluntary, and whether a reduction in real wages must accompany an increase in employment which workers may resist. The latter depends on whether there are increasing or decreasing returns to labour as output expands. If there are increasing returns, real wages may rise without profits suffering and employment and real wages can increase together. Monetarists insist on assuming that all unemployment is voluntary, that workers are always on their supply curve equating the marginal utility of the real wage with the marginal disutility of work, and that there are diminishing returns to labour, so that an increase in employment and a reduction in unemployment inevitably means a reduction in real wages that workers will eventually resist. 'Weak' monetarists assume that it takes time for workers to adjust wages to prices (adaptive expectations) so that there can be a short-run trade-off between inflation and unemployment whereas the 'new classical' macroeconomists assume rational expectations and instantaneous adjustment precluding even a short run trade-off. The implication is that governments can never apparently create 'real' (long-run) jobs by their own expenditure; there is a 'natural' rate

of unemployment determined by real forces in the labour market
and if governments attempt to reduce unemployment below this
rate there will be ever-accelerating inflation – as wages chase
prices instantaneously and equiproportionately.

The doctrine of rational expectations is used to deny the
existence of involuntary unemployment. According to the
doctrine, economic agents' expectations will not be systematically
wrong over time because any agent who forms expectations in a
manner that leads to systematic error will find himself
persistently making the wrong choices. By this argument, high
unemployment is explained by the expected rate of inflation being
above the actual rate of inflation and workers pricing themselves
out of jobs, not by a deficiency of aggregate demand. But rational
expectations predicts that they will moderate behaviour by
revising expectations and price themselves back into jobs. This is
akin to modelling the economy 'as if' all markets were clear. But
expectations can be rational and markets not clear. This is the
notion of a quantity constrained conjectural equilibrium where
transactors in a market are happy with the bargains struck, but
where there is still left a large unsatisfied demand or supply at the
ruling price.[25] In other words, there is a difference between
equilibrium and clearing. In classical monetarist theory, the two
are synonymous, but in practice they need not be. Also,
expectations may be rational, but markets may not clear
instantaneously. In this case, quantity signals (as opposed to
monetary signals) may become part of the mechanism whereby
the effects of monetary changes are transmitted to the behaviour
of prices. An obvious example is the moderating influence of
unemployment on wage behaviour, which has been the experience
of the United Kingdom in the 1980s. In this case, we are back in a
Phillips curve world of a trade-off between unemployment and
inflation.

The doctrine of rational expectations is a convenient supporting
belief for monetarist antipathy to activist interventionist policy by
governments in favour of non-discretionary rules for the conduct
of economic policy. The belief in rational expectations was not the
cause of this antipathy; rather the philosophic belief that
'governments are rarely more effective than when they are
negative' (Adam Smith) made belief in rational expectations
convenient. Under the rational expectations hypothesis there is no
room for active policy to influence events because if such effects
produced by policy are systematic, private agents will adapt to
them and thereby render the policy ineffective. In the case of
attempts to reduce unemployment, 'you can fool all of the workers

some of the time, and you can fool some of the workers all of the time, but you cannot fool all of the workers all of the time.' But if workers are *off* their supply curve with the real wage in excess of the marginal disutility of work, hundreds of thousands of workers may be willing to work at a lower real wage (if necessary) given the opportunity.[26] These workers are involuntarily unemployed which the doctrine of monetarism and rational expectations denies. Kaldor dismissed the concept of a 'natural rate of unemployment', based as it is on dubious classical labour market assumptions, and was contemptuous of the doctrine of rational expectations:

the rational expectations theory goes beyond the untestable basic axioms of the theory of value, such as the utility-maximizing rational man whose existence can be confirmed only by individual introspection. The assumption of rational expectations which presupposes the correct understanding of the workings of the economy by all economic agents – the trade unionists, the ordinary employer, or even the ordinary housewife – to a degree which is beyond the grasp of professional economists, is not science, nor even moral philosophy, but at best a branch of metaphysics. (1981c)

In 1979, the United Kingdom became a laboratory experiment for monetarism. The money supply was to be controlled and inflation was to be squeezed out of the system with only temporary losses of output and employment. Free collective bargaining was to be preserved because only governments cause inflation through monetary profligacy. The reality has been far removed from the theory. Judged by the evidence, the monetarist experiment has been an abject failure. The nominal money supply proved uncontrollable, at least by the chosen means of reducing the Public Sector Borrowing Requirement. High interest rates and a fiscal squeeze caused massive deflation, a fall in investment and a loss of jobs. The rate of wage and price inflation moderated as unemployment rose and world commodity prices fell, but nonetheless it was deemed necessary to introduce a wages policy in the public sector. There is nothing to prevent wage and price inflation accelerating if the British and world economy ever recover. The doctrine of monetarism, based on an identity, has proved to be a misleading and costly guide to the conduct of short run economic policy for the simultaneous achievement of full employment, steady growth and price stability. As Keynes reminds us, in both the *General Theory* and *A Tract on Monetary Reform* (1923), it is in the short run that we actually have our being: '[the] long run is a misleading guide to current affairs. . . . economists set themselves too easy, too useless, a task if in tempestuous seasons they can only tell us that when the storm is long past the ocean is flat again.'[27] In the real world industrial countries live on a wages standard and money is endogenous. This was Kaldor's message, amply vindicated by the British experience.

NOTES

1. *Report of the Committee on the Working of the Monetary System*, Cmnd 827 (London: HMSO, August 1959).
2. For a fascinating insight into the origins of the 'new classical macro-economics', and the characters involved, see A. Klamer, *The New Classical Macroeconomics: Conversations with New Classical Economists and Their Opponents* (Wheatsheaf Books, 1984).
3. D. Hume, 'Of Money', in *Political Discourses* (Edinburgh: A. Kincaid and A. Donaldson, 1752).
4. *General Theory*, p. 307.
5. p. 351.
6. Memorandum of Evidence to the *Treasury and Civil Service Committee on Monetary Policy* (London: HMSO, 17 July 1980). p. 122.
7. *Op. cit.*
8. Review of Kaldor's *Essays on Economic Policy* (Duckworth, 1964), in *Economic Journal*, December 1965.
9. Radcliffe Report, op. cit.
10. *Council on Prices Productivity and Incomes*, First Report (London: HMSO, 1958).
11. $P/K = g/s_p = (\Delta K/K)/s_p = (\Delta P/P)/s_p$, with constant distributive shares. This also shows that the rate of profit depends on how *fast* profits are growing *not* on relative factor quantities. This explains why the rate of profit in rich countries is higher than the rate of profit in poor countries despite large differences in the capital:labour ratio.
12. Evidence to the Radcliffe Committee (1958f).
13. A.W. Phillips, 'The Relation Between Unemployment and the Rate of Change of Money Wage Rates in the United Kingdom, 1861–1957', *Economica*, November 1958.
14. J.M. Keynes, *The Economic Consequences of Mr Churchill* (Hogarth Press, 1925).
15. To Walter Case, 14 September 1931, in D. Moggridge (ed.), *The Collected Writings of J.M. Keynes*. Vol. XX: *Activities 1929–1931 Rethinking Employment and Unemployment Policies* (Cambridge University Press, 1981), pp. 604–5.
16. J.E. Meade, *Wage-Fixing* (London: George Allen and Unwin, 1982). See Kaldor's article 'Lord Kaldor Replies to Professor Meade', in *Financial Times*, 16 December 1981.
17. R.F. Harrod, *The Life of John Maynard Keynes* (London: Macmillan, 1951).
18. 'Of Money', *op. cit.*
19. Ibid.
20. *Journal of Political Economy*, March/April 1970. An earlier statement which introduced for the first time the concept of the 'natural rate of unemployment' is contained in 'The Role of Monetary Policy', *American Economic Review*, March 1968.
21. Ibid.
22. More seriously, the effect of interest rates on the money supply may even work perversely. For example, a rise in interest rates to curb the growth of

the money supply above a target rate might swell bank deposits because buyers of gilt-edged securities postpone purchases knowing that if the money supply exceeds target, the rate of interest will rise and the price of gilts fall. On this behaviour, interest rates should be lowered to shrink bank deposits. Kaldor pointed this out in a letter to *The Times* (17 June 1978). Also if monetary contraction causes expectations that the real rate of interest will rise, borrowers may borrow more short term from the banks at lower rates, expanding the money supply.

23. M. Friedman and Anna Schwartz, *A Monetary History of the United States 1867-1960* (Princeton University Press, 1971).
24. M. Friedman, 'The New Monetarism: Comment', *Lloyds Bank Review*, October 1970.
25. An intelligible exposition of these ideas can be found in F. Hahn, 'Monetarism and Economic Theory', *Economica*, February 1980.
26. See A.P. Thirlwall, 'What are Estimates of the Natural Rate of Unemployment Measuring?', *Oxford Bulletin of Economics and Statistics*, May 1983.
27. J.M. Keynes, *A Tract on Monetary Reform* (London: Macmillan, 1923).

13 THE CHALLENGE TO
EQUILIBRIUM THEORY

No account of Kaldor's life-work would be complete without a more systematic statement of his challenge to the orthodox (neoclassical) theory of value based on Walrasian general equilibrium analysis, or what he called for short 'equilibrium economics'. This will provide an appropriate conclusion to the book since it is this challenge that preoccupied him in his later years and will remain one of his most important legacies. It was a bold challenge and a courageous attempt to induce economists, and the profession he loved, to be concerned with the real world around them and to build models and develop hypotheses based on empirically verifiable assumptions. It was not the notion of equilibrium as a concept that he objected to, but neoclassical modes of thinking, based on unsupported and unverifiable axioms, with their static emphasis on substitution and allocation to the neglect of the dynamic process of growth and change based on increasing returns. His publicly professed disquiet with the orthodox theory of value dates from the time of his celebrated retort to Samuelson and Modigliani in 1966 (1966a):

It is the hallmark of the neoclassical economist to believe that however severe the abstractions from which he is forced to start he will win through by the end of the day – bit by bit, if only he carries the analysis far enough the scaffolding can be removed, leaving the basic structure intact. In fact, the props are never removed; the removal of any one of a number of them – as, for example, allowing for increasing returns or learning by doing – is sufficient to cause the whole structure to collapse like a pack of cards. It is high time that the brilliant minds of MIT were set to evolve a system of non-Euclidean economics which starts from a non-perfect, non-profit maximising economy where such abstractions are initially unnecessary.

His assault on equilibrium theory gathered momentum in the 1970s with provocative essays on 'The Irrelevance of Equilibrium

Economics' (1972c) and 'What is Wrong with Economic Theory' (1975a) (see also 1979a; 1981f), and culminated in his 1983 Okun Memorial Lectures, *Economics without Equilibrium*, and his 1984 Mattioli Lectures on *Causes of Growth and Stagnation in the World Economy*, which both encapsulated his major criticisms of equilibrium economics and at the same time attempted to put economics on a sounder footing with a lucid and vivid account of how market economies actually function in time and space in the real world. Kaldor's complaint was quite simply that the framework of competitive equilibrium, within which most contemporary economic theory is cast, is, as he put it: 'barren and irrelevant as an apparatus of thought to deal with the manner of operation of economic forces, or as an instrument for non-trivial predictions concerning the effects of economic changes' (*Collected Essays*, Volume 5).

Kaldor was not a lone voice in his critique of trends in contemporary theory. At least three Presidential addresses from distinguished economists were devoted to this theme in the early 1970s expressing a similar disquiet,[1] and a major assault on the methodology of general equilibrium was also launched in 1971 by a fellow Hungarian, Janos Kornai, in a much publicised book, *Anti-Equilibrium*.[2] Kornai indicts equilibrium theory as a brake on the development of economic thought. The general equilibrium school is, he says, 'disorienting and diverts our attention from the most important task of economic science, namely the realistic description, explanation and formal modelling of the actual operation of the socialist and capitalist economic systems of the present era.' Not only can general equilibrium theory not cope with many types of behaviour observable in the real world, but the questions it asks are extremely narrow, making economics dull and uninspiring. Kornai throws out the challenge:

If only half or a quarter of the group of workers who now pick up the grains left by the 'great men' on the already harvested field of the general equilibrium theory began to investigate the really relevant problems of economic systems theory, results could be achieved perhaps in a few years. The map of our discipline is full of blank spaces. We hardly have looked into the internal structure of the functioning and control of economic systems. We know very little about the actual processes of planning, government control, price formation and the decision-making of the firm.'

The inspiration behind general equilibrium theory as formulated by Walras,[3] and later developed by Arrow and Debreu, was to explore in a decentralised market economy the conditions that must pertain for a stable equilibrium set of prices to exist, and for equilibrium to ensure an optimal allocation of resources. Arrow[4] and Debreu[5] showed independently in 1951 that competitive equilibria are optimal in the Pareto sense (i.e. that no one can be made better off without making someone else worse off), and that Pareto-efficient resource allocation will be associated with a set of prices at which supply equals demand in all markets. Later, together, they formally proved the existence of a competitive equilibrium.[6] The results hinge crucially on a number of quite stringent and unreal assumptions which pervade explicitly and implicitly much of orthodox analysis in the various sub-branches of economics such as international economics; monetary economics, labour economics and so on. Some of the assumptions are so far removed from reality that not only are many of the models irrelevant for understanding real world behaviour, but they can be a seriously misleading guide to policy formation. The equilibrium methodology is defended on two grounds: first, that it was never intended to describe reality – it was purely an intellectual experiment designed to find the minimum basic assumptions within a deductive system necessary to generate an equilibrium set of prices which is unique and stable; secondly, that it was intended only as an initial framework for an understanding of how decentralised market economies work, in the absence of which economics would lack intellectual coherence. The problem is, however, as Kaldor complained, that instead of being the starting point for an explanation of how capitalist economies work, the equilibrium framework has come to lead a life of its own, in some respects more remote from reality. It is true that refinements have been made to the Walrasian, Arrow-Debreu framework,[7] but the fact remains that the equilibrium story and neoclassical value theory has retained its grip on the profession with the tenacity of a limpet. Without much hesitation the general presumption is that economies do approach an equilibrium; that markets equilibrate through price adjustment; that prices reflect values; that factor prices reflect marginal products; that the economic system is efficient; that output at any point in time is resource constrained, and so on. Unlike in the physical sciences, the accumulation of empirical evidence to the contrary has made no significant dent in the axioms on which the equilibrium model is based. As Weintraub[8] remarks at the end of his historical survey of the development of general equilibrium theory: 'the "equilibrium" story is one in which empirical work, ideas of fact and falsification, played no role at all.'

The common core of explicit and implicit assumptions which characterise to a greater or lesser degree the various genre of competitive (equilibrium) models may be listed as follows: (a) wants and resources are given and independent; (b) producers maximise profits and consumers maximise utility; (c) outputs produced and consumed can be described by means of continuous variables – there are no indivisibilities; (d) the production set is convex implying non-increasing returns to factors of production and non-increasing returns to scale; (e) no technical progress so that there is no change in the production and consumption sets over time; (f) agents are price takers and act on the basis of price information alone, which is the only form of information in the system; (g) only producers and consumers exist – there is no role for dealers or merchants because all prices are known with certainty by agents; and (h) producers and consumers are indifferent with respect to who they buy and sell from. The static nature of equilibrium theory also means that history does not matter in determining the present or the future. Relaxing even one of the more crucial assumptions, such as convexity, optimising behaviour or that agents act on price information alone, has serious implications for the conclusions of the competitive (Arrow–Debreu) model, let alone relaxing them all as a concession to reality.

Kaldor's fundamental critique of equilibrium theory has three strands: the first is methodological; the second relates to the lack of realism concerning the role of markets and the way they function in practice, and the third relates to the implications of the neglect of increasing returns. His critique relates to equilibrium economics as a school of thought, and to the way that *in general* orthodox mainstream economics is taught and communicated in texts to students, and ignores the one-off papers in learned journals that modify one assumption here and there with little or no impact on the thinking of the profession at large.

METHODOLOGY

All models in the social sciences must, by their very nature, be abstract. Social systems are simply too complex to model precisely. But there are different forms of abstraction. In Kaldor's view equilibrium theory starts from the wrong kind of abstraction. The assumptions of the model are essentially *a priori*, or the axioms required to generate the result of a competitive equilibrium with Pareto efficiency. In this sense the model is, like mathematics, a tautological system that cannot be proved wrong. Yet if economics is to be a useful science, analogous to the physical sciences, the assumptions of the model need to be realistic and empirically verifiable. Many of the assumptions of equilibrium theory are either empirically false (e.g. agents are price-takers) or unverifiable (e.g. agents are maximisers). Like Kornai, Kaldor came to believe that 'the powerful attraction of the habits of thought engendered by equilibrium economics has become a major obstacle to the development of economics as a science – meaning by the term science a body of theorems based on assumptions that are empirically derived (from observations) and which embody hypotheses that are capable of verification both in regard to the assumptions and predictions' (*Collected Essays*, Vol. 5, p. 176). This methodological critique of equilibrium economics is closely related to the disquiet that many economists have expressed concerning the use of mathematics in economics which, for the sake of scientific impression, has led to the sacrifice of relevance for elegance. The assumptions of linearity, continuous variables and optimising behaviour, on which neoclassical theory is based, have an obvious mathematical appeal. In a letter to Kaldor, Robert Solow once wrote: 'the assumption of constant returns to scale is convenient for two reasons: mathematically because it simplifies calculation; and economically because without it competition runs into difficulties, and competitive systems are easiest to deal with. It is not quite true that neoclassical value theory is destroyed by increasing returns to scale. Competition breaks down but that is not the end of the world.'[9] In his Keynes centenary essay, Kaldor was at his most scathing, describing all the features of neoclassical economics as

the product of the feverish imagination of mathematical economists who invented them so as to make profit maximisation of the individual firm and perfect competition in perfect markets consistent with one another. Yet economic policies are based on models of the economy which are built with the aid of such assumptions, with far reaching consequences for the way the world actually develops. (1983d).

Kaldor was fond of quoting Alfred Marshall's comments on the use of mathematics in economics, (particularly as Marshall himself was a prize mathematician). In a letter to A.L. Bowley, Marshall wrote:

In my view every economic fact, whether or not it is of such a nature as to be expressed in numbers, stands in relation as cause and effect to many other facts; and since it *never* happens that all of them can be expressed in numbers, the application of exact mathematical methods to those that can is nearly always a waste of time, while in the large majority of cases it is particularly misleading; and the world would have been further on its way forward if the work had never been done at all.[10]

He goes on:

I had a growing feeling in the later years of my work that a good mathematical theorem dealing with economic hypotheses was very unlikely to be good economics, and I went more and more on the rules – (1) Use mathematics as a shorthand language rather than an engine of enquiry, (2) Keep these till you have done, (3) Translate into english, (4) Then illustrate by examples that are important in real life, (5) Burn the mathematics, (6) If you can't succeed in (4) burn (3). The last I did often.[11]

THE ROLE OF MARKETS AND HOW THEY FUNCTION

Apart from the methodological criticism, Kaldor's second major objection to neoclassical equilibrium theory was its emphasis on the principle of substitution and on the allocative function of markets to the neglect of the creative functions of markets and the complementarity between activities. Because of the implicit belief in the full employment, and optimal allocation, of resources, everything must be at the expense of something else; a type of 'tangential' economics as Allyn Young once called it. The problem of replacing substitution effects with income effects is, of course, that there are no neat equilibrium solutions, but this cannot be justification for elevating the principle of substitution to the centre of the economic stage. It is misleading because it ignores the important complementarities that exist in the real world between the demand for products; the demand for factors of production, and between activities in general. For example, capital and labour are for the most part complementary in the production process. It is possible that in response to changes in the relative price of factors manufacturers may seek to economise on one factor relative to another in the design of new machinery and equipment, but fundamentally, as the classical economists recognised, labour is required to 'man' capital. The demand for labour (employment) is determined by the rate of capital accumulation. Similarly, economic activities should be thought of as expanding together. Industry and services are complementary; industry and agriculture are complementary. The supply of one activity establishes the demand for others; the expansion of one sector stimulates the demand for others, and in the process of expansion resources are generated. In the presence of increasing returns all outputs are complementary (see later).

It is equally misleading to view the market as simply the mechanism for the allocation of resources, the orthodox view which led Lionel Robbins to define economics as the science which studies 'the allocation of scarce resources among alternative uses'. The allocation function is just one small facet of the market's role. Much more important is the role of markets in transmitting the impulses for change which characterise any economic environment in which tastes, technology and factor supplies are constantly changing. In many contexts it is even wrong to think of factors of production as being 'allocated' between sectors, as if sectors were competing for their use. For example, when labour is in surplus with a zero marginal product, as it is in agriculture and petty service activities across wide areas of the globe, it is meaningless to view the market as allocating this labour amongst alternative uses. Similarly, it is misleading to think of capital as being allocated between activities and sectors. Finance may be allocated, but capital is accumulated *within* sectors according to the demand for output and the rate of return. If there is a tendency for rates of return on capital to equalise between activities, this is not because capital is physically 'reallocated' but because a higher rate of production in sectors with a higher rate of return leads to a faster rate of capital accumulation.

A related criticism to the elevation of substitution and allocation to the forefront of economic analysis is the emphasis placed by neoclassical equilibrium theory on the price mechanism as the *deus ex machina* by which decentralised market economies function, as if agents act on prices and nothing else and prices perform no other function than to allocate resources. In the real world, other variables operate as a signalling system; agents are not simply price-takers and quantity-makers. On the contrary, in industrial economies, the presumption must be the other way round with producers as price makers and quantity takers, with quantity signals more important than price signals in the determination of producer behaviour. Kornai[12] has aptly referred to the 'stock adjustment principle' as characterising industrial producer behaviour and argues that such quantity adjustment represents a much simpler and more convincing account than the Walrasian system of equations of how impulses get transmitted through an economy.

Kaldor devoted his Okun lectures to describing in some detail how markets in modern capitalist economies appear to operate in practice. In passing he praised Arthur Okun as one of the few distinguished American economists to have been concerned not with the pursuit of economic theory for its own sake, based on unsupported axioms, but as an instrument for the practical pursuit of efficiency and equality. Okun supported Kaldor in the use of stylised facts as the only sure way for economics to be taken seriously and to progress as a science. Two types of markets need to be distinguished; commodity markets and markets for manufactured goods. Their behaviour is different, but in both cases it departs substantially from the Walrasian general equilibrium assumption. Walras, it will be recalled, admitted only two types of agent: producers and consumers. In the commodity markets, however, there are dealers or middlemen who hold stocks and act as intermediaries between producers and consumers. In a sense, the dealers fulfill the role of the Walrasian auctioneer, but the market behaviour is very un-Walrasian. Transactions do not take place at uniform prices, and it is clear from the evidence on stock variations that prices are not market clearing. Stocks are often run down in recession and built up in periods of boom, also indicating a substantial speculative element in the wide price variations observed in some of the commodity markets. It is also clear that markets are not anonymous in the sense that consumers and producers are not indifferent with regard to who they buy from or sell to. Loyalty, custom, goodwill and other intangible relations play an important part in market transactions, the more so where the product is not homogenous and producers are not price takers. In these markets, prices are mainly determined by costs plus a percentage mark-up, with demand influencing price primarily through changes in unit labour costs. With prices sticky, firms respond to quantity signals, which take the form of changes in stock holdings in the case of standardised commodities, or changes in the length of order books with more custom-made products. Notions of fairness and goodwill stop prices from being adjusted to take advantage of (temporary) conditions of excess demand, which does not square easily with the prevailing neoclassical assumption of universal profit-maximisation.

How prices are actually set in markets for manufactured goods is still something of a mystery. The fact that there are big differences in costs per unit of output and profits between firms in the same industry means that the mark-up cannot be the same for each firm; nor is it rigid over time. It would seem to be a residual between a firm's own costs and considerations of what the market will bear in relation to prices being charged by others. Some firms must take the lead and others follow. But who takes the lead? Who sets the position of the kink in the oligopolistic demand curve facing the firm? Is it the most efficient firm and, if so, how does it decide its own mark-up? Presumably it will not want to set it too high to lose market share, but not too low either which would force other firms out of business creating a monopoly situation.

These are fields of enquiry where much more empirical investigation is needed.

THE NEGLECT OF INCREASING RETURNS

It has long been recognised that increasing returns poses severe problems for the tenets of equilibrium theory. Marshall recognised the inconsistency in his *Principles:*

the statical theory of equilibrium is only an introduction to economic studies; and it is barely even an introduction to the study of the progress and development of industries which show a tendency to increasing returns. Its limitations are so constantly overlooked, especially by those who approach it from an abstract point of view, that there is a danger of throwing it into definite form at all.[13]

Competitive equilibrium requires perfect competition which is impossible if long-run marginal cost is below price. Marshall's reaction was to take refuge in the short run assuming capacity to be given and to treat increasing returns as 'externalities', preserving the U-shaped cost curve and the notions of the optimum sized firm and competitive equilibrium. It was Marshall's fudge which prompted Piero Sraffa's famous 1926 article on 'The Laws of Returns under Competitive Conditions'[14] which in turn led to the whole cost controversy in the late 1920s and 1930s (see Chapter 2). Increasing returns also worried Hicks who remarked in *Value and Capital:* 'unless we can suppose . . . that marginal costs generally increase with output at the point of equilibrium. . . the basis on which economic laws can be constructed is shorn away.'[15] The evidence for increasing returns in manufacturing is overwhelming: from empirically estimated production functions; from Verdoorn's Law; from the very existence of large firms and imperfectly competitive structures; and from the fact that despite large differences in the capital:labour ratio between countries, the capital:output ratio hardly differs. If countries were simply moving along a given production function, a higher capital:labour ratio would be associated with a higher capital:output ratio (and a lower rate of profit). This is one of the neoclassical parables taught to students. In reality, the degree of capital intensity depends not on the rate of interest but on the division of labour and the scope for specialisation which in turn depends on the scale of output permitted by the size of the market. Capital accumulation and increasing returns go hand in hand.

It was Adam Smith who first introduced into economics the notion of increasing returns based on the division of labour. He saw this as the very basis of a 'social economy'; otherwise everyone might as well be their own Robinson Crusoe. It also lay at the heart of his vision of economic progress as a self-generating process, far removed from the later statics of the neoclassical school. Unfortunately, however, having concentrated on the division of labour and the creative functions of markets in the early chapters of *The Wealth of Nations*, Smith turned his attention to how the prices of goods and factors of production are determined, and through the rest of the book assumed, in effect, constant costs, as did Ricardo and the other classical economists. The ground was laid for the theory of value. Smith's early vision of increasing returns lay dormant until Allyn Young (Kaldor's early teacher at the LSE before his untimely death in 1929) revived it in 1928 in his paper 'Increasing Returns and Economic Progress',[16] referred to in Chapter 7. Alas, the impact of the paper on the profession was minimal, and has remained so.

Young's purpose was to persuade economists to turn away from static equilibrium theory, back to the dynamics of Smith. He had written to Frank Knight (his former PhD student) in 1922: 'I have yet to see that the method of general equilibrium gives us anything at all that gets us anywhere'.[17] He believed the equilibrium methodology to be totally inappropriate and unsuitable for the analysis of change. There can be no doubt about Young's influence on Kaldor's thinking, although it was not immediate since in his papers in the 1930s which touch on these matters (e.g. 1934b) Kaldor was claiming that all economies of scale are the result of indivisibilities in the productive process, which is clearly not the case in Young. Young had a quite distinctive definition of increasing returns in contrast to the normal definition of a decrease in the average cost of production as output expands which could be the result of internal or external economies or the spreading of fixed costs. Increasing returns are defined as existing when an increase in the output of one product can be obtained at the expense of proportionately smaller quantities of other products. In other words, the production possibility curve is convex to the origin not concave.

The source of increasing returns is related to two aspects of the division of labour: first, and most important, the ability to break up complex processes into simpler processes, implying more roundabout methods of production permitting the use of machinery. In the use of machinery there is a further division of labour. The second aspect is specialisation among industries. Both aspects are dependent on the extent of the market. He stressed, however, that the mechanism of increasing returns cannot be discerned adequately by observing the effects of variations in the size of the individual firm or of a particular industry; increasing returns are related to the output of all industries which must be seen as an interrelated whole. For example, an increase in the demand for product X may make it profitable to use more machinery in its production which reduces both the cost of X and the cost of machinery, which then makes the use of machinery profitable in other industries, and so on. 'Change is progressive and propagates itself in a cumulative way'. The precise conditions in Young's model for a cumulative expansion to take place are that there are increasing returns and that the demand for each commodity is elastic in the special sense, as Young puts it: 'that a small increase in its supply will be attended by an increase in the amounts of other commodities which can be had in exchange for it'. Increasing returns lowers the exchange value of a commodity and demand must be elastic, so that producers of other commodities are willing to trade proportionately more of their products at a lower exchange value, otherwise demand for other commodities has not effectively increased. Take the example of steel and textile production. Steel is subject to increasing returns, its supply increases and its exchange value falls. If demand is elastic textile producers demand proportionately more steel (and offer proportionately more textiles). Textile production is subject to increasing returns; the exchange value of textiles falls and textile producers demand proportionately more steel and so on. Under these circumstances, Young concluded, 'there are no limits to the process of expansion except the limits beyond which demand is not elastic and returns do not increase'. In this whole process, the entrepreneur is the principal agent of change and progress in the search for markets on which specialisation and the division of labour depend. Kaldor agreed with Young's analysis of increasing returns but disagreed that 'elastic demand' is either necessary or sufficient for progress to be cumulative. What is important is that change should induce additional investment and that credit should be elastic to allow such investment to take place until saving has risen sufficiently to provide the 'finance' for it.

The implications and consequences of increasing returns for how economic processes are viewed are profound and far reaching. First, Kaldor was right to ask: what is the meaning of 'general equilibrium' when increasing returns will cause everything in the equilibrium system to change – resource availabilities, technology, tastes, prices and so on? The endogenous nature of change associated with increasing returns brings to the fore the importance of time in economics whereby the present and the future cannot be understood without reference to the past. How variables behave depends on what has gone before. History matters, in contrast to 'equilibrium theory' where the exogenous variables are given and assumed unchanging through time and where everything can therefore be predicted with certainty in advance. In the presence of increasing returns there can be no presumption that social and economic systems move towards an equilibrium (irrespective of speculative activity). A moving equilibrium is only possible if a constant rate of exogenous change is assumed, but this is completely arbitrary.

Secondly, once increasing returns are admitted, the concept of an optimum allocation of resources loses meaning, since the position of the production possibility curve will itself depend on the allocation of resources. The distinction between resource allocation and resource creation loses validity. The production possibility curve in the presence of increasing returns will be convex with a given quantum of resources, but what allocation of resources is 'best' in the process of change depends on the size of the market for the output of various activities. The focus of neoclassical value theory on the allocation of a given quantity of resources via the price mechanism becomes of subsidiary importance to the question of how the market generates resources in the process of change.

Thirdly, the existence of increasing returns undermines the neoclassical notion that at any moment of time output must be resource constrained. An economy is not resource constrained, in the sense that there is a physical limitation on output, merely because it is at some notional level of 'full' employment in the aggregate. For one thing, firms in imperfectly competitive market structures will have excess capacity. Secondly, unless productivity is everywhere the same, a reallocation of resources will itself create resources. There exist in every country large pools of 'disguised' unemployment on the land or in service activities, where productivity is low. The longer the time horizon the more elastic will be the supply of resources to the state of demand. If there is no lack of effective demand, the only true constraint on industrial output is the scarcity of non-substitutable natural resources (1986b).

Fourthly, increasing returns have serious implications for the neoclassical theory of the labour market and the diagnosis of unemployment. Increasing returns (with the capital : output ratio constant) means that real wages and employment will be positively not negatively related. This makes nonsense of the concept of a 'natural' rate of unemployment based on the assumption of diminishing returns and that an increase in employment requires a reduction in real wages which workers will resist leading to ever-accelerating inflation.

Fifthly, if supply and demand interact in the presence of increasing returns, many of the treasured theorems of equilibrium economics are rendered inapplicable. There is no reason why factor prices should equalise with free trade; there is no reason why factor migration should equalise factor prices or unemployment between regions or countries, and there is no reason why growth rates between regions or countries should necessarily converge. As was shown in Chapter 7, it is increasing returns which lies at the heart of what Myrdal originally called the process of 'circular and cumulative causation' in which economic success reinforces itself to the detriment of weaker economies. The geographic concentration of industrial activities in selected parts of the world is sustained and reinforced by this process. Orthodox theory, which assumes that economic and social processes work towards equilibrium if initial differences arise, finds it difficult to explain the divergent tendencies to be observed in the world economy.

Equilibrium theory itself does not recognise dualism and the different characteristics of the different sectors of the economy associated with it; particularly the fact that industrial activities are subject to increasing returns and agricultural activities are subject to diminishing returns. It is precisely because of these characteristics that levels of development may be unequal; that free trade may not be mutually beneficial, and that the full employment of resources cannot be guaranteed even in 'equilibrium'. Keynes undermined Say's Law at the aggregate level by showing that there is no reason why the money rate of interest should equilibrate real saving and investment at full employment. Say's Law is equally invalid at the sectoral level. If agriculture is subject to diminishing returns there is a limit to the level of employment on the land and therefore a limit to the demand for industrial goods and employment. This cannot be compensated for without limit by a rise in the price of agricultural goods in terms of industrial goods, since the price of labour in terms of food in the industrial sector cannot fall below subsistence level. Thus an 'equilibrium' terms of trade with unsold goods and surplus labour is quite conceivable. This poses problems for Walrasian equilibrium theory and the notion that economies in 'equilibrium' are resource constrained. For the economy to be resource constrained in the Walrasian sense, it is easy to see the importance of the crucial assumption of non-increasing returns in all activities. But this assumption is a far cry from the real world.

Kaldor admitted that as a young man he was caught in the equilibrium trap:

> most of my early papers were based on the deductive *a priori* method and concentrated on unresolved inconsistencies of general equilibrium theory but without questioning the fundamentals . . . Such was the hypnotic power of Walras's system of equations that it took me a long time to grasp that this method of making an abstract model still more abstract by discovering unsuspected assumptions implied by the results is an unscientific procedure that leads nowhere . . . 'It was a long journey' (1986a)

but he did escape.

CONCLUSION

Kaldor was a unique figure in twentieth-century economics. It was not only his intellect and his approach to economics that made him at one and the same time dominant and controversial; it was also his style, charm and sense of fun which made it impossible not to listen to what he had to say. In lectures and seminars, he would captivate his audience by the heavily accented flow of English prose which was so much a feature of his personality, and an endearing quality in itself. The image of a rotund and jovial medieval monk holding forth in intellectual discourse fits him perfectly. The acceptance of ideas often depends not simply on their intrinsic merit but also on the verve with which they are propagated. Kaldor, like Keynes, was a powerful publicist, who by perseverance and force of personality could wear an opponent down and achieve victory by attrition. He could be arrogant and stubborn on what he regarded as issues of principle, but he was more than ready to change his mind on any topic in the face of the evidence, as he did on several occasions, most notably on the causes of the slow rate of growth of the United Kingdom economy and on the role of exchange rates in balance of payments adjustment.

Kaldor's life was dominated by his love for economics, and his involvement in politics. His love for economics was superseded only by the love for his family, from which he derived much of his self-confidence and inner happiness. He had no hobbies such as music, gardening, collecting or the like, although he had a deep knowledge of European culture and institutions. He spent most days, all day, grappling with economic problems that fascinated and perplexed him at both the theoretical and policy level. His untidiness and forgetfulness in private life were legendary, but his academic mind was extraordinarily retentive and well-ordered. He could recall at an instant the debates and controversies of long ago (many of which he participated in), and he could pluck statistics from the air, like rabbits from a hat, in support of his case. He was not an avid reader, but he possessed an eye and a mind that could filter and photograph material simultaneously, and a memory that could store and recall it as the occasion demanded. This gift could make him devastating in debate.

While Kaldor worked away in his groundfloor study, the ever open door of his spacious home would see a succession of family and friends toing and froing. Kaldor might appear or might not depending on the urgency of the task at hand. He was egocentric, but could also afford to be generous with his time. He liked to compartmentalise his intellectual effort, working intensely for long periods and then relaxing. Nothing was allowed to interfere with family holidays at his home in France. There could never be complete relaxation, however. There were always articles to polish, lectures to prepare, and letters to write to friends and newspapers on topical matters of the day. He was the most prolific newspaper letter-writing economist of his generation, contributing to debates on social issues and defence as well as on economic matters. He had a passionate concern for the underdog which partly inspired his proposals for tax reform both in Britain and in the poorer countries. As is typically the case with European emigrés to Britain, he was in many ways more English than the English. He admired their history and culture and revelled in their institutions. His membership of the House of Lords gave him enormous pleasure, and he used the platform to great effect.

In his speeches, it will be difficult for economic historians to find a more lucid and pungent single commentary on contemporary economic problems or policies. While he enjoyed privilege, however, he was highly critical of the English middle-class and the social and economic infrastructure supporting them. He was particularly hostile to the public schools, the City of London, and the backgrounds and attitudes of the industrial managerial class. He saw no solution to Britain's deep-seated industrial malaise without reform of the educational structure and curriculum and a transformation in the dismissive cultural attitude towards industry.

There remains the question of what lasting impact Kaldor will have on the economics profession. One way to approach this question would be to consider how the history of economics and economic thought might have been different had Kaldor not become an economist and instead pursued his love of journalism or followed his father as a lawyer. Counter–factual questions like this, however, are notoriously difficult to answer, particularly in evaluating men and ideas in the social sciences where the concepts of invention and innovation are much more elusive and nebulous than in the physical sciences. Kaldor's work was not unified and sustained enough to be able to credit him with a major revolution of thought comparable to the 'Keynesian revolution' or the earlier 'marginalist revolution'. He was, however, particularly influential in turning the tide of thought on several matters, and he was a powerful Keynesian disciple who helped to keep Keynesian modes of thinking alive during their darkest days. In these two respects, his place in the history of economic thought is assured.

Thinking chronologically, I would highlight the following landmarks and contributions. In the 1930s he played a major intellectual and proselytising role in bringing about the acceptance of the Keynesian revolution. He converted Pigou; he influenced a whole generation of younger economists at the London School of Economics, and his 1939 paper on 'Speculation and Economic Stability' was the culmination of the Keynesian revolution in theory (as Hicks described it in private correspondence), although he received little credit for it at the time. During the Second World War, no economist did more than Kaldor to pave the way for the acceptance of Beveridge's proposals on social insurance and full employment. After the war he became renowned for his applied statistical work as the Research Director of the Economic Commission for Europe, charged with the task of producing an annual economic survey of Europe. The respect for the work done by the ECE must be attributed largely to Kaldor's vision and dynamism in galvanising a brilliant and enterprising staff. In the field of taxation, which occupied Kaldor in the early 1950s, there were few economists in the world, and no one in Britain, so concerned with the reform of taxation in the interests of equity and efficiency. His book on the expenditure tax remains a minor classic. In that intellectually fertile decade of the 1950s he was part of the nucleus of Cambridge economists who began to extend Keynesian theory to the long period, so linking the new revolution in macro-economics with the traditional preoccupations of the classical economists of growth and distribution. Kaldor, together with Joan Robinson, must be regarded as joint architect of the post-Keynesian school of economists. His path-breaking 1956 paper 'Alternative Theories of Distribution' re-opened the whole debate on distribution theory, and started in earnest the famous Cambridge assault on neoclassical growth and distribution theory.

The idea of the technical progress function to replace the neoclassical production function was a major innovation which played a central role in his own growth models. He never participated in the so-called 'capital controversy' but he had done enough to form a new school of thought which gathered disciples world-wide. Kaldor continued to be a thorn in the flesh of the neoclassical school of economics (largely based in the United States) for the rest of his life, widening his attack to encompass the whole range of assumptions underlying neoclassical value theory, which he called 'equilibrium theory' for short. He was a profound critic, not of the concept of equilibrium, but of the equilibrium methodology, and attempted to show in all his later work that the assumptions of equilibrium theory do not have to be made for economics to be interesting. As far as the applied economics of growth is concerned, he became more and more convinced that it is impossible to understand the growth process without making a distinction between increasing returns activities on the one hand and diminishing returns activities on the other. This distinction for Kaldor was virtually synonymous with the distinction be-tween manufacturing and all other activities. He attributed country growth rate differences to differences in the rate of growth of their manufacturing sectors, and his model of world growth was driven by the rate of growth of land saving innovations necessary to offset the effect of diminishing returns in agriculture on the growth of demand for manufactured goods. For open economies he believed that the growth of manufacturing depended fundamentally on export performance, and Kaldor was instrumental in reviving the doctrine of the (Harrod) foreign trade multiplier.

As a measure of his versatility he led world-wide the intellectual assault against the doctrine of monetarism, which in the 1960s spread from the United States with the virulence of a plague to infect thinking and policy-making all over the globe. Kaldor lost the policy battle, but it is now clear that he won the theoretical war. Cost push inflation can exist; there is a difference between commodity backed money and credit money, and a predictable velocity of circulation of money is evidence of the endogeneity of the money supply not evidence that inflation must be the result of prior increases in the money supply. In the political sphere, Kaldor probably had more influence on economic policy this century than any other economist apart from Keynes. Most of the major tax reforms during the period of the Labour government 1964–70, such as corporation tax, capital gains tax, selective employment tax, etc., owe their origin to Kaldor's missionary reforming zeal.

As a campaigner and espouser of causes he had no equals among his contemporaries. One particular political and economic issue that worried him greatly was Britain's entry into the Common Market which he strongly opposed on the proposed terms. He drew on Allyn Young's notion of increasing returns as a macro-economic phenomenon and Verdoorn's law (which he revived) to argue that if Britain started in a weak position it would get relatively weaker through the process of what Myrdal once called 'circular and cumulative causation'. His attack on the idea that Britain would gain 'dynamic' benefits from entry was devastating, and never answered. Again he lost the policy battle, but the evidence of growing divergence within the European Community and Britain's own position gives no comfort to equilibrium theory.

In all these areas of theoretical interest and practical concern, Kaldor attracted adherents and disciples, although perhaps not as many as he might have wished. Through his writing and disciples, his impact will continue to pervade the profession. Kaldor's legacy to the profession is listed in the bibliography which follows. It contains close to two hundred articles, pamphlets and books; but he never wrote a grand treatise in the tradition of Smith, Ricardo, Marx or Marshall. This is a pity since he had the vision, the intellect and the gift for writing, borne out of his early passion for journalism. He regretted it himself. His eight volumes of *Collected Essays*, however, are some compensation and will provide a lasting monument and testimony to his energy, creativity and endeavour. In reviewing some of these volumes, *The Economist* newspaper (20th January 1979) referred to Kaldor as the 'best known economist in the world not to have received the Nobel Prize'. He chuckled at that; let it be his epitaph.

NOTES

1. See E.H. Phelps Brown, 'The Underdevelopment of Economics', *Economic Journal*, March 1972; G.D.N. Worswick, 'Is Progress in Economic Science Possible?', *Economic Journal*, March 1972; W. Leontief, 'Theoretical Assumptions and Non-observed Facts', *American Economic Review*, March 1971.
2. J. Kornai, *Anti-Equilibrium: On Economic Systems Theory and the Tasks of Research* (Amsterdam: North-Holland, 1971).
3. L. Walras, *Elements of Pure Economics* (1874), translated (from the French) by W. Jaffe (London: Allen and Unwin, 1954).
4. K.J. Arrow, 'An Extension of the Basic Theorems of Classical Welfare Economics', in J. Neyman (ed.), *Proceedings of the Second Berkeley Symposium on Mathematical Statistics and Probability* (Berkeley: California, 1951).
5. G. Debreu, 'The Coefficient of Resource Utilisation', *Econometrica*, July 1951.
6. K. Arrow and G. Debreu, 'Existence of an Equilibrium for a Competitive

Economy', *Econometrica*, July 1954.

7. For illustrations and references see F. Hahn, *On the Notion of Equilibrium* (Cambridge University Press, 1973). Arrow and Hahn have provided a rigorous general equilibrium model with increasing returns and imperfect competition. Arrow–Debreu equilibrium may be shown to exist with increasing returns if increasing returns are small relative to the scale of the economy – although, in practice the increasing returns may not be small enough to have confidence in the closeness of the approximation.

8. E. Roy Weintraub, 'On the Existence of a Competitive Equilibrium: 1930–1954', *Journal of Economic Literature*, March 1985.

9. Letter dated 30 January 1961.

10. G.W. Guillebaud, *Marshall's Principles of Economics*, Vol. 2 (Notes), p. 774.

11. Ibid., p. 775.

12. J. Kornai, *The Economics of Shortage* (Amsterdam: North-Holland, 1981).

13. A. Marshall, *Principles of Economics* (London: Macmillan, 1890), Appendix H.

14. *Economic Journal*, December 1926.

15. J.R. Hicks, *Value and Capital* (Oxford: the Clarendon Press, 1939).

16. *Economic Journal*, December 1928.

17. Quoted in C. Blitch, 'Allyn Young on Increasing Returns', *Journal of Post Keynesian Economics*, Spring 1983.

CHRONOLOGY

1908	Born 12 May, Budapest.
1925	University of Berlin.
1927	Undergraduate, London School of Economics.
1930	Research student, London School of Economics.
1932	Appointed Assistant in Economics, London School of Economics.
1934	Married Clarisse Goldschmidt.
1935	Rockefeller Research Fellowship to the USA.
1938	Lecturer in Economics, London School of Economics.
1940	Evacuated to Cambridge.
1945	Chief of Economic Planning Staff, US Strategic Bombing Survey. Reader in Economics, London School of Economics.
1946	Adviser to Hungarian government.
1947	Adviser to Commissariat General du Plan, France. Resigned, London School of Economics. Director of Research and Planning Division, Economic Commission for Europe, Geneva.
1948	Berlin Currency and Trade Committee of the United Nations. *Advertising Expenditure and the Revenue of the Press* (with R. Silverman).
1949	Fellowship of King's College, Cambridge, and Lecturer in Economics, University of Cambridge. UN Group of Experts on National & International Measures for Full Employment.
1951	Royal Commission on the Taxation of Profits and Income.
1952	Reader in Economics, University of Cambridge.
1955	*An Expenditure Tax.* Honorary Member of the Royal Economic Society of Belgium.

1956   Adviser on Indian Tax Reform.
1958   Fiscal Adviser, Ceylon (Sri Lanka).
1959   Visiting Ford Research Professor, University of California.
1960   Adviser on Mexican Tax Reform.
        Essays on Value and Distribution and *Essays on Stability and Growth.*
1961   Economic Adviser to the Prime Minister of Ghana.
        Fiscal Adviser, British Guiana (Guyana).
1962   Honorary Doctorate, University of Dijon.
        Adviser on Turkish tax reform.
1963   Visiting Economist, Reserve Bank of Australia, Sydney.
        Fellow of the British Academy.
1964   Special Adviser to the Chancellor of the Exchequer.
1965   *Essays on Economic Policy,* Vols. I and II.
1966   Professor of Economics, University of Cambridge.
        Economic Adviser to Prime Minister of Iran.
        Causes of the Slow Rate of Economic Growth of the United Kingdom.
1967   *Strategic Factors in Economic Development.*
1968   Special Consultant to the Treasury.
1969   Special Adviser to the Department of Health & Social Security.
1970   President, Section F of the British Association for the Advancement of Science.
        Honorary Fellow, London School of Economics.
1974   Elevated to the Peerage as Baron Kaldor of Newnham in the City of Cambridge.
        Special Adviser to the Chancellor of the Exchequer.
        President of the Royal Economic Society.
1975   Retired from the University of Cambridge.
        Honorary Member of the American Economic Association.
1976   Fiscal Adviser, Venezuela.
1977   Foreign Honorary Member of the American Academy of Arts & Sciences.
1978   *Further Essays on Economic Theory; Further Essays on Applied Economics.*
1979   Elected Honorary Member of the Hungarian Academy of Sciences.
1980   Reports on Taxation Vols. I and II, completing eight volumes of *Collected Essays.*
1982   Keynes Lecturer, British Academy.
        The Scourge of Monetarism.
        Honorary Doctorate, Frankfurt University.
1983   *The Economic Consequences of Mrs Thatcher.*

1984   *Causes of Growth and Stagnation in the World Economy* (Mattioli Lectures).

1985   *Economics without Equilibrium* (Okun lectures).

1986   Died at Papworth Hospital, Cambridge, 30 September.

BIBLIOGRAPHY

BOOKS, PAMPHLETS AND OFFICIAL PUBLICATIONS

Translation of *Monetary Theory and the Trade Cycle* by F. von Hayek (with H. Croome), 1933.

Economic Reconstruction After the War (with M. Joseph), Association for Education in Citizenship, 1942.

Planning for Abundance (with J. Robinson, A.A. Evans, E.F. Schumacher and P. Lamartine Yates), Peace Aims Pamphlet No. 21, National Peace Council, 1943.

The Effects of Strategic Bombing on the German War Economy, US Strategic Bombing Survey, Washington, 1945.

A Statistical Analysis of Advertising Expenditure and the Revenue of the Press (with R. Silverman), Cambridge University Press, 1948.

A Survey of the Economic Situation and Prospects of Europe (co-author), 1948 edition, 1949 edition, 1950 edition, Economic Commision for Europe, United Nations, Geneva.

Report on National and International Measures for Full Employment (co-author), United Nations, Geneva, 1949.

Report on Full Employment Objectives in Relation to the Problem of European Cooperation (co-author), Council of Europe, Strasbourg, 1951.

A Reconsideration of the Economics of the International Wheat Agreement, Commodity Policy Studies No. 1, FAO, Rome, September 1952.

Memorandum of Dissent to the Final Report of the Royal Commission on the Taxation of Profits and Income, Cmnd 9474, HMSO, London, June 1955.

An Expenditure Tax, Allen and Unwin, 1955.

Report of a Survey on Indian Tax Reform, Ministry of Finance, Government of India, Delhi, 1956.

Suggestions for a Comprehensive Reform of Direct Taxation, Government Press, Colombo, Ceylon, April 1960.

Essays on Value and Distribution, Duckworth, London, 1960, 2nd edition 1980 (*Collected Essays*, Vol. 1).

Essays on Economic Stability and Growth, Duckworth, London, 1960, 2nd edition 1980 (*Collected Essays*, Vol. 2).

Ensayos sobre Desarrollo Economico, CEMLA, Mexico City, 1st edition July

1961, 2nd edition November 1963.

The Case for an International Commodity Reserve Currency (with A.G. Hart and J. Tinbergen), Memorandum submitted to UNCTAD, Geneva, 1964.

Essays on Economic Policy I, Duckworth, London, 1964, 2nd edition 1980 (*Collected Essays*, Vol. 3).

Essays on Economic Policy II, Duckworth, London, 1964, 2nd edition 1980 (*Collected Essays*, Vol. 4).

Causes of the Slow Rate of Economic Growth of the United Kingdom, Cambridge University Press, 1966.

Strategic Factors in Economic Development, Ithaca, New York, 1967.

A Monetary Policy for Latin America (with P. Uri, R. Ruggles and R. Triffin), Praeger for the Atlantic Institute, New York, 1968.

A Future for European Agriculture (co-author), Atlantic Institute, Paris, 1971.

Conflicts in Policy Objectives (edited), Basil Blackwell, 1971.

The Common Market—Its Economic Perspectives, Trade Unions Against the Common Market and NATSOPA, 1972.

The Case for Nationalising Land (with J. Brocklebank, Joan Maynard, R. Neild and O. Sutchbury), Campaign for Nationalising Land, 1974.

Further Essays on Economic Theory, Duckworth, London, 1978 (*Collected Essays*, Vol. 5).

Further Essays on Applied Economics, London, 1978 (*Collected Essays*, Vol. 6).

Reports on Taxation I, Duckworth, London, 1980 (*Collected Essays*, Vol. 7).

Reports on Taxation II, Duckworth, London, 1980 (*Collected Essays*, Vol. 8).

Origins of the New Monetarism, Cardiff University Press, 1981.

The Scourge of Monetarism, Oxford University Press, 1982, 2nd edition 1986.

Limitations of the General Theory (Keynes Lecture to the British Academy, 12 May 1982), Oxford University Press, 1983.

The Economic Consequences of Mrs Thatcher, Fabian Tract 486, January 1983, and Duckworth, London, 1983.

Causes of Growth and Stagnation in the World Economy (Mattioli Lectures, Milan, 1984).

The Failure of Monetarism (Chintaman Deshmukh Memorial Lecture, 18 January 1984), Reserve Bank of India.

Economics Without Equilibrium, (Okun Lectures, Yale University), University College Cardiff Press, 1985.

The Rise and Decline of Monetarism, Labour Institute for Economic Research, Helsinki, Discussion Paper 46, 1986.

ARTICLES

1932   a)   A Case Against Technical Progress, *Economica*, May.
        b)   The Economic Situation of Austria, *Harvard Business Review*. October.

1934   a)   A Classificatory Note on the Determinateness of Equilibrium, *Review of Economic Studies*, February.
        b)   The Equilibrium of the Firm, *Economic Journal*, March.
        c)   Mrs Robinson's 'Economics of Imperfect Competition', *Economica*, August.

1935 a) Market Imperfection and Excess Capacity, *Economica*, February.
1936 a) Wage Subsidies as a Remedy for Unemployment, *Journal of Political Economy*, December.
1937 a) Limitational Factors and the Elasticity of Substitution, *Review of Economic Studies*, February.
      b) The Controversy on the Theory of Capital, *Econometrica*, July.
      c) Professor Pigou on Money Wages in Relation to Unemployment, *Economic Journal*, December.
1938 a) On the Theory of Capital: A Rejoinder to Professor Knight, *Econometrica*, April.
      b) Professor Chamberlin on Monopolistic and Imperfect Competition, *Quarterly Journal of Economics*, May.
      c) Mr Hawtrey on Short and Long Term Investment, *Economica*, November.
      d) Stability and Full Employment, *Economic Journal*, December.
1939 a) Capital Intensity and the Trade Cycle, *Economica*, February.
      b) Money Wage Cuts in Relation to Unemployment: A Reply to Mr Somers, *Review of Economic Studies*, June.
      c) Principles of Emergency Finance, *The Banker*, August.
      d) Welfare Propositions in Economics and Interpersonal Comparisons of Utility, *Economic Journal*, September.
      e) Speculation and Economic Stability, *Review of Economic Studies*, October.
1940 a) The Trade Cycle and Capital Intensity: A Reply, *Economica*, February.
      b) Money Wage Cuts in Relation to Unemployment: A Comment, *Review of Economic Studies*, February.
      c) A Comment on a Rejoinder of H.M. Somers, *Review of Economic Studies*, February.
      d) A Model of the Trade Cycle, *Economic Journal*, March.
      e) A Note on the Theory of the Forward Market, *Review of Economic Studies*, June.
      f) A Note on Tariffs and the Terms of Trade, *Economica*, November.
1941 a) Rationing and the Cost of Living Index, *Review of Economic Studies*, June.
      b) The White Paper on National Income and Expenditure, *Economic Journal*, June–September.
      c) Employment and Equilibrium—A Theoretical Discussion, *Economic Journal*, December.
1942 a) The Income Burden of Capital Taxes, *Review of Economic Studies*, June.
      b) The 1941 White Paper on National Income and Expenditure, *Economic Journal*, June–September.
      c) Models of Short Period Equilibrium, *Economic Journal*, June–September.
      d) Professor Hayek and the Concertina Effect, *Economica*, November.
1943 a) The Beveridge Report II. The Financial Burden, *Economic*

Journal, April.

b) Export Costs and Export Price Policy, *The Banker*, June. Rejoinder, August.

c) The 1943 White Paper on National Income and Expenditure (with T. Barna), *Economic Journal*, June–September.

1944 a) The Quantitative Aspects of the Full Employment Problem in Britain in W. Beveridge, *Full Employment in a Free Society*, (George, Allen and Unwin).

1945 a) Obituary of Erwin Rothbarth (with D.G. Champernowne), *Economic Journal*, April.

b) The German War Economy, *Review of Economic Studies*, Vol. XIII, No. 1; also *Manchester School*, September 1946.

1946 a) A Comment on W.J. Baumol's Community Indifference, *Review of Economic Studies*, Vol. XIV, No. 1.

1947 a) A Plan for the Financial Stabilisation of France, in *Collected Economic Essays*, Vol. 8.

1948 a) The Theory of Distribution, *Chambers Encyclopedia*.

1949 a) The Economic Aspects of Advertising, *Review of Economic Studies*, Vol. XVIII, No. 4.

1950 a) Employment Policies and the Problem of International Balance, *Review of Economic Studies*, Vol. XIX, No. 1. Also in *International Social Science Bulletin*, Spring 1951.

b) A Positive Policy for Wages and Dividends, *Collected Economic Essays*, Vol. 3.

1951 a) Mr Hicks on the Trade Cycle, *Economic Journal*, December.

1952 a) Foreign Trade and the Balance of Payments, in *Collected Economic Essays*, Vol. 4.

b) Beschaftigungspolitik und Das Problem des Internationalen Gleichgewichtes, *Zeitschrift fur Nationalokonomie*, 15 January.

1954 a) The Relation of Economic Growth and Cyclical Fluctuations, *Economic Journal*, March: *Economie Appliquée*, January–June.

b) The Economic Effects of Company Taxation, *Transactions of the Manchester Statistical Society*.

1955 a) The International Impact of Cyclical Movements, in E. Lundberg (ed.), *The Business Cycle in the Post-War World*, (Macmillan: New York).

b) The Lessons of the British Experiment Since the War: Full Employment and the Welfare State, (Paper read to the Centenary Conference of the Royal Economic Society of Belgium) in *Collected Economic Essays*, Vol. 3.

c) Professor Wright on Methodology: A Rejoinder, *Economic Journal*, March.

1956 a) Alternative Theories of Distribution, *Review of Economic Studies*, Vol. XXIII, No. 2.

b) Characteristics of Economic Development, *Asian Studies*, November; also *Informazione Svimez*, May 1958.

c) Capitalist Evolution in the Light of Keynesian Economics, *Trimestre Economico*, July–September, also *Sankhya*, May 1957: *Rivista di Politica Economica*, February 1958: *Economie Appliquée*,

April–September 1957; *Journal of the Economic Society*, Hong Kong University, 1957; *Economica Brasileira*, No. 2, 1956.

1957 a) Caracteristicas do Desenvovimento Economica, Five Papers in *Revista Brasileira de Economia*, March.

b) Profit et Croissance, *Economie Appliquée*, August.

c) A Model of Economic Growth, *Economic Journal*, December: also *Trimestre Economico*, April–June 1958.

1958 a) Observations on the Problem of Economic Development in Ceylon, in *Collected Economic Essays*, Vol. 4.

b) Problems of the Indian Third Five-Year Plan, in *Collected Economic Essays*, Vol. 4.

c) The Growing Disparity Between Rich and Poor Countries, in *Problems of United States Economic Development*, Vol. 1 (Committee for Economic Development, New York).

d) Comment on 'A Note on Kaldor's Speculation and Economic Stability', *Review of Economic Studies*, October.

e) Sviluppo, Equilibrio e Squilibrio, *Informazioni Svimez*, June.

f) *Monetary Policy, Economic Stability and Growth*, Memorandum submitted to the Radcliffe Committee on the Working of the Monetary System, June 23, Memorandum of Evidence pp. 146–53, Minutes of Evidence, pp. 712–18, Cmnd 827, HMSO, London.

g) The Reform of Personal Taxation, *The Accountant*, 12 April.

h) Inflazione e Sottosviluppo Economico, *Informazione Svimez*, July.

i) Risk Bearing and Income Taxation, *Review of Economic Studies*, June.

1959 a) Tax Reform in India, *The Economic Weekly Annual*, January.

b) Economic Problems of Chile, *El Trimestro Economico*, April–June.

c) Economic Growth and the Problem of Inflation, Parts I and II *Economica*, August and November.

1960 a) La Rôle de l'instrument monetaire en matiere de croissance et de stabilité economiques, *Bulletin D'Information et de documentation* (Banque Nationale de Belgique), August.

b) A Rejoinder to Mr Atsumi and Professor Tobin, *Review of Economic Studies*, February.

c) The Radcliffe Report, *Review of Economics and Statistics*, February.

d) Report on Mexican Tax Reform, in *Collected Economic Essays*, Vol. 8.

e) Economic Growth and Distributive Shares: A Rejoinder to Mr Findlay, *Review of Economic Studies*, June.

f) Keynes' Theory of the Own-Rates of Interest, in *Collected Economic Essays*, Vol. 2.

1961 a) Capital Accumulation and Economic Growth, in F. Lutz (ed.), *The Theory of Capital*, Macmillan (paper prepared 1958).

b) Proposals for a Reform of Taxation of British Guiana, in *Collected Economic Essays*, Vol. 8.

c) Increasing Returns and Economic Progress: A Comment on Professor Hicks' Article, *Oxford Economic Papers*, February.

1962 a) The Role of Taxation in Economic Development, in *Collected*

Economic Essays, Vol. 3.

b) A New Model of Economic Growth (with J. Mirrlees), *Review of Economic Studies*, Vol. XXIX, No. 3.

c) Report on the Turkish Tax System, in *Collected Economic Essays*, Vol. 8.

d) A Proposal for a Levy on the Advertising Revenue of News-papers, (with R. Neild), in *Collected Economic Essays*, Vol. 7 (Memorandum to the Royal Commission on the Press, February).

e) Symposium on Production Functions and Economic Growth: Comment, *Review of Economic Studies*, June.

f) Overdeterminateness in Kaldor's Growth Model: A Comment, *Economic Journal*, September.

1963 a) Will Underdeveloped Countries Learn to Tax?, *Foreign Affairs*, January.

b) Comment on I. Svennilson's paper on Economic Growth and Technical Progress (OECD, Paris).

c) A Memorandum on the Value-Added Tax, in *Collected Economic Essays*, Vol. 3 (paper prepared for the Committee on the Turnover Tax).

d) Taxation for Economic Development, *Journal of Modern African Studies*, March.

e) El Papel de la Imposicion en el Desarrollo Economico, *Investigacion Economica*.

1964 a) Stabilising the Terms of Trade of Underdeveloped Countries, *Economic Bulletin for Latin America*, March; *Mondo Aperto*, April.

b) The Problem of International Liquidity, *Bulletin of the Oxford Institute of Economics and Statistics*, August.

c) Los Reformas al Sistema Fiscal en Mexico, *Comercio Exterior*, April.

d) International Trade and Economic Development, *Journal of Modern African Studies*, December.

e) Dual Exchange Rates and Economic Development, *Economic Bulletin for Latin America*, September.

f) Prospects for a Wages Policy for Australia, *Economic Record*, June.

1965 a) The Relative Merits of Fixed and Floating Exchange Rates, in *Collected Economic Essays*, Vol. 6.

b) Les Prélèvements fiscaux dans les pays en voie de developpement, in *Les Problèmes Fiscaux et Monetaires dans les Pays en Voie de Developpement*, Paris 1967.

1966 a) Marginal Productivity and the Macro-Economic Theories of Distribution: Comment on Samuelson and Modigliani, *Review of Economic Studies*, Vol. XXXIII, No. 4, October.

b) Economic and Taxation Problems in Iran, in *Collected Economic Essays*, Vol. 8.

1968 a) Productivity and Growth in Manufacturing Industry: A Reply, *Economica*, November.

1969 a) Choice of Technology in Less Developed Countries, *Monthly*

Labour Review, August.

1970 a) Some Fallacies in the Interpretation of Kaldor, *Review of Economic Studies*, January.

      b) The New Monetarism, *Lloyds Bank Review*, July.

      c) A Rejoinder to Professor Friedman, *Lloyds Bank Review*, October.

      d) The Case for Regional Policies, *Scottish Journal of Political Economy*, November.

      e) The Role of Modern Technology in Raising the Economic Standards of the Less Developed Countries, in W.L. Hodges and M.A. Kelley (eds.), *Technological Change and Human Development: An International Conference* (Ithaca: New York State School of Industrial and Labour Relations, Cornell University).

1971 a) The Economic Effects of Alternative Systems of Corporation Tax, House of Commons Sessional Paper in Minutes of Evidence to Select Committee of the Corporation Tax, in *Collected Economic Essays*, Vol. 7.

      b) The Existence and Persistence of Cycles in a Non-Linear Model: Kaldor's 1940 Model Re-Examined: A Comment, *Review of Economic Studies*, January.

      c) Conflicts in National Economic Objectives, *Economic Journal*, March.

1972 a) Advanced Technology in a Strategy of Development: Some Lessons From Britain's Experience, in *Automation and Developing Countries* (ILO, Geneva).

      b) Money and Gold, *Acta Oeconomica*, Vol. 9, No. 2.

      c) The Irrelevance of Equilibrium Economics, *Economic Journal*, December.

1973 a) Problems and Prospects of International Monetary Reform, *The Banker*, September.

      b) Tax Credits: A Critique of the Green Paper Proposals, House of Commons Sessional Paper, Minutes of Evidence to Select Committee on Tax Credits, in *Collected Economic Essays*, Vol. 7.

1974 a) The Role of Industrialisation in Latin American Inflations, in D.T. Geithman (ed.), *Fiscal Policy for Industrialisation and Development in Latin America*, (University of Florida Press).

      b) International Monetary Reform: The Need for a New Approach, *Bancaria*, February.

      c) Teoria del Equilibrio y Teoria del Crecimiento, *Cuardernos de Economia*, May–August.

      d) Managing the Economy: The British Experience, *Quarterly Review of Economics and Business*, Autumn.

1975 a) What is Wrong with Economic Theory, *Quarterly Journal of Economics*, August.

      b) Preface to *Economic Stability is Possible* by L. St Clare Grondona, (Hutchinson Benham).

      c) Economic Growth and the Verdoorn Law: A Comment on Mr Rowthorn's Article, *Economic Journal*, December.

      d) Why are Regional Policies Necessary?, in *Regionalpolitik und*

√

Agrarpolitik in Europe, Dunker and Humbold, Berlin.

e)   Capitalism and Industrial Development: Some Lessons from Britian's Experience, in D. Alejandro *et alia* (eds.), *Politica Economica en Centro y Periferia (Essays in Honour of Felipe Pazos)*, (Fondo di Cultura, Mexico): also in *Cambridge Journal of Economics*, 1977.

1976 a)   Observations on the Fiscal Reform in Venezuela, in *Collected Economic Essays*. Vol. 8.

b)   Inflation and Recession in the World Economy, *Economic Journal*, December.

1977 a)   The Effect of Devaluations on Trade in Manufactures, in *Collected Economic Essays*, Vol. 6.

b)   Is Capital Shortage a Cause of Mass Unemployment?, in H. Giersch (ed.), *Capital Shortage and Unemployment in the World Economy* (Institut für Weltwirtschaft an der Universitat Kiel).

c)   Discussant of 'Capital Requirements for Full Employment and Economic Growth in Developed Countries', by Klaus Wernerschatz, in H. Giersch (ed.), *Capital Shortage and Unemployment in the World Economy*, (Institut für Weltwirtschaft an der Universitat Kiel).

1978 a)   A New Look at the Expenditure Tax, in *Collected Economic Essays*, Vol. 7.

b)   Structural Causes of the World Economic Recession, *Mondes en Developement*, Centre Nationale de la Recherche Scientifique, No. 22, Paris.

1979 a)   Equilibrium Theory and Growth Theory, in M. Boskin (ed.), *Economics and Human Welfare: Essays in Honour of Tibor Scitovsky*, Academic Press.

b)   The Economics of the Selective Employment Tax, in *Collected Economic Essays*, Vol. 7.

c)   The Role of Fiscal and Monetary Policies in Latin American Inflations, *Interamerican Institute of Capital Markets*, Caracas, Venezuela.

d)   An Introduction to 'A Note on the General Theory' of Jean de Largentaye, *Journal of Post Keynesian Economics*, No. 1.

1980 a)   What is De-industrialisation? Comment on Sir Alec Cairncross's paper in F. Blackaby (ed.), *De-industrialisation*, Heinemann.

b)   Monetarism and United Kingdom Monetary Policy, *Cambridge Journal of Economics*, December.

c)   Memorandum of Evidence on Monetary Policy to the Select Committee on the Treasury and Civil Service, HMSO 17 July.

d)   Public and Private Enterprise—the Issues to be Considered, in *Public and Private Enterprise in a Mixed Economy*, ed. by W.J. Baumol, Macmillan.

1981 a)   The Foundations of Free Trade Theory and their Implications for the Current World Recession, in E. Malinvaud and J.P. Fitoussi (eds.), *Unemployment in Western Countries*, Macmillan, 1980; also in J. Los *et alia* (eds.), *Studies in Economic Theory and*

Practice, North-Holland.
b) Discussion of 'Verdoorn's Law, the Externalities Hypothesis, Kaldor's Proposition and Economic Growth in the U.K.', by M. Chatterji and M. Wickens, in D. Currie *et alia* (eds.), *Macroeconomic Analysis*, Croom Helm.
c) A Keynesian Perspective on Money (with J. Trevithick), *Lloyds Bank Review*, January.
d) Fallacies of Monetarism, *Kredit und Kapital*, Vol. 14, July.
e) The Radcliffe Report in the Light of Subsequent Developments in Monetary Theory, Radcliffe Lectures, University of Warwick, 18–19 May.
f) The Role of Increasing Returns, Technical Progress and Cumulative Causation in the Theory of International Trade and Economic Growth, *Economie Appliquée*, Vol. XXXIV, No. 4.

1982 a) Inflation: An Endemic Problem of Modern Capitalism, *Wirtschaft und Gesellschaft*, No. 2.
b) Keynes as an Economic Adviser, in A.P. Thirlwall (ed.), *Keynes as a Policy Adviser*, Macmillan.
c) Economic Prospects of the 1980s, *Economic Notes*, No. 2.

1983 a) Devaluation and Adjustment in Developing Countries, *Finance and Development*, June.
b) The World Economic Outlook in *Human Resources, Employment and Development*, Proceedings of the Sixth World Congress of the IEA, 1980 (London, Macmillan).
c) The Role of Commodity Prices in Economic Recovery, *Lloyds Bank Review*, July. Also *World Development*, May 1987.
d) Keynesian Economics After Fifty Years, in J. Trevithick and G.N.D. Worswick (eds.), *Keynes and the Modern World*, Cambridge University Press.
e) The Role of Effective Demand in the Short Run and the Long Run, Keynes Conference, Paris, September.
f) Contribution to the Conference 'Un Intellettuale Europeo del XX Secolo: Piero Sraffa, 1898–1983' at the Istituto Piemontese di Scienze Economiche e Sociali – A. Gramsci.
g) Gemeinsamkeiten und Unterschiede in den Theorien von Keynes, Kalecki und Rüstow, *Ifo-Studien*, No. 1.

1984 a) An Exchange Rate Policy for India, *Economic and Political Weekly*, Bombay, 14 July.
b) Piero Sraffa, (Obituary), *Cambridge Review*, July.
c) Joan Robinson (Obituary), *King's College Annual Report*.

1985 a) How Monetarism Failed, *Challenge*, May–June.
b) Lessons of the Monetarist Experiment, in C. Van Ewijk and J.J. Klant (eds.), *Monetary Conditions for Economic Recovery*, (Dordrecht: Martinus Nijhoff Publishers).

1986 a) Recollections of an Economist, *Banca Nazionale del Lavoro Quarterly Review*, March.
b) Limits on Growth, *Oxford Economic Papers*, July.
c) Piero Sraffa 1898–1983, *Moneta e Credito*, September.
d) 'Sraffa Come Critico Della Teoria Economica' in R. Bellofiore

(ed.), *Tra Teoria Economica e Grande Cultura Europea: Piero Sraffa* (Milano: Franco Angeli).

e) The Impact of Import Restrictions in the Interwar Period (with M. Kitson), unpublished.

1987 a) Piero Sraffa 1898–1983, *Proceedings of the British Academy.*

Name Index

Subject Index

Accelerator theory of investment, 50, 53–4, 176
Acorn Securities, 6, 231
Agriculture, 5, 106, 152–154, 187, 189, 193, 201–2, 204–21, 328
  see also Common Agricultural Policy
Anglo-Nippon Trust, 6–7, 231

Balance of payments
  adjustment, 8, 281–3
  constraint, 190, 194, 199n
  deficit, 229, 247–8, 249–53
  effects of EEC membership on, 264
Bancor unit of currency, 274–6
Berlin Currency Committee, 107
Beveridge Reports
  1942, 84–90
  1944, 90–5
Boom, causes of end of, 49–50
Borrowing, 79
  government, 305, 309–10
Brazil, 202–3, 216
Bretton Woods agreement, 8, 95, 233, 272–3, 280
Britain and the European Communities: An Economic Assessment, 260–1
British Guiana *see* Guyana

Capital
  accumulation, 172–6, 203, 205, 321–2, 324
  intensity, 41–7, 53, 324

gains, 122
scarcity, 47
transfer tax, 255
Capital Gains Tax, xi, 7, 114, 115–17, 119, 125, 230, 237, 239
Capital : labour ratio, 42, 166, 225, 324
Capital : output ratio, 54, 166, 167, 174, 176, 178, 179, 225, 324, 327
Capitalism, 162
  English development of, 204–5
Car industry, 98, 99
Causation, 307–10
  circular and cumulative, 202, 221, 328, 333
Ceylon *see* Sri Lanka
Child Benefit, 255
Chile, 202, 216
China, 161–2, 201
Choice of techniques, 177
Cobweb theorem, 40
Cohen Council, 296
Commissariat Général du Plan (France), 104, 130
Commod Control, 278–9, 280
Commodity reserve currency, 274–80
Common Agricultural Policy, 248–9, 258–9, 261–3, 269, 270
Common Market *see* EEC
Common Market Safeguards Campaign, 263

Ruth Cohen